Mrs. Marion France
22B Carriage Rd.
Clifton Park, NY 12065-7504

P9-DDG-097

HORSE PEOPLE

MICHAEL KORDA

HORSE PEOPLE

Scenes from the Riding Life

ILLUSTRATIONS
BY THE AUTHOR

HarperCollins*Publishers*

HarperCollins books may be purchased for educational, business, or sales promotional use. For information, please write: Special Markets Department, HarperCollins Publishers Inc., 10 East 53rd Street, New York, NY 10022.

All illustrations are by the author;
all photographs are courtesy of the author
unless otherwise indicated.

FIRST EDITION

Designed by Amy Hill

Printed on acid-free paper

Library of Congress Cataloging-in-Publication Data
Korda, Michael
Horse people : scenes from the riding life / Michael Korda.—1st ed.
p.   cm.
ISBN 0-06-621252-9 hardcover
1. Horses—United States—Anecdotes.   2. Horsemen and horsewomen—
United States—Anecdotes.   3. Horsemanship—United States—
Anecdotes.   4. Korda, Michael   I. Title.
SF301.K67 2003
798.2'0973—dc21   2002191940

03   04   05   06   07   NMSG/RRD   10   9   8   7   6   5

For Margaret
"la belle equestrienne,"
with love.

It is the seat on a horse that makes the difference between a groom and a gentleman.

—Miguel de Cervantes, *Don Quixote*

Hast thou given the horse strength? Has thou clothed his neck with thunder?

—The Book of Job, 39:19

CONTENTS

xi

Contents

HORSE PEOPLE

My Kingdom for a Horse

"'Aving trouble, sir?"

THE *Statistical Abstract of the United States,* a bottomless compendium of useless facts, indicates that there are over 5 million households owning a horse or horses in America today, and that the total horse population is, give or take a few horses, about 13.5 million.

That seems like a lot of horses in a country where most people had already made the switch to the automobile by the end of World War I, and in which horses—with a few exceptions like police horses, or carriage horses in places like New York's Central Park, or among the Amish—are no longer working animals, strictly speaking.

When I was a boy in England, the milkman had a horse that not only pulled his milk wagon but knew enough to stop at every house to which he delivered milk on his route, and fresh fruits and vegetables were hawked from horse-drawn carts, but all of that is long since gone. Even on cattle ranches, the horses are more ornamental and traditional than useful these days.

At the same time, horses aren't exactly pets, like dogs and cats. For one thing, they don't live in the house, or even visit it. However domesticated the horse is, he's not part of domestic life; his place remains firmly outside, in the field, the corral, the paddock, or the stable, depending on the part of the country you live in. You go to visit the horse, the horse doesn't visit you. In other cultures—among the Mongols, for example—horsemen sleep with their horses, for warmth, one presumes, but that has never been the Anglo-Saxon way, even among old-time cowboys. However fond the rider may be of his mount, it's our custom to bed down at some distance from it. Little girls may fantasize about sleeping with their ponies, but not many actually do it, which is just as well, since horses of all sizes are restless sleepers, and very likely to kick out when disturbed. In any case, horses do most of their sleeping standing up.

So the horse occupies a peculiar and privileged position, not quite a pet, no longer a working animal, rooted, for many people, in the past, but flourishing in the present, admired even by people who don't ride, and apt not only to survive but to thrive almost anywhere.

A few words about my own involvement with horses. I came to horses early in life—I have before me a picture of myself on a small, shaggy pony at the age of about six—but although I learned to ride, living as we did in Hampstead, on the outskirts of London, we never owned a horse.

My father Vincent and his two brothers, Zoltan, a few years older, and Alexander, the eldest, had grown up in rural Hungary before the invention of the motor car, so horses were neither a mystery to them nor an enthusiasm. Their father, Henry, a man with a fierce military bearing and mustache but with curiously melancholy eyes, had been a cavalry sergeant during his military service before he became the overseer of the immense estate of the Salgo family on the Hungarian *puszta*, or plains, and certainly he rode a horse to go about his job. Of his children, neither Alex nor my father rode as adults, though both had been on horses as children, if only to take them back and forth from the fields to the stable. When World War I began, however, my uncle Zoltan was called up for military service and actually became a lieutenant in a cavalry regiment in the Austro-Hungarian Army, unusual for a Jew in those days, particularly in the army whose most famous veteran was the title character in Jaroslav Hašek's classic novel *The Good Soldier Svejk.* Zoli saw combat on the Galician front and was wounded, gassed, and taken prisoner by the Russians. He rode in at least one cavalry charge, and perhaps as a result, in later years he showed no desire to mount a horse again. Uncle Alex's eyes were bad enough to exempt him from military service. My father was conscripted and sent to an infantry regiment, where the colonel soon discovered both his ineptitude as a soldier and his talent as a painter and promoted him to sergeant, giving my father a small, cozy cottage as a studio, where he busied himself painting portraits of the colonel, the colonel's wife, the colonel's daughters, and the colonel's dog (a dachshund), as well as nudes of the colonel's mistress, until the war was over and he could return to art school. When he was not painting, he looked after the colonel's horse, and in later life, whenever he saw a horse in the street, he would stop, pet it, and feed it one of the lumps of sugar that he took from restaurants and kept in his pocket for just that purpose. He remained distantly fond of horses, if only because they reminded him of his youth—the colonel's horse, he liked to say, had given him a good deal less trouble than the colonel's wife or mistress—but not so fond as to explain my own involvement with horses over the years.

On my mother's side of the family, which was staunchly English, it's harder to say for sure what part horses played. My great-grandfather was always described rather grandly by his daughters—Annie, my grandmother, and her more formidable older sister Maud-Mary—as "having owned horses all his life," which was true enough, since he had a horse-drawn cart pulled by a succession of bony old nags, with which he made his way daily around the Liverpool streets, crying out, "Coal, coal!" to housewives.

My maternal grandfather, Octavius Musgrove, must have been interested in riding at one time. I have before me a photograph of him, dressed to the nines as an Edwardian sportsman, in a tweed hacking jacket, a vest with gold buttons, well-cut riding breeches, and gleaming riding boots, one hand nonchalantly stuck in his pocket. My mother, at about the age of twelve, stands beside him, showing few signs of the great beauty she was to become, dressed in a schoolgirl's unflattering long-sleeved middy blouse and tie and a long, heavy skirt. Her cousin Madge Evans (who would go on to become a Hollywood child star and rival to Shirley Temple, and whose theme song would be "Pennies from Heaven") is on her knees in front of my mother, trying unsuccessfully to hold a

struggling Jack Russell terrier still for the photograph. The house in the background has columns and a lawn that suggests the presence of horses—why else would Ockie be dressed that way?—but no horses are visible in the picture. In later life, neither Madge Evans nor my mother ever expressed in my hearing the least interest in horses, however, and no photographs of them exist as equestriennes, though since they both achieved some measure of fame as actresses, they were photographed, once they reached Hollywood, playing, or pretending to play, almost every other sport.

I remember being taken to a riding school in Griffith Park, Los Angeles, when we moved to California in late 1940 so that my father could finish *The Thief of Baghdad* and make *The Jungle Book* and *That Hamilton Woman*. There I was introduced to western riding. When my mother moved to New York to play Irina in the Katharine Cornell production of Chekhov's *Three Sisters* on Broadway, I remember taking riding lessons at Durland's, a venerable old stable on West Sixty-seventh Street with an indoor ring, a glassed-in spectators' gallery, and an elevator that could hold a carriage and two horses, right where the ABC studios are now situated. Clearly, somebody in the family thought that I would benefit from riding, as well as learning to play the piano, to dance, and to speak French.

The piano lessons never stuck (nor the violin, an earlier experiment), and the dance lessons didn't stick hard enough to make me anybody's favorite dance companion in later life, but I can still speak French fluently and ride, so not all of the money was wasted. Over the years, as I grew up, I rode from time to time, when I was in the mood, where I could. Wherever you went in the world, I discovered, you were likely to find a stable if you looked hard enough. There was Lilo Blum's tiny stable in a mews off Hyde Park Corner, a ten-minute walk from the Connaught Hotel, where you could rent a horse to ride in the park, on Rotten Row. There were small stables hidden high in the fragrant hills above Cannes and Nice, where you could ride along dry, dusty trails in the pine forests, looking down at the Mediterranean, or take dressage lessons in a ring from a ferocious and unforgiving French instructor. I found places where I could ride in Switzerland when I was at boarding school, in Germany when I did my military service in the Royal Air Force there, in the Bois de Boulogne when the Royal Air Force unaccountably sent me to Paris to live with a White Russian family and learn Russian at the taxpayers' expense, and at Oxford, where the surrounding countryside contained stables that had catered to generations of foxhunting undergraduates.

Once I returned to New York, married my first wife, and found a job as an assistant editor in book publishing, riding was no longer on my mind—I worked long hours, reading and editing manuscripts until late at night, the normal demands of married life took up my weekends, and the birth of a son (to two woefully unprepared parents) took up whatever odd moments were left. I did not exactly *miss* riding, which had never in any case been a passion with me—it simply seemed like part of another life, something I had done a bit of once upon a time and was unlikely, on the face of things, ever to do again.

It was not until my son Christopher was about six years old—and my career as an editor had achieved a certain stability—that I had the leisure to pause, as if to draw a deep breath, and came to the conclusion that there was something missing from my life, something, in fact, that Chris and I might one day share, if he was introduced to it early on, and by a good instructor.

I had seen people riding in Central Park while I was pushing a pram, or later a stroller, on visits to the zoo, and it occurred to me that there was no reason why I shouldn't take up riding again, on a modest basis. I tried renting a horse from Claremont Riding Academy, the only remaining livery stable in Manhattan, a few grim blocks from Central park on West Eighty-ninth Street, but for one reason or another it did not at first appeal to me. I tried the stable in Van Cortland Park, in the Bronx, another on Sheepshead Bay, and a couple more in Brooklyn. In most cases, the horses were tired and shabby old nags, only a step or two away from the pet-food slaughterhouse, and the bridle paths exiguous, in poor repair, and fiercely contested by roving bands of juvenile delinquents.

Then one day, on the way home from a Sunday visit to the Coney Island Aquarium with Chris, I took the wrong fork in the highway and found myself crossing the Verrazano Narrows Bridge to Staten Island. I managed to get off the highway eventually, and looking for a place to turn around, I saw a sign that read "Clove Lake Stable—Two Miles." I followed it and turned off the road into an old-fashioned stableyard, with the familiar odor of manure and many dogs. There was a big barn, in poor repair, a large white clapboard house, presumably the owner's, a number of paddocks, and a fenced-in riding ring, at that moment full of small children not much older than Chris riding ponies, while a stout young woman with blond hair in pigtails, wearing boots and breeches, shouted, gestured, and cracked a long whip to keep them in line. Across the road stretched Clove Lake Park, hilly, heavily wooded, and apparently not "developed" the way Central Park was. Nothing suggested that we were still in New York City. The only competition to the stable as an attraction for miles around appeared to be a reptile zoo, to judge by a sign on the road.

Clove Lake Stable, as I soon discovered from one of the free brochures in a wooden box by the door to the office, was something of an old Staten Island institution. Owned by the Franzreb family for several generations (the girl in the riding ring was a Franzreb daughter), it was then managed by John Franzreb, a heavily built young man of Dickensian appearance, for his mother, who watched the cash register with a beady eye, like Mme Defarge in her husband's wineshop. The Franzrebs were urban equine entrepreneurs and John, by some kind of hereditary right of succession was entitled to blow the hunting horn signaling the beginning of the horse show in Madison Square Garden every year dressed in a scarlet tailcoat, a white waistcoat with gold buttons, white breeches, shiny black riding boots with brown tops, and a gray top hat.

Seen at the family business, he was bluff, busy, red-faced, and cheerful. If I was interested in riding lessons, I should go talk to his instructor, Paul Nigro, who ought to be coming in from the park at any moment. I walked off into the dusty stableyard just as a couple of riders appeared. One of them dismounted and walked off stiffly, as if in pain; the other, a short, slender, elderly man with bright red cheeks and fierce blue eyes, dismounted with easy grace and began to lead both horses to the barn. I walked over and said I was interested in riding lessons, for myself and perhaps for my son.

Nigro looked me up and down and shook his head mournfully. I was wearing jeans and a sweater. He wore a well-worn green tweed hacking jacket buttoned up over a tattersall waistcoat with gold buttons, a stock with a gold pin, tan breeches, and brown boots. His leather gloves were immaculate, there was a fresh flower in the buttonhole of his lapel, and he wore a jaunty black bowler hat cocked at a rakish angle.

"I guess I could make time for you," he said gruffly—he had a deep, gravelly voice and an old-fashioned New York City accent, with a definite hint of "deze, dem, and doze" outer-boroughs Irish, the kind of accent you still heard among people who worked at the track or older mounted cops. "You have to work all that out with dem in the office there, with John or old lady Franzreb."

I remarked that the two horses looked in pretty good shape—they did, too, compared to the horseflesh I had seen elsewhere in the city. "*Dese* two?" Nigro asked, with a laugh. "They're on their last legs, poor things, but I don't take 'em out until I've groomed 'em, and looked after their hooves and tidied them up a bit. The fellas they've got working here in the barn, they don't know what they're doing, that's the long and short of it," he said with a sigh, pointing his riding crop at a couple of men in overalls, who glared back at him angrily. "The dirty dogs," Nigro muttered angrily. "I won't ride a dirty horse," he said. "You go out with me, mister, you'd better be ready to take a brush to a horse if I sez so."

I said that was fine with me. I didn't much like grooming horses, but from time to time I'd done it, and cleaned a lot of things dirtier than horses when I was a recruit in the Royal Air Force.

That remark cheered Nigro up some—he had a lot of respect for men who had worn what he called "the uniform," irrespective of what it was, and what he most wanted from a pupil was a willing attitude and unquestioning obedience. He gave me a closer look. "You'll need boots, breeches, gloves, a hard hat, you and the boy. I don't take nobody out in jeans, that's the long and short of it."

At the other stables I had been to in the city, nobody seemed to care what the customers wore, so long as they paid in advance and signed a release form holding the stable free from any responsibility if the rider was injured or killed. I had long since lost track of my riding things, but I said that I had no objection to outfitting myself properly.

Nigro nodded solemnly, as if I had just passed some kind of test. He handed me a card. "Go see Charlie Kauffman, at Kauffman's Saddlery, in the city, down there on East Twenty-fourth Street, and tell him you'll be riding with me. He'll give you a good deal, and make sure you get the right things, not the kind of crap—excuse my French—you see a lot of people wearing around here, who don't know no better and don't want to be told."

With that, he touched the brim of his bowler and led his horses off to the barn. Seen from behind, he had the narrow bowed legs of the professional horseman—he might have been a figure out of a painting by Manet or Toulouse-Lautrec. Just before he entered the barn, he turned and shouted out, "Make sure you go to Kauffman's, like I told yez, not that other place, what's its name!" This, I was soon to learn, was a reference to Miller's Saddlery, also on East Twenty-fourth Street, a rival establishment, for which Nigro harbored such a great contempt that he would not even speak its name, despite the fact that so far as I could tell both places sold pretty much the same goods at more or less the same prices.

A few days later, when I presented the card to Charlie Kauffman in his vast, cluttered old horse barn of a shop, jammed to the cast-iron rafters and grimy skylights with every imaginable kind of riding clothing, tack, equipment, and harness, and redolent of the comforting smell of old and new leather, he handed it back to me with a sigh. "I hope you know what you're getting yourself into," he said to me, at the same time measuring Christopher for size with his eyes as he handed him a lollipop from a big glass jar labeled "Horse Treats."

I said I'd ridden before—a few lessons to brush myself up again didn't seem like a bad idea, and if that worked out Christopher would be taking lessons too—a father-and-son thing.

Kauffman nodded, as if he'd heard that song before. "Paul's one of a kind," he said, "a horseman of the old school. You don't see too many like him anymore, I'll tell you that." His tone was warily neutral, rather than enthusiastic, like that of a man who had seen as many horsemen of the old school as he wanted to in a lifetime of selling horse equipment. With Kauffman's help I selected what I needed, and also bought Chris a pair of jodhpurs, jodhpur boots, and, at Kauffman's suggestion, buckled straps to go below his knees, as well as the obligatory black velvet-covered hard hat with a chin harness, tiny gloves, and a riding crop. "He may as well have what Paul Nigro would want him to," Kauffman said. "Otherwise Paul will just raise hell and send you back to change it all, and who needs that kind of aggravation?"

Standing in front of the mirror in his tan jodhpurs and shiny brown jodhpur boots, with his black velvet hunt cap pulled down low over his eyes, Chris took on a whole new, and more serious, appearance, one that looked surprisingly familiar, until it occurred to me that he pretty much resembled photographs of myself at the same age on my way to or from a riding lesson.

Also, like myself at that age, his expression was guarded, as if he were saying to himself, What next? or possibly, Why me?

I put that thought out of my mind, packed our new belongings into the family Volkswagen, and took Christopher home so that he could model his new finery for his mother.

In the next few months Christopher and I rode at least twice a week with Paul Nigro, in good weather and bad, and sometimes even three times, for it turned out that one of Nigro's specialties was the Thursday-evening "musical ride," in which a mixed group of children and adults did precision team riding in the floodlit outdoor ring to a medley of Sousa marches and that old favorite of the Austro-Hungarian Army, the Radetzky March, all broadcast over and over again at earsplitting volume from the loudspeakers while Nigro rode up and down the center of the ring, tightening the ranks, speeding up the pace, demonstrating how to do a figure eight at the canter in columns of two, and generally acting the part of the riding master in a cavalry regiment. There were very few spectators (and what few there were, were mostly close relatives of those riding), but on a good night there would sometimes be as many as two dozen riders in the ring, most of them sweating bullets in case Nigro's eagle eye caught them cantering on the wrong lead, getting ahead or falling behind of the horse and rider next to them, or failing to sit to the trot when ordered to. If I close my eyes, I can still hear Nigro's voice, rising above the band music, shouting, "Keep your hands down! Keep your heels down! Remind the horse who's the boss!" as the rows of horses cantered past him in a cloud of dust, richly scented with manure.

On Saturday and Sunday mornings Chris and I would go off to Staten Island for our riding lesson in the park with Paul Nigro, at the end of which, if all had gone to his satisfaction and there were no mounted cops in sight, we were allowed a good, long gallop, or even a few jumps over low stone walls, after which we had to unsaddle our horses and hand-walk them until they cooled off, while Nigro walked beside us, giving us an assessment of our progress.

Praise did not come easily to Nigro, and his standards were both idiosyncratic and alarmingly high. Children who rode with him were expected to obey him unquestioningly, never to complain, and to always mind "their Ps and Qs." Once they could walk, trot, and canter to his satisfaction, with and eventually without stirrups, he taught them to ride standing up behind him at the canter on the croup of his horse, holding onto his shoulders if they were unsure of their balance, and to jump from that position to the ground, landing on their feet like acrobats. Riding, he liked to say, required good balance, courage, and horse sense, and he was determined to instill all three in his pupils. Although Nigro was himself an outspoken nonsmoker, his favorite test for adults was to have the rider take a pack of cigarettes and a book of matches from his or her pocket and light a cigarette at the canter, without slowing the pace, losing control of the horse, or dropping anything. He reminded me, not without a trace of nostalgia, of some of the older NCOs I had met up with in my time in the British armed forces—the kind of grizzled, old-fashioned, gray-haired regimental sergeant major who had a voice that could stop you dead in your tracks from across a parade ground, a stare of disapproval that could freeze your blood, and boots so highly polished you could use them as a shaving mirror. Nigro did not have the mustache or the martial background—he had served in the Merchant Marine, of all things, in World War II—and of course he wasn't English, but in every other respect he resembled one of those awesome and dreaded beings, with their impossibly high standards, their incomprehensible list of do's and don'ts, their fierce loyalty to traditions long since forgotten, abandoned, or ridiculed by the rest of the world, and their odd and unpredictable moments of kindness. It was as if I had been carried twenty years back, to my days as an RAF recruit, which perhaps explains my determination to live up to Nigro's expectations. His was a type I knew.

Years before, while riding in London's Hyde Park early one morning, I had encountered one of the last of this dying breed of warrant officers in peculiar circumstances. I had so far won the confidence of Lilo Blum, the owner of one of the small livery stables around the park, that she allowed me to take her own horse out by myself in the mornings instead of going with a group and an instructor. The horse was a dapper and rather flashy little Arab–Welsh pony cross that was just a little too small for me, but more than made up for that in good looks and character— he had, in fact, as it turned out, rather more character than was desirable. His name—which should have come as a warning to me—was Mephisto, and he was palomino, with a gleaming pale blond coat, a long, flowing silver mane and tail, and the large eye and neat little ears that are supposed to connote a lively intelligence in horses.

I never experienced any trouble taking Mephisto through the horrendous traffic around Hyde Park Corner—he didn't appear to care a bit about huge diesel lorries, buses, and taxis—and once in the park he drew a good deal of admiration, which he seemed to enjoy. In those days the early-morning park riders were a daunting lot. There were the flawlessly dressed young officers of the Household Cavalry on their own horses, troopers from the Life Guards or the Blues in uniform exercising their mounts, some of the queen's horses from the Buckingham Palace stables being worked by grooms in top hats and livery coats, and a few private riders, dressed to the nines as only the English upper class can be on horseback.

One day, for no particular reason that I could tell, Mephisto made his way with dainty steps through the early-morning traffic at Hyde Park Corner but seemed balky and unwilling to move forward once we were in the park. Perhaps he had been worked too hard the day before, or perhaps he wasn't feeling up to par, or perhaps he had simply taken my measure and decided that he could get away with misbehaving. I used my legs, made clicking noises with my tongue, and gave him a couple of taps with my riding crop, but to no effect—in fact, when he started to move, he went *backward,* straight toward the cold and uninviting water of the Serpentine, Hyde Park's large artificial lake. Once he was moving backward, however, there was no stopping him. Step by step he backed across the bridle path to the Serpentine, then began to back *into* it. I used the crop on him harder, but it didn't stop him from backing up. His ears were flat back against his head now—a sure sign of a stubborn determination to have his own way.

At first, I was embarrassed at this display of poor control over the horse on my part. I looked around, but the park appeared to be empty, so there was nobody around to laugh at me—or to help, either. Then embarrassment turned to apprehension. The Serpentine starts shallow, but very quickly becomes deeper. First Mephisto was in water above his hooves, then up to his knees, then, all of a sudden, the heels of my boots were underwater. A few more steps backward on his part, and I might find myself swimming in the Serpentine, in a tweed hacking jacket, breeches, and a brown velvet hunt cap.

I renewed my work with the riding crop, but it had no effect. Mephisto just rolled his eyes, snorted, and shuffled back a few more steps until the water was approaching the top of my boots.

At that point I saw, to my relief, somebody else on the bridle path. In the distance, moving at a sedate walk toward me, was a huge piebald horse, ridden by a man who looked like something of a giant himself. As they drew closer, I recognized the horse—it was none other than Clarence, the regimental drum horse of the mounted band of the Life Guards, who on parade bears a vast, heavy silver kettle drum on either side just ahead of the saddle. In full dress, the horse's reins are attached to the rider's stirrups, so the drummer's hands are free to use the big, padded drumsticks, while his feet control the horse. Clarence was a well-known and much-beloved horse, with hooves the size of dinner plates and thick, feathered fetlocks, a towering eighteen hands or more high and probably weighing over a ton—at least as big as the biggest draft horses, like the Scottish Clydesdale (famous as the "Budweiser horses" in America) or the Shire horse in England.

His rider, this morning, was none other than the regimental sergeant major of the Life Guards himself, well over six feet tall and a solid two hundred pounds or more, in a khaki uniform with razor-sharp creases, and buttons, badges, leather, and cap peak so shiny that it hurt my eyes to look in his direction. The RSM's neck was as thick around as my thigh, and bulged over the back of the high, tightly buttoned collar of his tunic. The gold-edged peak of his dark blue cap was pulled low so that it concealed his eyes—not that it mattered, since I had seen that same flat, bottomless stare often enough before on the parade ground from other senior warrant officers of the British armed services. His mustache was waxed into sharp, upturned points.

From his great height—horse and rider dwarfed Mephisto and me—the RSM gravely examined the situation in silence for a few moments. He did not laugh. "'Aving trouble, sir?" he asked in a deep, quiet voice, which, I knew, could rise in volume to make him heard from one side of a parade ground to the other.

I explained my predicament.

The RSM leaned his head a little to one side to have a better look—the peak of his cap no doubt rendered him blind to his immediate front, rather like a rhinoceros. "'Ave you used the whip on 'im, sir?"

I said I had, as hard as I dared.

"Ah." One look at the RSM's face told me that *his* definition of the hard use of a whip might be rather different from mine. Still he was not about to lay a whip on somebody else's horse, particularly one ridden by a civilian.

"They can be stubborn little buggers, ponies," he said. "Give me a big 'orse every time." He stared at Mephisto with intense dislike. Disobedience in any form, from man or beast, was, I had no doubt, the thing the RSM liked least, along with tarnished brass or dull leather.

"Mind if I 'elp, sir?" he asked, edging giant Clarence into the Serpentine to get closer to us. I indicated that help was just what I most wanted at present—the more, the better.

The RSM was close enough now to reach down and touch my horse. For a moment, it occurred to me that he might be planning to pull Mephisto out of the water—Clarence could probably have towed a Chieftan tank if put to the task by the RSM—but he merely grabbed one of Mephisto's dainty ears in his immense gloved hand and leaned over until his mouth was right next to it, like somebody speaking into an old-fashioned telephone. "Forgive me, sir," he said, then in a voice like thunder, he shouted into the pony's ear as loud as he could, "Get *out* of there, you fucking little bastard!"

Mephisto hesitated for no more than a second or two. Eyes rolling, ears pricked forward, he was out of the Serpentine in one long leap, and back on the bridle path, where he stood shivering, certainly not from the cold.

The RSM's voice had set the crows to cawing all over Hyde Park, not to speak of drawing people from out of the landscape as if they had heard the voice of God. Soldiers of all ranks for miles around no doubt straightened their backs, shot a desperate downward glance at their boot caps, tucked their chins in, and tried to think what on earth they had been doing to catch the Olympian attention of the RSM.

The RSM touched his riding whip to his cap as I thanked him. "'Appy to oblige," he said. "You shouldn't have any more trouble with 'im now, sir." He paused and got Clarence back on the bit again. "You just 'ave to speak firmly to 'em," he said. "If there's one thing your 'orse respects, it's firmness." And with that he and Clarence set off down the bridle path at a steady pace.

In his own way, Nigro was as great a believer in firmness as the regimental sergeant major of the Life Guards, and no slouch as an authority figure too. Remarkably, Chris's willingness to accept Nigro as yet another authority figure in his life was hardly less than my own, though in retrospect it occurs to me that Chris may have simply been humoring me, or happy enough to escape from his mother's far more exacting supervision for a few hours, even if it meant doing something totally alien to him, like riding a horse and being ordered around by a total stranger. No doubt, like many children, he had a natural desire to please grown-ups—a desire out of which he was very shortly to grow, once he approached puberty—and Paul Nigro, difficult as he could be, was a lot easier for Chris to please than his mother: all he had to do was to keep his heels down, his head up, his back straight, and stay on the horse. How much he enjoyed it is hard to say, but he certainly gave it his all, becoming a stylish, if not particularly enthusiastic, young rider and a great favorite of Nigro's, who in his own gruff way liked teaching children a lot better than teaching adults.

We were to see a lot more of Nigro over the next couple of years, and of Charlie Kauffman too, since as Chris grew, he needed to be reoutfitted at intervals, while Nigro persuaded me to buy my own saddle (it didn't take a lot of persuading). The purchase of the saddle was a transaction important enough for Paul Nigro to meet me at Kauffman's one afternoon, since he didn't trust me (or Charlie Kauffman) to select the correct one. Nigro was as authoritarian and opinionated off a horse as on one, and he and Kauffman fought like cat and dog over each saddle Kauffman showed me. "Don't show us no more of that Argent-teen crap, Charlie!" Nigro shouted, dismissing with one hand a whole wall full of Kauffman's stock. I was to have a saddle handmade in *England*, by Crosby, or better yet Barnsby, the latter a saddler so small that only Kauffman's still carried a few of their saddles, for those customers old enough (and sufficiently tradition-bound) to remember the name. It was to be a standard hunting saddle, without padded knee rolls ("None of that suede padded German crap, that's all wrong!"), with a deep seat, a high pommel so it would fit any horse, and a square cantle (round cantles were for women's saddles, square ones for men's, another of those all-important traditions which Nigro cherished and almost everybody else ignored, or simply didn't know about, to his fury).

Eventually, rolling his eyes and breathing hard after having moved half his stock around, Kauffman managed to produce a saddle by Barnsby that met with Nigro's approval, and they went off into a corner of the store, behind a pile of horse blankets, to argue about the price. Nigro came back red in the face. "Oh, he's a tough one, Charlie is," he whispered to me, quoting me a figure that was about 25 percent off the list price, "but I got him to throw in the stirrup leathers and the stirrups, as well as a saddle cover." He stroked the saddle gently. "You look after that, and it'll last yez a lifetime," he said.

That Nigro knew what he was talking about is evinced by the fact that I was still using that saddle day in and day out some thirty years later, and it showed fewer signs of wear than I did. He usually knew what he was talking about when it came to horses, tack, and horse etiquette, and was a sort of walking (or riding) one-man horseman's encyclopedia. On the subject of bits alone, he could name (and describe) dozens of them—a body of knowledge that was just about as widespread and commonplace in 1900 as that of carburetors and spark plugs and points by the 1930s, but has long since been forgotten by almost everybody.

Although Nigro drove a car—a huge great barge of a 1950s American car, of course, since he was of that generation of Americans who believed passionately in buying American, except when it came to saddles—he was totally uninterested in modern technology, or indeed the modern world in general; whereas on the subject of bits, for example, his knowledge was awesome, and his opinions fiercely held and argued, not that many people wanted to argue with him on the subject, least of all me.

He knew at a glance exactly what kind of bit he thought a horse needed, what size it should be, and how it should be fitted, and he had huge, long-running fights with John Franzreb, or the grooms at Clove Lake Stables (whom Nigro always referred to, I discovered, as "those dirty dogs"), who just wanted to get the horse out of the door and between the customer's legs, and didn't want Nigro bringing it back and telling them that it needed a pelham, or a kimberwick, or an eggbutt snaffle, or a double bridle in its mouth.

On the subject of martingales—the leather strap or straps used to prevent the horse from raising his head high enough to break the rider's nose—Nigro could argue with the passionate intensity and the absolute refusal to accept anybody's opinion but his own that are, so frequently, symptomatic of religious belief. Martingales, indeed, brought out the worst in him—it must be a *standing* martingale (fastened to the noseband) rather than a *running* martingale (fastened to the reins), and its length must be exactly as he prescribed it, to the inch, or else an explosion was certain, with Nigro eventually getting off his horse to carry the fight into the front office, where he and John Franzreb shouted at each other at the top of their lungs, eyes bulging and veins corded, until old Mrs. Franzreb managed to separate them and shoo Nigro back onto his horse again. He threatened to quit half a dozen times a month, but nobody else could have given the place the veneer of professional horsemanship that attracted the more committed students, in search, like acolytes, of absolute certainty.

For these, Nigro provided his own brand of religious faith, for the horse world is like a kind of secular religion, with its own cults and beliefs—in fact the worship of the horse is a good deal older than any known religion, going back to that point in prehistory when early man first started to use the horse to pull things rather than simply killing and eating it, and when, no doubt, his children learned you could get on a horse's back to take it to and from its field, leading the other horses behind you. In all cultures, horsemanship involves fiercely held or disputed do's, don'ts, and traditions, the origins of which are often lost, as they say, "in the mists of time," some of them based on many centuries of experience and commonsense, others idiosyncratic and impossible to explain. For example, since the majority of riders have always been right-handed, it makes sense that the horse is always mounted from the left—it is, in fact, almost physically impossible for most people to mount a horse from the "off" side—and for that reason too, most of the horse's tack is made with the buckles on the left side, so you can check and adjust things before you mount. That kind of thing makes sense, and is easy enough to explain and remember, but it is a good deal harder to explain, for instance, why the horse's mane is supposed to be brushed over until it falls to the right, even when nature clearly didn't intend it to, or the degree to which that kind of thing matters to purists.

Of course Nigro was the purist's purist: it *all* mattered to him, every detail. He knew for which occasions men should wear boots with a brown cuff around the top, and for which occasions they were inappropriate; which riders were supposed to wear the ends of the knotted ribbons at the back of their hard hats pointing down, and which ones were supposed to wear them pointing up, and why; he was a mine of information on how to tell the work of a good blacksmith from a bad one, the correct way to clean a hoof—all his pupils were encouraged to carry hoof picks, and to use them—and the importance of a clean saddle pad. Like some kind of equestrian high priest, he knew all the rules, as if he had learned the U.S. Army's last cavalry manual by heart. (He even gave me a copy, which I still have—*War Department Basic Field/Animal Transport,* "Prepared under the Direction of the Chief of Cavalry, FM 25-5, June 1939"—which no doubt reached the troops at about the same time the German army's panzers were decimating the Polish cavalry and inaugurating a war in which the care, training, and feeding of horses would no longer play a significant role.)

As with all high priests, Nigro's own version of the truth was the only one that mattered—he was deaf to anybody else's opinion—and when contradicted, he flew into a rage, then withdrew into moody silence. Even favorite pupils sometimes endured these outbursts, but at heart he was a decent soul, and if you turned up regularly and on time, whatever the weather, and did your very best with the horse you were given, he forgave you, and even sometimes gave you a sip of tea from his thermos, or split his candy bar with you. He always tried to ensure that his pupils were sent out on the best horses Clove Lake had, which wasn't saying much, despite what was clearly the intention of "the front office" and the grooms to sabotage him with the most intractable, hardmouthed, and difficult horses in the barn, the ones that knew every trick in the book about resisting a rider and getting him or her off, as opposed to the good ones, like Ocean Spray (the gray gelding that was my own favorite), which everybody wanted to ride. Once he even took Christopher and me to his home in the farthest reaches of Brooklyn, out toward Coney Island, to celebrate some triumph of Chris's in the children's horse show that Nigro organized once a year, where we met Nigro's family, none of whom seemed to have the slightest interest in horses, and sat down at four in the afternoon to an enormous Italian meal served buffet style, which, we discovered to our dismay, had been cooked by Mrs. Nigro entirely in our honor.

Sometimes when Chris, Paul Nigro, and I were out together, we rode in companionable silence—in bad weather we had the park virtually to ourselves. From afar you could occasionally hear the muted noise of traffic on the highway, or a ship's horn as it passed under the Verrazano Narrows Bridge; otherwise, the only sound was of the horses' hooves and their steady breathing—that and the jingling of a curb chain and the snort that is a horse's way of expressing relaxation, the feeling toward the end of the last ride of the day that all is for the best in the best of all possible worlds, with a good meal on the horizon and a long night of dozing and munching on hay in the company of a couple dozen other horses.

For most horses, heaven is other horses; quite the opposite of the human viewpoint, best expressed by Jean-Paul Sartre's comment in *No Exit*, "Hell is other people." Herd animals, horses are happiest when surrounded by their fellows—very few of them are loners. Although it is hard—and often misleading—to read human emotions into the facial expressions of animals, there is no joy quite like that of a horse on its own at the unexpected sight, even in the far distance, of another horse. The herding instinct never quite leaves horses, however well trained; it always remains buried deep in the horse's mind, perhaps even more strongly than the primal instinct of flight in the face of danger—which explains why horses that have been rescued from a barn that is on fire have been known to run back into it, and to their deaths, rather than be separated from their stablemates; also why it's important, even when horses have to be kept in separate paddocks or fields so they don't bite or kick one another, that they always be able to *see* each other.

It is because of things like this that riding is a sport like no other—it's not enough to learn how to *do* it, the way you might learn to play golf, for example, or to ski—it's also necessary to develop some understanding of the horse itself. The horse is not after all a golf club, or a pair of skis, but a complex living creature, with its own deep instincts, needs, and personality, and no two horses are alike, any more than two human beings. Of course plenty of people learn to ride without developing any particular empathy for the horse, but most of them eventually give it up, or get themselves hurt; the best riders not only master the *technique* of riding (whether "English" or "western" doesn't really matter), but learn to know, understand, and love horses, becoming not just good riders but "horse people."

Horses have been around people (and vice versa) for about ten thousand years, give or take a few, so both species have had plenty of time to get to know each other. The horse has come to symbolize, for humans, speed, strength, grace—it's amazing, when you think of it, how many cars are named after horses (Pinto, Mustang) or feature a horse on their nameplate or badge (Ferrari, Porsche)—and to judge from primitive cave paintings, these feelings of admiration for the horse were there from the very beginning. The horse must have been seen by early man as possessing so many qualities that man himself did not—absolute, unconditional loyalty to fellow members of the herd, awesome speed to escape from danger, a kick that would discourage all but the largest and fiercest of predators—that it is hardly surprising our ancestors ascribed to horses magical powers, and took such pains to paint them accurately on the walls of their caves.

What horses think of human beings is rather more difficult to guess—after thousands of years of living near people, do they see us as representing a sense of security?—but most horses are tolerant and trusting unless treated cruelly, as is, alas, all too often the case. Riding instructors have parroted to their students for years the old English adage, "The best thing for the inside of a man is the outside of a horse." Paul Nigro was no exception, but beyond the health benefits of riding (which is, in fact, better exercise for the horse than the rider), he managed to convey, more importantly, some feeling of partnership with the horse, the sense in which another living creature is involved in the activity, albeit not necessarily on an altogether voluntary basis.

This is something that even the most fervent of small animal lovers do not always find easy to accept, that the horse's own agenda, mood, experience, courage or fear, personality, and—not to anthropomorphize—*enthusiasm* are a vital part of the riding experience, from the little girl's pony to the highest and most glamorous level of competition. It is a constant wonder that even a small child can manage a large and powerful animal—that the horse is willing to put its strength and speed at the disposal of another, and very different, animal, so long as the bond of trust is maintained. "The horse has to trust you, and you have to trust the horse," we heard over and over again, as we walked, trotted, and cantered over the badly eroded bridle path of Clove Lake. Of course, like all simple truths, it was the hardest lesson to learn—or, in my case, relearn.

It should not have been so. Once, years before, Abby Hirsch, a friend of mine in the PR business, called in great excitement with a piece of good news. Would I like to ride in the opening parade on the first night of the annual Madison Square Garden rodeo? That sounded like something that might be fun to do, so on the appointed evening, I turned up at the Garden dressed as instructed in jeans, cowboy boots, a checked western shirt, and a Stetson. Deep in the bowels of the Garden, where the horses and rodeo stock were stabled, I was introduced to the famous western trick rider Danny Dakota, who would be leading the parade on his "wonder horse," King.

Dakota was a short, sinewy, bowlegged little man of indeterminate age, with a face as brown and deeply creased as a nut, and a ferocious expression. He was chewing gum fiercely. He and King were a star turn at rodeos, state fairs, and horse shows all over the West.

Mrs. Dakota looked to me several decades younger than her husband, a blond lady of stunning proportions in a skin-tight, sequined western riding outfit. She was holding the fancy bridle of "King the Wonder Horse," as he was always referred to, a placid, plump pinto. Trying to make polite conversation, I remarked on how hard it must be to have your whole act built around one horse—King could not only dance but count, all the way up to ten, tapping out the numbers with one hoof as Danny Dakota called them.

Mrs. Dakota gave me a bright smile—she had eyelashes like the ones later made famous by Tammy Faye Bakker—and shook her platinum curls. "Why, no, honey," she said sweetly, "that's no problem. Danny has a bunch of horses that all look exactly alike, all named King, see, so if one of them throws a shoe or goes lame or something, we just tack up another one."

So much for sentiment. Danny fixed me with a baleful glare. "Kin you ride?" he asked. "That PR gal sent me a whole bunch of people I swear don't know one end of a horse from the other."

I said that I thought I could manage. Danny did not look convinced by this display of British understatement. "Well, I got to have fifty of you, one for each state, so I guess I cain't be fussy. Here's the deal: you carry a state flag in your right hand, and we come on out of that chute there into the ring at a canter, then we do figure eights at a canter for a while. When the music stops, you halt, and you and your horse don't move a *muscle* while King and me do our number, you hear? Then the music starts up again, we do a few more figure eights, a final gallop round the ring, then you canter down that chute when it's your turn. Don't drop your flag, don't fall off, and don't screw up King's act, okay?"

An expression of doubt must have crossed my face, because Danny looked at me more closely, then pushed his big white Stetson back on his head with a sigh. It had, in fact, just occurred to me that I would be cantering a horse I'd never ridden before up a steep incline through a dark tunnel, emerging into the brightly lit arena of Madison Square Garden with maybe fifty thousand people watching me. The potential for making a fool of myself in front of a large number of people suddenly seemed excellent.

Danny put a hand on my shoulder reassuringly, horseman to horseman. "Listen, son," he said, slowing up on his chewing, "don't do nothing, just stay on the horse and let *him* do it all. He's done it a hundred times before, and I doubt he'll mess it up if you leave him alone. You just got to trust the horse, that's all."

I kept this thought firmly in my mind as Mrs. Dakota, still smiling brightly, handed me the state flag of New Mexico, and even managed to keep it there while the horse and I waited our turn at the bottom of the dark ramp leading up to the arena, in a dense mass of other horses and riders. The band was playing "California, Here I Come!" over and over again, as loud as could be; the horses were jostling, fidgeting, and flicking their ears nervously; the flagstaff in my hand seemed to weigh a hundred pounds. Then I heard somebody shout out, "Let's go, New Mexico! Ride 'em, cowboy!" and it was my turn. The next thing I knew, the horse and I were cantering up the chute in the darkness, then out into the blinding lights of Madison Square Garden with thousands of people shouting and cheering, and children swinging little flashlights, and the band playing louder than ever, and the smell of popcorn and horse and cow manure in the air.

I closed off my mind and did what Danny had told me to do—I could see him in the center on King, bearing the flag of the United States—while my horse, just as Danny had promised, cantered round the ring, did his figure eights, stopped when the band stopped playing, waited motionless while Danny and King did their number, then carried me safely round the ring again and down the chute.

Danny rode past me on King through the crush of horses in the basement corridor, still chewing gum, and turned in the saddle to give me a wink. "What did I tell you, pardner?" he said. "Trust the horse. How did it feel?"

I struggled for a tone of manly honesty—or perhaps found it naturally. "To tell the truth, I was scared shitless when we got out there into the lights," I said.

Danny wrapped Old Glory carefully around the staff and handed it down to Mrs. Dakota. He stared at me darkly for a moment or two. I hoped I hadn't offended him, but then he nodded and gave me a rueful, tight-lipped grin. "I'll tell you what," he said, "I been *there* myself a time or two, pardner."

Then he touched his hat and trotted off round the corner to return King to his stall, next to the other Kings, with Mrs. Dakota running behind him on the high heels of her cowboy boots, trying to keep up.

This is a book about horses, and "horse people"—people who love horses, or who know horses, or who make their living out of horses, or who just can't imagine what their life would be like without horses.

Most of them don't think you can make much headway with a horse by whispering to it—not unless a horse surprises us all one day by whispering back—but almost all of them have learned, as Danny Dakota put it, to "trust the horse," and from time to time most of them have been scared shitless too.

God knows I have, and never more so than in the very heart of horse country.

CHAPTER TWO

In the Heart of Horse Country

*Tally-ho – and
eyes front !*

IT WAS, IN FACT, a gift from Paul Nigro
that got me into trouble.

Nigro liked to spend his spare time repairing tack—another
vanishing skill—and could perform wonders with a broken-down
saddle or a worn-out bridle. On the grounds that no real lady could be
said to ride properly without knowing how to ride sidesaddle, he had
rescued, with Charlie Kauffman's weary blessing, a badly worn and damaged old sidesaddle from the basement of Kauffman's, and eventually
brought it back to something like its original state.

Of course it goes without saying that even Nigro's considerable
powers of persuasion were not sufficient to convince any of his female
pupils that they needed to learn to ride sidesaddle—hardly anybody
does today, except for the most dedicated and hidebound of tradition-
alists. Until World War I, however, it was unthinkable for a woman to
ride "astride"—women rode in a special saddle, with the right leg

pinned against a curved, projecting leather "horn" and the left leg in the stirrup, usually wearing a long skirt that covered both their legs. The sidesaddle looked cumbersome, but in fact a woman in a sidesaddle could ride (and jump) a horse as well as many men mounted astride, and far more gracefully. Empress Elisabeth of Austro-Hungary (Emperor Franz-Joseph's beautiful, unhappy, and reckless wife) was one of the most daring, admired, and skilled riders in all Europe, taking the most challenging of fences in the hunt field or on steeplechase courses, always on a sidesaddle, of course, so the thing *is* possible. Possible or not, however, none of Nigro's pupils wanted to put it to the test, to his great disappointment.

As it happens, in my role as an editor at Simon & Schuster I had recently bought on Larry McMurtry's suggestion a novel by a writer named Jane McIlvaine McClary, who lived in Middleburg, Virginia, perhaps the horsiest place in America. Her novel, which she had been working on for many years, was called *A Portion for Foxes*—it was huge, sprawling, melodramatic, romantic, the kind of vast literary chaos that in those days made my heart beat faster, a kind of *Gone With the Wind* of foxhunting, which to the surprise of my colleagues actually went on, after heavy editing and rewriting, to become a major best-seller. Jane was a horsewoman and foxhunter of international distinction, and knew that I rode—in fact, that was the main reason she had sent me her novel in the first place. During the course of our interminable discussions about how to cut *A Portion for Foxes* down to a reasonable length, Jane happened to mention that she was looking for a good used sidesaddle for herself. She had not been able to find one at a sensible price locally; might I happen to know whether she could find one in New York?

I was overjoyed, being perhaps the only person in Rockefeller Center who could have answered yes to that question. I called Paul Nigro at once, explained what a great horsewoman Jane McClary was, and asked if he would like to sell her his sidesaddle. As it happened, Nigro already knew her name—an avid reader of the *Chronicle of the Horse*, the weekly magazine of English riding in America, which is actually published (where else?) in Middleburg, he had read her columns, as well as accounts of her exploits on the hunt fields of Virginia and Ireland. Impressed that his saddle might be going to somebody who would not only appreciate it but *use* it, he insisted on giving it to me, as a present for her.

The sidesaddle was bulky, heavy, and valuable, so rather than try to ship it to her, I undertook at her suggestion to bring it down myself, spend a long weekend at her house, and go out with her on Saturday with the Middleburg Hunt. That sounded good to me, though when I told Nigro, he was apprehensive—I must not let him down. Above all, I must be properly dressed for a day out with one of the most famous hunts in America. He met me one afternoon at Kauffman's to oversee my purchase of the essentials. My boots, black jacket, breeches, and stock were okay, but if I was not to disgrace him in the field I needed the right kind of waistcoat, spurs, little leather straps like garters for the tops of my boots, plain dark leather gloves, a leather sandwich case to fasten to one side of my saddle, a long, thin flask in a leather case to fasten on the other side, and a hunting whip with a horn handle. Giddily, I wrote a check. Seen in the mirror at Kauffman's, I looked like a character from the work of the Victorian sporting novelist Robert Smith Surtees—perhaps Mr. Sponge, from *Mr. Sponge's Sporting Tour*, who memorably described foxhunting as "the sport of kings, the image of war without its guilt, and only five-and-twenty per cent of its danger."

Rereading Surtees before going down to Middleburg might not have been a bad idea—I would have had a better idea of just what I was letting myself in for—but unfortunately it didn't occur to me to do so. Surtees knew what he was writing about when it came to the danger of foxhunting.

We flew down to Dulles Airport, outside Washington, D.C., having bought four seats on the shuttle for me, my then wife, Chris, and the sidesaddle. The idea was that Chris and his mother would take the opportunity for a couple of days of sightseeing in Washington, while I got my fill of the Virginia horse world. Jane's house, when we finally found it, might have come straight from the pages of Surtees—a huge, timbered, sprawling old mansion, the kind of place that people always describe as having been built "before the Crash," full of dogs, very English, surrounded by big old trees and gardens run to seed, with a large, well-cared-for barn and many acres of horse pastures. Inside, as outside, the dominating themes were the horse, the fox, and the hounds. Almost everything in sight was decorated with one or the other, or where possible, all three. Fox heads appeared everywhere, engraved on the glasses and silverware, painted on the china, carved on the posts of the banisters and at either end of the mantelpiece, embroidered skillfully or amateurishly on pillows, adorning the ashtrays, the bookends, the wastepaper baskets, Jane's writing paper, the doorknobs, the fire irons, even the telephone, where a fox wearing a hunt cap grinned from beneath the little round plastic disk where, in the days of rotary telephones, the home number usually appeared.

The walls were covered with paintings and drawings of horses, framed photographs of people on horseback going back to the 1920s, and group photographs of polo teams, eventing teams, and hunt meetings. Everywhere there were signs of horsey activity. The mudroom was jammed with riding boots and Wellington boots, spurs, Barbour rain gear, hunt caps and whips of every size and type, dog leashes, a corkboard with rows of fading ribbons, and a glassed-in cabinet full of silver riding trophies and horse sculpture. Odd pieces of tack and horse blankets were hung up to dry in every bathroom and from the bedroom doorknobs, and there was everywhere a strong prevailing odor of wet horses and dogs. It was the look that, in a highly sanitized form, would later be parodied and merchandised so successfully by Ralph Lauren to the new rich. In Jane's case, of course, her family had been among the *old* rich until the Crash, and had muddled along in a state of dazed and penurious shock ever since. A couple of marriages and a stint as a journalist had allowed her to keep her head just above water (and feed her horses), but with or without money she was "gentry," part of the small number of people who decided who got invited to what in Middleburg. She had the firm, natural authority of somebody who had been born to money, whether there was any left or not. Paul Nigro would have loved her.

Jane herself, though it was lunchtime, was still in her tan corduroy riding breeches, with the distracted look of somebody who can't for the moment remember why she invited these guests, and who has a dozen horses and a pair of donkeys to worry about.

I trooped out to the barn with her, carrying the sidesaddle, which pleased her as much as Paul Nigro could have wished, and did the obligatory tour of the barn, noting that, like so many horse people's, Jane's tack room was a good deal neater and better looked after than her house. Though Jane had scarcely bothered to introduce her children or name them, I was given the name, the breeding, the current state of health, and the age of each of her horses. Much as I was hungry for lunch, I knew enough to take a minute or two to admire each horse individually, while Jane beamed, patted, stroked, and gave them treats from her pocket. She was wearing a rakish white tam-o'-shanter with a green shamrock pattern, and a matching sweater—both appeared to have been knitted by not particularly skilled hands—souvenirs of her last hunting trip in Ireland, in honor of another guest, Thady O'Neil, master of one of the most famous and hard-riding hunts in Ireland. Thady would be arriving later, and the three of us would go out together tomorrow with the Middleburg Hunt, after which we were invited to a big dinner party at the house of the famous sportsman Jimmy Quick. On Sunday morning I would go riding with one of Jane's friends, who owned so much land that he was known locally as "the Duke of Rappahannock," followed by a round of hound shows that Thady, a respected international expert on foxhounds, would judge. The weather promised to be cold, rainy, and windy, but that, she guessed, would not dismay a real sportsman like myself—in any case, there were plenty of slickers and wellies in the mudroom to choose from, and I should have no trouble finding something that fit. I said that sounded fine to me, although there was a small, persistent thought at the back of my mind that I would rather have been home in New York, with my feet up, reading a manuscript—that all this was at once an imposture and a mistake. I felt like the hero of Gogol's *Inspector General,* and had very little confidence that I could make it through the weekend without being exposed as a fraud. It occurred to me, a little late, that I might have inadvertently oversold myself to Jane as a rider.

Lunch was served amid a chaos of barking dogs of every size and breed. Christopher and his mother were to go off to Washington to visit the Smithsonian, while Jane announced that she had a special treat in mind for me—the two of us would hack over for a look at the farm of a friend who trained horses for the Middleburg Gold Cup.

For those who don't know, the Middleburg Gold Cup is a major sporting event, an amateur steeplechase race over huge brush fences, modeled after those of the more famous Grand National at Aintree, in England. Riders are "amateurs" in the sense that they can't be paid professional jockeys, unlike "flat racers," and Gold Cup day is an almost unique spectacle, perhaps the most exclusive haut-WASP tribal gathering of the year. The notion of riding half an hour or so in the pouring rain to look at replicas of the Gold Cup fences was not one that instantly appealed to me, but it clearly meant a lot to Jane, so I went off to the mudroom in search of rain gear.

At the barn I was introduced to the horse I would be riding, Black Jack, a large, muscular thoroughbred of some age and experience, who rolled his eyes, showing rather more white than I would have liked—usually a sign of bad temper in a horse. Black Jack, Jane promised me, was my kind of horse—a real goer, reliable as the day is long, the kind that always looks after his rider. He was no slowpoke, and needed *riding,* mind you, but that should be no problem for someone like me.

Now was my chance to say that I would prefer the slowest and most reliable old plug in the McClary barn, something so placid you could put your grandmother on it and not worry, or even that I wouldn't mind going by car, but I didn't want to shatter Jane's image of me as a daredevil horseman, so I mounted, and together we set off at a brisk trot in the pouring rain.

Middleburg, seen through the rain on horseback, looked very much like England, perhaps not surprisingly, since here was a place in which most people's highest ambition was to be mistaken for an English country gentleman or lady. There was the same profusion of gift shops, antique shops, and quaint old hotels that you could see in landmark English villages like Broadway, in Gloucestershire, except that there everything *is* old, whereas here it has merely been artfully (and expensively) made to *seem* old. This being Virginia, there were also a good many more black people than you would expect to see in Gloucestershire, of course.

The farm, when we clip-clopped through its entrance and onto the well-tended fields also resembled England. As Jane gave me a brief, sodden tour of it, she explained that this was a rare and unusual privilege—she had had to pull in all sorts of markers to get us permission to ride here, but she had told everybody that she didn't want to disappoint her editor. I mumbled my gratitude, though I didn't see why her friends would need to make a fuss about our riding around their farms. "Better tighten your girth and check to see your hat is securely on," Jane said firmly, and before it had quite dawned on me what was happening, she put her horse into a trot, swung onto the training course, and headed for the first brush fence at a brisk canter.

If I had been thinking more quickly, I might have pulled Black Jack up, but it would not have been easy. He was certainly, as Jane had promised, a "goer"—he had a big, powerful stride—but he was also one of those horses that deeply dislikes being behind another horse, and above all hates to be alone. Once Jane set off at a canter in front of Black Jack, that was it—he put his head down and set off to catch up with her, and pulling at the reins only brought his head lower and made him that much more determined. I reminded myself of Monty Montana's advice and grabbed Black Jack's mane with both hands.

I watched Jane jump the first fence in front of me. It was higher than anything I had ever jumped—ever dreamed of jumping, in fact—but clearly Black Jack was going to jump it—would in fact jump *anything*, so long as Jane's horse led the way—so I simply shut my eyes, held on as hard as I could, and hoped for the best. I was glad that Jane couldn't turn her head and see me—she would have seen me grasping the horse's mane as if for dear life, riding toward each fence with my eyes shut, an expression of abject terror on my face. On the other hand, I was absolutely determined not to fall off. You can say what you like about riding being a dangerous sport, but so long as you're actually *on* the horse, you can come to no real harm; it's only when you and the horse part company that it becomes dangerous.

I don't know how many fences we jumped or how long it took, I just remember that when Jane cleared the last one, I was right behind her, hyperventilating and suffering from the headache of a lifetime. "Bravo!" Jane said. "I *knew* that would be a treat for you. I'm afraid the rest of the weekend may seem a little tame for you after that."

I could have done with a bit of tameness at that point, but in the meantime we slogged back to Jane's home at a slow walk, to cool the horses, while the rain poured down. By the time we got the horses put away, it was dark—there was just time for a quick hot bath and a shot of Jack Daniel's before dinner. It dawned on me that before the hunt tomorrow I would have to dry my breeches, dry out and polish my boots, and clean my spurs. I was reminded, without pleasure, of my days as a recruit in the British armed services.

Thady O'Neil, when he finally arrived—cocktail hour at the McClary's seemed to stretch on indefinitely, long past the point when the cook had begun appearing from the kitchen from time to time to announce that everything was burned to a crisp and would be inedible if we didn't sit down immediately—had been taking a few drinks on his own "to keep the chill out" on his way across the Atlantic from Shannon to Dulles. He was dressed as only the Irish (and the English gentry) can be, as a result of living in houses without central heating—layers of bulky tweed, with the consistency and color of a used Brillo pad, a green waistcoat with gold buttons, apparently cut from billiard-table cloth, a checked Viyella flannel shirt, a tie embroidered with fox heads, shoes and socks suitable for a polar expedition. Jane introduced me as her editor from New York, then took him aside to give him a glorified description of my exploit that afternoon. Who else in the New York publishing world could have followed her over those fences, she asked?

O'Neil came over and clinked his glass jovially against mine—even from a distance he exuded a slight but by no means unpleasant odor of Jameson Irish whiskey and the stable. "That's the way to go, boyo," he said. When Jane—God bless her, he said, lifting his glass vaguely in her direction—had first arrived in Ireland to hunt, she had taken one look at the fences—bloody huge they are, with bloody great ditches on the far side that you can't see—and wondered how she would do over them, and on a strange horse, mind you. Throw your heart over the fence, then ride after it, he had told her, and by God, had she not done just that? Was that not what the sport was all about, after all? Not about the fox, not ever for a minute—Jesu, the bloody animals rights people never could understand that!—but about not listening to your own fears, about throwing your heart over the wall, or the fence, or the ditch, or whatever, and going on.

As we sat down to table, urged on by the scolding cook, Thady O'Neil reached over and touched his glass against mine a second time—I noticed it was full again, with no sign in it of ice or water—and promised me we were going to have a great day tomorrow, by God. He would stick close to me and make sure I followed the right line. Other people might opt to go around an obstacle rather than jumping it, but not us—we would jump over bloody *houses* if we had to, we would show them what a fox hunter was, the two of us—or rather the three of us, he added, waving his glass at Jane, then empty-ing it in one gulp. It would be not just a pleasure, but an honor to ride with a real horseman like me. He held his empty glass up for a refill. One of these days I must come to Ireland and hunt with him, and bring my charming wife with me.

My charming wife shot me a look from the other side of the table that said, Over my dead body! together with, What am I *doing* here, and why did I let you talk me into coming? I put this down to the fatigue of plodding around the Smithsonian—that and a natural Shaker Heights, Bennington College, and New York City impatience with horse talk in general and foxhunting talk in particular.

I slept that night like the dead—it was, in fact, all I could do to stagger upstairs on trembling legs, drop my clothes on the floor, and fall into bed, what between total exhaustion, the aftermath of fear, and the amount I'd had to drink during the course of the evening. A good night's sleep was probably a blessing, since it prevented me from thinking about the morning, and the notion of what it was going to be like galloping toward a big fence with forty or fifty other riders, while Jane and Thady O'Neil urged me on.

I woke up early and went downstairs to clean my boots and brush off my breeches—a task that also had the advantage of taking my mind off what was in store for me. At breakfast Thady O'Neil appeared in his full glory as a visiting MFH (master of foxhounds), wearing a splendid cream waistcoat with gold buttons, spotless whipcord breeches, and a white stock secured with a big gold pin. His heavy scarlet hunting coat—too thick to wear comfortably indoors—was hanging on the back of his chair. Jane too was dressed in the full fig of the Middleburg Hunt. Outside, it was a cold late-autumn day, foggy and damp, with intervals of light rain. We ate a huge breakfast—like the last meal of a condemned man, it occurred to me—eggs, local bacon, Virginia ham, sausages, grits, and endless slices of toast. There was a pitcher of Bloody Marys on the sideboard, for those who believed in a bit of "the hair of the dog that bit you," and some kind soul had ensured that our hunting flasks, which lay neatly on the hall table beside our gloves, hunting whips, and hats, were filled with Madeira, "just to keep the cold out," as they say.

If Jane and Thady O'Neil had hangovers, they showed no sign of it. Both of them helped themselves to a good-sized Bloody Mary before settling down to breakfast. Since it seemed like the thing to do, I had one myself. "When in Rome, do as the Romans do," I told myself, and indeed I soon felt a good deal more optimistic about the whole day, and the pounding in my head from last night's drinking began to retreat. It actually occurred to me that the day might turn out to be good fun.

This illusion was somewhat shattered once we got to the stable. Black Jack, who had been docile enough the day before until Jane started to go over fences, was in a wild-eyed lather this morning. Jane's groom was trying to keep him still with the chain of a halter wrapped around the horse's nose, but even so, he was dancing on his feet, snorting, trying to throw his head around, gnashing his teeth, weaving from side to side, and rolling his eyes. "Good old Jack," Jane said. "He knows when it's a hunting day. They all do."

They all did too—every horse in the barn was in a state of high anxiety, as if they could already hear the sharp, high-pitched sound of the hunting horn, and the barking of the hounds. In the end it took the groom, Jane, and Thady O'Neil to hold the horse still long enough for me to mount, and the moment I was on him, I realized that Black Jack felt like a totally different horse from the one I had ridden yesterday— there was a high-stepping, nervous, twitchy quality to his movements, and a reluctance to pay any attention at all to the bit. I was already sorry I had buckled on my spurs, blunt though they were, but it was too late to take them off, since Jane and Thady O'Neil were already mounted. Before I could gather my wits about me, we clattered out of the courtyard and set off down the road at a brisk trot. From time to time Black Jack broke into a nervous, unwelcome canter, which sent him skittering about on the slick, wet surface of the paved road—an unpleasant sensation for his rider, who expected at any moment to go "ass over tit," as we say in England, or to end up on the hood of a car. "Damn all that eagerness, boyo," Thady O'Neil shouted cheerfully. "Hold him back a bit."

But holding Black Jack back was no easy task—he was determined to get ahead of the other two horses, and then, when I finally got him where he wanted to be, he shied, skidded, or reared up at anything that caught his eye, from a school bus to a squirrel running across the road. When he shied, it brought my breakfast back up into my mouth—his neck would stiffen when he saw something he didn't like, his ears would go forward as he looked at it more closely, then he would plant them flat back against his head and take a sudden, huge lurch sideways away from it, without giving any thought to where that might land us: in front of a car or a truck on the other side of the road, or through a shop window, or down a steep embankment. The only thing you could say in favor of his shying was that it was a lot more scary when he decided to rear, but either way promised to put me on the pavement with Black Jack on top of me. I was grateful he was wearing a double bridle, but it didn't seem to be slowing him down much.

I gave a sigh of relief as we turned off the main road into a narrower, but quieter, dirt one, then, after what seemed like a long time, onto the gravel of a driveway that took us around the side of a magnificent old brick mansion to a vast expanse of lawn, on which I saw two or three dozen more horses and riders, mixed in with a lot of well-dressed people on foot—for foxhunting is as much a social occasion as a sport, in which seeing who is there and being seen are perhaps more important to most people than killing a fox. I was introduced by Jane to the master, a tall, stately older gentleman who lifted his hat to me and said that he'd heard I was a real daredevil on a horse. Then a butler with a silver tray handed me up a "stirrup cup" of sherry, which I drained at a gulp. Several people rode up to me and asked if I was Jane's editor from New York, the one who turned out to be such a daredevil of a rider? I had a couple more sherries while I tried to explain that my reputation was grossly exaggerated.

The presence of a large number of other horses had momentarily calmed Black Jack, but the arrival shortly afterward of the hounds undid him completely. They came out of a black van, barking and baying, and eddied around the horses' legs, tails up, while the red-coated huntsman and his assistants cracked their long whips to get them back in order. Had I been watching it on foot, I would have found it an interesting and colorful spectacle; seen from the saddle, it gave me the same kind of unsettling feeling in the pit of my stomach that soldiers must have experienced in the trenches on the western front during World War I, just before being ordered to go over the top and move forward into no-man's-land.

The huntsman mounted his horse, cracked his whip, and gathered the pack of foxhounds; the butler then collected the last glasses, and all of a sudden the hounds, the master, and the hunt servants moved off the broad lawn and down a country lane, followed by the rest of us, in a large, untidy clump of horses and riders. I did my best to stay at the back, and for a brief few minutes congratulated myself that I was doing pretty well. Certainly, I could see that there were other riders who were having more trouble with their horses than I was, and even riders who looked more nervous—though the bulk of them looked only too eager for a hard cross-country gallop, with plenty of ditches and stone walls to jump, "hard thrusters," as Surtees called them in his novels.

The hounds were moving faster now, the sharp noise of the hunting horn sounding more often as the pace picked up. We swung into a big, rough plowed field at a trot, then moved uphill into a canter. In front of me I could see a stout stone wall topped with brambles. There was no way to guess what was on the other side. Horses and riders were jumping over it, bumping into each other as they jostled for a straighter line. I shut my eyes, felt Black Jack leave the ground, and opened them to see that there was a huge drop on the other side. As Black Jack landed, I could see that there was also an opening in the wall that some riders were prudently taking, instead of jumping it, but it was too late now, as we galloped across another field over another wall, and into somebody's backyard. I caught a brief glimpse of washing on the line, a couple of small children clinging to their mother, a pigpen with startled, indignant pigs; then we were over another fence and onto a dirt road, with the horses in front of me sending up a shower of mud that instantly covered my glasses, leaving me partially blind. Pieces of gravel pinged off the lenses of my glasses like shotgun pellets, or stung my face. A rider whacked me hard on the shoulder with his whip to get me out of his way; then I heard Thady O'Neil's voice shouting, "Turn hard to your right, for the love of God, boyo!" and followed him blindly in a stomach-churning leap over a muddy ditch with steep banks, in which several riders had come to grief. Using the gloved fingers of one hand, I managed to scrape enough mud off my glasses to make out Thady's broad scarlet back. I had lost a stirrup somehow, I was breathing harder than the horse, and I was drenched in sweat, though it was a cold, wet day—but at least I was still on Black Jack.

I was not in control of him, however. Ahead of us were loud cries and shouts, the shrill sound of the horn, and the noise of the hounds "giving tongue," as the phrase goes—thanks to Surtees again!—a sure sign that the pack had found a fox.

We rode cross-country for what seemed like an eternity, over stone walls, ditches, fences, across fields, and into people's backyards—it was astonishing how many people kept an old-fashioned washing machine on the back porch in rural Virginia—then into a dense wood, where I crouched low against the horse's neck as branches banged against my hunt cap and threatened to knock me off the horse. They did not slow Black Jack up a bit—he had a sure instinct for places where the branches were just high enough off the ground to give him room to canter under them, but low enough to sweep me right off my saddle or knock my brains out. By the time I emerged on the other side of the wood, I looked around and realized I was alone.

Black Jack was by now willing enough to stop and catch his breath. I managed to get my right foot back in the stirrup where it belonged, carefully unfastened my expensive crystal hunting flask, and took a deep, soothing drink to steady my nerves. I had no idea where I was, and I didn't care. All I had to do was walk Black Jack quietly until we found a road, and then ask for directions home.

At that precise moment, I felt Black Jack tense his muscles. Ahead of us, on higher ground, I saw a flash of orange, moving slowly. I peered at it. It crept forward carefully, stopped, raised its head to look in my direction. I had a momentary feeling that it was a stray cat, or perhaps a dog, but then I looked more closely at the tail—or "brush," as foxhunters call it—and the face, or "mask," and realized I was looking at a fox! Not just *a* fox, of course, but *the* fox, the one we were hunting, the star, as it were, of this elaborate production.

Had I been a real foxhunter, I would have cried out to attract the huntsman's attention, but the truth was that my sympathies, to the extent that they were in any way engaged, were on the side of the fox. He was as sleek, well-groomed, and shiny as a Park Avenue matron's dog, but a good deal shrewder. Looking at him, I thought he was a lot more attractive than most of the people hunting him, and very likely more intelligent too.

The fox may have guessed my ambivalence. He gave me a grin, then made his way daintily into the woods, in no particular hurry. A moment later there was a wild burst of noise and the hounds appeared, following his trail. The huntsman cantered after them as they milled around the spot where the fox had paused. "Which way did he go?" he shouted at me.

"Which way did *who* go?" I shouted back.

"The *fox*, man! He must have gone right past you! Right under your nose, for Christ's sake!"

I shook my head. "I never saw hide nor hair of him."

The huntsman gave me a look of disdain. The master and a couple of the more senior members of the hunt rode up now, and paused while the huntsman pointed his whip at me and explained, I had no doubt, what had transpired.

The master gave me a look of even greater disdain and set off at a canter after the hounds. Since Black Jack was all atwitch to follow on, I let him have his head—I was afraid that if I tried to hold him back, he would simply buck me off—and we pounded after the master, perhaps fifty yards behind, back through the wood, over a fence into another backyard—with another washing machine on the back porch—and out onto a muddy, rutted dirt road, where Black Jack began to pick up speed alarmingly.

Thoroughbreds—and Jack was a thoroughbred—are, as everybody knows, born and bred to race. Of course some of them are faster or slower than others, or there'd be no point to horse racing, but the one thing most of them have in common is that they want to be in the lead. Oh, occasionally you'll find a thoroughbred horse that prefers what he perceives to be the safety of being in the middle of the pack to being alone in front, and such horses are quickly sold off the track to some other occupation than racing, but most thoroughbreds live to be out front, and Black Jack was no exception.

More than most sports, foxhunting is full of unbreakable rules and traditions, but the two things that matter most are never passing or riding ahead of the master, and never riding into the hounds. The latter is obvious, even to a neophyte—a runaway horse galloping full tilt into the hounds is bound to kill or injure a few of them. The former is not necessarily so obvious. In a very few moments Black Jack had narrowed the gap separating me from the master, then pushed on until we were galloping almost side by side, our stirrups occasionally clanking as they touched.

I caught a glimpse of a crimson, furious face and saw a hunting crop brandished in front of me. "Get back, get the hell back!" I heard the master shout, but now that Black Jack saw his way clear past the master's horse, it would have taken a stronger rider than me to hold him back. We passed the master, spattering him with mud—even I could tell by now, from the shouts coming from behind me, that I had committed some kind of monstrous hunting faux pas—and made a beeline for the pack of hounds in front of us. I could see the huntsman glaring back over his shoulder. It was dawning on me at last that unless I did something, we were going to gallop right through his hounds, with undesirable results.

Since I couldn't stop Black Jack, I looked to either side wildly, until I saw an opening in the hedgerows, and leaning forward until my hand was practically in his mouth, I pulled the right reins as hard as I could until his head was facing in that direction. If you turn the horse's head, the old saying goes, the rest of the horse will follow, and so it proved—Black Jack didn't slow down, but he turned sharp right into somebody's driveway, dodged between a couple of cars, and jumped a low wire-mesh safety fence that landed us just short of a swimming pool. Fortunately, he didn't take the plunge—the sight of the pool stopped him dead, perhaps because he had never seen one before, and anyway, it was too wide to jump. He put his head down and began to eat grass.

I swung off the saddle, drained the rest of my flask, and leaned against Black Jack until my heartbeat had returned to normal. Then I opened the gate in the pool fence, led him through, and took him out into the driveway. A woman opened the front door, but before she could object to my intrusion—or to the big holes Black Jack had made in her turf—I swung myself back into the saddle and asked her the way to Middleburg.

Within an hour or so I was back, leaving the horse in the hands of Jane's groom and peeling off layers of wet, muddy clothes to take a hot bath.

By the time Jane and Thady got home, it was teatime. They had had a couple of really good runs, they reported, but no further sighting of the fox. I was glad of that, but wisely kept my mouth shut on the subject.

Jane, still in her breeches, with her boots removed, stuck her toes out toward the fire and sighed.

"You didn't happen to see the fox, did you?" she asked.

I shook my head.

Jane nodded. "I told the huntsman you couldn't have, or you'd have shouted out, wouldn't you?"

"Definitely."

"That's what I said to him. He must have been mistaken." She paused. "Did you ride right past the master?"

"Up to a point. That I *may* have done, yes." I knew better than to put the blame on Black Jack. You can't criticize the horse somebody has lent you—it just isn't done.

Jane chuckled. "Nobody's done that in *years*," she said. "He looked as if he was about to have apoplexy, didn't he, Thady?"

"Aye, that he did," Thady said contentedly. "I told him that's what happens when you get a real daredevil in the hunt field. In Ireland, I said, the master just rides faster than anybody else, damned if he tries to slow them down like a policeman at a crossing." He sipped his tea, into which Jane had poured a generous shot of Irish whiskey. "I'll tell you what, though, laddie," Thady continued, "he won't forget *you* in a hurry."

The same thought had occurred to me, which perhaps explains why I never repeated the experience.

Dinner at Jimmy Quick's was a big event, for which I had been instructed to bring down my dinner jacket. On arrival I felt as poorly dressed, however, as a moth among butterflies. Many of the men were wearing hunt evening clothes—scarlet "tails," with silk lapels in the hunt colors, white waistcoat, a row of gold buttons—while even those dressed as "civilians" ran to items like tartan trousers, velvet slippers with embroidered gold fox heads, flamboyant waistcoats, or ties in startling colors. Jimmy Quick, our host, a wizened gnome of a man who held himself up by means of two aluminum canes on which his forearms rested, wore a velvet smoking jacket. Bald, deeply tanned, with broad, muscular shoulders, Quick must once have been a powerful figure of a man, but a lifetime of polo accidents had broken almost every bone in his body at one time or another, and it was only sheer pride that brought him out of his wheelchair for his guests.

He was rich, in a way that reminded me of Tom and Daisy in *The Great Gatsby*, with a huge house here (and another in Palm Beach), innumerable black servants, room after room done in the style of—and perhaps in fact by—"Sister" Parish, the society decorator. In its own way, the house was as horsey as Jane's, but at a higher, wealthier level: wonderful paintings of horses, including a few by George Stubbs himself, bronzes of horses from every era, shelf after shelf of gleaming polo trophies, some of them works of art in themselves. There was a pianist at the big white Steinway grand playing tunes from Cole Porter, Noel Coward, and Rogers and Hart, while the butler circulated through the room refilling people's glasses. It was all like stepping back into the 1920s.

Quick buttonholed me in the library, surrounded by silver-framed photographs of himself in his younger days, playing polo with the Prince of Wales and just about everybody else who played polo back then, when he had been the top-ranking polo player in the United States. "I hear you're a goddamn daredevil of a rider, young man," he said to me fiercely. "Don't get many of those from New York."

I raised an eyebrow. "Winston Guest? Cornelius Vanderbilt Jr.? Averell Harriman?"

Quick gave me a malicious leer. "That wasn't what I meant, and you know it."

Mine is not an ear necessarily finely tuned for anti-Semitism, but I knew exactly what he meant. Still, I wasn't going to quarrel with my host before dinner was even served, and in any case I didn't want to embarrass Jane, so I kept my mouth shut.

"Heard you rode past the master out hunting, too. Pushy, eh?" He winked.

I decided to ignore that too. I knew what kind of New Yorkers were described as "pushy" in high-WASP circles.

He grabbed the sleeve of my jacket in one of his clawlike hands. "I'll tell you what, though, I used to be a daredevil on a horse myself, by God. Many a time I've ridden past the master, out hunting. I've ridden hard, played polo hard, broken every goddamn bone in my goddamn body, and I wouldn't have missed a goddamn *moment* of it, you hear me? Aches, pain, broken bones, *these* goddamn things"—he slapped a hand against one of his canes—"I don't regret a thing. I'd do it all over again if I could." He shook his head. "More than I can say for any of my marriages, young man," he said, with a wild cackle of laughter; then he stumped off in the direction of the prettiest young woman in the room, still laughing.

Dinner, when we sat down to it, was formal, with perhaps two dozen people seated at a long table, in the middle of which was a sterling silver statue of a horse and polo player about four feet high, and place-card holders in the form of small crossed sterling silver polo mallets. The food was from Jimmy Quick's farm, and when the roast beef was served, he not only told us the name of the Black Angus steer it had come from but also recited its pedigree. Although the dining room was full of black servants, Quick inveighed at length against civil rights demonstrators, occasionally asking one of the servants what he or they thought of "outsiders stirring up the colored community," and whether people weren't happy and well treated just as things were—a display doubtless put on for the benefit of those of us who were visitors from the North, then almost de rigueur at social occasions below the Mason-Dixon line. The servants smiled, chuckled, and swore they were indeed happy with things just the way they were, but I was reminded of similar scenes in English colonies like Kenya, just before the servants took to the forest to join the Mau Mau and reappeared to chop their former employers to death with sharpened pangas.

Jane and her husband were, I knew, unusual for the area, since they were both Democrats with strong liberal sympathies—indeed, Jane had helped introduce Jacqueline Kennedy to the Middleburg horse world, and sent me a photograph of herself showing a mightily bored and impatient-looking President Kennedy around her barn—but she gave me a firm look from across the table, which clearly signified, "Don't argue with your host!"

I hadn't the slightest desire to, as a matter of fact. The food and wine were excellent, and although every muscle in my body throbbed and ached from the day out with the hounds, I felt the sense of peace that comes from having survived unscathed. After dinner, the ladies left the gentlemen to sit at table with their cigars, while port and brandy was passed around. Quick called me over to sit down next to him. He pointed at the big silver sculpture on the table. "That's me, you know," he said, "back in the twenties." I looked at it more closely and saw indeed that the face on the rider was Quick's. "Those were the days," Quick said. "I'll tell you this, my young friend from New York, I'm an old man, and I'm going to be dead soon, but I won't be sorry to go. I've had a good run for my money. Anyway, this country is finished. It hasn't been a fit place for a white man to live since the day Franklin and Eleanor Rosenheim moved into the White House and sold the country out to the niggers and the Jews."

I was so startled by this old-fashioned view of FDR, which had once been common among wealthy Republicans but was now a caricature, like the elderly clubmen in a Peter Arno cartoon, that I choked briefly on my brandy.

Quick patted me on the back hard with a gnarled fist, until I caught my breath. Now that he had vented his spleen about politics, he was solicitous and anxious to play the good host. "Where are you going tomorrow?" he asked.

I explained that Jane and I were going for an early-morning ride with somebody she referred to as "the Duke of Rappahannock." Quick looked sad. "I envy you," he said wistfully, and for a moment it was possible to feel sorry for him, with his crippled hands and legs after a lifetime in the saddle, living proof of the fact that polo is a dangerous sport. "I'd give anything to get on a horse again, one last time," he said. "And the Duke's got land to ride on—more land than anybody else around here." He puffed on his cigar—a big Churchillian Montecruz. "Mind you, he's no daredevil on a horse. Good enough horseman, but cautious, you know—never had a bad fall, never broken a bone." He squeezed my knee sharply. "A rider ought to have a bit of wildness in him. Well you know that, even if you are from New York. Don't suppose you play polo, though?"

I admitted that I did not.

Quick smiled shrewdly. "No, I didn't think so," he said, less amiable now. "It takes guts, polo does. Separates the men from the boys." With that, he dismissed me, waving his cigar like a wand.

I had the curious sense that Quick had seen through me—had understood that I was skating on a reputation acquired by a couple of lucky rides, in which terror and sheer stupidity had contrived to prevent anybody from noticing my incompetence.

I reflected, as we moved in "to join the ladies," that in its own way this was a kind of privilege, not just a look at a vanishing world but an opportunity to see the horse in a new light, as a symbol of social opportunity and a sign of wealth. What is it, after all, that men do when they acquire money in large amounts? For many of them, owning horses is the fastest way to enter the ranks of the upper classes, among whom the horse has always played a symbolic, not to say a totemic, role. Ownership of a racing stable, learning to play polo, foxhunting, sending one's wife or daughters out onto the show jumping circuit—in countless ways the horse signifies rank, class, money, and has done so from the very beginning of history, separating the knight from the common foot soldier, the caballero from the peasant, the lordly plantation owner from the lowly dirt farmer, the glamorous cavalryman from the muddy infantryman. The horse stood, among other things, for social superiority, mobility, and not getting your feet wet and muddy like ordinary folk.

In the American West, the artifacts, vocabulary, and clothing of Spanish horsemanship were transferred intact, along with the horse itself, which had never been native to America until the Spanish brought theirs with them to the New World. The Spaniards wore boots with high heels and sharp toes, and although cowboys were later to rationalize the shape of their boots by arguing that you could dig your toes into the sand when you were trying to wrestle a calf to the ground, or that the high, slanting heels were a safety measure that would prevent your foot from slipping through the stirrup, the simple truth was that the Spaniards deliberately wore boots that were difficult to walk in to demonstrate that they didn't *need* to walk. They were horsemen, caballeros, for whom walking was a thing that peasants, beggars, and Indians did. The more uncomfortable and hard it was to walk in a pair of boots, the more clearly they stamped one as a person for whom walking was beneath one's dignity—a gentleman, in short.

Those who had horses rode with their heads high above the common people, looking down on them, or later in carriages protected from the elements, with blinds you could pull down so you didn't *have* to look at them. The horse was for centuries the key factor in establishing and maintaining social distinctions, and horsemanship was the common bonding factor between the upper classes of almost every civilized nation and culture. The one thing the British officers and civil servants of the Raj had in common with the Indian princes was a love of horses, of horse racing, and of dangerous horsey sports like polo (which originated in Afghanistan) and pigsticking (which originated in the Punjab), as well as an admiration for elegant, reckless horsemanship in all its forms. The same was true for the wealthy, the aristocratic, and the officer class of every European country. Winston Churchill, for example, not only served as a cavalry officer as a young man but rode in the last big cavalry charge of the British army, at the battle of Omdurman against the dervishes in 1898, played polo well into his fifties, and was photographed foxhunting with the Old Surrey and Burstow Hunt in 1948, three days before his seventy-fourth birthday.

Not only individuals but whole nations, some with few other claims to power or greatness, like Hungary, were respected for their skill in riding or in breeding horses, or for a reputation for fearless horsemanship. Both King Louis XVI of France and King George III of Great Britain won more acclaim for their skill as horsemen and their courage on the hunt field than for their politics, and the passionate interest of the present-day British royal family in horses is well known—one of the few occasions where the queen is actually photographed smiling is when she watches her horses run at race meetings, and among the many qualities that endeared the late queen mother to the country is that she read the racing papers religiously and loved to bet on horse races as much as her countrymen.

Middleburg, Virginia, represents this side of horse ownership—both the tendency of the upper classes (or "old rich") to identify their status by means of horses, and the determination of the ambitious "new rich" to win acceptance by spending lavishly on horsey pursuits—although there are plenty of other places in the country where the same thing is going on in different forms, from the polo fields of Palm Beach to the racing stables of Kentucky, and from the show jumping circuit to the world of three-day eventing. Wherever you look, nothing sanctifies new money more quickly than the smell of horse manure.

"America is a wonderful country: from Poland to polo in one generation," the screenwriter Joseph Mankiewicz joked famously when he heard that movie producer Sam Goldwyn (né Gelbfisz) had taken up polo, but it was not only in Hollywood that mounting a horse was seen as the first step to social acceptance. Jimmy Quick's father was the son of an impoverished Irish immigrant who went on to make a fortune in the Chicago meatpacking business, thus giving Jimmy the chance to make his mark as a polo player, and thereby vault into high society. Of course Middleburg was famous for its foxhunting, but like a lot of other places in the country (Southern Pines, North Carolina, comes to mind) it resembled a kind of horse theme park, with people involved in show jumping, three-day eventing, thoroughbred flat racing, steeplechase racing, breeding—almost any horsey activity you could think of, except eating them. Not a few people in the area had their own private race-tracks, one of them belonging to Mrs. Randolph Dupont Scott, a Dupont heiress who had married a handsome "poor white trash" hunt servant named Randolph Scott, who went on to become a Hollywood star. Mrs. Scott was at the apex of the horse world, higher even than Paul Mellon, who had more money, but slightly less horsey cachet. The Duke of Rappahannock, with whom we were to ride the next day, was right up there with them, though, Jane assured me on the way home, with his own racecourse, his own racing stable, and his own stud farm, a patron of several local hunts and a very grand personage indeed.

We were up at the crack of dawn to prepare ourselves for the occasion, Jane and I, shining our boots until they gleamed as we ate an early break-fast. Although Jane lived in a place where snobbery was by no means un-known, she was not herself a snob—she had too much of a sense of humor and too many "unconventional" opinions for that—but she made no secret of the fact that the Duke's opinion mattered to her, in much the same way that it might have had she lived in the English countryside and had he been a real duke. To her, he stood for certain things that had no doubt been drummed into her mind when she was a child—respect for property, a sense of noblesse oblige, old-fashioned good manners, and perfect horsemanship. I should not, therefore, have been surprised when she put her new sidesaddle in her truck, fastened a long sidesaddle skirt over her breeches, and placed a bowler hat on her head.

The Duke's land was far enough away that we had to transport the horses in a trailer. The weather was unseasonably—even uncomfortably—warm, but showed signs that this might change later in the day. Huge dark storm clouds were rolling over the Duke's land as we parked, backed the horses out of the trailer, and tacked them up, Jane and I struggling to get the sidesaddle just so, but as if on command the clouds parted and allowed the sun to shine through just as the Duke himself rode up to greet us, followed by a couple of well-mannered big dogs.

He was a small, robust, elderly man, with a grave, courteous southern-patrician voice and manner, perfectly turned out on a horse that looked as if its groom had spent all night getting it ready—even its feet were polished until they glittered in the sun like jewels.

He and Jane chatted about various friends in common as we finished tacking up the horses. The Duke's lands, as they stretched before us, were magnificent—endless gently rolling hills, stretching to the horizon, with the morning mist gradually lifting in the sun. It was not an English landscape—the hills were a little too steep for that, the woods thicker and more widespread, and in the very far distance, as the mist cleared, the sharper ridges of the Blue Ridge Mountains were visible against the sky—but it would have delighted Reynolds or Stubbs to have painted it, no doubt with the Duke on his magnificent horse in the foreground.

I bent over to give Jane "a leg up"—the hardest part of riding sidesaddle is mounting the horse from the ground—while the Duke rode around to the off side of Jane's horse to hold the saddle as she mounted, so it wouldn't slip. I checked her girth, then mounted my own horse.

Seen at closer range, he was older than I had thought—still very much in the Duke of Omnium mold, but wizened around the edges. He nodded approvingly at the sight of Jane riding sidesaddle. "My mother always preferred a sidesaddle," he said. "In her day it was the thing to do. Of course things have changed since then." He frowned at the thought.

He looked out at the landscape—*his* landscape—and gave a small, discreet smile of satisfaction, as if to confirm that here, at least, nothing had changed, that God was in his heaven and all was right with the world. We moved off at a brisk walk, three abreast, with Jane in the middle, the dogs close to the Duke's side, and the Duke himself on Jane's left, exactly as Victorian etiquette books would have placed us when the queen herself was still alive.

In the Duke's presence, even the normally outspoken Jane seemed slightly subdued, though it's possible that the sidesaddle had something to do with that. It requires just that much more concentration to ride sidesaddle, together with a strong back—the correct position doesn't allow the rider to slump or bend forward; in fact it's like a training position for perfect posture, giving much the same effect as walking around with a couple of heavy books balanced on your head, as girls used to be obliged to do at the better finishing schools—the kind that, as it happened, Jane had attended.

"Your reputation has preceded you—I hear you're quite the daredevil," the Duke said to me, without a trace of approval.

I demurred, while Jane once again burnished my reputation. I had come to realize that while she was in most respects almost alarmingly truthful, she had somehow committed herself to the notion that she had the only editor in New York City book publishing who was a daredevil on horseback, as if it were part of *her* legend. She had transformed my one awful moment at the Madison Square Garden rodeo into a whole rodeo career that made me sound like Montgomery Clift in *The Misfits*, so determined was she to make me more interesting for her friends.

In any case, the Duke all too sensibly took this with a grain of salt, to the extent that it interested him at all. He was not a daredevil himself—he rode with simple perfection, like the photographs in a riding instruction manual that make the reader feel he or she is, by comparison, a sack of potatoes on horseback. In that sense, he reminded me of the legendary nineteenth-century dressage expert James Fillis, a Scot who in his heyday could fill the huge Vélodrome d'Hiver in Paris with people just to watch him ride perfectly. Fillis was a celebrity, like a rock star or a sports star today, whose most famous act was cantering a horse *backward,* something that would be hard to believe if we didn't have early serial photographs of him doing it. In later years he went to Russia at the invitation of the czar to reform the training of the Russian cavalry, and in his great old age was invited to give an exhibition of his skill for Kaiser Wilhelm II. The kaiser watched with growing impatience as the old man rode his horse at a walk around the dressage ring at the Potsdam Palace several times. When Fillis came to the halt, the kaiser said, "Now that you're warmed up, Herr Fillis, what are you going to show us?"

There was an uncomfortable moment of silence, then Fillis said in pained reproach, "Your Imperial Majesty has just witnessed the most difficult of all achievements in riding a horse—*the perfect walk!*"

Fillis was born a great showman and one of the nineteenth-century popularizers of the art of dressage, the system of classical riding that goes back to the sixteenth century and is still practiced extensively, both competitively and in training horses to a higher level of perfection, the haute école.

The Duke gave much the same impression of riding with effortless perfection as Fillis must have, so much so that, despite no physical resemblance to the character, I felt like Sancho Panza bumping along on his donkey next to him. Jane, I was not surprised to see, was a natural at riding sidesaddle, pretty much a forgotten art. The great difficulty for most women is that both the rider's legs are on the same side of the horse, the right leg cocked over the horn of the saddle, the left leg in a more or less normal position, with the foot in the stirrup. Horses are used to "contact," the feel of the rider's leg on both sides of the horse's ribs, and a well-trained horse will move away from contact, so pressure from the right leg will tend to move the horse toward the left, and vice versa, while equal pressure from both legs will move the horse forward. Since a woman riding sidesaddle has no contact on the horse's right side, she usually carries a long, thin whip with which to touch (not hit) the horse on the "off" side, thus replacing what would normally be the effect of her right leg against the horse's side. The inability to do this properly shows itself in the tendency of the horse to move constantly toward the right, away from the rider's left leg, instead of proceeding in a straight line, and neophyte sidesaddle riders tend to move in a series of zigzags as they overcompensate for this, tacking like a sailboat in the hands of an inexperienced helmsman. Jane, of course, kept her horse moving in a perfectly straight line along the long, meticulously swept and raked gravel paths of the Duke's domain.

The Duke didn't actually *say* anything, but he looked pleased. He himself, he told us, was doing a lot of driving these days, hence the gravel paths. Driving is one of those complicated and expensive sub-worlds of horsemanship, that was beginning to have a rebirth back then in the early 1970s. The Duke mostly drove "two in hand," that is to say controlling two horses pulling an open vehicle, usually a shooting brake or something like it, in which the driver sits up front, meticulously dressed, with the reins from the pair of horses in his hands, or, when he needs to use the whip, neatly gathered between the fingers of one hand. Not getting the reins tangled up seems to the onlooker the most difficult part of it all, but once you get up to driving "four in hand" or beyond, like the coachmen of yore, it takes skill, courage, strong, agile fingers, and much practice to make sharp turns (the outer horses have got to be going faster than the inner horses, for obvious reasons), let alone to race a coach-and-four over open country against the clock, a form of competition which was increasingly popular in England (where Prince Philip was a determined four-in-hand competitor), France, and Hungary, and was becoming more so in the United States.

Of course it is the perfect aristocratic sport—expensive, difficult to master, linked to centuries of tradition, and something you can invite your friends along to as passengers, dressed up in period costume, if you have a mind to. Mrs. John D. Rockefeller was known to begin the day by driving two in hand at a spanking clip along the perfectly manicured paths on the Rockefeller estate at Pocantico, New York, with a rug over her knees and a groom in full livery and a top hat seated behind her, facing backward, arms folded, as he would have been in the eighteenth or nineteenth century. When it came to taking tradition seriously, though, I guessed that the Duke would make old Mrs. Rockefeller look like a flapper.

We rode past his herds of prize beef cattle, between rolling meadows full of his horses, past the breeding shed, the barns; we saw his full-size racetrack, complete with a starting gate and everything else a track might need, in fact, except a grandstand, of course, since here there was only one spectator. We rode on and on, past model farms in which the fields were plowed as if by the use of a ruler, and back toward where we had left the truck and trailer.

On the way there, we reached a huge field with high fencing, substantial stuff designed to keep in bulls rather than horses. The Duke stopped at the gate, a fairly formidable obstacle in its own right, and for a moment I thought he expected us to jump it, with Jane flying over it sidesaddle, like Lucy Glitters in *Mr. Sponge's Sporting Tour* ('Clear the way, then!' exclaimed Miss Glitters, putting her horse back, eyes flashing as she spoke). I half wondered if this was yet another test of my supposed qualities as a "daredevil" rider, but the Duke must have guessed my train of thought and shook his head. I offered to dismount and open the gate, but he said that wouldn't be necessary—somebody would open it for us. I looked across the field, and there, perhaps a mile away, I saw what appeared to be a very old black man running toward us, one hand on his head to steady his hat. It was warm, by now—too warm to be running, I thought—but the old man kept coming, flailing away across the gently sloping field to where we waited. Jane and the Duke chatted about mutual acquaintances until the old man, now drenched in sweat, arrived at the gate. He removed his battered old hat, wiped his forehead with a bandanna handkerchief, and bowed slightly. "Good mornin', sir," he said to the Duke, who lifted his hat a fraction and said thank you back as the old man opened the gate for us. As we set off across the field, I heard him close the gate; then, to my surprise, he appeared in front of us, still running as fast as his old legs would carry him, clearly in order to reach the far side before we did, so he could open that gate for us. Which was exactly what happened. The Duke thanked him in a distant, courteous way, as if this was an everyday occurrence, which perhaps it was. Jane looked mildly embarrassed. "What a nice old man," she said. "Such good manners."

The Duke had to think for a moment about that. He wasn't sure whose manners were being praised, his or his employee's. When the penny finally dropped, he nodded and said, as if explaining something basic, "Yes, he knows *his* place all right, no doubt about that." I shot Jane a glance that read, So much for the New South! but she was look-ing straight ahead, determined, no doubt, not to catch my eyes.

A station wagon waited for us. A butler had laid out a late breakfast on the tailgate—there was champagne in an ice bucket, sherry and Madeira in crystal decanters, a silver thermos of coffee, a wicker picnic basket from Asprey's of London containing a Virginia ham (from one of the Duke's own prizewinning pigs, of course), hard-boiled eggs, fresh bread—everything, in short, one could want. A groom waited to take our horses. We dismounted, and the butler opened the champagne and passed us china plates and silverware from the basket.

"Don't know how you fellers can stand it in New York City," the Duke said. "I never could. Give me the simple life down on the farm, eh, Jane?"

Jane agreed that she too preferred the simple life; then we finished our champagne and our snack, put the horses back on the trailer, and thanked the Duke. "Anytime," he said with a genial wave and a smile. He shook my hand. "Always glad to see a city boy who isn't afraid to break his neck."

Shortly after we left the Duke's, the clouds blotted out the sun, the tem-perature dropped, and it started to pour rain. It was, I thought, typical that none of this should happen until *after* we had left the Duke's land, and doubly unfortunate because Jane's plan for me for the rest of the day was to visit a whole series of hound shows, which Thady O'Neil, whom we would meet up with at the first one, was judging. Was I a real fancier of foxhounds? Jane asked—if I was (and her expression made it clear that the notion I might not be had never crossed her mind), I was in for the time of my life.

Ever the good guest, I said that while I was no expert, nothing would give me greater pleasure. Despite the rain gear that Jane carried in her truck, the first of the day's hound shows was not something I would normally have lingered at, given a choice. Under a pouring rain, in now near-freezing temperature, we stood ankle deep in mud while Thady O'Neil examined a long row of hounds, with the look of a man completely absorbed in his subject. All the hounds looked pretty much alike to me, but to Thady each was different, and he conversed at length and with great authority with the masters, the huntsmen, and the hunt servants before awarding the prizes. He took ages to examine each hound. Being Irish, he was used to rain, and behaved as if he had all the time in the world, as if indeed nothing could hurry him, or persuade him to get under cover. From time to time he was offered a shot of whiskey from somebody's flask, "to keep the chill out," and so fine were his manners that he never refused once. By the time he got in the truck with us to go to the next hound show, the fumes of Irish whiskey were enough to bring tears to one's eyes; on the other hand, he was certainly not feeling the cold and the rain the way I was.

The next hound show was miles away, and by the time we got there it was even colder and wetter. Thady took a deep, prophylactic pull from his own pocket flask and squelched off through the mud in his wellies, beaming in delight at the sight of another couple of dozen hounds that looked exactly alike.

At the third or fourth hound show, I gave up and, to Jane's distress, insisted on staying in the truck, pleading fatigue, the beginnings of pneumonia, and so forth. Thady, who thought I was looking a little blue—he meant the color, literally, my fingernails having already turned a dark purplish blue from the cold—gave me a few nips from his capacious flask to keep me going, with the result that I had to be helped out of the truck and into the house when we finally arrived there.

"What's the matter with him?" I heard my wife ask as I dragged myself upstairs to collapse into a hot bath. "He looks drunk."

"Never in life!" Thady said. "It's the way it is with daredevil riders like him, you see. They take these huge great bloody fences at a gallop, don't even give it a thought, but afterwards, ah, *afterwards,* you understand, it hits them dead on. Delayed reaction, you might say."

"Delayed reaction? He looks drunk to me. And what's all this stuff about 'daredevil riders,' if you please?"

Thady coughed nervously. "Ah, well," he said, "Surtees, as wise a man as ever was about horses and riders, once wrote, 'There is no secret so close as that between a rider and his horse,' and let it be so. A hot bath and a cup of coffee, and he'll be as good as new." And so it proved to be, more or less, though my legs were still trembling when we boarded the last shuttle back to New York that night.

Jane begged us to come back soon. She was worried that the weekend had been a little tame for me. Perhaps next time we should go out with the Rappahannock Hunt, which rode hell-for-leather over *really* rough country—huge stone walls, with big drops on both sides—and was known locally as the "Break-Your-Neck Hunt." It had been George Patton's favorite hunt, in his hunting days, before World War II.

I promised we'd take her up on the offer soon, but the truth was that I considered myself lucky to have escaped unharmed, and had no desire at all to try to live up to my reputation.

A couple of years later, when Jane's novel was—at last—edited and cut down to a reasonable size, I had the idea of presenting it to the Simon and Schuster sales force on horseback, dressed up in full hunting fig like one of the characters on the cover of the book, in a scarlet coat, white breeches, and black boots with buff tops. I had no difficulty in pulling together all the clothing, thanks to Paul Nigro and Charles Kauffman, and a visit to the Claremont Riding Academy on West

Eighty-ninth Street elicited from the owner, Mr. Irwin Novograd, a promise to rent me a horse and truck it down to the St. Moritz Hotel on Central Park South. Mr. Novograd had not blinked at my request—he behaved as if this were the most normal thing in the world, something that happened every day. They had a few horses that were used for photo shoots and circus acts, he told me, dead calm even in a hotel ballroom, he promised.

The hotel manager assured me that there would be no problem putting ramps down to get the horse into the ballroom, but then at the last minute Richard E. Snyder, then president of Simon and Schuster, got word of the plan and, calling me to his office, put an end to it instantly. It was too risky, our insurance wouldn't cover us if there were an accident, one of the sales reps might get hurt if the horse panicked, we could end up looking like a bunch of complete assholes.

He ran his hands over his eyes—as if to say, The things I have to deal with!—then gave me a hard but not altogether unaffectionate stare. "You want to be a fucking daredevil," he said gruffly, "you go do it on your own time."

So I presented the book in hunting dress standing on the dais, tooting a hunting horn to attract the reps' attention, but it didn't feel the same.

I never did go back to Middleburg for a second crack at breaking my neck, and Jane stopped asking me after the book made her comparatively rich and famous—and something of an outcast for painting the morals of the foxhunting world in an unflattering light.

Perhaps it's as well. Riding a horse was about to change my life completely.

CHAPTER THREE

A Girl and Her Pony

"If you can get 'er 'ome, you can 'ave 'er."

IRCUMSTANCES SOON DREW ME back to Claremont Riding Academy, on West Eighty-ninth Street, just off Amsterdam Avenue. Christopher's schoolwork was mounting up—and turning serious as he grew older—while Paul Nigro's difficulties with the management of Clove Lake Stables seemed to be accelerating. Besides, it was tempting to be able to ride in Central Park early every morning during the week before work—it was only a fifteen-minute taxi ride from my apartment to Claremont Riding Academy, and about ten minutes by subway from there to Rockefeller Center, where my office was, a far cry from the hour or more it took to drive to Staten Island.

"Claremont," as insiders always called it, was at that time the last livery and boarding stable in Manhattan, where before World War II there had been half a dozen or more, and at the turn of the century, when the horse was still dominant in urban transportation, probably thousands. It was not just the age of the horse that had passed Claremont by; the entire Upper West Side around it had plunged from being a neighborhood of middle-class brownstone houses, genteel, tranquil, and prosperous, into a vast slough of urban decay, crime, and drug dealing. The city, the state, and the federal government had from time to time announced ambitious and often conflicting plans for renovating the Upper West Side by building public housing, but these plans began and ended with the ruthless bulldozing of most of the buildings around Claremont, leaving the stable standing until recently in the middle of a sea of rubble, burned-out and gutted houses, and empty lots.

By a bizarre twist of fate typical of New York City real-estate politics, Claremont was awarded "landmark" status at some point, thus ensuring that while it could not be torn down, it also could not be significantly altered or improved either, so that it survived in a kind of limbo, the subject of weighty editorials and passionate letters to the editor of the *New York Times* from preservationists, and the object of neighborhood fury and juvenile vandalism from those who saw it as a bastion of white upper-class privilege—the rights of horses and riders being put above those of the urban poor, in this view.

Throughout it all—the decades of press conferences, the appeals to the parks commissioner and the mayor, the endless stormy sessions at the district board's hearings—Claremont continued to house, in the basement, about two dozen "school horses," used for giving lessons or rented out to ride in the park, and upstairs, on the second floor, about a dozen or so privately owned boarders. Both private horses and hacks lived in conditions of Dickensian squalor, not unlike those of Fagin and his brood in the London rookeries. Horses came tottering up from the basement or slipping and sliding down from the second floor by means of extremely narrow, steep ramps—an ancient, cranky elevator was used for moving loads of hay and bedding in, and fifty-five-gallon steel drums of manure out. The ground floor contained a small, grimy, poorly lit indoor riding ring with an overhead garage door opening onto Eighty-ninth Street, and an office and waiting room, with a big window looking out onto the ring.

Behind this window sat the proprietor, Irwin Novograd, hunched over his big, old-fashioned account book, a stained fedora pulled low over his eyes, keeping up the daily struggle to account for every grain of feed and stalk of hay and if possible to charge it to one or another of his "boarders," whose detailed monthly bills were like works of art—hardly surprising, since Novograd was an accountant first and foremost, rather than a horseman. In his case, the pen was mightier than the whip—he had in fact been doing the accounts for the owners of Claremont when they eventually gave up the ghost and sold him the business, horses and all, for a song, and over the years since then he had learned a good deal about horses, without ever having felt the slightest desire to get on one.

What he *did* understand, above all, was how to make money out of horses—most important, how to get them out to the park with a paying customer in the saddle (a journey of one block uptown and two blocks crosstown through heavy, impatient, and often antagonistic traffic), no matter how spavined, lame, or weary the horse might be, or how barely competent the rider. Mr. Novograd was also a horse trader in the old-fashioned sense of the term, in touch with the horse netherworld, where you bought horses cheaply at livestock auctions by the job lot, then got rid of the ones you didn't want by selling them off as carriage horses, or to brokers who provided horses for summer riding camps, or, at the very bottom end of the feeding chain, to people who bought the hopeless rejects for the pet food companies. The sounder ones he kept to rent out for use on the bridle paths of Central Park, or as school horses, for giving riding lessons. The odd good-looking one that showed up—usually a problem horse sold "down" from hand to hand because it bucked, reared, or kicked uncontrollably, or had some other secret vice—Mr. Novograd tried to sell to those of his customers who were in the market for "a horse of their own."

I very soon fell into that category, in part because social life in the early mornings at Claremont, such as it was, revolved around the private owners, who if not exactly glamorous were certainly a distinct urban subspecies. In those days, before the running craze started, the half a dozen or so "early birds" had the park pretty much to themselves, and viewed it with a certain feudal sense of proprietorship. They did not mix easily or willingly with lesser mortals who merely rented one of Mr. Novograd's hacks; indeed their relationship to Novograd himself was fraught with the kind of suspicion and hostility on both sides that is common to the traditional New York City landlord/tenant relationship. The boarders suspected Novograd of padding their bills, underfeeding their horses, and providing inadequate or incompetent care, while Novograd viewed the boarders as spoiled, greedy children, who made unreasonable demands and complained at the drop of a hat. At the same time the boarders, however aggressive, could only complain so far—if you wanted to ride your horse, or even *his* horses, in Central Park, Novograd's was the only game in town, and that was that.

Since I was out in the park on one of Mr. Novograd's hacks every morning, it did not take long before I knew most of the early morning crowd. There was Mr. Lipper, a man of mystery who was reputed to carry a pistol and owned Cavalier, a gaited horse that—shades of Danny Dakota and King the Wonder Horse—could count up to five by tapping on the ground with a forefoot, and on command would get down on its knees. There was Mr. Schleiker, a bulky, crimson-faced, and quick-tempered old man, always faultlessly dressed, who owned Ladidah, a gaited mare even worse tempered than her master, and Mrs. Schleiker, who sometimes accompanied her husband in the mornings on one of Novograd's horses, or rode Ladidah in the ring in the afternoons. Mrs. Schleiker was courteous but shy; Mr. Schleiker was grumpy, and took an aggressive attitude toward people who got in his way in the streets or taunted him in the park. As a result, he had been pulled off his horse and badly pummeled on occasion by the local juvenile delinquents and street toughs. There was Liz Black, a lawyer, and Margaret Sacre, whose life seemed to revolve largely around the ownership of an overweight palomino mare which she had bought from Novograd, and last but not least, Murray Ramson. Murray was the most visible of the early birds, and by far the easiest to know.

Short, florid, with a silver mustache and hair and slightly protuberant eyes, he looked like Esky, the debonair little man-about-town and *boulevardier* who for years was the trademark of *Esquire* magazine before it turned literary and stopped featuring improbably long-legged pinups by Alberto Vargas and recipes for a perfect Manhattan. Murray, though married and the father of two boys, did in fact see himself very much in the image of man-about-town and *boulevardier*—at the sight of a pretty girl he would stroke his mustache and chortle like a stage villain. He drove a dashing vintage Jaguar E-type 2+2, dressed in English suits or tweed sports jackets with tailored "cavalry twills," and in general presented himself as a figure straight from the pages of a man's magazine of the late 1940s or early 1950s. Murray's horse was a handsome chestnut Arabian gelding named Fabab, with a broad white blaze, white stockings, and a splendid, flowing mane and tail.

Arabs are among the prettiest of all breeds of horses, though because of their relatively small size and the fact that they're not generally used for foxhunting, three-day eventing, flat racing, or steeplechasing, they have never had a lot of respect in the English-speaking horse world. Perhaps this is also because Napoleon is always portrayed riding one. Though they are in fact tough little horses, and perform spectacularly in long-distance endurance riding in the desert or the mountains, they tend to be looked upon with the kind of disdain that owners of sporting or working dogs have for breeds that are merely flashy and showy. Perhaps because of this, Arabian horses and their owners form a small, inbred world of their own, in which pedigree and appearance (of the horse, at least) count for a lot. Although a lot of the best breeding has been done outside the Arab world for many years—in California and Poland, particularly—Arabs still carry with them a kind of romantic desert-sheikh appeal for a lot of people, of whom Murray was one.

Murray lavished on "Faby-baby," as he called Fabab in his tenderer moments, the kind of care and attention that some thought he might better have directed toward his long-suffering wife Elaine. Fabab had his own set of Mason-Pearson hairbrushes for the grooming of his mane and tail, and unlike many of the private owners at Claremont,

Murray mostly took care of Fabab himself, rubbing and brushing the horse until his coat gleamed like burnished copper and his tiny hooves twinkled. In the afternoons Elaine, who was equally devoted to Fabab, would often come over and ride him in the ring—Fabab was not entirely reliable about such things as manhole covers, city buses, and umbrellas, so the trip from Claremont to the park was not thought to be safe for her on her own—then groom him all over again before he was put away for the night, wearing his own monogrammed sheet or his Baker blanket in cold weather. Fabab's birthday was celebrated upstairs at Claremont, with—what else?—a carrot cake specially ordered for the occasion from the then fashionable New York City bakery of William Greenberg Jr., and coffee, cocoa, and drinks laid out on Fabab's tack trunk.

To say that Fabab was spoiled would be putting it mildly, but he retained a certain independent spirit, occasionally throwing Murray in the park and on one memorable occasion breaking both of Murray's wrists. Murray was nothing if not a dedicated rider—whatever the weather, he was out in the park on Fabab every morning by seven.

Murray was the first of the early birds to invite me to ride with him. We soon became friends, and thanks to him I became a regular upstairs when the private owners got together to share a hip flask, or grouse about Novograd, or speculate on the future, if any, of Claremont. It did not take long before I persuaded myself that it would surely be cheaper and more satisfying to own a horse of my own than to rent one of Novograd's, and no sooner had the thought entered my mind than Novograd was producing horses for me to try.

Since the ethics (and methods) of the used-car business derive more or less directly from those of the horse business, there is no real need to describe the unsuitability of most of the horses that Novograd produced for me, or the kind of bargaining that ensued when he finally found one that seemed, despite numerous defects and problems (and a mysterious background), close to what I was looking for in terms of age, price, experience, and soundness. With horses even more than with cars, there is always a good reason why somebody is selling one—a reason that is, moreover, unlikely to become apparent until you own the horse, at which point it's too late.

The horse trade has always been one where the phrase *Caveat emptor* ("Let the buyer beware") was the motto, even back in the days when Latin was still the language of choice for buying a horse. Any horse trader worth his salt knows how to make an old nag look like a desirable horse—gypsy horse traders, for example, have long been skilled at turning old white horses into young dapple grays with a hard-boiled egg dipped in ink rolled skillfully onto the horse's coat, and every old-time horse trader knows how to measure out just enough arsenic onto the small blade of a pocket knife to give a horse a temporarily shining coat and get him to drink enough water to plump him up for a prospective buyer. Mr. Novograd, it is only fair to say, was not in that class, but he was pretty good at selling horses in his own way.

I was smart enough at any rate to take Murray's advice and have his vet examine the horse I finally chose for soundness. He could find nothing obviously wrong, beyond the fact that his estimate of the horse's age was a good deal higher than Novograd's. "He's seen some wear and tear," the vet said. "Are you sure this is something you want to do?" I wasn't sure at all, but I was determined to do it, and thus I joined the ranks of the private owners in one fell swoop for $1,250, about half of what Mr. Novograd had been asking, and more than twice what Paul Nigro thought the horse was worth when he came from Brooklyn by subway especially to see it.

Never mind—nothing could dim my enthusiasm. I went downtown on my lunch break to see Charlie Kauffman, with a list of things I needed, drawn up by Murray Ramson, Frank, the dignified old West Indian groom who looked after the private owners' horses at Claremont, and Paul Nigro, and returned with a secondhand tack trunk so full that it took two people to carry it to the taxi: a Baker blanket, a sheet, a full kit of grooming essentials, my own bridle with an eggbutt snaffle bit, a standing martingale ("Don't you *dare* ride that horse without no martingale!" Nigro had warned me at the first sight of him), a halter, a lead rope, leg wraps, saddle pads, sheepskin foot warmers to slip over the stirrups on cold mornings, hoof dressing, glycerin saddle soap, vitamin supplements. As Frank and I lugged the trunk across the ring to the ramp, past Mr. Novograd's office, he glanced up at us from his account book and said, "You won't ever use half of that stuff," and he was absolutely right.

It took some vigorous prodding from Novograd, Frank, and two or three others before Malplaquet, as I had renamed him, after one of the duke of Marlborough's famous victories over the French (in 1709), could be persuaded to leave the ring and walk out the door onto Eighty-ninth Street for the journey through the streets from Claremont to Central Park. In the end, Frank and Mr. Novograd pulled him forward with a canvas strap around his hind legs, while I used the whip and two other grooms held on to his bridle, but at last Malplaquet found himself outside the building, eyes rolling. "Don't worry, Mr. Korda," Novograd shouted to me from the doorway. "He'll settle down before you know it." He instantly shut the overhead electric garage door to discourage any second thoughts on the part of the horse, or me.

Apprehensively, Malplaquet followed Fabab to the park. Subsequent months were to prove full of adventures on the city streets—at one point I was thrown onto the hood of a taxicab, at another the horse kicked a passing taxi, leaving a deep dent in the driver's door. Eventually we reached a kind of nadir when the horse, startled by a noisy bus on Columbus Avenue, took refuge on the sidewalk, scattering pedestrians on their way to work, kicked in a telephone booth, then tried to back his way through the door into the White Tower hamburger shop on the corner of Columbus and Ninetieth Street, while the counterman and the customers shouted and pleaded at us in Spanish to go away.

In the end Malplaquet settled down, just as Novograd had predicted, though he had a habit of throwing his head back at the first sign of danger, which would have broken my nose many times over but for Paul Nigro's sage advice to keep a standing martingale on him. He retained a pronounced dislike of buses and trucks with noisy exhausts, large groups of children shouting at him or throwing things (particularly unfortunate, since there were a couple of schools full of troublemakers on the way), cars with souped-up engines and no mufflers, ambulances and police cars with sirens going and flashing lights turned on, open umbrellas, and street fairs of any kind. Except for the umbrellas—and, after all, who knows what an open umbrella looks like to a horse?—I dislike all these things myself, so we had no basic disagreement, though from time to time I was as scared as I had been in Madison Square Garden or at the Middleburg Gold Cup course, in fact maybe more scared, since here it was possible to be thrown in front of a speeding taxi, or for the horse to slip on a slick manhole cover in the rain, or for a gang of juvenile delinquents to give me a working-over like Mr. Schleiker. But in the end, nothing as dramatic as that ever happened to me, even in years to come when we rode down Fifth Avenue to the skating rink at Rockefeller Center, then back to the park again up the Avenue of the Americas, or when we rode to Rumpelmeyer's, the famous tea shop on Central Park South, and tied up our horses to the parking meters while we stood on the sidewalk and sipped Rumpelmeyer's famous hot chocolate with whipped cream.

In short, a whole new social life opened up for me, thanks to the horse, though most mornings it merely consisted of riding in Central Park for an hour or so, either alone or in the company of Murray Ramson, and sharing a thermos of coffee with a shot of brandy in it on cold winter mornings while we were putting away our horses. In fact it was Murray, with his unerring eye for women, who first told me that the attractive blond woman who had taken to riding in the park in the early morning on one of Novograd's best horses was English.

I had already noticed her, of course—hers were a face and figure that would hardly go unnoticed anywhere—and also noticed that she rode well enough to make even one of Novograd's horses look good. There is an art to this, by the way. It isn't just that certain people look better on a horse than others, though that's obviously true; it's that people who *really* know how to ride have a way of reminding the horse of whatever it was taught earlier in its life, a kind of natural combination of empathy and dominance that the horse automatically recognizes and respects.

Of course even the best rider can't overcome the horse's physical limitations or make it do something it hasn't ever been taught, but almost every horse is able to sense and respond to the presence of somebody on its back who knows what he or she is doing. Even the oldest, dullest, and most bloody-minded of hacks or school horses tends to come alive at the feel of a real rider's hands on the reins—the neck arches; the head comes down; the horse begins to mouth the bit, sensing that it isn't going to be used as a punishment, instead of pulling or leaning against it; the ears point forward, signifying perhaps interest, curiosity, or simply the dim memory of happier days; and the gait becomes crisper, sharper, instead of a slovenly, pathetic shuffling along.

You can't perform this kind of miracle with the whip or with spurs—old school horses have learned to put up with physical punishment and respond to it with mulish resistance, often by simply standing still and refusing to move. It's done by means of establishing a mutual emotional bond as well as a physical one, requiring, on the horse's side, the same kind of instincts that enable a cat to tell who is "a cat person" and who is not. Much is made of the fact that a horse can instantly recognize fear in its rider, but fear isn't the only negative emotion horses can sense in a human being—anger, impatience, incompetence, ignorance, indecision, and indifference play a part too. On the other hand, they have a pretty good nose for a gentle pair of hands, strong legs, and self-confidence in the saddle, and can usually tell a good rider from a bad one before he or she is even mounted.

In any event, whatever gifts were required to make Novograd's horses look good on the Central Park bridle paths, this blond Englishwoman clearly not only had them, but used them effortlessly, as if there were nothing to it. What was more, she made a striking figure on the bridle path. With her long blond hair, her skintight stretch breeches—then still something of an innovation, the riding equivalent of the first bikinis on the beaches of Saint Tropez in the 1950s—and dramatic tops, she was not the usual Central Park morning rider. Far more than Jane McClary, she seemed to me like a latter-day version of Lucy Glitters, the daring equestrienne and charming companion of Lady Scattercash, who so attracted Mr. Sponge when he first met her in the hunt field. (To quote Surtees: "'Run him at it, Lucy!' exclaimed Mr. Sponge, turning his horse half round to his fair companion, 'Run him at it, Lucy!' repeated he; and Lucy, fortunately hitting the gap, skimmed o'er the water like a swallow on a summer's eve.")

It took some time before Lucy Glitters and I were on speaking terms,

"Lucy Glitters"—Margaret and Tabasco in Central Park.

perhaps partly out of English reserve, perhaps also because of a mutual attraction strong enough that both of us may have sensed that this was unlikely to develop into a simple, easy friendship, with no consequences. For a long time we rode around the reservoir in Central Park, as if by mutual agreement, in opposite directions, nodding every time we passed, but inevitably we ended up riding out to the park together one morning, and were soon riding together every day. Margaret Glinn turned out, as one might have guessed, to be a model, was married to the well-known Magnum photographer Burton Glinn, and led what seemed to me at the time an almost unnaturally glamorous life. The Glinns had a huge apartment overlooking Central Park; they seemed either to give or to go to dinner parties every night of the week, and in the winters rented a house in Cuernavaca, Mexico, which they shared with such friends as John Chancellor and David Halberstam and their wives.

Margaret had modeled for her husband all over the world—there seemed to be no place, however far or exotic, where she had not been— but of late, she intimated, she had lost the taste for travel. Riding in the park was a way of returning to some form of her roots, for despite the aura of urban glamour and the sophistication, she was a farmer's daughter from Gloucestershire, in the heart of the Cotswolds, who had grown up with ponies and horses.

I did not realize then that Margaret's early-morning rides were a small, but significant, step in her growing independence from Burt; that by deciding she would no longer travel with him, and taking up again, in a very modest form at first, on Novograd's horses, what had been an important part of her life until she married Burt, she was distancing herself from her marriage perhaps further and more quickly than she realized, or intended. Nor had I realized the extent to which riding had for me become an escape from my own marriage, a way of spending a couple of hours a day doing something in which my then wife had not the slightest interest. In short, despite a slow beginning on the bridle path, Margaret and I were riding in the same direction, though perhaps at different speeds and for different reasons, and before very long she was going through the same stages I had. Her riding wardrobe grew, we went to Kauffman's together so she could buy her own saddle, and eventually, like myself, she bought her own horse from Irwin Novograd—in her case a big, flashy, copper-chestnut thoroughbred named Tabasco, with a habit of running away with inexperienced riders in the park, as if the bridle path around the reservoir was the track at Hialeah, and a mysterious past.

Even Mr. Novograd recognized that Tabasco was too much horse for most of his customers, and was cautious about putting riders on him, very few of whom in any case asked for the horse a second time. Tabasco was not the horse for everybody—he did not suffer fools gladly. Heavy hands on the reins or an incautious snap of a whip were likely to produce an explosion, and being a big, long-legged horse, he could buck a rider he didn't respect right off, or failing that, gallop for home, gathering speed at an alarming, and unstoppable, rate.

It was to Margaret's credit that she could not only *ride* Tabasco, but sensed that he was basically an elderly aristocrat fallen on hard times. Though he was far too thin—he was a restless, nervous horse, and a "poor keeper," as they say about horses which are fussy about their food and don't gain weight easily—he had the elegant grace that comes naturally to thoroughbreds, a long, powerful, muscular neck, and a noble head, with a trace of sadness in his eyes, as if he knew he had been bred for better things than Irwin Novograd's barn. It did not take long before Margaret had brought his coat to a bright, coppery shine, though nothing could conceal the nicks and scars of a hard life at the track and elsewhere.

At first, Margaret shared him with an attractive young woman called Jo-Jo Temerson, whose life was almost as much of a mystery as the horse's past, and who left almost immediately for Paris to become—or to live with—a jockey (it was never quite clear to me which), leaving Margaret as sole owner. (It was typical of Mr. Novograd that on the day Margaret was to purchase Tabasco from him, she had to wait, check in hand, for the horse to come back from Central Park, since Novograd had been unable to resist renting him out one last time.)

Once Margaret had become a private owner, she set about making the second floor of Claremont more lively. Nothing could alter the essential dinginess of the place—it was essentially slum housing for horses—but before long the quick cup of coffee after riding was transformed into a longer and more sophisticated occasion, with pastries brought in, and Irish coffee on cold mornings. It was as if she had somehow managed to transform this small group of people whose life revolved around the ownership of a horse in Manhattan into a glamorous group of sportsmen and sportswomen. Frank opened up a small locker room, which appeared to have been untouched since before World War II, where men had once changed into formal riding clothes before going out to the park, and where, Frank assured us, their boots had been polished and neatly put away by the attendant. This became a kind of "club room," and a source of deep and gloomy suspicion for Mr. Novograd, who, like all landlords, didn't like to see his tenants getting too friendly with each other.

Margaret jumping Tabasco over a police barricade, Central Park, N.Y.C.

Margaret and Tabasco, winter, Central Park, N.Y.C.

The riding became livelier too. Margaret took to jumping police barricades in the park, which was strictly forbidden by the park rules but which the mounted cops didn't seem to mind (the cops in police cars minded, but weren't about to get out of their cars to do anything about it). We explored whole areas of Central Park on horseback, far beyond the bridle paths, as if it were a private estate. In the winter Margaret rode Tabasco through the snow wearing a fur coat with an immense fox collar that framed her face, and a fur cap, like a character out of *Dr. Zhivago,* or perhaps Natasha in *War and Peace,* and when summer came, she took to riding in an embroidered Russian shirt, which made her look like a Cossack maiden. Soon all the private owners—except the Schleikers, who were impervious to fashion—started to blossom out into more exotic clothes.

Gradually, Margaret and I began to spend more time together, even when we weren't riding. On Saturdays and Sundays we would often stop for long breakfasts before going home, and it was at one of these, over bacon and eggs at a coffee shop on the West Side, that I happened to ask her how and when she started to ride. Of course, like all such stories, it began with a girl and her pony.

In England, you have to understand," Margaret says—giving me a look that means, Take this seriously!—"there's a whole lifestyle that revolves around ponies, like the one in the Thelwell cartoons, full of cross-looking little girls in pigtails, with velvet hard hats and jodhpur boots, and tiny, fat Shetland ponies, each with a mind of its own. In the English countryside, a pony gets passed on from child to child as it gets outgrown, like clothes in a large family, so most of them don't stay at one place all that long."

Still, Margaret can remember the names of all hers, as well as those of her friend Nancy, and ticks them off, beginning with her own Snowy and Rip, and Nancy's Bess, Chips, and 'Khana. . . . Of course that's not so surprising, I reflect. From a child's point of view, a pony in those days involved some of the same desires that center on learning to drive and owning a car today for teenage Americans—freedom to come and go as you please, responsibility ("You can have it, but you have to look after it."), a sense of power and control, on top of which, unlike a car, a pony is warm, furry, accepts—indeed *expects*—treats, and responds to love, affection, and attention. If not quite as cuddly as kittens and the smaller breeds of dog, small ponies—Shetland ponies particularly—have a lot of charm, as well as strong individual personalities, and are built on a scale that doesn't seem threatening to children, though the first thing a child learns is that they can kick, bite, buck, and refuse to go along with the program like any large horse.

The whole notion of the little girl and her pony is deeply entrenched in English life, and also provides an early statement about class, status, and athletic ability, very much part of the Diana the Huntress syndrome that permeates a certain stratum of English society when it comes to little girls. I have already seen a photograph of Margaret as a little girl, riding her pony down a village lane, followed by her friend Nancy, on her pony, past a dozen or so village children, who look at them as they ride by. The village children are on foot; she is mounted. Everybody in the photograph looks happy enough—they all seem to be having a good time—but there is a clear social dividing line between those who are on the ground, and Margaret and Nancy who are not.

I remind myself (and her) that this is the same old dividing line that exists—has existed for thousands of years—between the man on horseback and the man on foot, between the cavalryman and infantry, between cowboy and farmer, and that explains the enduring qualities of such myths as the centaur. Since the horse was not native to the Americas, the Indians of the Southwest at first jumped to the conclusion that the mounted Spaniards they encountered in the sixteenth century were, like centaurs, a single creature. They soon worked out that the Spaniards were merely riding an animal, though, and very shortly afterward, starting with Spanish horses that they had stolen or that had escaped from the herd, the remuda, and run wild, they became horsemen themselves, though they never completely gave up the idea that the horse was magic—hence the elaborate way in which they painted their ponies for war, and the central role that horses came to play in their culture. The Indians, who had always gone on foot, leaped in a couple of generations to mounted status, and soon developed in their turn a deepseated contempt for those who went—or fought—on foot.

In England too, the horse has divided, since the Norman conquest, gentry from common folk, those who live in "the manor house" from "villagers," the well-to-do from the poor, perhaps more decisively than almost anywhere else in the world. English class distinctions, coupled with the English fondness for animals, gave the horse a special place in English life, not just as a class symbol but as an appealing, if slightly zany, national passion. The English love of horses was fabled, and deeply rooted—flat racing, steeplechase racing, and in modern times show jumping were, and to some extent remain, major national sports—as was the belief, among those who could afford it, that ownership of a horse or pony was a character-building experience for a girl.

Margaret nods, as if to say all this may be so, of course, and is very interesting, but we're talking about *her* pony—*revenons à nos moutons.* Ponies, she points out practically, need a lot more looking after than cats or dogs, and for all but the very rich, who have stables and grooms, they involve a good deal of hard work and responsibility on the part of the child—not a bad thing by itself. Of course there's also the thought, somewhere back in the minds of most parents even today, she agrees, that the longer you can keep a girl interested in horses, the longer you can put off the moment when she starts being interested in boys. From that point of view, encouraging a girl's interest in riding early on can be seen as a prudent step, even if it accomplishes nothing more than keeping her away from boys for a crucial year or two of her adolescence.

The expression on Margaret's face makes it clear that this didn't work in her case, but I reflect that undoubtedly a certain innocence seems to attach itself to the whole idea of owning a pony, as if the pony were a way of prolonging childhood dreams and fantasies. Surely it's no accident that one of the few books that never rates anything less than a misty-eyed five-star review from its readers on the Amazon.com Web site is *Misty of Chincoteague,* with *My Friend Flicka* (admittedly the latter is about a boy and his pony, but most of the readers seem to be girls) a close second.

Such considerations were doubtless not far from Paul Mogford's mind when he began to ask about after a likely pony for his five-year-old daughter Margaret; being nobody's fool, he can hardly have failed to look ahead to the future with the thought that a pretty girl on a pony might be engaged in wholesome and innocent pursuits a lot longer than a pretty girl in the passenger seat of an MG or a Jaguar.

Margaret smiles at the thought of her father's illusions on that subject. We are seated next to the window, in a coffee shop on the West Side, and outside the morning traffic jam fills the streets. I ask her at what age she started to be interested in horses. She looks out the window, eyes slightly veiled as her mind goes back to England and her childhood. "I can't remember a time when I *wasn't* interested in horses," she says at last. After all, growing up on a farm in wartime England brought her close to horses from the time she could walk. There were plenty of horses in rural England in those days—many of them sturdy working animals—and the war had briefly halted, even reversed, the process of replacing them by machines that had begun before World War I. Gasoline was strictly rationed, and country people fell back on the horse. With the car laid up for the duration, people went visiting by pony and trap, used horses to bring in the hay from the fields, and made deliveries with a horse and cart, just as their grandparents had. The horse had been a vanishing part of English rural life; now it became once again essential.

Margaret's desire to own a horse was clear enough early on in her life, by the age of four, when she came across two farm laborers having their lunch by the side of a lane while the horse that had been pulling their farm wagon, removed from the shafts, grazed nearby. It was a draft horse, a huge mare with feet as big as dinner plates, a massive neck, thick feathers around her fetlocks, and big square leather blinkers shading her eyes. Like most draft horses, she was friendly—sheer size seems to make such horses gentle—and more than willing to be patted by a little girl.

It didn't take long before Margaret's proprietary instincts were aroused, and she asked if she could take the mare home. The older of the two farm workers put down his bread and cheese and nodded—perhaps with a wink to his companion—then smiled. "If you can get 'er 'ome, you can 'ave 'er," he said, no doubt as a harmless piece of fun. In any case, Margaret took him at his word. So far as she was concerned, it was a bargain—the mare was as good as hers.

She took hold of the mare's bridle and pulled on it. The mare snorted, dropped her head, and continued to graze. Margaret pulled harder, tugging with all her might, but the harder she pulled, the more firmly the mare dug her feet in and stood rooted in place. She even tried to pick up each huge foot to get the mare moving, to no effect. Meanwhile, the two farm workers roared with laughter at the sight of a little girl, tears in her eyes, trying desperately to drag a horse that weighed close to a ton home with her. It's hard to know which was the most painful—the humiliation of being laughed at by a couple of loutish grown-ups, or the fact that the horse wouldn't budge for her.

Margaret pulled and pulled, but there was no moving the mare an inch. If there's one thing a big old draft horse knows, it's not to let itself be led away by a total stranger, however small and endearing—particularly when it's eating its lunch.

In the end Margaret went home without the mare, having learned a few valuable lessons from the experience—first of all, no doubt, not to put too much faith in men's promises; secondly, that the hardest way to move any horse is to stand in front of it and pull; and, finally, that what she wanted most in the world was to have that horse—or another horse—at home, *hers*.

. . .

"The most important lesson of all—not to be frightened of horses—I already knew," she says, eyes still a little misty at the memory of that draft horse she failed to take home. By the time she was four she had learned how to climb up onto the manger in a horse's stall, and from there to swing herself up onto its back and sit there. "You don't know what it's like for a little girl to sit on a horse's back in a dress, with your bare legs pressed hard against all that warmth and power," she goes on. "We'd sometimes sit three in a row on a cart horse, and inevitably the girl on the end would fall off and pull the rest of us off with her. The horses never minded, you know—they were always good-natured."

That sense that horses are your friends and mean you no harm is vital for a young rider—one of those things, like a natural sense of balance, that can't be learned later on as an adult, no matter how many lessons you take or how hard you work at it. It's why the Indians of the American West could outride cavalry troopers, I tell her—and do so without a saddle, or stirrups, or even a bit, with just a blanket folded up on the horse's back and a rope around his muzzle, so at ease with the horse that they could lean back and shoot an arrow with deadly accuracy at a full gallop. They too grew up learning to know and trust horses—the horse was their "little friend." Being friends with a horse, or pony, isn't just a metaphor either, or peculiar to Native Americans. For a little girl like Margaret, an only child living in a small English village, a pony would be not only a friend, but a *best* friend.

Snowy came into her life at the age of five, a Welsh pony "with some mileage on him," when she was living in Tiptree, Essex, where Margaret's father Paul was managing the orchards of the famous maker of jam. Margaret describes Snowy with a wealth of exact, remembered detail, including where he came from. "He was found by Dick Porter, a friend of Paul's who was a dealer in cattle and horses, and famous for his wonderful eye for a good horse," she says. "Porter was quite a character. He went up to Yorkshire once to look at some cattle—it must have been during the war, so he was picked up at the station by the farmer with a horse and trap. Porter took one look from the platform and said to the farmer, 'I'll buy that horse from you right out of the shafts.' He took the horse back home, and it went on to become the top point-to-pointer in England.

"Porter had previously loaned Snowy to some American officers on an Essex air base, who used him and the trap to get around the base, and kept a cake tin full of sweets under the seat of the trap; when they wanted him to stay in place while they did something, they simply opened the tin and put it in front of him on the ground. He was smart, cunning, very knowing, which isn't too surprising—most ponies *are* smart, to begin with, smarter than horses, anyway. And of course a children's pony usually has a lot more experience with the pony-child relationship than its owner, as well as a more clear-cut agenda."

Margaret remembers another detail. Snowy came along with a Victorian pony trap (a two-wheeled, two-person vehicle), in dark blue with pale blue decorative trim, and Margaret's introduction to the world of competitive horsemanship at the age of five was in a driving class, with Snowy between the shafts of the trap. Driving was very much in vogue in those days, with gas strictly rationed—not that it has ever really gone out of fashion, even today, but then there were plenty of adults driving a pony and trap to do their shopping, so it was anything but an exotic or esoteric mode of transport. Margaret had learned to drive at once, trotting Snowy at breakneck speed through the orchards with her father beside her—she was strictly warned against cantering Snowy between shafts. Driving without her father beside her was something of a problem, however, since the trap had to be in balance, and by herself she didn't weigh enough to do the job. Her father solved that problem by slipping an old tractor crankcase weighing one hundred and fifty pounds or so under the seat.

Unfortunately for Margaret, the judge weighed over sixteen stone (two hundred and twenty-four pounds) and had to ride beside her in the trap, and the moment he stepped in and sat down, what with his weight and the crankcase under the seat, the trap tipped over backward, almost lifting Snowy off the ground between the shafts. Her father had to run over and remove the weight before Snowy could move. Nevertheless, she still managed to win second place, and for many years treasured the blue certificate.

For riding, Snowy had a child's felt saddle, with a handle at the front and a leather crupper that went down his back and around the base of his tail. Many ponies are so round that a normal saddle just won't stay in place, and you can still see the old-fashioned felt ones offered for sale today in the catalogs of the more upmarket eastern tack stores. They have the further advantage of making it very hard for a child to fall off, though not impossible, of course.

Like a lot of little girls in those days, Margaret didn't get any formal riding instruction—the pony was her teacher, basically, and she learned to ride by trial and error, which, when combined with instinct, boldness, watching other people ride, a natural sense of balance, and the well-known ability of a child to survive unharmed from falls that would break an adult's bones, was enough to point her in the right direction. As in mountain climbing, probably the first thing to learn in riding anyway is never to look down—"Look straight ahead between the horse's ears!" may be the best (and most frequent) piece of advice offered to a beginner. To a child that comes naturally, Margaret explains, along with a certain feel for what's going on in the horse's mind.

That makes sense to me. After all, the children of the Plains Indians didn't get any riding instruction either, I point out. At some age, they simply managed to get on a pony's back and learn by doing. Margaret learned to ride in much the same spirit.

She stirs her coffee, and shrugs. The Plains Indians don't interest her that much when she's on the subject of Snowy. Shortly after getting him, she continues, the Mogfords left Essex and moved to Overbury, in Gloucestershire, where Paul took on the management of the Holland-Martin family's big farm. That was, and is, real riding country—rolling wooded hills, big fields, stone walls and dirt lanes, the beginning of it all, really, little legs in jodhpurs and jodhpur boots, blond hair flying in the wind, out the garden gate to freedom. It's hard to go back from there to boarding-school discipline and lessons, she says sadly, and I realize that in some part of her head Margaret never has. For her, freedom and happiness would be forever defined by that moment, associated in some way with having your hands in a horse's mane, feeling its stride, and the sound of its hooves and breathing.

There wasn't anything formal about the way Margaret kept Snowy, or the way the friend she had made in Overbury, Nancy, kept *her* pony, Bess. Any moment they could, they simply pulled their ponies out of their fields, tacked them up, mounted, and galloped off. "All we did," Margaret says, "was throw a leg over and go." A certain amount of grooming took place—on the whole, little girls enjoy grooming a pony almost as much as the pony enjoys the attention—and an occasional stab at cleaning the tack, but that's about it. It's a heady thing—little girls are bossed around by almost everybody, but in the relationship between a little girl and a pony the little girl is boss, or is supposed to be. And the pony is there, close at hand, part of the rural landscape, ready to go when she is, always happy to see her, visible in its field through the window even on rainy days when it's not going to be ridden—and it's hardly surprising that Margaret, like a lot of little girls, dreamed of marrying her pony (though an alternative ambition was to marry her dog).

She and Nancy were "holy terrors" on their ponies. She remembers having to pull Banks, the local blacksmith, out of the pub to shoe their ponies. Nancy's Shetland pony had to be coaxed into standing on a couple of boxes, since, drunk or sober, Banks couldn't bend down low enough to work on its feet otherwise.

Ponies, like children, Margaret goes on, are always full of surprises. Nancy's pony Chips, who was thought to be too fat for her own good, surprised everybody by suddenly giving birth to a foal one day, out of the blue, in the cherry orchard—nobody had even guessed that she was pregnant—the day after Nancy competed on her in the school gymkhana. The foal was named 'Khana, of course. Margaret remembers Nancy's father trying to corner and catch the recalcitrant Bess after she had escaped from her field—when ponies don't want to be caught, they can avoid capture for hours—until he finally lost his patience. "All

*Margaret and Rip,
1949.*

right, you bugger!" he shouted; then he threw away the carrot and the halter, charged down the field, the perfect English gentleman, in his suede ankle boots, flannel trousers, and tailored blazer, and brought the astonished pony down with a flying rugby tackle.

Margaret laughs, then looks out at the traffic and the city streets wistfully. "It's hard to imagine that kind of thing happening these days," she says. "A grown man tackling a pony. . . . It's like something out of another world, isn't it?"

On the face of things, sitting in a coffee shop on the West Side, yes, I can't deny it. I glance at my watch and call for the check. I'm late for work, and Margaret has to get home to her husband, her life, her apartment; we're a long way from a neatly dressed gentleman tackling a pony in a field in the English countryside. All the same, as we gather up our things to get on the subway—What *can* people think of us on the B train at ten in the morning, I sometimes wonder, two people in riding breeches and boots, one of them an attractive blond lady carrying a whip?—I can't help wondering if it isn't more a question of parallel worlds. Somewhere out there, beyond New York, there are still plenty of children whose life revolves around a pony, and no doubt a good many fathers who have been tempted to tackle the pony, if they have not actually done it.

Margaret's apprehensions all that time ago about the world of ponies were, as it happens, misplaced. Nothing much has changed. I am sitting, some twenty years later, on a fence rail by a large field just outside Shekomeko, New York, near Pine Plains, watching two little girls trying to round up a pony. They circle it, making soft clucking noises. The older one—they are five and seven—carries a lead rope hidden behind her back. The pony's head is down as it grazes, and it doesn't seem to be paying any attention to them, but every time they get within reach, it raises its head for a good look at them and moves a few feet away. So far it has managed to evade them for about fifteen minutes, moving several hundred yards across the big, rolling field.

The girls aren't as impatient as Nancy's father was—nor big enough to tackle the pony—but they have promised to ride it for me, and are worried that I might lose interest and go away. On the way to the field, they admitted to me that their father sometimes has trouble getting his hands on either of their ponies. "You have to sneak up on mine," the younger one says of hers, "pretending you don't want her, then— *Wham!*—you have to grab her before she knows it." Apparently this is true of the older girl's pony too, which is the one they're after. Eventually the two girls regroup, make a whispered plan of attack, then walk away, pretending that they're really after one of the other horses—the ponies are in a field with three or four full-size horses—while the pony continues to graze, tail switching, eyes watchful.

Eventually, the girls get behind a horse, use it as camouflage, and manage to get close enough to the pony to grab it when it has wandered into a corner of the field, hard by the fence line, where it's trapped. The pony looks surprised and annoyed at its own stupidity as the older girl snaps on the lead rope.

They return in triumph to where I'm sitting, pulling the pony behind them, spirits high again; I swing the gate open for them, refasten it— they both warn me sternly to be absolutely sure the chain is secure, like adults talking to a child—and follow them back to the barn.

As if to prove that *plus ça change, plus c'est la même chose,* I recognize the pony now that I'm close to her—or at any rate, I remember her name, which I see engraved on a brass plate on her halter. Tiddlywinks, a bay Shetland/Welsh pony cross, had been something of a fixture around us at events, ridden for many years by Ashley Jaeger, the diminutive daughter of a local vet. Ashley Jaeger took Tiddlywinks hell-for-leather over fences that would have given a full-size horse and rider pause, and were usually in the ribbons at the end of the day. Ashley was a formidable competitor, even as a little girl, but was also locally famous for the fact that everything she owned was decorated in her colors, turquoise blue and bright pink. Her tack trunk, her helmet cover, her back protector, even Tiddlywinks's saddle pads and leg wraps, were all in Ashley's signature colors, a kind of equine fashion statement that made her instantly recognizable.

I ask Hope, the seven-year-old, who now owns Tiddlywinks, what her pony's age is. Hope and her five-year-old sister Ky roll their eyes at each other, as if I'd posed them a tough math question. They are both blond, pigtailed, and sunburned. "Pretty old," Hope says, shrugging. They have Tiddlywinks hooked to the cross ties as Hope goes over her lightly with a brush, raising a cloud of dust and loose hair—it's early spring, and the pony is shedding. "She's my fourth pony," she adds. She counts them up on her fingers, reciting their names.

I do a quick calculation in my head. When did she start riding, I ask? Hope thinks about that one. She got her first pony when she was three, she says, or maybe three and a half? That seems like a lot of ponies, I say. Hope nods. The ponies come and go as other kids outgrow them; some of them work out, some of them don't. Anyway, her first couple of ponies were tiny Shetlands, like her sister's pony Schmoo, and she quickly outgrew them. Tiddlywinks, she thinks, will probably stay for a while.

Their mother, Louise Merryman, appears to check on the proceedings. Louise is a successful three-day event rider and an instructor, a woman whose life revolves around horses. Tanned, with a silver-blond pigtail, she looks like a taller version of her daughters. Tiddlywinks's age is hard to know, Louise says, but thinks she is probably over thirty—a fabulous age for a horse, but then ponies live a lot longer than horses. By now the two girls have given Tiddlywinks as much brushing as she's going to get; Hope leans over and carefully cleans out each hoof with a hoof pick. The only problem they have is in bridling their ponies, for which they have to stand on an upended bucket.

It is cool and pleasant in the big, open aisle of Louise's barn. We are watched by two large dogs, which are quietly but fiercely protective of the two girls. Somewhere around is Ky's cat, which she desperately wanted to show me, and in pursuit of which we climbed a huge pile of hay bales, but which has apparently gone to ground at the approach of a stranger. She has shown me its litter box and water bowl instead, perhaps afraid that if I don't see them, I won't believe she actually has a cat.

Hope puts on her miniature back protector and hard hat, and we follow her to the outdoor ring, since she is determined that I should watch her jump. The girls ride every day, Louise tells me, all year round. Sometimes, in the winter, if the school bus bringing Hope home is a little late, Louise meets her down the road at the bus stop, leading Tiddlywinks already tacked up and ready to go, so as not to miss the last bit of daylight. Of the two girls, Hope is the more determined rider, something of a cowboy, in fact, I think, as she mounts, takes up her reins, and takes off around the ring. She clearly has complete faith in her pony, and with some reason—though in human terms Tiddlywinks is probably over ninety, she seems indefatigable and still eager to please. Much to Hope's displeasure, Louise and I lower a few rails and watch her sail over them effortlessly, though a little too fast. "Keep your hands down," Louise tells her. "And don't lean into a turn. Sit straight in the saddle." Hope corrects both flaws while Ky fidgets, waiting for her turn, bored with watching her sister ride.

There is a line of barrels painted white set up on the sand of the ring. Hope shouts out that she's going to jump them, scoots around the ring like a barrel racer, neglects her mother's instructions about keeping her hands low and sitting straight, and comes tumbling off her pony at the jump, landing in a cloud of dust. The pony stops on the other side of the jump and looks back with mild interest or concern. Ky giggles. "Hope fell on her butt," she says. "You say things like that about your sister, and you can go right back to the barn," Louise says back to her, eyes on Hope, wondering no doubt, like most parents, how bad the damage is. But there are no tears. Hope scrambles to her feet and dusts herself off, none the worse for wear, and apparently eager to get back on the pony—a good sign.

Louise helps her back on, and Hope takes the barrels again, keeping her hands down this time, goes right over them, then trots out of the ring, off toward a bank and a stone wall, scattering dogs right and left, while the three of us—Ky reluctantly—go running after her. She jumps the wall and the ramp successfully, then trots back to give her sister a chance.

"This isn't my pony," Ky tells me, having last-minute second thoughts, but Louise shortens the stirrups, checks Ky's helmet, and lifts her onto the pony. "I don't want to trot," Ky says. "It's too high up." I see her point. Ky is less than three feet, six inches tall, and from her point of view Tiddlywinks might as well be a draft horse. Louise walks her around the ring, warning Hope not to make clucking noises, since Tiddlywinks takes them as a signal to trot. After fifteen minutes— during which Hope simmers gently at the sight of her younger sister on her pony—Ky has had enough, and we go back to the barn. Tiddly-winks looks as if she's good for another couple of hours, but it's late in the afternoon, and the two girls are showing signs of hunger—or per-haps the thrill of having me here watching them is simply wearing off.

Louise removes the saddle and the bridle while the girls give the pony another brush. I compliment her on the girls' behavior and riding. It's hard not to push them, Louise says, but you have to let them go at their own pace. Ky is still a little timid—though less so on her own pony—while Hope is a little overconfident. . . .

I look around us. The farm is on a county road, with almost no traf-fic, and Shekomeko is such a tiny hamlet that you can drive through it before you've even realized you're there. Its one commercial establishment, a country store, seems to have given up the ghost. It's not such a different life, I think, from Margaret's childhood in England. At any rate, the pony culture still seems to be going strong, whatever else has changed in the world since then.

I mention this to Louise, who brushes the hair out of her eyes and watches the girls go off, leading the pony back to its field, tail snapping briskly back and forth with the satisfaction of a job well done and dinner on the way.

Louise laughs. "No," she says, "a little girl and a pony, that's a story that never changes, isn't it?"

And never will, I think, as I head back to my car.

Photo courtesy of Dean Niezper

CHAPTER FOUR

The Seat on a Horse

T DID NOT TAKE LONG before Margaret's life and mine began to center on the horses to a remarkable degree for two city apartment dwellers. Because of them, we met every day, after all—something which would surely otherwise have begun to look suspicious to our spouses sooner or later.

We didn't need, at first anyway, an excuse to meet—each of us arrived at Claremont separately at seven in the morning, greeted Mr. Novograd, then went upstairs to collect our horses from Frank. Most mornings we had breakfast together afterward before taking the subway, Margaret back to her home, and I to my office in Rockefeller Center. When eventually we became lovers (no surprise to anybody at Claremont, especially the eagle-eyed Mr. Novograd), we first had to pull off each other's riding boots, as if in a scene from *Tom Jones*. On the weekends, like most of the "private owners," we tended to stay at Claremont a good deal longer than was necessary, cleaning tack, concocting

Irish coffee in the winter, and talking horses with Murray Ramson and whoever else was there. There was no great compulsion to go home, and, as always with horses, there was usually something to do.

Occasionally, somebody new would turn up and make their way into the group: there was Julie Vitullo-Martin and her husband Tom, owners of a handsome gelding named Brian Boru, and a tall, good-looking young man named Arno Mares, an entrepreneur before the word was commonplace, who brought in a succession of different horses and seemed to be as much in the horse business as Mr. Novograd, and a natural rider as well. Lean, laid-back, and good-humored, Arno was one of those riders who could make any horse look good—a valuable gift in the horse trade—and in his cowboy hat and suede schooling chaps, he set hearts aflutter all over Central Park. The Vitullo-Martins, movers and shakers in the world of public policy and urban planning, were both young and energetic and determined to shake things up at Claremont, which certainly stood in need of a good shaking. Mr. Novograd was soon scrunching down behind his ledger, his fedora pulled low over his eyes, at the first sight of either of them. Both Vitullo-Martins were fiercely committed activists—they lived in a big, old-fashioned West Side apartment building where the tenants, under Tom Vitullo's leadership, had been on a rent strike against the landlord for so long that the story regularly appeared in the *New York Times*—and thanks to them Margaret and I were drawn into the interminable campaigns to "save Claremont," or at least to change it.

In this sense, if no other, Mr. Novograd resembled Louis XVI—he did not wish to be saved by his own boarders, still less to be re-formed by them. Nevertheless, for a heady period Margaret and I attended community board meetings, lobbied the mayor and the parks commissioner, and tried to interest the police department in taking over a decaying storage facility in Central Park as a combined public and police stable (Julie Vitullo-Martin even became, for a while, one of New York's few mounted police volunteers), none of which led to anything much. In the meantime, though, horses seemed to have taken over our lives, as they do everybody who gets involved in riding or owning them.

Of course all hobbies have an element of the obsessional built into them—who has not felt that, for example, when watching grown men and women down on their hands and knees as if in prayer beside a gleaming car at a concourse, doing a last-minute final check for dust before the judge arrives, armed with Q-tips and a 100 percent cotton towel sprayed with Pledge, or for that matter at any dog show?—but horses have been around humans for a very long time and played a vital role in war, sports, and agriculture. As a result, most people who own a horse or horses begin to feel that as central to their life, not something you can take up and then put away for a while, like skeet shooting, say, or collecting stamps. While we were not perhaps as obsessed as Murray Ransom—whose idea of a quiet domestic evening well spent was to sit in his favorite chair with a glass of wine after dinner, catching up on back numbers of the *Arabian Horse World* magazine, the *Arabian Horse World Calendar* on the wall beside him and black velvet slippers decorated with an Arabian's head in gold thread on his feet— the way we spent our time (and money), the way we dressed, the fact that we had met in the first place, was to some degree a result of owning horses.

From time to time it occurred to us that what we were doing was unusual. Once, when I was having lunch with a couple of Hollywood agents, having as usual gone directly from Claremont to the office, no doubt with the faint odor of horses still on my clothes, I noticed one of them looking increasingly preoccupied and puzzled. Eventually I asked him what the matter was. He sniffed. "I don't know what the hell it is," he said, nervously glancing around the restaurant as if his mind was playing tricks on him, "but somehow I keep thinking that I'm at the track."

We didn't notice it ourselves, in much the same way that we came to consider it normal that our day should begin at dawn as we clip-clopped across Ninetieth Street, weaving in and out of traffic, to Central Park, and had the entire park to ourselves for an hour or so as the sun came up. Occasionally we saw somebody we knew—Jacques d'Amboise, the choreographer and dancer, who was a great admirer of Margaret's, would sometimes run around the reservoir, bare-chested, holding onto Margaret's stirrup—but for the most part, except for the other riders, we were alone. Not that we complained about it—we were happy enough to be alone.

Nothing lasts forever, of course. As time went by, both of our marriages got shakier, neither of them helped much by an ill-starred vacation to San Miguel Allende, in Mexico, where we had arranged to rent a house and take lessons with an instructor from the Mexican cavalry school, together with the Vitullo-Martins. At the last minute Margaret's husband Burt, who was becoming suspicious of me, with good reason, decided not to go on the trip, which was further complicated by the fact that my then-wife neither rode nor had the slightest interest in horses. The Vitullo-Martins were placed in the unenviable role of appalled spectators of a domestic commedia dell'arte, and perhaps as a consequence those of us who rode did so with a combination of lunatic daring and sheer bravado, as if serious injury or death would be more tolerable than another sticky evening in our rented house, with its glamorous pool and pretty gardens that had failed to dissipate the underlying tension.

Mexico was an eye-opener in more ways than one. Here, at any rate, was riding that made the dangers of hunting in Middleburg (or even skidding around on a nervous, balky horse through rush-hour traffic on Amsterdam Avenue on an icy winter morning) pale by comparison. There was no fuss here about wearing a hard hat, and every ride ended with a plunge straight off a barranca—a steep drop, almost a perpendicular wall—into a deep arroyo, with the horse sliding down on its haunches, then climbing up the opposite side, almost vertically, while the rider clung for dear life to the horse's neck, the kind of thing you see done by stunt men in westerns. In case that excitement wore thin, there was jumping over high walls of living cactus, on which a fall would have made

Photo by Tom Vitullo-Martin

the rider look like a pincushion, urged on by a well-mannered but firm, cavalry sergeant who seemed determined to make the gringos whimper.

In Mexico, we soon realized, the culture revolves around the horse to a degree that puts even England to shame. Perhaps even more than the Spanish language, the horse there is the ultimate symbol of status, defined by the word *caballero,* "horseman," used as a mark of respect. Because so much of Mexico is still poor and rural—even the part that isn't aspires to be and has its roots in a rural, almost feudal society—the horse is still omnipresent, even in cities. Horse-drawn carts still make deliveries, and on festive occasions the horse comes into its own.

On Saturday evenings in the plaza of San Miguel Allende, it's crowded and noisy. Several bands compete, the open-air cafés are full, and the modest, chaperoned mating ritual, in which the girls walk arm-in-arm in pairs clockwise around the square, under the trees strung with lights, giggling to each other while the boys walk in groups in the opposite direction, is in full swing, carefully observed by aunts, uncles, parents from under the awnings and café umbrellas.

Then all of a sudden a clatter of hooves announces a line of horses, maybe a dozen or so, each ridden by a man in the full regalia of Mexican horsemanship: huge-brimmed sombrero, short jacket, and fancy tight, flared trousers decorated with silver conchos, gleaming boots with high heels and pointed toes (the ancestor of our cowboy boots), and shiny silver spurs with jingling rowels. Behind each man a young woman sits modestly astride on the horse's croup, her long skirt covering her legs, one arm around the rider's waist, a bit like Audrey Hepburn riding pillion on a Vespa motor scooter in *Roman Holiday.*

The men look serious—clearly it is important for them to present what the Italians call *una bella figura*—but the girls are having a good time, laughing and waving at friends. The horses are immaculately groomed, and their tack sparkles with highly polished silver decorations—they have long manes and tails like the Paso Fino, and the traditional high-stepping gait, their thick necks deeply curled like horses in a Renaissance painting. From time to time a few more riders turn up, including some older couples, just as elaborately dressed, the men a little thicker at the waist, with heavy white mustaches, the women motherly or even grandmotherly in appearance, but sitting just as gracefully as the younger ones.

The riders don't actually *do* much—reins hanging from the little finger of the left hand, they parade around the square at a leisurely pace, apparently for no other reason than to offer people the pleasure of looking at them, simply doing a mounted version of what everybody else is doing on foot. Occasionally somebody hands up a bunch of flowers to one of the girls—nothing personal, it appears, just a gesture of good-natured admiration for the spectacle. When one of the girls accumulates more flowers than she can conveniently hold on to, she tosses a couple of bouquets to her girlfriends on foot, like a bride leaving her wedding, and like bridesmaids, they giggle and compete to catch it.

After half an hour or so of this, the riders leave the square, clattering down a narrow cobbled side street past the church steps, headed back to the barn or the corral, the horses flicking their ears and picking up the pace a bit at the prospect of going home. Is it perhaps a riding club of some kind? I ask the barman of the café, the terrace of which we're sitting on. He shakes his head, a little puzzled by the question. No, no, he says, people come and do this every Saturday night for their own pleasure, sometimes more of them than tonight, sometimes less, depending on the weather and so on. There's nothing formal about it at all, it's what caballeros have always done on Saturday night, before dinner. I reflect that Saturday dinner is probably somewhere between ten and eleven in the evening in Mexico, so of course there's plenty of time to dress up, make the paseo, get the horse put away for the night, then sit down to dinner in one's fine clothes, with the kind of good appetite that comes from keeping up an old tradition and putting on a good show—pretty much what foxhunters feel at the opening meet, when you get right down to it, though for my money the Mexicans put on a better and more civilized show. Certainly the girls, in their long skirts and embroidered blouses are prettier, and seem to be having more fun, than most of the women I've seen foxhunting.

It occurred to me then, sipping my drink on the terrace of a café in San Miguel Allende, how much of the passion for horses involves dressing up, display, putting on a show. Some aspects of that are obvious—the showy costumes of the Mexican riders, echoing an older Spanish tradition, the scarlet coats of foxhunters (referred to as "hunting pinks," to the confusion of outsiders, not because of the color, which is supposed to be a rich, deep red like that worn in full dress by the foot guards in England or the Mounties in Canada, but because the most popular sporting tailor in London of the early nineteenth century was a Mr. Pink), the embroidered, spangled parade outfits of western riders, the cavalry uniforms of those few countries that still maintain mounted units—others more subtle.

Riders have always sought to put on a good show—Native American horsemen painted not only their ponies but themselves, in matching patterns and colors—but also to define status (and exclude outsiders) by means of small but all-important details, perfectly symbolized by the many distinctions of dress that so obsess foxhunters. Riders permitted to wear "the hunt colors" (i.e., a scarlet coat with the hunt's special buttons and collar) must wear black boots with brown tops (women wear black boots with black patent-leather tops), while a rider who isn't yet permitted to wear the hunt colors wears a black coat instead, with plain black boots. And so on, ad infinitum.

Anybody who thinks that this kind of thing is simply East Coast or British sartorial snobbery on horseback need only look through any riding apparel and tack catalog to discover that it's universal. Western riders obsess about things like the exact cut and type of chaps, and endless variations of hat creases and boot patterns, while riders of saddlebred horses wear outfits with flared trousers, a long, waisted jacket, and a bowler hat, often in fantasy colors. Polo players, Mongolian herders on their shaggy ponies, officers of the United Kingdom's Household Cavalry, New York City's mounted cops—any group that rides, in fact—bring to the horse their own special costumes, traditions, customs, conventions, and prejudices, and the same people who will raise an eyebrow and give a condescending smile at the spectacle—no other word will do—of somebody riding a saddlebred around Madison Square Garden wearing what appears to be a raspberry-colored nylon suit and a matching bowler hat, legs stuck straight out like a Harley-Davidson rider's, with long, flowing hairpieces attached to the horse's mane and tail like those of a star on Oscar night, while the crowd shouts, "Rack 'im! Rack 'im!" to urge horse and rider on, will turn puce in the face with fury at the sight of somebody in the hunt field with the ribbon on the back of their hat turned up when it should be down, or vice versa.

The Mexican riders in their fancy outfits are not just part of their own tradition, derived from Spain, with flamboyant Mexican additions, but also part of the larger worldwide tradition of dressing up to ride a horse, which reached perhaps its peak in medieval Europe, when horse and rider alike were dressed in long, flowing garments of cut velvet and gold embroidery, intended to awe the onlooker on foot and project an image of magnificence and unassailable superiority.

Even up to the recent past, looking good on a horse mattered. Long before he became famous for other reasons, George Washington was regarded as perhaps the finest horseman in colonial America, and people came from miles around merely to watch him ride, in an age when riding was regarded as an art, rather like the ballet today. Ulysses S. Grant earned the highest marks ever awarded for horsemanship at West Point, and as a boy was famous not only for his seat on a horse but for his skill at calming and breaking difficult horses. In later life even those who thought he was a drunk, or who had fought on the other side in the Civil War, admired his horsemanship—indeed Grant was regarded by his fellow officers as the best horseman in the U.S. Army, and certainly as the best horseman in the White House since Washington.

Washington was something of a beau, while Grant was notoriously disheveled and shabby, but both had that hard-to-define combination of physical elegance and complete control that we have in mind when we talk about somebody's "seat on a horse." It was Cervantes who wrote, in *Don Quixote,* "It is the seat on a horse that marks the difference between a gentleman and a groom," and he knew what he was talking about, having also written in the same great novel, "*Religion es la cabalerria,*" a sweeping statement which can be interpreted both as "Knight-errantry is a religion" and also "Horsemanship is a religion," the two being linked, if not always identical, in the sixteenth-century Spanish mind.

"The seat" is the ability to sit tight on a horse, gracefully and without apparent effort, under any circumstances, a state of being-at-one with the animal that involves all sorts of muscles but has to look easy and natural, as if the rider weren't doing anything at all.

A famous story of riding instruction has the teacher watching a pupil ride around the ring, sweating bullets as he attempts to do everything he's been told—keep his heels down, maintain gentle pressure on the reins, straighten his back, look between the horse's ears, press the horse forward with his legs, and so on. After a few minutes of this, the teacher calls the pupil over and says, "Very good. Now go back and do the same thing again, please, but less of it."

Bingo! In riding, less *is* more.

Not everybody who can ride can teach. It's like anything else: the patience, the ability to put something subtle and complex into words, the combination of authority and self-confidence that teaching anything physical requires, simply isn't programmed into most people, however well they may do it themselves. At the same time, picking up horsemanship the natural way, like Plains Indians in the eighteenth and nineteenth centuries, isn't going to happen for people who don't live their lives around horses.

At Claremont, city children—those wealthy and privileged ones who get riding lessons—can be seen waiting with varying degrees of patience for the horse to be tacked up and brought down the ramp to them, just the way their fathers wait, no doubt tapping their feet impatiently or filling in time with their cell phone, while somebody goes downstairs at the garage in their building to bring their car up. They don't tack the horse up, feed it, groom it, sit on it bareback, learn about horses from the horse, as American Indians used to when they were still famous for their horsemanship, or as little girls in the country or an English village still do today.

Pupil and horse meet for the lesson, often for the first time, since they can't always be given the same horse. There's no feeling of continuity, no relationship or bonding, no time to figure out what's on the horse's mind, or even to give any thought to the fact that the horse *has* one, and it is this attitude, very common among people who have learned to ride as adults, which leads to the kind of impatient horsemanship in which the rider assumes it's the horse's job to figure out what's expected of it, and do it pronto, with as little fuss as possible.

Whenever you see a horse going round and round a riding ring with a pupil on its back and its attention firmly fixed on the person standing in the center of the ring with a whip in his or her hand, you know what's going on. Riders who learn that way may look good—even splendid— in the ring, but they very often get into big trouble the first time they're out on their own, since they've learned riding skills without acquiring any real horse sense, and seldom develop a real affection (as opposed to a sentimental one) for the horse, let alone the kind of empathy that is required to make mutual understanding and communication between the two of them possible.

Horses may learn slowly—after all, they have their own issues and priorities, which aren't necessarily the same as ours—but they have a good memory, particularly for things they fear or dislike, among which impatience ranks high. Shouting at a horse, raising one's voice at it, tapping it with the stick in lieu of giving it a clear command with the legs, hands, and back, treating it brusquely, while not as bad as outright cruelty, are seldom effective. They merely lower the horse's confidence in the rider, without which nothing can be accomplished. The hunt field, the polo field, even the worlds of show jumping and combined training, especially at their lower levels, are full of people who learned to ride without ever developing any special intimacy with a horse, and for whom riding therefore remains an essentially mechanical exercise, in which it's assumed to be the horse's job to make the rider look good and to compensate for his or her mistakes. All too often it's also the horse's job to take the blame when things go wrong; hence the occasional overuse of the whip or the spurs, and the rider's temper tantrums when things go from bad to worse, or when the rider feels he or she has been humiliated in public by the horse.

It's hard for most people to develop any kind of intimacy with an animal that weighs a thousand pounds more than you do, can accelerate from a full stop to thirty miles an hour without breaking into a sweat, and jumps cleanly over fences and ditches that you could hardly even *climb* over or across on all fours, and do all this (and more) with you on its back. You can't pick it up and cuddle with it, like a kitten, or curl up in front of the fire with it, like a dog; for the most part it doesn't stand around moping for you until you come home, and although it may recognize the sound of your voice, it will not as a rule respond to the sound of its name. In short, the horse, though domesticated, remains wild at heart, a peaceful, grass-grazing herd animal, to be sure, always on the lookout for danger even in the safety of a fenced-in paddock or corral, and apt to kick out and break into a gallop when alarmed.

It's hard for a lot of people to figure out what's going on in a horse's mind, but it shouldn't be. Watching zebras in the wild, or in nature films, is all you need to do to understand how a horse's mind works. The horse is *prey*, and in its own mind the only thing that stands between it and being killed and eaten by predators is constant awareness and the ability to outrun an attacker. As a herd animal, the horse craves and needs the company of other horses—there is safety as well as companionship in numbers. Even the most restless of horses is likely to stand quietly in its field so long as it can see, however far away, other horses, but left on its own, it may start running until it loses a shoe or injures itself.

As potential prey, the horse is always watchful—horses sleep standing up, for the most part, for just that reason, and lie down as seldom and little as they can—ready at any moment to make the mad dash for safety on which survival may depend. Hence horseracing in its various forms merely exploits the horse's natural instinct to run fast, and to compete with other horse's to see which one can run the fastest.

Given all this, for the horse to place its trust in the hands of another species, learn to overcome its natural instincts—flight, sticking close to the herd, avoiding anything which it might perceive as a threat—and instead go where the rider wants to go and stop when the rider wants to stop requires an enormous mental shift on the part of the horse, and a degree of trust that is truly unique in nature. A large part of riding instruction traditionally consists of building up "the confidence of the rider," but as every rider sooner or later learns, the *horse's* confidence in the rider is the real issue.

We may marvel at the sight of a police horse weaving in and out of fast-moving traffic on city streets, or a cowboy's pony "cutting" a single steer out of the herd, while keeping clear of all those horns, but it's worth remembering that neither vehicles nor cattle are perceived by the horse as potential predators. The real wonder is that a little girl in a hard hat and jodhpurs can get a horse to move away from its fellow horses (or the barn, which a horse is likely to see as a place of safety because it contains other horses) merely by pressing her legs against its sides or telling it, in a gentle voice, to get a move on, and slow it when it starts to gallop merely by squeezing the reins with her fingers.

All "aids" (as signals to the horse are called) benefit from being gentle, precise, and easy for the horse to identify and understand. Horses don't respond well to mixed signals (pulling on the reins while squeezing the horse with one's legs is just like stepping on the brake pedal of a car and the accelerator at the same time), and much of riding instruction focuses on getting the rider to have a clear idea of what he or she wants before asking the horse to do it. Horses aren't mind readers, but it's pretty clear that the rider's attitude signals itself to the horse. A self-confident, determined attitude communicates itself to the horse, and so, unfortunately, does a fearful, uncertain, and mentally unprepared one.

No telepathy is involved—it's simply that the horse is superbly equipped by Mother Nature to respond instinctively to small signals, which is to say that when you're riding, your breathing, your rate of perspiration, your level of anxiety, and your pulse rate are all being communicated constantly to the horse, which draws from all these things its own conclusion about what's going on up there in the driver's seat.

Horses pay attention, in ways and to a degree that we can hardly even imagine. When horses are grazing together in apparently peaceful contentment, they are in fact in constant communication with each other, their ears flicking back and forth as they listen for any sounds from their companions that might indicate a threat on the outskirts of the herd—a sudden head movement, a change in the rhythm of some other horse's breathing. The horse is always alert and tuned in to signals so fine that no human being would even notice them—that's how you stay alive if you're a herd animal—so it's almost impossible for a horse *not* to pay strict attention to its rider, or to the people who work around it in the barn. You don't even have to speak to a horse to communicate with it—you're communicating with it all the time, whether you want to or not. The fact that it's eating, or dozing, or appears to be ignoring your presence doesn't mean that its senses aren't fully focused on you, or that your feelings about the horse, and to some degree your intentions toward it, haven't been communicated. Given the difference in size between horses and people, and their very different order of priorities, the relationship between these large, four-hoofed creatures and us small, two-footed primates is bound to be full of difficulties and misunderstandings. By and large, though, it's the horse that listens, with an acuteness that no animal that talks can approach.

On the other hand, how does somebody who doesn't live around horses learn to communicate with them? How do you get close enough to horses, over a long enough period, to develop some real sense of what they are about? Whatever else it may be, the horse isn't a piece of sports equipment that you can take out, use, and put away again, at will. Of course some horses are specialized—racehorses, for example—and in some horse activities the connection between horse and rider is necessarily blurred. Polo players arrive for a game with a "string" of polo ponies—six or eight is not uncommon—and change mounts at intervals during the game, called chukkers, as the horse is "blown" (exhausted and winded), and are therefore less likely to have the kind of close relationship with a single horse that a show jumper, or an eventer, or a westerner who rides a cutting horse might develop over time.

One reason (apart from economy) why cavalrymen, cowboys, and the mounted police are assigned a horse and have to look after it themselves is that this will foster a close relationship between horse and rider. In the days of cavalry, it was axiomatic that a trooper's ultimate responsibility was for his horse—its welfare, its soundness, its cleanliness, were his first concern, and even the most dim-witted of troopers developed a certain feel for his horse, on which, after all, his life might some day depend.

Few kids these days, however horse-struck, are likely to have that kind of relationship with a horse unless they live in the country, with their own barn on the property, but it's the whole theme song of riding camps and dude ranches that cater to children, the ultimate sell for the city girl or the girl from the suburbs who loves horses—or whose parents think she ought to.

These days, of course, it's mostly girls that are horse-struck. Boys can take horses or leave them, but with girls it's as if the teenage Elizabeth Taylor in *National Velvet* were part of their gene pool.

Sitting under a large white plastic tent, eating an ice-cream cone, some twenty-five years after I first met him, Arno Mares, my old friend from Central Park, now director of the International Riding Camp, surveys his kingdom, where sixty to seventy girls aged seven to seventeen spend the summer getting close to horses and riding their hearts out. Arno is as rakish, attractive, and genial as ever, though he's acquired over the years a certain ability to play a figure of authority. Having dabbled in businesses as far removed from horses as international express delivery—he, his brother, and a partner were doing what Federal Express now does on a larger scale when Arno was just out of college— he eventually decided to enter the horse business when the proprietor of a Catskill riding camp for girls where Arno had worked as a counselor and riding instructor during summer vacations from college in the late 1960s made up his mind to retire, and sold the whole place to him in 1981. When he isn't busy running a summer riding camp for girls, he takes people to Argentina for an intensive polo course, or on riding vacations in Russia, where they spend days in the saddle and nights in Stalin's former dacha. Arno is one of a growing number of horse entrepreneurs, busy finding new ways in which to turn riding into a branch of the worldwide tourist industry, though his core business remains his camp near Ellenville, surrounded by mysteriously named Ukrainian cultural centers buried in the deep woods up dirt roads and the remnants of what was once a thriving center of Jewish summer camps for children and adults—Marjorie Morningstar country.

The girls don't resemble Marjorie Morningstar, however, at least not at first glance. Without exception they are dressed in riding breeches and T-shirts, midway through a day that revolves almost entirely around riding, at least two hours in the morning and two in the afternoon, with special camp trips that involve trucking girls and horses to the city for a guided riding tour of Central Park's bridle paths (Arno's old haunt), followed by lunch at Tavern on the Green and a shopping trip to F. A. O. Schwarz and Miller's, New York's last riding apparel and tack shop (Charlie Kauffmann having long since closed down his store), or out to the island for a weekend at Southampton, with early-morning rides on the beach and afternoons of watching polo. For those who ride well enough, there is the possibility of polo lessons or going out "cubbing" with the Rombout Hunt in nearby foxhunting country.

One of Arno's most popular innovations, he tells me, is a "Mother and Daughter Week" twice a summer, in which mother and daughter share a room (or share it with another mother and daughter), all of them in bunk beds, and go through the riding program together. "Lots of the moms tell me that they drop fifteen years off their lives during their week up here," Arno says solemnly, and certainly it must be a change for adults to sleep in a bunk bed, rise and shine at seven, spend most of the day on a horse, and retire, no doubt sore and exhausted, at ten, after having shined their boots and washed their riding breeches for the next day. For those girls who have a surplus of energy, there are lessons in ballet and in pottery making, and certainly there is a pool as well as a couple of tennis courts. Between riding lessons, cleaning tack, gymkhanas and horse shows, looking after the horses, and polishing their boots, however, the girls don't look as if they get much free time for anything that doesn't involve horses, or would want it, frankly—they are here "to ride their little butts off," and that's it. As Arno puts it, looking them over as they eat cold pizza and talk about their morning riding lesson and searching for the secret of his success, "They come here because they love horses." He gets up and strolls through the tent, stopping at each table to chat with his campers, and show that he knows what they've been doing and how well they've been doing it. "These are girls who *dream* about ponies and horses," he says to me proudly.

Clearly he's right. It's a hot day, and lunch is just over, but already the girls are getting ready to ride again. Nobody is in the pool. Down at the stables, there are two long lines of horse stalls, each with a tack room at the end. The girls tack up the horse they're going to ride and do a good deal of grooming, though they don't actually look after the horses as such—there are grooms for that, plus a certain number of "working students," girls whose parents pay up to $5,200 so their daughter can "ride twice a day and assist with barn chores, including, but not limited to, feeding, cleaning stalls, painting fences and assisting riding instructors with lessons." This is the kind of onerous hard labor which only a horse-crazy adolescent girl would persuade her parents to pay for the privilege of letting her do—after all, in this day and age it's hard enough to find people who want to muck out stalls for a *salary*—but for well-to-do city or suburban girls who don't have a barn near the house, or a paddock with a pony in it visible from the bedroom, this is the place to be. There are nearly seventy horses and ponies here, plus Arno's polo string, and their presence is inescapable; they are hardly ever out of sight. There are horses being led back and forth to graze, horses in fields, horses back in the barn area, horses being loaded into Arno's big rig for a polo game later in the day, horses everywhere you look, and most of the waking day revolves around their needs and schedule.

In one of the outdoor riding rings, two beginners are already receiving a lesson, a younger one on a flashy-looking but experienced pony, an older one on a small horse that has the expression of an animal who has seen it all before. The instructor, a young woman, is standing next to a couple of low, simple jumps and cavaletti, rails placed on the ground at precisely measured spacing, so that the horse has to step across them briskly, lifting up its feet. Arno and I lean on the fence around the ring and watch. I ask how many of his campers know how to ride before they come here. He shrugs. "A lot of them *think* they can ride," he says. "We start them all from scratch—it's like learning how to walk all over again." The girls get a strong dose of "safety orientation." They start by learning how to saddle up their horse; they have to make sure the tack is on properly, with all the keepers (those little leather loops that hold the ends of leather straps, and without which bits and pieces of the bridle would stick out and flap around, distracting the horse) in place; they have to master the elements of "horse first aid," enough at least to recognize the signs of lameness, cuts, and bruises. They get a strong dose of "the basics," whether they think they need it or not; then they're separated into groups by experience and ability, and after two weeks even the beginners are ready for "a little schooling show."

Arno eyes the two girls critically as they ride around the ring. "We teach them the basic two-point position," he says, demonstrating what he means. "They have to stretch up out of the saddle, put ninety percent of their weight on the stirrups and lower leg, and get used to doing that. Then we teach them good pelvis position—not to slump, and all that—so they have a secure seat before they start jumping."

The instructor looks over in his direction, and he nods. The girls, both beginners, are ready to jump. The younger one on the pony crosses the ring, picks up a canter, and pops her horse over the jump effortlessly—no encouraging clucking sounds, no use of the crop, no kicking her heels against the pony's side. Whatever is going on between rider and pony is invisible. Of course it's partly that the pony is well schooled, experienced, and willing—Arno goes out west and buys whole lots of horses before the season begins, giving himself enough time to weed out the difficult ones and move them on. What does he do with them in the winter, I ask him? "They're profit centers on four legs," he says. "A lot of the girls fall in love with their favorite horse, and persuade their parents to lease it for them. They take the horse home at the end of September, at $250 a month, and we pick it up in May."

I ponder this insight into the economics of running a riding camp—that, plus the fact that the girls virtually feed themselves, since they can buy pizza in Arno's store with the weekly pocket money their parents provide, explains a lot—as the older girl circles the ring, leans forward, and takes her horse over the jump. "Nice!" Arno shouts. He turns to me. "Three weeks ago neither of those girls could ride. Now they're tacking up their own horse, and jumping like pros."

I comment on how effortlessly they seem to ride. He nods. "Well," he says, "that's what they have to learn, isn't it? It shouldn't ever *look* hard." He pulls down the brim of his hat as we go off to watch his polo ponies being loaded up.

"Less is more," I say.

Arno thinks about it and nods. "I guess so," he says. Then he grins: "That, and keeping your butt in the saddle."

CHAPTER FIVE

The Backyard Horse

Murray grooming Faby-Baby

LAREMONT EVENTUALLY began to pall on us, partly because of the rapid deterioration of the Central Park bridle paths, which came to resemble rocky arroyos or mud baths according to the season, partly because Claremont was deteriorating even faster, and with even less likelihood of repair, partly too because having moved in together at last, Margaret and I wanted a larger measure of freedom in our lives—wanted, in effect, to stop skulking around, whether on horseback or not. We cast around for an alternative, and eventually decided upon the Sleepy Hollow Country Club at Tarrytown, New York, close by the Hudson River, perhaps three-quarters of an hour's drive from our West Side apartment (except at rush hour, when the sky was the limit).

Neither Margaret nor I was then (or is now) a clubbish sort of person, and the membership of Sleepy Hollow, with its golf course, restaurants, tennis courts, squash courts, and pool, did not at first glance seem to be our cup of tea, nor we theirs, to be sure.

Conceived before the Crash, in an age of prosperity, the club was, to put it mildly, built on the grand scale, the clubhouse itself having been designed by Stanford White, apparently with instructions to re-create Versailles at Tarrytown. Much of the reason for the club's existence lay next door, in the vast Rockefeller estate at Pocantico. Old John D. Rockefeller, the family patriarch and founder of the fortune, had acquired, with every form of guile and ruthlessness, thousands of acres around Tarrytown and cleared them of farms and buildings to create the Rockefeller family estate. He may have felt that some concession to the locals—at least to those who fit the description of white, Protestant, and upper-middle-class—would smooth relationships between future generations of Rockefellers and their neighbors, and perhaps discourage the latter from trespassing, or worse yet turning up in the form of an angry mob like the Parisians who marched to Versailles with pikes and muskets to seize the king and queen during the French Revolution.

A lavishly appointed country club must have seemed just the ticket *pour épater les bourgeois,* and it seems a shame that Louis XIV didn't have a similar notion when he built Versailles. In any event Sleepy Hollow Country Club helped to maintain a cordial (if slightly *de haut en bas*) relationship over the years between America's richest family and its neighbors. One sign of this was that riders who kept a horse at Sleepy Hollow's stables were allowed to use the bridle paths on the Pocantico estate; in fact the entire stable and its lavish and enormous indoor riding ring—again from the hand of Stanford White—had once been the Rockefeller family's own private stable, back in the days when keeping a hundred or so horses and a small army of grooms in a vast stone neoclassical building seemed the natural thing to do, in case your guests wanted to ride.

At some point, the family had cannily passed this enormous and costly white elephant on to the country club, together with the vast expense of maintaining and staffing it, so the club was eager enough to rent out stall space to boarders who in the ordinary way might not otherwise qualify for membership. "Riding members" were not given full use of the club (and were discouraged from appearing there), but so long as you had a horse and a checkbook, you could board there, and quite a place it was—a striking contrast to the cramped, narrow conditions of Claremont. Here, the stalls were huge, the wide stone aisles were like those of a cathedral, and the roof vaulted to a high ceiling. It was the kind of stable that could only have been built in an age when money was no object, and by a family whose idea of a good-sized building project was Rockefeller Center or the Cathedral of St. John the Divine in Morningside Heights. The indoor riding ring, though no longer perfectly maintained, was if anything even more impressive, with a vaulted glass ceiling, comfortable viewing galleries, and endless vistas of carved stone, polished wood paneling, and painted murals, all of it decorated in the classical horsey style.

Our new routine now consisted of driving up to Tarrytown before dawn, riding, then driving back to the city, the main disadvantage being that we were in a fairly constant state of exhaustion, and in my case, apt to fall asleep over the luncheon table—something of a problem in an industry where most serious business takes place over lunch. As for the horses, they settled into unfamiliar comfort with no trace of surprise. Every morning we would tack them up—we arrived too early for the grooms—and set off on horseback to explore Pocantico, which in its own way was like a secluded and secretive kingdom, Oz perhaps, since the Rockefellers themselves remained invisible.

Riding a horse seemed to render us invisible too. Although there was a good deal of security around the estate, and trespassers were vigorously discouraged, nobody seemed to pay any attention to people riding on the bridle paths, which wound endlessly throughout the estate, revealing occasional glimpses of Rockefeller family life—a medieval Belgian village, imported stone by stone from Belgium and reassembled on the spot, right down to the narrow cobbled streets, immense David Smith metal sculptures placed in rolling, grassy fields with herds of prizewinning Black Angus cattle grazing around their bases, a man-made swan pond, looking like the setting for *Swan Lake*, groves of rare trees, each one carefully labeled, and for that matter Pocantico Village itself. An American version of the famous "Potemkin villages," which that canny prince caused to be constructed along Catherine the Great's way as she toured Russia, so she would only see smiling faces and neat peasant dwellings, Pocantico was like a movie set of a small village. Its neat rows of tidy white houses betrayed no trace of commercialism; the children playing on their bicycles looked straight from Central Casting, and the interior of the handsome church had been decorated somewhat incongruously, but handsomely, by none other than Henri Matisse.

From time to time, in the early mornings, we saw a trace of the Rockefellers themselves—David Rockefeller's jet helicopter would go roaring overhead, carrying him down the Hudson to his office at the Chase Manhattan Bank, or old Mrs. John D. Rockefeller Jr. would be seen briskly driving a pair of horses, whip in hand, a blanket neatly folded over her knees and the aforementioned groom seated facing to the rear behind her on the back seat of a four-wheeler. It was, we gathered, largely on her behalf that the bridle paths were kept in such perfect shape, the gravel raked carefully, horse droppings removed, fallen leaves swept away almost as soon as they hit the ground. The great Rockefeller mansion itself was hidden away, perhaps deliberately hard to find even on horseback, but the lesser Rockefeller houses could be seen from the bridle path, along with the occasional oddity, like the Japanese teahouse that Japan had given Nelson Rockefeller, and which a crew of Japanese builders came from Kyoto to assemble on the site, or the huge stone causeway for the construction of which a small army of Italian stonemasons was imported early in the twentieth century, and which helped to separate Pocantico from the rest of the world.

The horses had no trouble fitting into more glamorous surroundings, and seemed a lot happier not having to go back and forth to Central Park through heavy traffic—at Sleepy Hollow you just walked them across a narrow bridge that linked the stables with the estate, and there you were, in Rockefeller country, where you could ride until you or your horse was worn out without, as a rule, seeing another soul, and get lost

Photo by Stanley Tretick

Margaret and Michael on Missouri and True Grit at Pocantico, N.Y.

among sweeping vistas that nobody, including the Rockefellers, seemed
to have visited in years. To be fair, there was an element of Disneyland
to it all, for concealed behind the landscaping in the ambitious style of
England's Capability Brown, with every mossy boulder and clump of
trees artfully placed for a natural but dramatic effect, a small army of
caretakers, like invisible gnomes, brushed, weeded, and tidied to the
required standard of perfection. At one point Margaret and I were startled when a good-sized tree seemed to have moved overnight. Discreet
inquiries produced the information that old Mrs. Rockefeller had complained that the tree blocked her view of the Hudson from her bedroom
window, so it had been moved a few feet during the night to correct the
problem, and fresh turf laid down to cover the scars. When Mrs. Rockefeller had her breakfast in the morning, she could look out the window
and see what she wanted to see, as if God had simply plucked the tree

up at her request and deposited it where He should have put it in the first place. Run in this spirit, Pocantico was always full of surprises. Old John D. Rockefeller's landscape architects, for instance, had scattered rare trees from all over the world on the property, so that while at first glance it looked like the rest of the northeastern United States, on closer examination it was like a beautifully planned and cared-for botanical garden on a huge scale.

This became the center of our world, so far as the horses were concerned, for a good long time, while many of the other Claremont boarders moved up to Sleepy Hollow, including Murray Ramson and the Vitullo-Martins. Had I given the matter any thought, I would have realized that we had all taken another, deeper step in horse ownership by moving the horses out of the city. Pocantico was still close enough to New York to be almost urban, like a more luxurious (and private) extension of the park system, but to the north as well as across the river, in New Jersey, was the beginning of more serious horse country. One of the chief boarders at Sleepy Hollow was Janet Black, a noted dressage teacher and judge, who kept a whole lot of her horses there, with her own groom, and no small number of distinguished riders from the various competitive worlds stabled their horses from time to time at Sleepy Hollow. Most of the more serious riding happened, as it usually does, in the outdoor and indoor rings, while we were still exploring the Rockefeller estate in the early mornings, but there was a subcurrent, a whiff, as it were, of real competitive horsemanship at Sleepy Hollow that had not been present at Claremont.

Horses have a way of taking over people's lives. Of course, there are people who can simply relegate them to a corner of their life, as just another sports interest, like a few day's sailing in the summer on the Vineyard or in Maine, or the occasional golf game, or tennis when they're in the mood for tennis. Not everybody who enjoys fly fishing, after all, ends up building their life around trout fishing, spending the long winter months indoors tying flies and reading the vast literature of fly fishing while waiting for the magic moment when it's time to pull the waders back on and start fishing again, though some, as we all know, do. Horses, however, are not just the basis for any number of sports; their relationship with men and women is ancient, complex, and demanding; looking after them is bred into the gene pool—or certain gene pools, anyway. The horse simply has no equivalent in man's relationship to animals, except for the dog, and the dog has on the whole adapted to man right from the beginning, rather than the other way around. For plenty of people, there's no going to bed without a walk down the fence line or through the barn in the dark, to hear the horses gently snorting to acknowledge their presence, to reach out and pat a couple of warm, velvety muzzles, perhaps to pass out a few sugar cubes or apple slices, and in general to make sure—as cowboys still say, even today—"the stock is all right" before getting into bed. My friend Larry McMurtry's father, a rancher in Archer City, Texas, would no more have thought of going to bed without going outside to check on his horses than he would have thought of getting into bed with his boots on. It can have come as no shock to his family when, after his wife divorced him in their old age, much to his chagrin, he died and left his money to support his favorite quarter horse in comfort for the rest of its life. No man ever felt cheated on his deathbed by a faithful horse.

No admirer of General Robert E. Lee will be surprised that after saying his prayers in early morning, he invariably started his day by walking out to say good morning to his horses, the famous Traveler and Miss Lucy, before having breakfast himself. Nor is this feeling confined to the nineteenth century or to the rural South. The horse may live outside the house, unlike the dog, but the affection between man and horse is none the weaker for that.

It was hardly surprising, then, that after Murray Ramson's divorce—another Claremont drama, this one apparently ignited by his long-suffering wife Elaine's discovery that Murray did not have just *one* subscription to the *Arabian Horse World* (and the *Arabian Horse World Calendar*), but *two*, one for home, and one delivered to the apartment of his long-term girlfriend. Naturally a man devoted to his routine and his comforts, Murray had apparently duplicated everything he enjoyed at home a few blocks away—the same comforting pile of magazines, the same black velvet slippers with a horse's head and his initials embroidered in gold on the instep, the same Arabian calendar, the same cocktail glasses engraved with high-trotting Arabians. Perhaps, this parallel world of Arabian tchotchkes, more than all the other more familiar signs of womanizing, triggered the end of the marriage. In any event, Murray ended up with custody of Fabab, the Jag, and the faithful girlfriend, though Elaine got visitation rights to ride Fabab in the afternoons, in the ring at Claremont. He settled down to what would turn out to be a long and happy second marriage.

Eventually, Murray would move his horse to Sleepy Hollow, and some time later, bought a house close to Pocantico trails, and moved Fabab there, to become a real backyard horse at last. For Murray, despite the English blazer, the well-pressed gray flannel trousers and the Gucci loafers and the *boulevardier* air, owning the horse, riding it, was never enough—Murray wanted the horse there, visible from the kitchen window, a living presence at the end of the fence line. In Tarrytown, of all places, with the noise of the trains on the old Grand Central tracks cutting through the clear, cold night air in the winter and the hum of traffic from 287 just behind the trees—where despite a valiant fight on the part of Robert Moses, the highway takes a wide, inconvenient curve miles out of the way so as not to cross the Rockefeller estate—Murray found what he was looking for.

Between Murray's tastes and his divorce, it must have strained his finances to set up a place where Fabab could be stabled at home in the lap of luxury, but although riding is generally thought of, by those who don't know any better, as "a rich man's sport," the truth is most of the people who keep horses in the United States today aren't rich, or even particularly well-to-do. Otherwise sane people will make great sacrifices to keep a horse or a pony at home, and there are plenty of cities where it's still perfectly legal to do so—it's actually in the suburbs where the codes against keeping horses are more likely to exist and be enforced. I live now not far from Poughkeepsie, New York, and am sometimes amazed by the sight of a backyard horse behind somebody's garage, in a row of houses that's maybe half a mile from a shopping mall and a short walk from a retirement home and a car wash. What's the horse *doing* there? I ask.

A day spent out on calls as I write this with one of our own veterinarians, Dr. Paul Mountan, provides an eye-opening glance at the secret horse world all around us. Paul, whose practice, Rhinebeck Equine, covers a huge and growing area, has at least six other vets working for him, nearly six thousand clients, and five phone lines that never stop ringing. At a quarter to seven on a quiet summer Monday morning the big Chevrolet Suburbans and trucks the vets use are drawn up in front of his building, being loaded by the assistants like an invasion fleet. Each vet has an assistant, enough supplies to cover any problem or emergency, and a cell phone linking him or her to the office—it's the reverse of a small-animal practice, where you bring the dog or the cat to the vet's office. Here, the vet pays house calls, crisscrossing the countryside from patient to patient. Paul, a wiry, good-humored man with a cheerful and optimistic bedside manner, is going over his schedule, trying to make sense of it in terms of driving time, while his assistant Christine continues to cram supplies into the vehicle.

Paul shakes his head. There is no sensible way to approach his day, except to get moving. "Cool," he says, his trademark comment. Before we go, however, Paul and Christine bring in his own horses and pay a visit to Paul's pig, Injun. Half Duroc, half Florida wild boar (with the tusks to prove it), Injun was part of a team of steeplechasing pigs that played the Florida agricultural fairs until Paul rescued him from show business. Injun appears, devours an apple, flashes his tusks.

I ask Paul how many animals he has on the property. He thinks for a moment. "Four horses, Injun, and right at the moment twenty-five Jack Russells." Paul's wife Dale, whom he met when she was still a sweetheart of the rodeo, is nationally famous for rescuing Jack Russell terriers and placing them in good homes, and also creates and publishes the *Jack Russell Calendar.*

We climb in and drive off, with the car phone already ringing. Paul drives while eating a breakfast roll, drinking a V-8 juice, and juggling appointments. This is the easy time of year, he explains apologetically—nothing like the breeding season, when it isn't even worth taking your boots off to go to sleep, or midwinter, when you get to do all this in the dark, in the middle of snowstorms and sub-zero temperatures.

We are beginning the day on a high note, visiting the barn of a famous television producer in the rolling hills behind Millbrook— beautiful, lush country, enormous estates, carefully maintained dirt roads. When we get there, it's like a barn out of a movie, all polished rare woods, gleaming copper, shiny brass, with floors made from antique bricks. There are English horse paintings on the walls, and a tack room you could live in. This is that rare barn in which you could, if you wanted to, eat off the floor. Framed in glass facing the entrance are the riding clothes the owner's wife wore when she won her first blue ribbon at, one would guess by the size of them, the age of six or so—a tiny pair of jodhpurs, a black jacket, a pinny with her number on it, and of course the ribbon itself.

Paul is only here to give a couple of shots, but the barn is empty. We explore it for a few minutes, then the manager, a blond New Zealand lady, and a friend ride up out of the mist, which is beginning to lift, revealing impeccably mowed fields and trimmed bushes and hedges. The horses are perfectly groomed—they not only shine, they gleam. Paul gives them their shots, asks after their general health, exchanges a little horse-world gossip, says, "Cool," and immediately we're off again, downhill onto the flats, the big estates soon behind us.

We drive for what seems like hours until we're in downtown Newburg, surrounded by pizza places, used-car lots, and Jiffy Lube outlets. We turn down a residential street full of modest, run-down homes on half-acre lots, turn again into a bumpy driveway almost blocked by overhanging trees, and come to a stop in front of what looks like a garden shack that is about to collapse. There is no sign of horses. "Cool," Paul says. "See how the other half lives."

He unfastens a garden gate attached with twisted strands of baling wire, stoops under an overgrown grape arbor, and leads us into the garden shack, where, to my surprise, a very skinny white Arabian is standing in the dark. The ceiling is just low enough to touch the horse's ears, perhaps, as I quickly realize, because the shed has never been swept out, so the horse is standing on several feet of dry horseshit—years worth of it, I guess aloud.

"Could be," Paul agrees equably. "They don't make any big fetish of cleaning out stalls here." There are more thick clusters of cobwebs in the corners than in old Miss Havisham's chamber in *Great Expectations*. Paul and I have to bend over like coal miners in a seam to get close to the horse. The horse has foundered, and isn't pleased to see Paul, whom it clearly associates with injections and worse. Still, it doesn't have any place to go, so it stands there patiently while Paul makes new protective pads for its front feet out of thick Styrofoam, cuts the old ones off, tapes on the new ones, and admires his handiwork. He uses a big, curved blacksmith's knife. "Old-time blacksmiths used to say, you want a lame horse, just put a knife in a vet's hand and let him near a hoof." He laughs.

He moves the horse out of the shed into a small backyard—a garden run to seed, really—to watch it move. To my great surprise, three more horses appear. One horse had already seemed astonishing—four seems like a clown act. The sides of the garden are banked up with old horseshit—it must be years since anybody has taken a shovel or a backhoe to it. Still, the horses aren't in bad shape at all. "You'd never know they were back here from the street," I say.

Paul nods. "That may be the point." It occurs to me to wonder whether anybody in fact knows that there are four horses back here. On hot days, the neighbors must surely be able to smell the manure, but no casual passerby would ever suspect their presence, in a space that might be thought confining for a couple of large dogs, and the neighbors may be people who have secrets of their own hide.

"Do they ever get ridden?" I ask.

Paul rolls his eyes. "Ridden? No, nobody rides them. Where would you ride them to anyway?" He gestures toward the narrow street, full of double-parked cars, which leads down to a derelict-looking little shopping mall, and beyond that miles of urban sprawl. He puts the Arabian back in the shed and pats its nose. "This fellow's lucky," he says. "He'll never be sound. There's no way he'll make a full recovery, so he'll always shuffle along like a cripple, and have a certain amount of pain. . . . If the owner wanted to ride him . . ." He shrugs, leaving unsaid what would happen to the horse if the owner was determined to ride it. "But people have all sorts of reasons for keeping a horse," he says, cheerful again. "Some of them want to ride. Some of them just want a horse in the backyard, like a garden ornament. That's cool too."

The phone rings, and we zoom north up the Taconic to check on a horse that may be about to colic. "Before we had all the medications for this kind of thing, we sometimes used to have to do surgery," Paul says. "The old-timers used to say about that kind of surgery, 'Big incision, big bill, dead horse,' and it was mostly true."

Majestic Acres Horse Farm turns out, despite the grand name, to be small, dusty, guarded by dozens of dogs, and situated invisibly off the road, as if it were being hidden away from the zoning authorities. The horse turns out to be all right, but Paul stays to watch while another horse he has been treating for one of those interminable, mysterious problems of lameness is lunged by the woman owner, a hearty lady who seems to know what she's doing, and to rely on an endless number of small daughters for her workforce. Paul suggests putting shoes back on the horse and walking it a bit, then we get back into the truck.

"That's the way it is, mostly," Paul says, "the fancier the name, the smaller the place. The places with real simple names turn out to be huge." He glances at his call sheet, and indeed, End-of-the-Road Farm, which we visit next, seems to cover several thousand rolling, wooded acres, with magnificent barns, hundreds of thousands of dollars' worth of fencing, and a whole staff of people in matching polo shirts in the farm colors zipping back and forth on brand-new bright green John Deere four-wheel-drive vehicles, in touch with each other by radio.

During the course of the day, we will see plenty of both kinds—and of places, often within a few minutes of each other, that range from luxurious to the horse equivalent of *Tobacco Road*, including one in which a couple of thoroughbred horses, one a real beauty, a big, flashy chestnut gelding with four white socks (known in the trade, Paul explains, as "heavily chrome plated") are standing around in a garage full of partially dismantled vintage tractors (how do the horses manage not to get injured or hurt?), and another in which two miniature horses, with hooves so long that they look as if they're standing on tiptoe, share a dusty paddock that seems to have been made out of an old aboveground swimming pool. But it's not just the contrast that's extraordinary, it's the sheer *quantity* of horses, the sense that everywhere you look, even where you least expect it, somebody has jury-rigged a place to keep a horse, or even a lot of horses, utterly confident that they will survive and even thrive, despite the absence of all those safety items and comforts the necessity for which many horse owners (including Margaret and myself) take for granted. It's as if there's a whole secret, burgeoning world out there, a horse population hidden from view in places where you'd least expect to find it.

What dream makes somebody put a horse, let alone four horses, on a half-acre plot behind a modest, vinyl-sided bungalow on a city street, or keep a couple of thoroughbreds in a garage, between old tractor parts?

But I already know the answer. People who want their horse or horses at home will go to any lengths to get them there and keep them there, and not just in the northeastern United States. When people think of the West, they think of sweeping vistas, big skies, *space*—but anybody who has actually lived out West knows that you can find backyard horses on pieces of property that hardly seem large enough to contain a trailer mounted on cinder blocks and the owner's rusted-out old car, let alone a corral for Old Paint, yet there Old Paint stands, right behind the trailer, big as life, eating two squares a day while the family lives off food stamps.

Well, you don't even have to go out west. Take Rita Dee, a sculptor with two kids and a husband who is a hospital executive, who lives not far from us today. Now in many ways Rita Dee is an extraordinary horse person, a painter (mostly of horses) who started to do life-size statues of horses made out of pieces of wood that she finds while she's out walking—like driftwood, except that it's lying out in the woods, not on a beach, what the French would call *des trouvailles*. She makes something of a fetish of not cutting or altering the pieces of wood she finds, so of course it's important for her to find a piece with the right shape to be the jaw or the side of the head, and with the right kind of natural knothole to simulate an eye, or the nostrils, as well as the longer, flowing, curved pieces for the back and the legs. When she began, she started by constructing a steel or iron framework and assembling the pieces of wood around it until she got it right, but Rita is also something of a purist, and eventually she discarded the metal framework in favor of a horse that's all wood, and perfectly balanced on its own feet—trickier to achieve, but more satisfying, and more spectacular to look at. She has the wood primed by an assistant before putting it into place, fixed with wood screws, and later adds color, usually terra-cotta, faded turquoise, sandy red, white, or gray, which somehow makes the horse seem as if it's in motion, reflecting the sunlight even on dark days. I see a lot of horse art—the horse is perhaps the single most frequently sculpted animal of all—and much of it seems either sentimental or a poor imitation of classical sculpture, but for no very good reason that I can think of, Rita Dee's horse sculptures are fun to look at, and convey motion as the central element of the horse in a way that more conventional statues usually don't. They actually do seem to be moving, stretching, galloping, as you look at them.

She started early, making horses out of wire in art class at school, then branched into painting until she developed a deadly allergy to paint and linseed oil. At Bard College, her professor suggested she take up welding, and the life-size horses gradually developed from there. Her professor told her, "If you love horses, *do* horses!" and that was that. They sell for five to ten thousand dollars, depending on size, pose, and how much Rita likes the finished product herself, and they can be kept outdoors with no ill effects; indeed, they seem to improve with exposure to the elements.

Rita has three children, two dogs, three cats, and seven horses, and both the children and the horses seem to run free. The horses clatter in and out of the barn as the mood takes them, kept in control by Gus, the dominant horse of the herd, whom Rita describes as "a great, wise leader." Due to the absence in large part of conventional fencing and gates, the horses sometimes end up across the road, on the property of Rita's neighbors, but Gus eventually gets them back unharmed.

When Rita and her husband first bought the farm, she had to chose between building the barn or the house, and decided to begin with the former, since winter was coming on, and she needed someplace for the horses. As a result, she and her family ended up moving into the barn as it was built, and spent a year living in one of the stalls with the horses. During a considerable part of that time there was no electricity—her favorite pony Jerry had died, and the excavator digging a hole to bury him in cut through the primary electric cable, severing it completely. For some reason Rita had been anxious to bury Jerry under the over-hanging gables of the barn, at dead center, but hadn't known about the electric cable. The first day after Jerry's death, "everybody cried"; then, on the second day, Rita made a life-size plaster cast of him in sections, and on the third day he was finally buried, exactly where she wanted him to be, so the whole family would always know where he was. Rita and I walk through the barn and stand, briefly, on the spot. The excavating man had been so saddened by Jerry's death—as well as feeling a certain amount of guilt for having cut the cable—that once Jerry was finally buried he told Rita, tears in his eyes, "I'm not going to charge you for this," and to her astonishment, he didn't.

We are standing in the barn, while the horses walk in and out at will, roughly where the Dees camped out, while I try to imagine what it would be like to live here in the barn with them. It must have been pretty cold come January or February, I suggest, but Rita says brightly that, no, it wasn't all that bad, actually—the horses develop a tremendous amount of heat. It was tougher on her husband—he had to keep his clothes up in the hayloft and climb up there every morning to put on a suit before going to the office—but the rest of the family settled in without any problems. As for the children, they loved it, and since there was no electricity, they grew used to being without television, and are still "TV-free," as Rita puts it proudly.

At one end of the barn, out in the open, next to a lean-to full of Rita's wood collection, is her latest horse sculpture, slowly taking shape, while her own horses walk around it as if it were just another member of the herd, which in a way it is, of course. We walk up to the house—it

Photo by Andy Wainright

finally got built—followed by horses, dogs, and kids. Somewhere along the way Rita seems to have conquered her allergies well enough to take up painting again. Above the fireplace is a painting of—what else?—a horse, and what's more, a horse I recognize, one of my own, Zapata, whom we retired to Rita's farm, where one of Margaret's old horses, Zenith, also lives. It's a big canvas, and captures Zapata perfectly, chunky, thick-necked, and defiant, eyes rolling. The decor is horsey— photos of horses, drawings and paintings of horses, antique horse arti- facts hanging from the huge stone fireplace and mantel. Outside, on the porch, visible through the windows, stands a maquette, a half-size model of one of Rita's horses, which looks as if it's galloping round the house.

We chat over a cup of coffee, and then I walk back to the barn with Rita to say good-bye to Zapata. The horses follow us curiously, occa- sionally going off to explore something on their own, then circling back. There are no gates—nothing to stop them from getting out onto the road, or going AWOL completely. I ask Rita if that doesn't worry her.

She thinks about it for a moment, then shakes her head. "Why would they run away?" she asks, in genuine puzzlement. "This is their home. They're family."

As I drive off, I take another look at the barn and try to imagine what it must have been like to live in it for a year with the horses. Well, why not? People lived with their livestock in medieval Europe, and the kaiser had the imperial apartments placed above the stable in Potsdam Palace because he believed that breathing in the smell of horse manure pre- vented colds.

I reflect that Rita's children look healthy enough to make it possible to imagine that the kaiser was right.

Of course you don't have to be poor to live next to your horses, or have them dominate your life. Even in Millbrook, New York, where there are plenty of rich people, the Tobers, Barbara and Donald, are seldom mentioned without some comment on how rich they are, or more important, how perfect their farm is, despite the fact that their property abuts that of two neighbors who are, if anything, even richer and have even larger horse farms, and, if anything, an even more intimidating reputation for perfectionism. Yellow Frame Farm, however, is special, perhaps because the Tobers' lives revolve around their horses to a degree that is rare, even in horse country. I have come over for lunch, and had the obligatory tour of the showplace barn, the well-stocked goldfish pond, with its two-foot long golden koi, and the outdoor sculpture garden. Yellow Frame Farm is big, though dwarfed by its imposing neighbors.

Donald Tober, a successful New York businessman, points to the hill on the far horizon, where there is a forty-four-acre field he wanted to buy from his neighbor "Libet" Johnson (of the Johnson & Johnson family) as additional pasture for his horses. "Her business manager heard me out," he says, chuckling at the memory, "then he said, quite stiffly, 'I'm sorry, but Miss Johnson *never* sells land, you see—she only buys.' "

We both laugh. "She only buys" says it all—it describes a whole point of view about country life and about money. Tober, however, had the last laugh in this case. A careful study of the deeds on his part, he says, down at the Millbrook town hall revealed that the land in question belonged to him in the first place. His neighbor had mistakenly assumed for years that it was hers, while, as for Tober, he had been mistakenly trying to buy his own land, all of which tells you a lot about Millbrook. The big estates there are really big, big enough so nobody's quite sure where their property line runs. Big wealth is taken for granted, slightly better if inherited than if made, but people are beginning to be less fussy about that these days, though it's still something of an invisible dividing line between the Tobers and their old-money neighbors.

Tober takes me over from the small house where he and Barbara live, right next to the barn, to "the guest house," a mile or so away, a far more elaborate place, in front of which a swimming pool is overlooked by a huge bronze statue of galloping horses, their forelegs reaching out dramatically over the pool. The Tobers keep six of their own horses here—they move them to their farm in Upperville, Virginia, in the winter—and board others, including a couple of Paul Newman's, one of which is a pony so old as to qualify as a miracle. A fence line runs behind the pool, enclosing a sloping pasture, and from time to time horses appear to look at the pool—for the Tobers too, in their own way, live close to their horses and enjoy having them in sight, though they might draw the line at living in the barn with them.

Still, you never know. "My happiest moments have been on horses," Barbara says as we sit down to lunch. Barbara grew up in horse country in southern New Jersey and at one time taught riding as a girl, in fact earning her first money that way, with which she bought herself a Box Brownie camera and a copy of Audubon's book of birds, but Donald's interest in horses didn't begin until he met her. On their first weekend together, she casually asked him if he liked to ride, and he said yes, so they rented a couple of horses. "How about a canter?" she called out to him, and he said, "Sure!" When she looked behind, she saw him ashen-faced and clinging to the saddle, and realized that he couldn't ride at all—love at first sight.

Donald started to ride, took lessons ("He learned to ride, and I learned to ski," she says). Quickly, they were riding together at Greenbrier, and in North Salem, where they lived for a time, and pretty soon Donald fell in love with horses. "I like being there," he says, speaking of riding. "I like the musculature of the horse, the freedom." Gradually, step by step, their shared interest became a passion, and led to all the predictable steps—marriage, foxhunting, the farm near Millbrook, another in North Carolina, which didn't work out, then Upperville, where they now winter. At one time they owned Sweet and Low (the name is a reference to Donald's interest in the artificial sweetener), a seventeen-hand gray that held the record for puissance jumping for many years (at seven feet, seven and a half inches), but now they mostly own horses for their own pleasure. Their hobbies, apart from collecting art and furnishing their homes, are all horse-based. They travel all over the country to ride in cavalry reenactments—Princeton, New Jersey, where they charged with cannons; Yorktown, Virginia, where they participated in the reenactment of Cornwallis's defeat; even Paris, where they rode down the Champs-Elysées in a reenactment of the signing of the Treaty of Versailles, in a company of riders led by the duc de Lauzan. They have ridden among herds of giraffes in Tanzania, and in the uniforms of almost every historical era. Barbara, Donald says affectionately, has agreed to give up jumping ("I just told her, 'Barbara, it's time to stop,' " he says), and Donald has given up foxhunting, though in fact his worst injury in the field was a dislocated thumb.

As we are served luncheon outdoors, with the bronze horses and the real ones all about us, Barbara says that she just can't imagine life without horses. "They're my friends," she says, waving toward the rolling pastures. "If a horse trusts you, he will climb the stairs for you." She lifts her sunglasses and examines the bronze horses that seem to be charging right at us. "In fact," she goes on, "I once walked my horse Judy up the stairs at home to my mother's bedroom. Just to make a point."

I tell them a bit about "backyard" horses, and she smiles. "That's what we've got," she says. "That's exactly it." I nod as the maid and the cook clear the table, bring out the dessert, and offer us an espresso or a cappuccino.

It's just a bigger backyard, that's all.

I ask Barbara Tober if she's looking for a new horse. She nods. "Aren't we all?" she replies. "Still looking for the perfect horse?"

CHAPTER SIX

The Perfect Horse

"The Perfect Horse"

O

F COURSE it almost goes without saying that there is no such thing as the perfect horse. Perfect for whom? Perfect for what?

It isn't even a question of money, or bloodlines, though both these things matter. Most people spend years buying the wrong kind of horse before they stumble across the right one, which quite often turns out to be very different from what they've had in mind all along. Many people—particularly those with plenty of money to spend and an exaggerated opinion of their own skill as a rider—end up buying a horse that's too "hot" for them, or whose flashy good looks conceal a whole lot of problems and vices, and therefore end up "overmounted," an old-fashioned word used to describe a rider on a horse he or she clearly isn't up to handling. Those who go this route very often end up badly hurt, or simply get scared off riding for good.

In the old days this problem was solved by having the stable boys ride the horse until it was exhausted before the owner arrived, though that doesn't always work with real problem horses, which, like problem children, tend to have an inexhaustible supply of energy. Nowadays the problem is more likely to be approached chemically, the horse being injected with a hefty dose of tranquilizer before the owner gets on it. This isn't foolproof either, however—some horses have unpredictable reactions to medication, and even those that are effectively tranquilized may, just like people on drugs, stumble, lose their concentration, and end up injuring themselves or their rider.

In any case, the perfect horse, if such a thing exists, should clearly not need to be medicated to make it rideable, nor to make it go, or starved into submission, or worked like a mule before it's ready for the owner to mount—anyway, none of these things will necessarily stop a horse from running away with its rider like an express train, or bucking him or her off if it's inclined to buck, or shying at every leaf, or digging in all four hooves and refusing to move, if that's what it has in mind.

Self-image inevitably plays a large role in the choice of a horse—much larger than common sense does, as a rule. Some people, like my old friend Murray Ramson, the owner of Fabab, can only imagine themselves riding an Arab, with a long, flowing mane and tail, and nothing else will do, while others, like another friend of ours, wouldn't be caught dead riding an Arab, but only like big, *big* horses that are "just a little bit too much for them," as the saying goes. Then there are people who aren't interested in owning anything except paint horses, or Appaloosas, or palominos—the so-called color breeds, each of which has its own association and registry—not to speak of enthusiasts for such special breeds as the Morgan, the quarter horse, the Paso Fino, or the many variations of "warmbloods," all essentially a cross between one kind or another of working horse and sport horse, often with a dash of thoroughbred. Each of these breeds has its own association and devoted, not to say obsessed, followers and true believers, as well as people who have spent a lifetime trying to define exactly what the breed is, and, more important, what its determining characteristics should be.

In all of this, the great model is of course the thoroughbred, since all thoroughbreds can be traced back to three original sires in seventeenth-century England, and their ancestors and pedigrees are carefully preserved on both sides of the Atlantic. There is no animal so zealously documented as the thoroughbred, and breeding thoroughbreds is at once a big business (because of horse racing), an art, a science, and the ultimate expression of man's knowledge about horses. There are very few families, even at the very highest level of nobility or royalty, in which genealogy has been pursued with such ferocious attention to detail, or with such a single-minded determination to improve the breed. Horse breeders, from the beginning, have always succeeded rather better at this than have royal or princely families, and to this day very few owners of thoroughbred horses, if any, are nearly so well-bred or attractive as their horses.

Of course with thoroughbreds, the ultimate goal is simpler than it is with humans—a horse that can run faster than any of its fellow thoroughbreds, and also has that indefinable quality of "heart" that provides the will to win. If to those qualities are added good looks, a pleasant disposition, and a certain physical grace and elegance, so much the better (the great Secretariat, winner of the Triple Crown and supreme equine media celebrity, was the perfect example of a horse that combined all these qualities, though ultimately he lacked the ability to pass his speed and will to win on to many of his descendants), but speed and heart are what matters most—indeed, the *only* things that count. An ugly horse that wins races is more valuable than a handsome horse that loses, and that's that.

As a result of this, there are a lot of thoroughbreds around that have breeding, looks, and stamina, yet aren't worth a dime in the racing world because they can't, or won't, win races. There are also plenty of people around who only feel comfortable riding a thoroughbred, and fortunately for them the supply always exceeds the demand.

This is because breeding thoroughbred horses is, in itself, an addictive form of gambling, even if you never go up to the window and place a bet on one. Up where I live, in Dutchess County, New York, at plenty of tiny horse farms tucked away on dirt roads somebody is spending big bucks to breed horses for the track, and going quietly broke doing it, what between having to pay stud fees, training fees, and all the other expenses of breeding and producing a horse, only to find that despite its pedigree, it doesn't win races. It's not uncommon to spend one hundred thousand dollars to find this out, and most of the people who do it labor at other jobs, go into debt, and mortgage the farm (would mortgage the children if they could) in pursuit of the dream of turning out a backyard winner.

I have been on such a farm—a couple of paddocks squeezed between other people's backyards, and a kind of jerry-built toolshed which also serves as a barn. Here the entire hopes of the owners are vested in a magnificent-looking two-year-old, such a big, handsome, flashy, strongly built horse that I would be tempted to bet on him myself—or even to buy him for Margaret—if the vet hadn't already told me that he was suffering from a fracture of the sesamoid (a tiny bone behind the fetlock), and when I asked what the chances were of a full recovery, rolled his eyes and changed the subject. I stand there looking at him—he's a real beauty, the kind of horse that's a pleasure to look at, which makes it all the sadder—and note that he has four white "socks" (that is to say, his legs are white from his hooves to more than halfway up his cannon bone). The old English horseman's rhyme on this subject goes, "Two legs white, buy 'im; three legs white, try 'im; four legs white, go 'ome without 'im," which seems to hold true in this case.

I look at the proud owners as they stand on either side of him, patting him, feeding him carrots, still hoping against hope that he'll eventually recover and race, and that one day they'll be standing on either side of him just like this, only in the winner's circle, with a jockey on his back. The homebred backyard colt that goes on to become a champion is one of those enduring legends, like the hometown girl who's discovered waiting on tables in a diner and goes on to become a movie star, and it happens just often enough to keep people going into hock to pay for stud fees all over the country, and in the process produces an awful lot of thoroughbred horses that aren't going to win races, or even get on a racetrack to begin with.

Ideally, thoroughbreds have a degree of athletic ability and speed that most other breeds lack, though set against this is a certain tendency toward nervous and flighty behavior—"high-strung" is the usual description. Many of the other, noncolor breeds of horse result from mating thoroughbreds with hardier pony stock, or draft horse stock, to produce a horse that combines the endurance and physical hardiness of "colder" breeds with the thoroughbred's qualities. Throughout the second half of the nineteenth century—indeed right up through World War I—the U.S. Army funded an ambitious program that made available thoroughbred stallions at no cost to mate with western stock horses to provide a reliable supply of good cavalry mounts, as the British did in Ireland for the same reason. Apart from improving the quality of horses in general, some of this cross-breeding has long since paid off in the form of whole new breeds, like the quarter horse, which derives its name from horses bred especially to sprint the quarter mile in colonial America, a form of racing that demanded a horse with powerful hindquarters—in modern automotive terms, a drag racer, as opposed to a Formula One race car.

By the nineteenth century the quarter horse had developed into an instantly recognizable breed, almost as well-defined and zealously protected as the thoroughbred, and the American Quarter Horse Association in Amarillo, Texas, is something of a shrine, as well as the last word on what is and is not a quarter horse. It keeps a painstaking registry to back it up, not to speak of sending out plastic models and four-color posters of what constitutes the ideal quarter horse. Although smaller in numbers, the Morgan horse too has its own association (the American Morgan Horse Association, which puts out among other things a seventeen-point checklist on how to recognize a Morgan, as well as an anatomical chart of the ideal Morgan), and a history going back to colonial America (the founding father of the breed was owned and promoted as a stud by Justin Morgan, a Vermont music teacher and part-time entrepreneur who correctly thought there would be a ready market in New England among thrifty farmers for a stylish, high-stepping riding horse that could also pull a carriage or a plow), as do most of the various horse and pony breeds throughout the world, however humble their origins may once have been, or "lost in the mists of time," as books of genealogy like to assert.

Since ultimately somebody has to be able to sit on a horse and ride it from point A to point B, the variations between the breeds, however much passion they generate among the cognoscenti, are inevitably less extreme and bizarre than those of dogs, and to non-horse people most horses, color apart, tend to look pretty much alike, except perhaps for really big draft horses (like the Budweiser Clydesdales), which are a rare sight these days, or, at the other extreme, the smaller breeds of children's ponies, like the Shetland.

Of course many horses—most horses in fact—don't belong to any particular breed, and simply represent a happy, or on occasion unhappy, mix of different breeds and types. Margaret's beloved Tabasco was a thoroughbred, but without the papers or registration to prove the fact, which means that very early in his life somebody decided he wasn't going to make it on the track, while my horse Malplaquet was simply "a horse," of no identifiable breeding or type, the kind of animal that, seventy years earlier, would have ended up pulling a hansom cab or a light wagon, if he'd had the temperament for it, which he didn't. Examples of this type can still be seen today in the sad and scruffy little collection of horses lined up on Central Park South, in New York City, to pull tourists around Central Park in what is usually a lame and shuffling clip-clop, the end of the line for horses, only one step away from the pet-food slaughterhouse.

One thing is sure: if there were such a thing as a perfect horse— sound, good-tempered, handsome, well-bred, and exactly suited to your needs or mine—it probably wouldn't be for sale. The very fact that it *is* for sale usually means that something has gone wrong somewhere, either with the horse or between the horse and rider. As with people, the only way to find out is to bite the bullet, bring the horse home, look it in the eye, and hope for the best.

With Tabasco, for example, there was never any question that Margaret had found the right horse—from the very beginning they simply bonded. Other people, certainly me, found Tabasco difficult and uncomfortable to ride, with a tendency to give wild and unpredictable bucks, and more alarming still, to take off at high speed like a race car without brakes, but Margaret rode him with ease, looked good on him, and could make him do just about anything—even slow down. Still, Tabasco, there was no doubt about it, was beginning to show his age. He had neither the temperament nor the robust, sound legs for jumping—like a lot of unsuccessful thoroughbreds, he had probably been worked hard and carelessly too early in his life, when his bones were still soft, and though he was a tough old fellow, he wasn't up to regular hard work, or to the pounding of the show ring if Margaret wanted to compete there.

Already, while we were still at Claremont, Tabasco had had his problems, bringing gloomy looks to the faces of Frank, the head groom, the blacksmith, and the vet, and eventually it became necessary to send him away to convalesce from surgery in a setting where he could receive better care than in New York City. This we were to find at Katherine Boyer's Hidden Lake Farm, in Staatsburg, Dutchess County, part of that wide sweep of New York State that New York City residents refer to as "upstate," encompassing everything from Yonkers to the Canadian border and from the Hudson River to Lake Erie. Tabasco's extended stay with Katherine Boyer was to have a whole lot of unintended consequences, among them our eventual move to a farm of our own only a few miles away from hers, but one of the most immediate was Margaret's reexposure to the world of serious horsemanship.

Katherine Boyer was, at first meeting, a little forbidding, a horsewoman through and through, whose only standard was perfection. At Hidden Lake Farm, bridles were not just cleaned after every use (an idea foreign to Claremont) but stripped down to their many component pieces, each piece of leather saddle-soaped until it looked like new, all the metal—buckles and bits—burnished until they shined, then the whole thing painstakingly reassembled, and hung up in exactly the right place (and exactly the right way) to be ready for the morning. Here things were done to an exact schedule, and with a thoroughness that would have pleased a regimental sergeant major of the Household Cavalry, had one ever turned up. In most people's barns, you worried about getting your shoes dirty; in Katherine's, you worried about tramping dirt from your shoes onto her aisle.

She was, in short, a perfectionist. When it came to horses, she always knew what she was talking about, knew exactly what she was doing, and in her care even the most unpromising of horses began to look good. Horses recognize firm, unyielding authority when they see it, and one glance from Katherine was usually enough to convince even the most recalcitrant animal that she was the boss, failing which a couple of brusque words would do the trick. The horses in her barn gleamed from their hooves to the tips of their ears, and were fed exactly on time and looked after with punctilious care, but they knew their place.

Looking after horses—which also means managing a barn and the people who work there—is one thing, while riding is another, and it is very seldom that the two go together, but Katherine was not only a good rider, she was a great one. Tall, thin, wiry, with immensely long legs, she rode with the kind of old-fashioned, formal grace that one sees at the Spanish Riding School in Vienna, or among the members of the French army's Cadre Noir at Saumur, able to make even the clumsiest horse look good. She had been, in her day, a top-level dressage rider, and framed photographs of her riding on her famous stallion Appomattox hung in rows on the walls of her crowded tack room, testaments to a happier, more elegant time, before arthritis had begun to stiffen her fingers. Even so, to watch Katherine ride was to see something very special, much as it must have been to watch the great Fillis ride in the last days of the nineteenth century, when the motorcar was just about to render his genius obsolete.

In Katherine's case, it was not just that she approached the act of riding with total seriousness, even, when riding indoors in the ring, with a certain solemnity, but that she seemed somehow perfectly made for riding. Her long legs never moved, her posture was superb, even the most bloody-minded of horses appeared to calm down when she mounted it, as if the horse felt obliged to live up to Katherine's expectations and uncompromising standards. Horses that were brought to her by their owners with a long list of complaints put their ears forward when Katherine took their reins in her hands, and went round the ring as obediently as if they had been trained at the Spanish Riding School. She carried a whip, but almost never used it—the sound of her voice, then a deep, gravelly smoker's voice, either praising or expressing discontent, was enough, that and the pressure of her long legs driving it forward into the bit like a coiled spring. It was a sight to behold.

Like most people whose first interest is dressage, Katherine was of that somewhat old-fashioned, classical European school that holds that dressage is the basis for everything else—the solid foundation without which nothing else could or would go right. In her day, she had jumped successfully and foxhunted regularly, but her heart was in the haute école, the pursuit of absolute perfection in the dressage ring. Her impatience with anybody who was unwilling to pursue that kind of perfection, was only too apparent, though it has to be said that she made an exception for me, and to a degree, for Margaret.

In any case, once Tabasco was dispatched to Hidden Lake Farm and Margaret started to drive up there for the day every so often to visit him, Katherine Boyer, who had hitherto been only a voice over the telephone to me, all the more imposing because, having discovered that I speak French, Katherine tended to give me the punch line to whatever she had to say in that language. Having been partly brought up in France, she spoke almost the most perfect French I have ever heard from an American.

Katherine's passion for dressage I understood, to a certain degree, without sharing. Several of the stalls at the Sleepy Hollow Country Club stable were rented by a robust young South African woman, Janet Black, who was not only a dressage instructor but a mover and shaker in the then relatively small world of American dressage—a branch of sports split by at least as many feuds over orthodoxy, personal rivalries, and divergent beliefs as any major religion. Rather than Rome, the center of the dressage world was Vienna, where the Spanish Riding School is situated, and where, in the view of purists, dressage was still taught in its perfect form, unsullied by commercialism (the riders were merely paid salaries as Austrian civil servants), or the need to educate the audience to the subtleties and perfection of what was taking place in the ring, or to compete for interest with show jumping, three-day eventing, rodeo, western reining contests, or horse racing. Though the religious comparison comes to mind quickly whenever I hear anybody talking about dressage, another comparison might be to ballet, in which, for most of the twentieth century, the heart and soul of pure ballet—the real thing, as it were—remained in St. Petersburg (or Leningrad), at the Bolshoi, where the classical method of training and the repertoire were unchanged and unchangeable, although no two teachers ever agreed with each other.

Classical dressage as such had never caught on in the United States, any more than it did in the United Kingdom, where it was regarded, even as long ago as the seventeenth century, as foreign, "continental," overformalized (like French or German ideas about gardening), and unsuited to the three basic uses of horses, which were, in English eyes, foxhunting, horse racing, and the cavalry charge.

So great was the English belief in foxhunting as the true test of horsemanship that Wellington encouraged all his officers to foxhunt in Spain during the Peninsular War, and even had foxes brought over from England, since they were in short supply there. As for cavalry, Field Marshal Sir Douglas Haig believed so strongly that cavalry was the way to beat the Germans in World War I that he kept a force of nearly 100,000 cavalrymen behind the lines for four years, waiting for the moment when the infantry would break through the German trench system deeply enough to let the cavalry charge past them to the open country beyond and end the war with the saber and the lance—this despite the fact that more modest attempts to use cavalry against the Germans on the western front were invariably stopped dead by a combination of machine-gun fire, hopeless ground, and rapid artillery fire. Even the British secret weapon the tank was thought of primarily as a means of punching a hole in the German trench system so the cavalry could deploy en masse rather than as a breakthrough weapon in its own right. To the very end, the illusion that the war would be won by a mass cavalry charge persisted, indeed flourished, at British GHQ in France, at home in the War Office, and in the mind of the king, and helps to explain why the British army lagged so far behind the Wehrmacht in the design, production, and strategic use of tanks in 1939. As late as 1937, one design for a tank turret was rejected by the War Office on the grounds that it would be difficult for an officer to get in and out of the hatch while wearing spurs, and the British army training manual urged officers and NCOs to think of the tank "as an armored, mechanical horse." Given this mindset, it is easy to understand the prevailing, touching, but seriously misplaced belief in English military circles that mass charges of Polish cavalry—for the Poles were even greater believers in the horse, the saber, and the lance than the British—would halt the German Blitzkrieg dead in its tracks.

To people for whom the real test of horsemanship lies in risk—riding hell-for-leather over stone walls and ditches after a fox, or the cavalry charge, or rodeo, to take just a few examples—the sight of a group of riders trotting around the ring to music, however beautifully done, fails to stimulate much in the way of excitement, but dressage, like gymnastics, is the culmination of a long process of training and experience, in which the communication between horse and rider is brought to its highest point.

As with human beings, there is no shortcut to achieving perfection; in the horse world there are, and have always been, a lot of "miracle cures" for "the problem horse" (and for that even greater challenge, "the problem rider"), and some of these have become so famous that they reach out beyond the world of horses into popular culture—the idea of "the horse whisperer," the man who communicates directly to horses, has been out there in various forms for hundreds, perhaps thousands, of years, in every culture. Monty Roberts is simply the latest in a long line of people who talk to horses, or whisper to them, or breathe in their nostrils, or pat them down gently, to communicate.

While it's certainly true that a gifted trainer can often accomplish miracles by means of patience, gentleness, and some understanding of the horse's mind, and may even undo much of the harm that has been done by overreliance on the whip and the spurs, not everyone will agree that talking to horses, or listening to them, for that matter, will always do the trick. William Steinkraus, one of the most celebrated riders in American show jumping history, who rode in five Olympics and won four medals, including America's first individual gold medal, talking about the Monty Roberts phenomenon when Roberts's book first made the best-seller list, remarked to the noted horseman "Cappy" Smith, "Cappy, you listen to horses too, but the difference is, you make sure they listen to *you!*"

There is a great deal of truth to this. Experience has demonstrated over and over again that the one who is in the saddle should be in charge, not the one which is under it, and that any ambiguity on this score is certain to lead to trouble sooner or later, as well as the risk of severe injury. A respect for horses, and for the fact that riding them is a cooperative effort on the part of horse and rider, is one thing, but the horse can't be the one to make the decisions—it has to be able and willing to obey its rider instinctively at all times.

This too is an aspect of dressage, which is supposed to increase the horse's sensitivity to the rider's "aids" (the pressure of legs, seat, and fingers on the reins), while making the rider more conscious of what he or she is doing—not so much "a miracle cure" as the patient, step-by-step building up of the horse's suppleness and obedience by means of a series of formal exercises (or "movements") that can be (and are) objectively judged. In some respects it is not unlike yoga, except that the spiritual aspect is lacking (some dressage riders would deny that), and of course the horse is in constant forward motion, but the main difference lies in the fact that dressage is, and has always been, a form of entertainment, though not one as appreciated in the Anglo-Saxon countries as it is "on the Continent."

In a different form, of course, it still remains part of the repertoire of the circus, the familiar act in which white horses canter obediently around the ring, with young women in spangles, sequins, and Spandex standing up and doing gymnastics on their backs. This act goes back pretty much unchanged to Roman times, except for the Spandex, and was as popular at fairs and carnivals in medieval times (when it was done by gypsies) as it is today.

The sight of pretty young women doing somersaults on the backs of perfectly trained horses was a surefire crowd pleaser even in Nero's day, and has now been elevated into a demanding, fast-growing, and competitive sport, in the form of national championship vaulting, sponsored by the American Horse Show Association and American Vaulting Association. In this series of events, young women (and men) vault on the back of a cantering horse, as well as perform gymnastics and even dances—one event involves a pas de deux performed flawlessly on horseback, for instance.

Given this long involvement of horses and show business, it is hardly surprising that the magical Zingaro can still fill a circus tent with people sitting breathless to watch horses and riders perform equine ballet, and in New York City at least, not many in the audience appear to be the kind of "horsey" people who would normally be likely to attend, say, the Horse Show in Madison Square Garden, or who ride themselves. They are simply people prepared to sit for two hours on hard wooden bleachers to watch perfectly trained horses perform to music, and to admire the interaction of horse and human, as the riders leap on or off the galloping horses, do somersaults on their backs, and guide the horses through intricate movements without reins, saddle, or stirrups.

The fact is, there is always an audience for watching something that looks difficult or impossible performed on horseback. Large crowds attend the four-day International Horse Archery Festival in Fort Dodge, Iowa, where competitors shoot arrows at a target seventy-five yards away while riding a galloping horse, a skill that was highly prized among Native American warriors of the Plains tribes, and with which the Saracens surprised the Crusaders, but which has few uses today, while bronc-riding remains the emblematic event of rodeos. (For those eager to pursue mounted archery, you can learn more at www.mountedarchery.com, and for those for whom even *this* isn't an exciting enough sport, there is "mounted shooting," in which the rider "gallops full blast," according to my informant, the Santa Fe sculptor and equestrienne Star York, through "an obstacle course lined with barrels to which balloons are attached." Riders shoot at the balloons, carrying and using two pistols, and the winner, needless to say, is the one who shoots the largest number of balloons in the shortest time. In both this and mounted archery, the ability to ride without reins is an obvious asset, and the spectator is advised to keep his or her head down.)

Dressage has never had this kind of popular audience—popcorn is never going to be hawked at a dressage show—and even among seasoned riders, it inspires respect rather than high levels of excitement. Some dressage people attribute that to the formal costume that is obligatory for dressage at the higher levels—a silk top hat, a black tailcoat with brass buttons, a white waistcoat, stock, and breeches—and have suggested that dressage could be made more popular if the riders dressed up in cowboy clothes, or perhaps as gauchos. Much as people like western chic, however, it seems to me unlikely that a mere change in costume would be sufficient to make dressage a popular spectator sport, or would be acceptable to most dressage riders, a fairly conservative and tradition-bound lot.

Certainly photographs of Katherine Boyer riding during her heyday (and that of Appomattox, her stallion) are very formal indeed, both horse and rider clearly aware of the importance of the moment, and caught by the camera in a way that reveals both the formality of dressage riding and the immense forward-moving, contained energy of the horse. In hardly any other form of riding is the horse's power so apparent, or the rider's ability to control and hold that power in with nothing more than the pressure of the fingers on the reins and the calves against the horse's side. The horse is coiled like a spring, every muscle sharply defined, but instead of galloping flat out like thoroughbreds on the racetrack or jumping over amazingly high obstacles like puissance horses, all that energy is being applied to precise, stylized movements, as intricate and carefully meshed as the mechanism of a fine Swiss watch. To look at the photos that line her tack-room walls is to be struck by the sheer grace and momentum of dressage riding—and by the thought that changing the riders' costume would be as pointless as trying to popularize classical ballet by asking the members of the Bolshoi to dance *Swan Lake* in denim overalls and work boots.

In any event, when Margaret decided that she needed a younger horse than Tabasco and that he would have to be honorably retired, Katherine—who has a good eye for a horse—not only found a place to retire Tabasco to but also found Margaret a young dapple-gray quarter horse gelding whom Margaret named Missouri, after his birthplace, to replace him. Missouri was of a very different temperament from Tabasco—living proof of the American Quarter Horse Association's claims for the quarter horse's superior intelligence and common sense.

The truth is, when Americans think of a "cow pony," what they're mostly thinking of is the quarter horse, thanks in large part to the movies. Quarter horses tend to be compact, solidly muscled, with big, powerful hindquarters and a broad forehead that suggests equine intelligence. Most of the horses that cowboys rode in the Old West were in fact a scrubby lot, as photographs and the paintings of artists like Frederic Remington demonstrate, pretty much the bottom of the equine barrel, at least so far as looks are concerned. After all, what rancher in his right mind would waste good horseflesh on a bunch of cowboys, who were the nineteenth-century social equivalent of migrant fruit pickers? From the very beginning of the motion picture industry, however, a huge effort was made to prettify the West, and that applied to the horses cowboys rode just as much as to the cowboys themselves and the girls they pined for. The worn-out whores working out of the cribs and bars of Abilene didn't make it to the screen any more than did the worn-out, underfed workhorses of the remuda, with their big heads, mule ears, swaybacks, and saddle sores, part mustang, part just plain ordinary horse.

There was a lot to be said for the quarter horse. It was American, plenty were being bred in the West as racehorses or pleasure horses by the time the movies started to film westerns on locations farther west than Brooklyn or New Jersey, and as a breed they were photogenic, with a graceful neck, small, delicately pointed ears, and broad chest, the kind of horse that could carry a big man and make him look good as well. By John Wayne's time—even long before his time, come to that—the image of the quarter horse was firmly established in the American mind as the way a western horse should look, although it would have been as unlikely to see one in a real nineteenth-century western cow town as to see a sheriff's wife there who looked like Grace Kelly in *High Noon*. In photographs of Teddy Roosevelt taken during his brief incarnation as a rancher, for example, he is shown on shaggy-coated, big-headed cow ponies the likes of which he would hardly have ridden when going out foxhunting on Long Island, but after World War II the better quarter horses began to look more and more like thoroughbreds, and were just as much at home on the hunt field or in the show ring as on the range. Like blue jeans and cowboy boots and a lot of the things that came from the American West, they had become fashionable without altogether losing the practicality that had defined them in the first place. Brooke Shields in her modeling days in skintight blue jeans might present a very different appearance from the average ranch hand (or even the average ranch hand's wife or daughter), but her blue jeans remained practical, hard-wearing, and easy to wash; and in much the same spirit the quarter horse, however refined by breeding, remained a tough, sturdy, strong-boned horse that didn't need a lot of coddling and was unlikely to be temperamental and high-strung.

Missouri had all these virtues, as well as a relatively placid disposition and striking good looks. He had the big, powerful hindquarters, the stocky build, broad chest, thick neck, and fine features that are the trademarks of the quarter horse, and was "close-coupled," as horse people say, meaning that he had a short back, presenting a compact, powerful appearance—a chunky-bodied horse with "a leg at each corner," another of those old-time horseman's phrases that is hard to explain, but makes perfect sense when you see it (or it is pointed out to you) in the flesh.

Photo by Michael Korda

Margaret and Missouri eventing, Millbrook, N.Y.

What's more, he was willing. Horses, like people, have personalities. Some of them are eager to learn, and take a positive attitude toward life; others don't. Up to a point, they can be coerced, but coercion has its limits with an animal that weighs as much as ten times what its rider does, and it often backfires, producing a horse that's "sour"—mean, cranky, crabby, and unwilling to learn anything or do more than is absolutely necessary, results that paradoxically can also be obtained by not disciplining the horse or giving it enough work to do.

With horses as with people, initial character counts, and can only be changed so far, by however ambitious a system, so it helps to start with a horse that has a sunny, even disposition, takes pleasure in learning things, and seems to be having a good time doing what the rider wants to do. Horses don't have expressions as such—they don't smile any more than dogs or cats do—but their attitude shows through unmistakably, in the way they go about their work as well as the way they behave around people and other horses in the barn. Unhappy horses (although there are exceptions) tend to *look* unhappy, with ears pinned back flat against their head, teeth grinding away or bared, tail thrashing irritably, and one hind leg always cocked, ready to kick, while contented horses usually *look* contented—ears forward, alert, muscles relaxed, and eyes reflecting a certain curiosity and a benevolent interest in the world around them. Missouri (or "Mizou," as Margaret soon came to call him) had his strong likes and dislikes—he greatly preferred women to men, for example, particularly on his back—but he was and would remain exactly the kind of willing and able horse that everyone wants to own, a kind of living testimonial to the more extravagant claims of the American Quarter Horse Association, which refers to the breed rather grandly as "America's Horse," thereby overlooking, among others, the Morgan, the Tennessee walking horse, and the Appaloosa.

My own horse, Malplaquet, had been retired some time ago, in his case to upper New York State, in the Adirondacks. It is strange how certain decisions lead to major life changes—my acquiring Malplaquet from Mr. Novograd led to my meeting Margaret, to our subsequent divorces, then to our marriage, and eventually to our moving to an eighteenth-century farm house in Dutchess County, with a barn where Margaret could at last keep her own horses. None of these things could have been predicted the day that I wrote Mr. Novograd a check for $1,250 at his counter overlooking the riding ring at Claremont Stables on West Eighty-ninth Street, while he signaled frantically to Frank, the head groom, to get the horse back upstairs before I changed my mind— a check that was to change my life, as well as Malplaquet's.

Some people love horses with a deep passion—Margaret, for example—while others, like myself, although fond of horses, don't necessarily attach to them the kind of warm, fuzzy feelings that cats and dogs so easily inspire. But Malplaquet, for all his faults, his ungainly build, and Roman nose, was not just a horse but a symbol of the many ways in which my life changed during the years I owned him, and on those grounds alone, despite his modest price, I was deeply in his debt. On the other hand, inexpensive as his purchase price had been, his veterinary care was not. A long life in the hands of many owners, long before he hit bottom as one of Novograd's school horses, meant that Malplaquet was lame as often he was sound. It wasn't just that he had all the wear and tear of a hard lifetime; his was also, as a more astute judge of horseflesh than myself might have pointed out, the kind of conformation that inevitably leads to trouble.

A horse's conformation is not just its overall appearance, but more important, the angles at which bone, muscles, and sinew meet, the shape and proportions of the horse's skeletal structure itself. A long, straight back, for instance, will cause problems for the horse (as well as being uncomfortable for the rider), as will a narrow chest, or a steep shoulder, or a pastern that is too straight, not to speak of innumerable irregularities of hooves. The horse is an athlete, and as with most human athletes, the harmonious appearance of the body is of vital importance. Special shoeing, careful dressage work, and so on can all help to correct any deficiencies the horse may have, but only up to a point. A horse that isn't "put together" right in the first place probably won't *go* right—not in the long run, anyway—and the ability to evaluate a horse's conformation in a single glance is perhaps the one that matters most in selecting and breeding horses. And in buying them, of course.

It isn't the same thing as "soundness." Anybody in their right mind will have a horse examined for soundness by an experienced horse veterinarian before buying it, but that merely tells you the horse in question isn't lame, doesn't have any major physical problem, and is in general good health, as well as giving you a more accurate idea of its age than you are likely to get from the seller. Judging a horse's conformation is a more intuitive matter.

In any event, it was Malplaquet's conformation—that and a certain stubborn wariness in his eyes—that had caused Paul Nigro to shake his head when he got his first look at the horse, not his soundness. To Nigro, the proverbial old horseman, he looked like a horse of no particular breeding, which would sooner or later have problems, and this indeed proved to be the case. Even "Chick" Gandal, the genial vet who examined Malplaquet for me, had been cautious rather than enthusiastic about my buying him, though he could find nothing obviously wrong. A person who is determined to buy a horse, rather like a person in love, is in any case not normally in a state of mind in which he is likely to listen to good advice, let alone pay attention to it. Nothing short of the vet's actually shouting, "Don't even *think* of buying this horse, you fool!" is going to stop the infatuated buyer from writing out a check. It's just like friends telling a man who's in love that the object of his affection has been married three times, has rendered countless men miserable, and is probably at least five years older than she says she is, and that her wide-eyed stare is not a sign of passion but merely the result of the fact that she's half blind without contact lenses. . . . Lots of luck.

It's usually harder to get rid of horses than to replace them, and for obvious reasons, the older and lamer they are, the harder this becomes. In Malplaquet's case, the replacement was provided by Mr. Novograd, of all people, in the shape of a smallish, very handsome and lively bay quarter horse mare, attractive enough for me to forget the old adage "Once bitten, twice shy." True Grit, as we renamed her, after Charles Portis's novel of the same name, was a great-looking horse, with everything going for her except temperament. If I had not been so instantly smitten with her, I might have wondered just why a horse like "Grits," as her name eventually became, had ended up in Mr. Novograd's hands in the first place, for sale at a price that seemed disarmingly reasonable. Grits, it turned out as soon as the ink was dry on the check, had the kind of hair-trigger temper that made even Frank, who had spent a lifetime around horses, keep well clear of her when she was standing in the aisle upstairs at Claremont, and carry a stiff brush to whack her with if she tried to bite or kick him. "She *nasty!*" Frank would say, staring at her darkly from under the brim of his cap, while she stared right back, waiting for the moment he dropped his guard or turned his back. It was pretty clear that she had bitten or kicked one owner too many before she got "moved on" to Claremont, and even old Mr. Novograd, eager as he was to sell the mare, moved cautiously around her, making soft, clucking noises like a hen as he did so, while she pinned her ears back flat against her head and waited patiently for an opportunity to sink her teeth into him.

All this I might have noted—indeed, it would have been difficult to miss—if I hadn't ridden the mare, found her comfortable, and most of all, not only liked her looks but fancied myself on her. She was the right size for me, she had a quarter horse's dashing good looks, and when I caught my reflection riding her in shop windows on Ninetieth Street on my way to Central Park in the morning, we made a striking impression to my eye, in contrast to poor old Malplaquet, who even to the non-horseman, looked a little "as if all the bits and pieces had been put on wrong." That Grits ground her teeth alarmingly, hated traffic, small children and other horses, and tried to bite anyone who got close to her I did my best to ignore on the grounds that her behavior would certainly improve as she got to know me better—an illusion, needless to say, with horses as with people.

An equal illusion is that environment is the answer to behavioral problems. Moving Grits from her cramped and dirty quarters upstairs at Claremont to the comparative luxury of Sleepy Hollow, with its big stalls and wide aisles, had no more effect on her personality than moving a teenage hoodlum from a bad neighborhood to a better one. People who knew anything at all about horses still moved around her cautiously, while Grits ground her teeth at them, waiting for the opportunity to land a solid kick. Outside the stable, she seemed fine—the Rockefeller estate at Pocantico contained, after all, no small children or loose dogs, nor was there any traffic at all to contend with, so it should have been ideal for her. Of course, some days it was, but other days it wasn't. Grits had a high level of moodiness, and it was difficult to predict what might irritate her. In Central Park she had kicked dogs and bitten joggers who got too close to her on the bridle paths, which didn't disturb me all that much, since the dogs should have been leashed and the joggers had no business being on the bridle path in the first place; at Pocantico, cattle, swans, and geese upset her, but fortunately they remained out of Grits's reach. She could grind her teeth at them, and make the occasional lunge in their direction, but that was about it. No admirer of nature, she even snapped at passing butterflies.

With the arrival of Murray Ramson and Fabab, soon followed by the Vitullo-Martins and their horse Brian Boru, we were beginning to reconstitute the Claremont "group" in Tarrytown, though without the intense camaraderie that came in part from a shared antipathy—or sense of persecution—at having Mr. Novograd as our landlord. At Sleepy Hollow, the management was distant, and its being a club, there wasn't the day-to-day friction of keeping a horse in a place where the owner's eye is on every flake of hay or grain of oats. During the early morning hours, which is when we rose during the week, there was nobody there at all—we usually groomed and tacked up our horses long before the help had arrived for work, and were on our way back to the city by eight o'clock in the morning. The hours were, in fact, a little brutal—we rose at five and were in the garage by five-thirty or a quarter to six, winter and summer, which meant that by the time Margaret had dropped me off at my office in Rockefeller Center at nine o'clock, it felt like noon, and by seven in the evening we were ready for bed, and had to pinch ourselves to stay awake if we were to have any sort of social life at all. On those rare mornings when I did not go up to Sleepy Hollow to ride with Margaret, Murray Ramson picked her up in his E-type Jaguar, which, though dashing in appearance, lacked a reliable heater, so that in the winter it was necessary to huddle under several layers of blankets, while in the summer one sweltered, as if in a Turkish bath on wheels. It was this sense of being set apart from most of the other boarders in the stable, who tended to live in Westchester and ride in the afternoon, that led us to consider Murray's suggestion (at the time he was still married to Elaine) that we should drive upstate one weekend and visit my old horse Malplaquet in his retirement home.

Liz Black, one of our fellow riders at Claremont, had volunteered to take Malplaquet—volunteered with a degree of enthusiasm that I found surprising, in view of his age and numerous physical problems.

I met Liz early on in my time at Claremont, before I had bought my own horse, when I used to ride one of Mr. Novograd's favorite school horses, a solidly built palomino named Fancy, a handsome, good-natured, broad-backed old mare with a long, flowing, ash-blond mane and tail. I liked the mare well enough to have thought about buying her—she was as comfortable to sit on as an old-fashioned Victorian sofa—but years of pounding up and down the city streets to the park had made it improbable she would pass any vet's test for soundness. Unlike most of Novograd's horses, the mare was plump, absolutely round in cross-section, so much so that no matter how hard you tightened her girth, the saddle tended to slip. One morning, when I was out in the park on her, the saddle started to slip sideways as we were trotting down the bridle path, and before I could lean over and tighten the girth, I had listed forty-five degrees to port, then, in full view of a group of astonished park workers having their breakfast, the saddle slipped all the way under the horse, so I was suddenly upside down under her belly, held in place only because I was clutching to the saddle for dear life, anxious not to smash my head on the cinders of the bridle path or get kicked in the head, since the mare was still trotting along briskly, placid as anything, as if nothing at all unusual was happening. Liz Black, passing by on her own horse, very luckily for me brought Fancy to a halt and advised me sharply, once I was on my feet and brushing myself off, to insist on having a breastplate put on the horse before I rode her again, and perhaps to check my girth every once in a while.

Liz had the brisk voice and manner that suggested a certain amount of authority, and a refusal to tolerate any nonsense, but this, as I soon discovered, was merely a way of concealing extreme shyness. She cut a mildly eccentric figure in her bulky, rust-colored tweed hacking jacket and her thick twill jodhpurs, cut the old-fashioned, unflattering way, swelling out at the hips and bagging at the seat. She was one of the few boarders at the approach of whom Mr. Novograd hid his head behind his pile of ledgers, pretending to be busy in the hope of avoiding a lecture on the poor quality of his hay or the inadequacy of his bedding.

In conversation, Liz frequently referred to somebody called "Studs"—Studs would know what to say to Mr. Novograd about the hay, Studs would know how to fix the electric hot plate on which the boarders heated up their coffee so it didn't blow every fuse in the building, Studs would know how to deal with Frank the groom when he was in one of his surly, difficult moods, a sign of which was usually a flat pint bottle of Southern Comfort stuck in the seat pocket of his jeans. I heard so much about Studs that I had come to the conclusion that he didn't exist, that he was probably just a figment of Liz Black's imagination. I had formed a mental image of Studs as the Marlboro Man—Liz was full of stories about Studs's daring as a rider, Studs working as a ranch hand, Studs's skill at shoeing horses and resourcefulness in emergencies—so it was with some interest that I heard from Frank, after returning from my ride one Sunday morning, that Studs was actually here, on the premises, having a cup of coffee in the old dressing room the boarders had appropriated as a kind of clubhouse, much against Mr. Novograd's wishes. I asked what Studs was like, but Frank was in no mood to say. He simply rolled his eyes, handed me my saddle, and stumped off down the aisle, muttering darkly to himself.

I stumbled into the darkness of the room—Mr. Novograd's revenge was to limit the lighting to one bare forty-watt bulb high in the ceiling—carrying my saddle, and before my eyes had adjusted to the gloom, I heard a deep voice say, "Let me help you with that, sonny." Studs grabbed the saddle out of my hands as if it were weightless, placed it on the saddle rack, and shook my hand. Studs had a big, roughly calloused hand, with short, blunt, strong fingers and a grip like a plumber's pipe vise. I received a squeeze hard enough to bring tears to my eyes. For a moment I thought Studs might be planning to arm wrestle me, but eventually my numb fingers were released.

I took my pipe out of my pocket—in those days, when almost everybody still smoked, I was a pipe smoker—and Studs took a wooden kitchen match, struck it against the heel of one battered, well-used cowboy boot, lit a hand-rolled cigarette, then handed the match to me. I lit my pipe. Studs sniffed the aroma of my Dunhill's Private Blend tobacco. "Smells good," Studs said. "I'll have to try that in my pipe one of these days. Might be a little too aromatic for me, though." Did I detect a certain suggestion that *real* men don't smoke aromatic tobacco? No doubt Studs preferred something stronger and more masculine— Bull Durham, perhaps, the kind of tobacco that could turn you into a confirmed nonsmoker overnight.

In the smoky darkness I could see that Studs wasn't quite as big as I had imagined. In blue jeans, boots, and a well-worn western work shirt, Studs was about my height, but chunkier, with much broader shoulders and more muscular arms. Height aside, in a battered straw cowboy hat, seated on a pony, Studs would have made a pretty good Marlboro Man, I thought—then, as the initial puffs of smoke began to clear, I looked more closely and realized that however many horses Studs had shod,

Studs wasn't going to be the Marlboro Man, for the very simple reason that Studs was a woman.

The face was rough-hewn, the hair cut short, the jawline firm, and the eyes challenging and pugnacious enough for any cowboy, but there wasn't a hint of beard—this was a Marlboro Man who had never shaved, and would never need to. "I'm Liz's friend," Studs said unnecessarily, and sipped her mug of coffee. I said I'd guessed that, trying for the right note of easy acceptance, though this was in fact some years before that kind of relationship would be accepted as commonplace or ordinary, which no doubt accounted for Liz's skittish behavior on the whole subject, as well as Studs's hearty truculence. Studs, we were subsequently to learn, had at one time in her life been a conventional wife and mother, before she started rolling her own cigarettes and walking with a cowboy's rolling gait.

I never saw Studs on a horse—she remained a visitor at Claremont, and when she was there Liz played, improbably, the role of a *jeune fille en fleur*, while Studs roistered around like a sailor on shore leave, accusing poor Murray Ramson, who had actually *been* a sailor, of having a weak handshake and of eyeing her girl. It was enough to keep Mr. Novograd hidden away behind his counter all day, with the martyred expression of a man whose patience is being sorely tried, and even Frank, who was pretty broad-minded when it came to the boarders, looked as if he expected the angel with the flaming sword to appear in the aisle at any moment. Still, Studs, in her gruff, man-to-man way, quickly settled into the private boarders' tack-room society, although she wasn't, as she liked to point out, "a real city kind of person," and much preferred life on her little "spread" up in the Adirondacks. The occasional visit to the big city to see Liz was as much of New York as she wanted to see, and the sooner Liz moved up north, she let it be known, the happier she would be.

Eventually, that is exactly what happened. Liz gave up being "a poverty lawyer" and moved north to live with Studs, taking Malplaquet with her for an honorable retirement and the occasional light hack. I had no qualms about letting him go—whatever else you could say about Liz and Studs, they were crazy about animals. Even Studs, who liked to affect a kind of tough-guy lack of sentimentality, turned into a lump of melting sugar at the sight of a stray dog or cat, or a horse in any kind of distress. Anytime we wanted to visit him, we should feel free to, Liz and Studs emphasized, but it was Murray's idea that the four of us—he and Elaine, Margaret and myself—should take a weekend off to do so, at Thanksgiving. Out of sight was out of mind, so far as I was concerned, but of course Margaret and the Ramsons felt that this was heartless of me, so it was three to one. Anyway, I consoled myself, we would no doubt have a scenic drive, stay in an interesting hotel with great log fires in the room, and find a really good restaurant nearby. Murray got on the telephone with Liz Black and made all the arrangements, promising us a Thanksgiving weekend in the country that we would never forget.

What neither Margaret nor I had reckoned on was that the Ramsons were going through a terminal crisis in their marriage at the time, and although Elaine put a brave face on things, she sniffled gently all the way from New York City to the Adirondacks, going through a full box of Kleenex before we had even reached the Rip Van Winkle Bridge. A cold rain poured down from minute one of the day, and far from being scenic—I had imagined something resembling the hills of Austria or Bavaria—the route Murray had selected took us by crumbling two-lane county roads through miles of what looked like sodden tundra, sparsely populated with run-down farms, scrap heaps of old trailers, tar-papered shacks, goat farms, and collapsing tourist courts. I would not have imagined that it was possible to see so many miles of drenched Faulknerian poverty in New York State, which I had ample opportunity to observe in detail, since we sat in stony silence until well north of Albany.

The hotel, when we finally reached it, consisted of a few dilapidated plywood cabins partly clad in decaying fake log siding, huddled behind a defunct German restaurant on a narrow dirt road, set in a dark, gloomy pine forest. The place had the look of a small concentration camp hastily constructed in some faraway part of the Reich, like Thuringia, and what with the rain, the mud, and the many dusty deer heads mounted on the walls, we were drinking Jack Daniel's out of my pocket flask by four in the afternoon. The proprietress, an elderly lady with a goiter and a thick though distinctly *ungemütlich* German accent, took us to our cabin, which was arranged so that in order to reach the bathroom, Margaret and I would have to go through the Ramsons' room. I asked for another cabin, but the proprietress announced with great satisfaction that all the other cabins were occupied, despite the fact that ours was the only car parked in the muddy parking lot, so we settled down as best we could.

The Ramsons had moved fast enough to grab the larger of the two rooms, the one with direct access to the bathroom. Ours was rather like a rabbit hutch, both in size and a certain moldy smell that hinted at the occasional presence of some wet animal. The heating system produced short bursts of hot air that might have come straight from a blast furnace, followed by a longer period in which the temperature dropped to the point where you needed to put on a couple of thick sweaters, while through the thin wall came the sound of Murray raging and banging away fruitlessly at the thermostat, which was on the Ramsons' side of the cabin. We were not a happy group, and I became still less happy when it was made clear to me that far from eating in some interesting roadside restaurant—assuming such a thing existed within driving distance—we were going to have dinner at Liz and Studs's place. For some reason this part of the outing had passed through one ear and out the other. They had, apparently, been cooking for days and nights in anticipation of our visit, and there was no way out of it.

Just in case their heating system didn't work any better than the motel's, we dressed in many layers of flannel and wool and set off for their house, stopping—wisely, as it turned out—on the way to buy a few bottles of wine at the liquor store in the nearest town. The town itself was a dispiriting sight. Most of the buildings on the short main street were boarded up and abandoned, and there seemed to be a singular absence of men—almost everywhere we saw women, in blue jeans, boots, and parkas, many of whom made Studs look as feminine as Little Bo Peep. We followed the directions carefully, but nothing approaching a farmhouse was visible—the only inhabited place we could find was a single-width metal trailer set in the middle of a muddy field, surrounded by rolling hills covered in pine forests. We decided to ask for directions, but as we stopped by the mailbox, we discerned through the pouring rain our hosts' names on it. There was a moment of surprise and dismay in the car as it dawned on the four of us that we had actually arrived.

We squelched through the mud to the front door and squeezed our way into the narrow interior, where in a kitchen about the size of the toilet in a commuter plane, Liz—whose domestic skills had not hitherto ever been in evidence—was busy cooking a full Thanksgiving dinner. I glanced at the paper bag Murray had carried in with the wine, and raised an eyebrow. Murray nodded. It was not clear how long it would be before dinner was served, but he opened a bottle, and we started right in on the wine. Sometime around the third glass, I glanced out the window and saw, through the pouring rain, a familiar sight: Malplaquet, wrapped up in his rain sheet, was standing in the field, staring at the trailer wistfully, up to his hocks in mud, his big head cocked to one side as if he were silently asking me why he had been sent away.

I pulled the curtain closed. I knew that he was in good hands and that, old, lame, and cranky as he was—all of which could only worsen in the Adirondack winters to come—he would be looked after as well as he could be. Liz had already showed me the bowl of carefully cleaned carrots ready for his daily treat, the premixed bran mash, kept warm on the stovetop next to the vegetables cooking for our dinner, for his evening meal, the bags of feed stored in the tiny trailer bedroom so that mice or dampness couldn't touch it, the winter blanket drying out in the even tinier bathroom, confident that Malplaquet would live to great old age.

That night we slept in cold, miserable discomfort, or *tried* to sleep, while Murray snored and Elaine cried. At times, when one or the other of us simply *had* to use the bathroom, it was necessary to open the door to their room and tiptoe past the sleeping Murray, lying on his back with his mouth wide open, his dressing gown neatly spread out to keep him warm and his fur-lined slippers on the floor beside him, and Elaine, whose large, tearful eyes seemed to glow in the dark, like the radium dial of a watch or clock. The toilet was one of those old-fashioned ones with a tank, which made a noise like Niagara when you flushed it, but of course *not* flushing seemed rude, and pointless, since Elaine wasn't going to sleep anyway, while nothing short of a thousand-pound bomb going off in the parking lot outside would have woken Murray.

During the interminable trip home the next day, it was easy enough to reflect that when you have given an animal away, it is perhaps better not to go visit it, but the trip to see Malplaquet may have had the opposite effect on Margaret, because she not only went to visit Tabasco regularly in his new home but would eventually decide to take him back, when it seemed to her that he was not being properly looked after.

He was, when all was said and done, that rarest of creatures, the perfect horse for her, and you don't send the perfect horse off to grow old in the hands of strangers, not if you love horses.

CHAPTER SEVEN

"Well, I Guess You Know Best"

Ready for the hunt

T'S HARD TO DESCRIBE the intense camaraderie that develops between people who ride together in all kinds of weather, sometimes soaking wet, or numb with cold, or close to heat-stroke, or the kind of closeness that comes from watching somebody you know get bucked off a horse, or seeing them fail to negotiate a jump with disastrous consequences.

There's an affection blended with the toughness that seems to be part of the riding experience, bolstered by old "war stories" of people getting back on their horse to continue hunting despite a broken leg, or continuing over jumps with a cracked vertebra. These tend to come with the territory. On one of the few occasions when I rode Tabasco, back in our Central Park days, he threw me over his head, and I broke my collar bone on landing. It never occurred to me not to get back in the saddle and ride him back to the stable, and continue riding with my arm in a sling for the next few weeks against my doctor's advice, though it did somewhat shake my confidence when it came to riding Tabasco again, who had a tendency at the canter to gather speed in enormous strides, and had the kind of big, bouncy, stiff-legged way of going that turned easily into a buck once he was really moving. His bucks weren't small, timid affairs, either—if you weren't ready for them, he could launch you into the air like a V-2 rocket leaving its pad.

As Margaret was fond of saying, it was all part of the game—riding was a risky business, was her philosophy (and a lot of other riders'), and that was that. When Grits eventually blotted her copybook by kicking out and breaking Margaret's leg while we were riding side by side at Pocantico, Margaret took the incident calmly and went out of her way to find an orthopedic surgeon, Dr. Maurice Carter, who was not only willing to give her a cast in which she could continue to ride but also worldly-wise enough not to try and argue her out of riding with a compound fracture. Well, why not? Murray Ramson continued to ride Fabab with both hands in plaster after Fabab threw him, breaking his wrists, though it's true that most people thought he was crazy.

Still, from a certain point of view, Margaret was right. It *is* all part of the game—anybody who rides gets injured, eventually. It's a long way down, and the faster the horse is moving, the harder you hit the ground. Small children falling off their ponies mostly bounce. Past a certain age, that's no longer the case.

Hardly any feeling is more distressing than the certain knowledge that you and the horse are about to part company, and it's remarkable how threatening even the softest, grassiest turf suddenly begins to look when you realize you're about to hit it hard, head- (or shoulder-) first. Many years ago, during my service in the Royal Air Force, I received basic parachute training, and remember that by far the most unpleasant part of it was rolling off the back of a truck that was being driven over rough ground at thirty miles an hour in order to prepare us for the real thing. "Just land on your side and keep rolling, and you won't feel a bloody thing," our corporal instructor said. "Piece o' cake."

But in fact it was not a piece of cake, and when I tumbled off the bouncing truck, eyes closed and arms wrapped tightly across my chest like a mummy, I felt a paralyzing stab of fear that erased from my memory all the good advice the corporal had told us, followed by an impact that took my breath away. To my astonishment, I rose shakily to my feet, unharmed except for some abrasions on my face from gravel—no sprains or broken bones—and it occurred to me as I brushed off my coveralls that I had experienced worse falls than that from a horse, though I had the sense not to tell that to the corporal when he came back to round up those of us who were uninjured and tell those who were to lie still until an ambulance got there.

No doubt statistics can prove that it is more dangerous to be a passenger in a New York City taxicab, say, than to ride a horse, but every rider is familiar with the absolute importance of staying on the horse, which only makes it that much more ironic that Margaret's leg was broken while she was firmly in the saddle, at a gentle walk. Grits had let off a high, sideways kick that caught Margaret halfway up the front of her boot, audibly snapping the bone. Margaret rode back to the barn, gritting her teeth, a model of sangfroid in the best English tradition.

True to form, when we had reached the local hospital in Tarrytown and it was clear that the boot would have to be cut off, Margaret prevented the emergency-room nurse from cutting down the side of it with surgical scissors, and calmly made her cut the stitches down the seam of the boot instead. There was no point, she insisted with remarkable self-possession, on ruining a comfortable, well-worn-in pair of boots, and she was right, since I had the seam restitched, and she was still wearing the same boots more than twenty years later. That is more than can be said about Grits. Margaret certainly forgave her—she is incapable of bearing a grudge against an animal—but she made no secret of the fact that the sooner Grits moved on, the better.

In the meantime we had bought a house in the country, with a barn of our own, to which our horses would eventually be moved, including Tabasco, about whose well-being Margaret had been brooding ever since she let him go, and whom she visited frequently. She did not think he was doing as well as he would in her hands, and she was surely right, since once she had him back, he lived to an amazing, if short-tempered, old age. (Grits, by a remarkable coincidence, would eventually be retired by her new owner to a farm less than a mile away from our own, after a short career as a foxhunter, and although slowed down by ringbone—a degenerative bone disease of the pastern joint—gave birth to a foal, though she proved, not surprisingly, to be rather short of the motherly instincts.)

In any event, once we were moved into our house in the country, surrounded by many acres of fields, the notion of keeping our horses at home seemed altogether a natural one. We were not, after all, in suburbia—down the road was a horse farm where a local printer, Frank Costello, raised draft horses for show and occasionally came clattering down the road in a horse-drawn wagon; across the road was another horse farm, owned by Sheila Melville, joint master of the local hunt, while between them was a dairy farm owned by the elderly and reclusive Plankenhorn brothers (Lester and Earl) and their even more reclusive sister Ermintrude, none of whom showed any interest in horses but kept a prizewinning herd of Holstein cows. One of our neighbors raised donkeys; another had a son who, when he wasn't in and out of one of the many local psychiatric institutions, sometimes rode across our property bareback on a farm horse, grinning maniacally. Insane or not, most of our neighbors kept large animals at home and seemed to think nothing of it, so it was hardly surprising that Margaret should want to do the same.

Out toward Millbrook, on the other side of the Taconic Parkway, only twenty minutes away from us to the east, barns have become something of a status item, really the first place that visitors get shown, as opposed to the house or the guest house. Rare paneled woods, crystal chandeliers, tack rooms that look as if Ralph Lauren had designed them, these are common enough. Excess scarcely even raises eyebrows, and it's a rare barn that isn't an architectural showpiece, complete with a sculpture garden and a beautiful view over the wooded, rolling hills, most of it long since bought up by the owners of the barns or their neighbors, so that the prospect of development is slight. Here, the next home is out of sight—a long way out of sight—and is very likely to be even larger and more expensive than your own, and the chance of a trailer park or rows of houses on half-acre lots appearing overnight to blight the view is remote.

On our side of the Taconic, neighbors and their animals are closer to hand, and the animals are less likely to be gleaming hunters exercised by an English stable manager than donkeys, cattle, and ponies with a winter coat like a buffalo's. Nevertheless our barn, when we looked at it more closely, seemed, at any rate to Margaret, to have "possibilities," as compared to most of the ones around us, which were frankly collapsing. In the first place, the roof wasn't falling in, the beams weren't rotting, and much of the siding was still more or less in place, or could be put back in place by somebody who knew what they were doing. Inside, it was admittedly less appealing—cracked, grimy windows revealed that it had been used to house sheep for some years. Apparently it isn't usual to clean out sheep pens regularly, or at any rate, these had not been. A thriving population of bats had added to the mess underfoot, while everywhere spiderwebs hung down to the level of your face. It looked to me as if the only sensible approach would be to tear it down and start from scratch, which I didn't think we could afford to do, but Margaret took one look at the massive, hand-hewn eighteenth-century beams and the solid timber of the old horse stalls, with their thick, heavy doors hung on old-fashioned wrought-iron hinges, and declared that all it needed was a little cleaning up. The evidence of the sheep (not to speak of rats, mice, and bats) would have to be removed, the ancient water hydrant with its graceful cast-iron handle would have to be reconnected, electric lighting would need to be installed—but in the right hands all this should not be an insuperable task.

To give Margaret credit, she did not for a moment assume that mine were the right hands, even had they been willing ones. We had already discovered that almost anything I did needed to be done again by somebody who knew what he was doing, and I did not see myself turning the barn into a happy learning experience, or an opportunity to learn construction on the job. I was, on the other hand, pretty good at writing checks, a basic skill without which nothing gets done, though it seldom gets much in the way of attention or praise.

Happily, this problem sorted itself out in no time. Margaret had acquired the services of a groom, Roxanne, who in return for living in one wing of our house would look after our horses before she left to put in a full day working at Katherine Boyer's farm and when she came home after work. In addition, Roxanne was marrying a young man, Richard Bacon, recently out of the navy, who could do anything from carpentry to wiring, and for whom the restoration of our barn would be a snap.

This proved to be true. Richard set to work in his overalls, and before our eyes the barn took shape. Twenty years of debris and sheep droppings vanished, the broken glass was replaced, the wire netting that had held the sheep was removed, the inside was whitewashed or painted barn red, an electric line was run to the barn and lights installed, the plumbing reconnected—and voilà, a cozy, working barn, perhaps not an architectural showplace like some of those in Millbrook, but clearly a feasible place in which to keep five or six horses, with space left over for a modest tack room, which Richard soon added on, complete with paneled walls, fluorescent lights, and a rack for cleaning saddles. Nobody could have mistaken it for the work of a decorator, but it was functional, and with minor changes, it is still in use basically unchanged over twenty years later.

Richard was large, bearded, and monosyllabic, except when it came to explaining electric circuits, when he tended to talk very slowly and with a steadily fixed glare like that of the Ancient Mariner, as if that would help make things clearer. Roxie, on the other hand, was short, solidly built, pink-cheeked, and cheery, at any rate on the surface. Perhaps more than anybody I've ever known before or since, she qualified as a real "horse person."

At one time she had worked for Janet Black—not an easy taskmaster, however quiet her voice—and for several years she had worked for Katherine Boyer at Hidden Lake Farm. Roxie had worked for Janet during the period when the American Dressage Institute—itself one of those relatively small, beleaguered bastions built around the teachings of a single prophet, which sought to establish the true faith in dressage in the United States—moved from the relative comfort of Skidmore College to the frozen wilds of Maine, sort of a dressage gulag. Roxie was, as it happens, almost completely impervious to cold—on days that had most of us slipping hand warmers into our gloves and boots, and still unable to move cramped fingers, Roxie would work on the horses with her mittens hanging loosely from her sleeves, apparently unaffected by wind-chill factors of many tens of degrees below zero—but all the same the mere mention of looking after horses in the long Maine winters tended to bring a certain haunted look to her eyes, which told the whole story. To say that Roxie came of sturdy stock was putting it mildly. Even Katherine Boyer, who was pretty tough herself, was in awe of that side of her.

One of Roxie's two favorite expressions was, "Righty-oh!" which indicated a willingness to get right down to whatever work might be called for, however difficult the circumstances; the second, less cheerily, was, "And so forth, and so on," which usually served as a warning of something she didn't want to say, or repeat, or do.

Thus, if asked to get a horse ready for the vet earlier than had been foreseen, Roxie would say, "Righty-oh!" and go off through the mud to bring the horse in and clean it up. If, on the other hand, the vet happened to come while you were out, and you asked Roxie what the problem was, she would sometimes go on with whatever she was doing, studiously avoiding eye contact, and say, "Oh, no problem really, but he took the shoe off and thinks the leg ought to be hosed twice a day, and so forth, and so on." In general the phrase meant bad news, with more to come, which she was reluctant to reveal herself or admit responsibility for.

In 1939 there had been a huge hit song in France—a kind of story song, featuring a famous *chansonnier* of the time brilliantly playing both roles—in which a titled lady calls home from Paris to her château in the country to see how things are going in her absence, and the elderly butler replies, *"Tout va très bien, madame la marquise, tout va très bien, tout va très bien"* (Everything is going well, *madame la marquise,* everything is going very, very well).

On further inquiry, however, the butler reports one disaster after another to madame, each one more serious than the one before, leading finally to a stable fire, which spread to the château, destroyed it completely, and killed *monsieur le marquis,* but after every piece of bad news madame extracts from the reluctant butler, he replies, always anxious to please, *"Mais à part ça, madame la marquise, tout va très bien, tout va très bien"* (But apart from that, *madame la marquise,* everything is going very, very well).

It is easy, of course, to understand why the song became so popular in 1939 and 1940, as one piece of bad news led to another, each accompanied by an invariably optimistic bulletin, culminating in the occupation of Paris, the collapse of the French army, and the surrender of France, but for me the old music-hall number on everybody's lips in the France of my childhood—and which remained a kind of national theme song for decades afterward—came back irresistibly to my mind whenever Roxie said, "And so forth, and so on." The words always made me prepare myself for disaster of one sort or another, once the details had been extracted from her one by one like pulling teeth—they were Roxie's equivalent of General Weygand's "The army of France is pulling back in magnificent order to well-prepared defensive positions," followed shortly thereafter by the arrival of the Germans at your front door.

Really bad news, on the nonhorse front, Roxie tended to leave to Richard, who always prefaced whatever was coming with the warning, "You'd better sit down before you hear this." Of course at the beginning of our relationship, none of this was self-evident. The Bacons moved into the empty wing of our house, and Roxie, for whom a working day that began at four or five in the morning was normal, was seldom around at times when we were up. (Richard worked shifts in the control room at the local power company, so he was, if possible, even less visible.) The horses and the barn were looked after with a care and attention to detail that was altogether new to me, though not to Margaret. In Roxie's barn, there was not only a place for everything, and everything in its place, but everything gleamed and shone. Of course it quickly became apparent that the downside to this was that you couldn't change, or even touch, anything.

Once, early in our relationship, I caught sight of a rusty old tin garbage bin and thoughtlessly replaced it with a brand-new one prettily painted in red, white, and blue with Pennsylvania Dutch motifs that I picked up from the local hardware store, only to find that I had created a crisis which required one of Richard's rare personal interventions ("You'd better sit down before you hear this!") because the old one had been Roxie's storage bin for horse feed ever since she was a little girl. In the end it had to be retrieved from the dump, and the new one went unused for the next ten years or so, in shiny reproach.

Roxie could not only look after horses, she could *ride* them. Nobody who had worked for Janet Black *and* Katherine Boyer (who was *still* working for Katherine Boyer, come to that) would ever have any difficulty getting on a horse and making it look better—and go better, too. Roxie might not be built on the tall, thin model—she was in fact solid, chunky, and muscular—but once she was seated on a horse, it perked up its ears and paid attention.

For me—less so, perhaps, for Margaret—horses had always been a part-time occupation, as they were for most of the other people I knew in the horse world, even the so-called professionals, for whom horses were a job rather than a hobby, but Roxie was the first person I had ever lived at close quarters with whose whole life was horses, and who was as sure of herself with them as she was shy, easily wounded, and ill at ease with human strangers. With horses, her touch was sure, she was in control of herself and of them, her instincts were almost always correct, her opinions, however eccentric or opposed to conventional wisdom they might occasionally be, usually worth listening to carefully. Arguing with her was in any case a losing proposition, since another of her favorite phrases was, "Well, I guess it's up to you," signifying that she washed her hands of the whole matter.

Untutored as Roxie was in some ways (she always referred to the *Omnibus*—the United States Combined Training Association's annual list of events and rules—as the "Ominous"), her knowledge of horses, sharpened by years of working for demanding taskmasters who were unapologetic perfectionists, made it difficult to disagree with her in matters affecting the barn, which in any case she came to regard almost from the beginning as her private domain, and where everything was arranged by Richard to meet her own requirements. Just as the inadvertent replacement of her old, rusted-out feed bin led to a major scene, so did any alteration, however small or innocent, of the way things were kept or done in the barn. I was constantly saying, "But that sounds crazy," whenever Margaret reported on some new crisis, or when Richard, a dour expression on his face, waylaid me in the driveway and took me to one side to warn me in a hoarse whisper about whatever had happened. I soon learned that, crazy or not, it would have to be dealt with, and that if Roxie wanted the red plastic manure buckets piled separately from the blue plastic ones, there was a reason for it, in her mind, at any rate.

Tiny things—or at any rate things that might have seemed tiny to anybody else—produced disproportionately large (and long-lasting) sulks and scenes, all of which had to be placed in proportion because both Bacons were invariably superb in a *real* crisis. A horse colicking late at night, a pipe bursting while we were both away in the city, a horse with a deep, open wound, an unexpected snowstorm that isolated the farm and risked crushing the roof, all these things brought out the best in the Bacons. You could be absolutely certain, beyond even the smallest doubt, that Richard would take care of whatever happened in the house, and that the horses and the barn were safe in Roxie's care, whatever disaster occurred, and we often found ourselves repeating this like a mantra to each other when one or the other of them was "in a mood" about something—though it would have been hard to find two people more affected by each other's moods than the Bacons.

The Bacons came to us as a couple from the beginning, thanks to Katherine Boyer, and we had even attended their marriage in a strange, cramped, gothic-looking little wooden church of uncertain denomination (Richard's family was Catholic, Roxie's not) on a hill opposite Southlands, a riding establishment then of some size and note on the outskirts of Rhinebeck, where Roxie, like practically everybody else in the horse world around us, had once worked for riding lessons.

Southlands was owned by an elderly lady named Deb Dows, an authentic member of the rapidly vanishing Dutchess County landed gentry, a genial and slightly dotty autocrat whose life revolved largely around horses, dogs, and people of all ages who rode or wanted to learn to ride, and it was appropriate that from the windows of the little chapel one could see, across Route 9, the dilapidated riding ring and barns of Southlands.

There was a whole world up here, between Poughkeepsie and Rhinebeck, along the Hudson, that still centered on the horse (and the pony), with its dominant *grandes dames*—Deb Dows somewhere near the top, and perhaps slightly below her, Katherine Boyer, as well her neighbor, the redoubtable Betty Davis, wealthy landowner and doyenne of the local hunt, then *our* neighbor Sheila Melville, who ran a boarding stable from her home, less than a mile away from our house, with a decided bias in favor of foxhunters, then the loyal followers—horse owners, foxhunters, people who lived to compete in horse shows, or eventing, or hunter trials—and its equivalent of the loyal, hardworking peasantry that made all this possible, of which Roxie was an example of sorts.

This was a world from which the shopping malls and housing developments a few miles to the south were hardly visible, let alone the grow-ing black slum neighborhoods of Poughkeepsie, with their social prob-lems, or the advancing tide of automobile dealerships and fast food outlets moving north at a rapid pace along Route 9. In this world, old money was still decidedly more acceptable than "new" money (though that distinction was ebbing fast, as the landed gentry began to sell off chunks of their family estates to Wall Street speculators, computer mil-lionaires, and wealthy "people from the city" in general), and the total number of acres you owned still counted for something, as well as the number of generations that land had been in your family's hands; it was a world as well in which a certain degree of eccentricity, a good seat on a horse, and an autocratic presence counted even more than mere wealth, a world of big estates, riverside mansions, and dirt roads. Deb Dows could recall as a teenager riding over to her family's neighbor's home at Hyde Park on her pony for lunch, the neighbor being Franklin D. Roosevelt, and sitting afterward on the lawn talking to Winston Churchill while her pony grazed. It was a world, in short, perhaps mar-ginally less inbred, showy, and social than Middleburg, Virginia, and far too American ever to be confused with the more openly feudal English countryside, but still revolving very much around the horse as the center of attention, as well as the deciding factor in who "belonged" and who did not. Remnants of that culture existed all around us—a near-neighbor with a decaying full-size trotting racetrack on her property, complete with a small, personal grandstand; Sheila Melville's annual hunter pace, held across the road from us, which featured most of the more hell-for-leather members of the Rombout Hunt and combined heavy drinking in the refreshment tent with flat-out hard riding over stiff fences; and the annual opening meet of the Rombout Hunt, which took place at the end of our road, about a mile and a half away, and in those days mixed the remnants of the local gentry with those "locals" who either worked for them or were employed in one role or another as "hunt servants." In short, "horsiness" was not in short supply, despite the many social changes since World War II (let alone World War I) and the increasing encroachments of housing developments, trailer parks, and commercial establishments.

Of course real old-timers like Deb Dows remembered what Dutchess County had been like before the Crash, which had led to many of the bigger estates being abandoned, sold, or broken up. Most of them had vast stone stables, suitable for a medieval castle, that would never be filled again—along the Hudson River there were plenty of estates with empty stables, windswept tennis courts long since gone to ruin, miles of riding trails reverting to second growth, carriage houses full of dusty carriages, pony carts, and piles of harness, a whole world that had once revolved around the horse and had been dying a slow, lingering death ever since the Crash turned off the flow of money and the war gave the children of the locals a chance to escape from the narrow confines of mild rural feudalism or hardscrabble farming to new technologies, businesses, and opportunities.

Very few of those who returned from the war wanted to clean tack, muck stalls, empty manure buckets, and groom horses for their betters as a living, any more than they wanted to pick apples or milk dairy cows— still less so after IBM opened a big mainframe computer factory outside Poughkeepsie, bringing with it hundreds of new businesses in most of which it was, by and large, possible to work indoors, comfortable and dry, with clean hands, as opposed to standing around in overalls holding a pitchfork or a shovel and doffing your cap while Miss Dows or Mrs. Davis fussed around their horse before mounting and riding away.

The horse might still be enshrined as a symbol of rural status, but looking after it was not, and when horse people got together, what they mostly talked about was the difficulty of finding help, or, having found it, keeping it. Whatever role horses may play in people's lives, they are not in the final analysis pets, and they require a tremendous amount of care and cleaning. Some people don't mind doing this for themselves, and they may even enjoy it, but it's pretty much a full-time occupation looking after horses, and a fairly risky one at that. Statistics on the number of people who get injured caring for horses are hard to come by (all the more so since many of the people who do barn work these days are either amateurs, children, or illegal immigrants, for the most part from Mexico), but most people who work around horses have some scars to show for it, or at the very least some scary stories.

Most horses (there are exceptions) are not ill-natured, but any animal that weighs over a thousand pounds and can put an iron-shod hoof down on your toes without noticing it, or kick you out of sheer indifference or annoyance, or pin you against the wall of its stall with its full weight, or give you a good, hearty bite when you're least expecting it, is not to be treated carelessly, or looked after by people who don't know what they're doing. And, on the whole, a great many horses *are* looked after by people who don't know what they're doing, to the detriment of both species.

It isn't just a question of danger to people—though barn work, like most agricultural work, is inherently dangerous, even at the basic level of handling heavy weights (try picking up a bale of hay, and now try doing it a couple of dozen times, if you want a taste of what that kind of thing can do to your back!), and of dealing with large animals at close quarters. The horse is at risk too in the hands of people who don't know much, if anything, about it. It can slip on ice, with disastrous consequences; it can get too hot, too cold, too wet; it can develop colic and die in agony, or injure itself, sometimes fatally, in countless ways in the barn or the paddock. It is, in short, not an animal that thrives without an experienced horse person's eye on it and its surroundings.

Good horse people develop a kind of natural instinct for potential dangers to the horse—rakes or pitchforks placed carelessly in the barn, loose wire or broken posts on which the horse may impale itself, holes in fields or on trails in which it can break a leg, to name only a few. Hornets' nests pose a threat—a horse may be stung badly enough to start running and lose a shoe or lame itself—not to speak of ticks—horses catch Lyme disease just like humans—or countless other insect bites that produce violent reactions and mystify vets.

There is an old Arab saying that goes, "The eye of the master makes the horse grow fat," which just about says it all. A real horse person *no-tices* things about a horse, looks for troubles and warning signs, can tell when the horse, for whatever reason, just doesn't *look* right, is, as they say on both sides of the Atlantic, "off." As the number of people who can—or want to—do this diminished after the war, a lot of horse owners, the more serious ones, anyway, gradually took over this role themselves, fulfilling the Arab proverb. We hadn't been up in the country long before it became clear that certain people's lives revolved full-time around their horses, that they could never be "off the place" for more than an hour or two at a time, that if you invited them out, they needed to eat dinner early so as to be home in time for "barn check" (that last look to make sure that the horses are all right), that they had long since given up on certain things like shopping for new clothes, or getting their hair done, or a weekly manicure (not that horse people are likely to put a manicure as high on the list of priorities as the blacksmith's visit), because their presence was needed at all times. We were surrounded by people whose social life—whose life, period—was determined by the need to look after the horses, not really very different from the way that the Plankenhorns' lives were fixed by the routine of their dairy cattle (up at two in the morning to start the milking, straight to bed after an early, frugal supper and a last, careful look at the herd). Looking out for the horses, however, was something the gentry did—that part of the gentry that couldn't get really experienced barn help anymore, or couldn't afford it—whereas looking out for the cattle was something their farmer neighbors did, and slightly down the social scale, if you cared about that kind of thing, and a lot of people around our way still did.

Having Roxie Bacon living in a wing of our house relieved Margaret of much of that. Whatever else you could say about the Bacons, who soon became like family, Roxie's eye was the equivalent of the owner's in the Arab proverb, and she had a natural instinct for noticing that a horse looked, as she would put it, "peaky," coupled with the knowledge of what to do (a hot bran mash, or half an hour of being walked back and forth), together with the common sense that knows when it's time to give all that up and call the vet. With her own schedule rigidly fixed, it was Roxie who saw the horses first thing in the morning, and Roxie who did barn check last thing at night, and unclear as her focus sometimes seemed to be in other directions, when it was fixed on the horses, she didn't miss a thing. You could leave the place for a week—for a month—secure in the knowledge that everything in the barn would be "Righty oh," down to the last detail, as long as you were gone. While Richard made sure that plumbing, electricity, the roof, and the gutters were looked after perfectly, Roxie went about her routine as if Katherine Boyer or Janet Black were looking over her shoulder as she worked.

Roxie was, in fact, what locals describe as "a work horse," somebody who never seemed to get tired (or let it show), and who never leaves anything half done or unfinished. With Roxie you never had to write down a list of things to do and when to do them; all that was imprinted in her mind, carved in stone, worked into her daily routine so she didn't need to think about it, let alone be reminded of it. When we heard other people's horror stories, we knew we were lucky, and so, in their own way, were the horses, whether they knew it or not.

We started with two horses, Missouri and Hustle, the horse I bought from Katherine Boyer to replace the ill-tempered Grits, who, pretty as she was, was by now chiefly known as the mare that broke Margaret's leg. Hustle, like Missouri and Grits, was a registered quarter horse youngster, about three years old, a big, handsome chestnut, with a broad white blaze on his face. Hustle wasn't quite as compact as Grits and Missouri—he was a little more sprawling and long in the leg and even looked, at first glance, a trifle awkward and clumsy, though he more than made up for it in his disposition, which was everything the American Quarter Horse Association promised in their promotional material, and then some.

Hustle was genial, easygoing, patient, and unmistakably friendly, as free from bad habits as it is possible for a horse to be, and despite his youth had a certain gravitas, a freedom from all that flightiness that often comes with young horses—shying at their own shadow or a squirrel running across the trail, bucking when other horses take off suddenly, taking it into their head not to do today what they did perfectly easily yesterday—as well as a natural athleticism, with talents far beyond my capacity to use. Katherine Boyer, who had found him for me—the sooner I moved Grits on the better, had been her advice—made no secret of the fact that Hustle was a better class of horse than a rider like me deserved. As I mounted him in Katherine Boyer's ring—he wasn't that much bigger than either of my previous horses, but it seemed higher up—Katherine said, "This horse will move you up a notch," and it was certainly true that Hustle, with his gleaming copper coat, his good nature, his long, swinging stride, and his eagerness to please, felt from the beginning like a lot more horse than I really needed, or would ever be able to use. Still, he was not only very reasonably priced, he was Katherine's choice for me. I felt myself privileged that she had found a horse for me—argument, hesitation, or doubt hardly seemed possible once Katherine had said that this was the horse for you, such was her tone of authority, and anyway, I could see her and Margaret nodding contentedly in the center of the ring as I trotted around it, feeling, as I always did when Katherine's eye was on me, clumsy and graceless as I posted to the trot. The deal was as good as made before I was even on him, and once Margaret had mounted him, it was confirmed and the check as good as written—the only question in anybody's mind was whether I would be able to live up to Hustle.

Hustle was such a good horse that it always remained a mystery to me why anybody lucky enough to own him in the first place would sell him. With some horses it is only too evident why they're up for sale—they may be mean-tempered, stubborn, too much horse for the owner, or not enough, or there may be a simple change-of-lifestyle explanation, like a young woman going off to college. Every once in a while you see a horse for sale that makes its owner downright nervous—it is always a bad sign, for instance, when the person selling a horse walks around it nervously, or tries to hustle you out of the barn while it's being tacked up—but the great advantage of relying on Katherine was that most of these problem horses were eliminated; the horse you saw at her place was the one she thought you ought to have, and that was that.

There are those, of course, to whom horse shopping is a real pleasure—a greater pleasure, one sometimes supposes, than riding. You read the classified ads in the back pages of *Chronicle of the Horse,* or its western equivalents, make a lot of telephone calls to people who are only home in the evening, go visit horse dealers or people with a horse to sell, stand around with one foot raised on a lot of fence rails, see a lot of horses, and ride a few of them. Some people I know can do this for years, make it a full-time occupation, in fact, and still not buy a horse, but I'm not one of them, so Katherine's way of selling horses was ideal for me. I went to her barn, rode Hustle a couple of times, and bought him, subject to his passing the vet's test, which he did with flying colors, to nobody's surprise. "He'll make you a great hunter," Katherine said, and I had no doubt she was right, nor that I wanted one.

There were none of the hesitations or little problems that usually come up when buying a horse, with the vet saying there *might* be signs of a little bit of stiffness here or a little problem there, or shaking his head over the X rays, or wondering if the back is really 100 percent right (although probably nothing that a different saddle, or a different rider, or six months of acupuncture, or equine chiropractic manipulation, or regular shots of this and that, won't cure, of course). Hustle was built like a tank, back in the days when we knew how to build tanks, and seemed about as healthy and indestructible as a horse can be. He was young too, a horse you could expect to keep for many, many years without having to coddle him—for just like people, some horses are high-maintenance animals, fussy about what they eat, prone to pick up colds or suffer from mysterious pains in the joints, allergic to insect bites, a challenge to fit with a shoe, prone to bad coughs if their hay is dusty, requiring almost every bit and piece of their tack to be sheathed in sheepskin before it is put on. . . . You only have to look at the layers of fancy gel-filled or hypoallergenic saddle pads you see on many horses in competition to guess how much care is needed to keep the horse in work and prevent a sore back, and appreciate how much it means to own a hardy, sensible animal that doesn't need to be treated like a sensitive plant.

Hustle, once he was installed *chez nous*, fitted in as if he had never lived any place else. Margaret and I rode both horses over from Katherine Boyer's farm the day Richard finished work on our barn, following the myriad of hunt trails through the woods and across open fields, and for the first time approached our property from behind, instead of turning down the driveway off the road in a car.

The distance wasn't great—perhaps five or six miles as the crow flies, but of course we weren't crows. Hunt trails meandered, led into other trails, wandered around ponds, crossed people's backyards, merged with deer trails, from time to time crossed roads, some of them known to us, which gave us a bearing, others whose existence we had never suspected.

At one point, on the homestretch, skirting a lake we recognized in front of Bob Smith's horse farm—familiar territory indeed—we saw a line of tiny russet triangles on top of a crumbling stone wall beside the trail, and, coming to a halt, realized that we were looking at a row of baby foxes staring intently back at us, ears pricked forward at full alert. Their mother was nowhere to be seen—had she been close by, they would doubtless have been kept hidden behind the wall, but in her absence their curiosity overcame their caution.

Behind them, on the lake, were Canada geese, some swans, and domestic geese—it was familiar territory, the view from the end of our road. There on the lake, as usual until it iced over in the winter, was an elderly black man from Poughkeepsie, a retired police officer who spent most of his afternoons sitting in a boat, fishing for God knows what, a familiar, friendly sight. We waved to him, turned onto another hunt trail, skirted the lake, and descended a series of long, sloping hayfields that belonged to a farmer named Krayenbrinck—like the Plankenhorns half a mile further on, his was one of those old Dutch farming families that had been here since New York was a Dutch colony, and an English name was still an unwelcome novelty. We paused to listen for shots—Krayenbrinck had a shooting range dug into the hill behind his house—then rode on past his front door. Mrs. Krayenbrinck came out onto the porch, wiping her hands on her apron, to wave at us. We crossed Netherwood Road and rode on past a farm with donkeys and guinea hens. Hustle snorted slightly at the noise of the guinea hens but didn't shy or stop, which was just the behavior you want from a sensible horse. Then we turned down the gravel driveway of an A-frame house that was to become locally famous when a young boy shot and killed his mother with his father's pistol there, and on into the woods, where the trails, once you knew them, would bring you directly to our barn by the back way, through an overgrown apple orchard, with huge trees that looked old and gnarled enough to have been brought here from Holland as saplings by the first settlers.

Roxie fussed about the horses and got them settled in. All of a sudden they were no longer quite the same horses. Before they had belonged to us, certainly, but now they became almost automatically a part of our lives (a much larger part of Margaret's than of mine, to be sure), and their presence and well-being would henceforth be a dominant factor in how we lived. There was no calling to see how they were, or to say that we were going away for a week or two—Roxie might be here to look after them, but there was a riding schedule, and from some of the windows of the house, those that looked out towards the north, you could catch sight of them in what was then our one paddock, grazing, pacing, passing the time the way horses do. They were, in short, "our" horses now, in a whole different way from when they had been "our" horses being boarded elsewhere, and the change was going to be a major one.

Of course, you could say the same thing about a lot of animals—dogs and cats affect their owners' lives in all sorts of ways, after all—but horses are bigger, more demanding to keep. They can't easily be put in a carrying case and taken to the city, or down to the vet's to be boarded for a few days while their owners fly to Jamaica to catch a little sun or just go away for a weekend on the spur of the moment. Horses make an altogether different set of demands on those who own them, an expectation that they will be used on a regular basis, as well as looked after, a sense in which the small local world that is home will revolve around them. They are not "fashion accessories" like some dogs, or part of the furnishings like some cats, aloof, able to look after themselves a good deal of the time, content to be left alone. They need constant care, supervision, a firm schedule, and in bad weather, careful treatment, well thought out in advance. If it's going to pour rain, or turn freezing cold, or if a snowstorm is on the way, thought has to be given about what to do with the horses, and preparations made in advance. The middle of a winter night during a bad storm, with snow and ice on the ground, is not the time to be going out into their fields in boots and pajamas to get their halters on and bring them into the barn, or putting salt down on the paths so they don't slip. You need to decide in advance where they're going to go, what they're going to wear in the way of clothing, which ones can't be put next to each other because they'll bite, or kick, or fool around. You have to make sure that they've got fresh water, and that it won't freeze solid on them in the winter and they can't kick it over accidentally in the summer, and that they've got plenty of good hay where it can't get wet or muddy, if possible, and that there's nothing in their field or paddock they can hurt themselves on. It's not that the horse is stupid, even compared to a cat or dog; it's that he's big, powerful, and a herd animal, so his instinct, once he senses danger, is to start running, in the direction of the barn if possible, which for domestic horses represents safety. Anything that's in the way, whether it's you or a wire fence or a carelessly placed wheelbarrow, is likely to come to grief or cause grief to the horse when that happens.

Roxie, having spent a lifetime looking after horses, was seldom caught by surprise. She thought ahead automatically, and was prepared for emergencies. The whole business of keeping horses was very different than it had been at Claremont, for all its faults, where the horses were basically indoors in their stalls most of the time, as city horses have always been. Neither Margaret nor Roxie liked to see the horses "inside" more than was absolutely necessary—at night during the coldest part of the winter, from first thing in the morning to late afternoon in the hottest part of the summer, to give them a break from the sun and the bugs—so most of their time was spent outdoors, where we had fenced in a number of paddocks for them, on what used to be pasture turned to scrubland. The former owners had kept sheep here, and their predecessors had kept cows, but although we did not yet know it at the time, no amount of hard work or money was going to turn *these* acres into the kind of grassy, rolling fields dotted with galloping foals and mares that appear in television commercials for banks and insurance companies every year about the time of the Kentucky Derby. Dutchess County is just close enough to New England to qualify as rock country—plowing, even raking, merely brings up the next layer of loose rocks, and the soil is spread thinly over layers of solid rock. It helps to remind oneself from time to time that the chief geological event in this part of the country was the Ice Age, and what the mile-high wall of ice did as it moved south was to scrape away the surface of the earth below it like a giant Brillo pad, right down to the bare rock, which explains why nobody ever got rich by farming in this part of the world, and why we don't have the equivalent of Kentucky bluegrass.

Whatever we had, Hustle ate. He was "a good keeper," one of those horses that has a good, healthy appetite, eats what he's given, puts away plenty of hay and grass, and turns it all into solid, gleaming muscle. Despite the traditional warning against buying a horse with four white socks, he was as free of physical problems as it is possible for a horse to be, with the kind of hooves that don't give a blacksmith any problems. His expression was lively, benevolent, friendly, with what seemed to be a smile on his lips, even to somebody as little given to anthropomorphizing horses as I am. I carried a whip while riding him, but purely out of habit—Hustle rarely if ever needed pushing along or punishing, and was in any case very sensitive to the rider's tone of voice. He was, as horse people say with admiration about a certain kind of horse, "a real gentleman." Praise made him happy, while a chiding tone set his ears at a wistful, sorry angle and made him try harder. It would be difficult to find a horse so superior to his rider as Hustle, or so easy to please—a couple of gentle pats, a word or two of praise, an apple or carrot at the end of a ride, and he was happy. Having owned two horses, neither of which was particularly eager to please, I found this a revelation.

If you got into trouble, Hustle would do his level best to get you out of it. A gifted natural jumper, Hustle would eye a fence, gather himself up, and get you over it somehow. Even if you had approached it from the wrong angle, or jabbed him in the mouth rudely at the wrong moment, or got completely unbalanced in the saddle, or had to put your arms around his broad neck to keep from coming off, Hustle would get the job done for you. At worst he might give you a reproachful look after he had landed, as if to suggest that a few jumping lessons might be in order, but there was never any doubt that Hustle would get you over anything you aimed him at, and do his best not to let his rider disgrace himself. Big, challenging jumps, ditches, stone walls with no clear view of what was on the other side—none of the things that tend to make horses refuse gave Hustle a moment's pause. The only dangerous thing about Hustle was that he had a tendency to give me a greater confidence in my own ability than was merited, objectively.

In an effort to be worthy of Hustle, I found myself buying new breeches and in general giving a little extra polish to my appearance, and even took a few jumping lessons from Roxie, whose theme, rather like Paul Nigro's, was, "You can do it! Come on! Show him who's boss!" But I never truly felt that I was Hustle's "boss"—at most, I aspired to a partnership.

One thing about Hustle is that he produced in all those around him, except perhaps me, a great desire to get out there and compete. First of all, he himself seemed to like competition, as well as the praise and attention that come with winning, and secondly he was the kind of horse who *could* win—who *would* win, given the right rider. It wasn't as yet a consuming interest—we didn't have a trailer, for example, or a vehicle appropriate to tow one—but Roxie knew a woman who would lend us one when it was needed, and before very long Missouri was turning out to be a winner for Margaret at those harmless dusty weekend shows where little girls on ponies mix with grown-ups on full-size horses, or hunter paces, over a course of jumps and natural obstacles. As for Hustle, he always did his best, and he never seemed to put a foot wrong or to go lame.

I didn't compete on Hustle, much as Roxie was dying to get me to, but Roxie did, and when Margaret's goddaughter, Tamzin, came over from England to look after the horses during Roxie's first pregnancy, she took Hustle to horse shows with Margaret, as her mother did when *she* came over. Wherever we went, people who knew horses would nod at the sight of him and say, "Good old Hustle," affectionately, as if he were an old friend, and he usually ended up with a ribbon pinned to his bridle. He *looked* about as friendly as a horse can look, with big, trusting eyes and a slightly droopy lower lip when he was relaxed or bored, and the look was genuine. He never did anything foolish or dangerous, unlike one horse of Margaret's which startled people at the local Pleasant Valley Horse Show by trying to scramble out of the trailer over the closed, waist-high back doors, or other horses that bit, kicked, and made a fuss about crowds, noise, small children, or dogs. Everybody who saw him took a moment to pat him on the neck and say, "He'd be a fine hunter."

So great was everybody's confidence in Hustle that I was encouraged by Margaret and Roxie to go to the opening meet of the Rombout Hunt, which was then held about two miles down the road from our house, in a big, rolling field next to the lake—familiar territory for us. In those days, twenty or so years ago, the road was quiet enough to ride on—we often trotted the horses down the side of the road, on the grassy verges, and people almost always slowed their cars and waved at us. Hustle, of course, didn't mind the road work a bit. Even a big eighteen-wheeler roaring past him, or an oil truck with noisy air brakes, didn't upset him a bit—he didn't necessarily like motor vehicles, his expression seemed to say, but he was willing to live and let live. I therefore had no qualms about riding Hustle to the meet, but my experience in Virginia had made me wary of trying to repeat my success there. Besides, challenging as the hunting was in Virginia, Rombout Hunt territory seemed to consist mostly of crumbling stone walls, with a steep drop on the other side. It was agreed that Hustle and I would "make an appearance" at the opening meet, to show a solidarity with local foxhunting that we were in fact very far from feeling; then I would either join Margaret and Roxie in the hunt or trot home by myself. We had recently acquired yet another horse, a smallish bay gelding whom we renamed Sundance, and Roxie would ride him. Sundance, owned by one of the local highway superintendents, had been going so cheap that it seemed impossible not to buy him. The highway superintendent was going to prison, like many of his fellow highway superintendents, who had been caught in a variety of schemes that involved, among other felonies, rigging bids for equipment and salt and renting out town equipment for private use. Sundance, who lived in his backyard, was an expense nobody wanted during his prison sentence. Sundance himself had a quizzical look and gentle manner, as if he had figured out that he was lucky to have found a new home, and was anxious to please.

That, of course, is the problem with having six stalls in a barn—there is a natural tendency to fill them. In any case, as Hustle was competed more and more, I got to ride Sundance when Hustle's schedule got too busy for the occasional morning hack. Sundance was a pretty nice little horse, though he was eventually to go lame, but he was no Hustle, in either looks or performance.

Very early on—even before we had brought the horses to the farm—the question of foxhunting had proved to be a matter of some delicacy. As horse owners—and, more important, landowners—we were expected to be fervent supporters of the hunt, and indeed we were made honorary "landowner" members of the hunt more or less automatically, thus confirming the hunt's right to cut trails on our property and to hunt over it. I had not given the matter much thought—it seemed like a clear case of noblesse oblige. Anyway, everybody in the local horse world seemed to expect it of us—Katherine Boyer, our neighbor Sheila Melville, who was a major figure in the hunt, and the formidable Betty Davis (not the actress, of course, but Mrs. Putnam Davis of nearby Staatsburg), a lady who was, to put it mildly, difficult to refuse, even had we been inclined to do so.

Betty Davis was very definitely of the ancien régime, insofar as that phrase could be applied to Dutchess County, with her ramrod-straight back, patrician features, steely eyes, and slim figure, her iron-gray hair always tightly gathered in a rider's hairnet as if she had just taken off, or was about to put on, a black velvet hunt cap. She was married to Putnam Davis, a gentleman of the old school, good-looking, soft-spoken, wealthy, with perfect manners and a wardrobe full of the kind of country clothes Ralph Lauren has since made a fortune imitating. A quietly convivial drinker (and chain smoker), "Put" Davis, as he was universally known, was widely respected throughout Dutchess County—it was impossible to find anybody, at any social level from top to bottom, who had a bad word to say about him. Even those who feared Betty would always add, when speaking of her, "Well now, but Put, that's a whole different story. . . ."

Put was an avid horticulturist and seemed in his own effortless way to know everything there was to know about gardens, flowers, and plants. Sometimes he dropped round to give Margaret something for our garden, to fill in a gap, or plant in a shady place where nothing else would grow.

Betty took hunting and horses as seriously as anybody in Virginia did. She was held in awe by many people, not because of her skill with horses but because of her unassailable position in the foxhunting, landowning world, which intersects with the horse world but is not necessarily the same thing. The Davis's house was, by local standards, large, old, and handsome, located down the road from the Rombout Hunt kennels—her barn was run by Stanley Money, an old-time horseman of great local repute, who was also the hunt's whipper-in—and a visit to her farm would have pleased Surtees himself.

Early on, perhaps as part of the campaign to make us supporters of the hunt, perhaps merely as a gesture toward new landowners, we were invited to the Davis house for dinner. Like similar houses in Middleburg, Virginia, the decor featured horses, hounds, and foxes in various combinations, the table talk was mostly about horses, and our hostess knew and shared with us the name of the steer who had contributed the roast beef that was served.

Foxhunting, she pointed out to us, was the basic glue that held things together up here—take away foxhunting, and what had you got? The hunt was threatened by land developers, by unsympathetic locals who saw foxhunting as an extension of class warfare, by new people moving in—not people like *us*, of course!—who didn't know any better, who didn't cherish the traditions and the values of foxhunting, who had never been privileged to enjoy a day out on horseback in the open air.

I had heard this song before, of course, both in England and Virginia (in England, as I write, it is being sung louder than ever as Tony Blair's Labour government moves to ban "blood sports" altogether in the United Kingdom), and much as I admire the way foxhunting *looks*, and the deep traditions behind it, I have never been totally convinced. It made sense of a kind, no doubt, when the countryside was sparsely populated by rural people who kept chickens and were, in principle, grateful to their social betters for keeping down the number of predators, but people weren't raising chickens in the middle-class housing developments that were fast replacing the farms, and the fox, far from being a nuisance or a threat to them, was an endangered species. People were thrilled to see a live one, or at any rate their children were, and their hearts were no longer stirred by several dozen hounds and scarlet-clad riders dashing hell-bent across the countryside determined to kill it. Many hunts, in fact, had scaled back to "drag hunting," in which the scent of a fox is carried back and forth across the countryside by the huntsman the day before the hunt to give the hounds something to chase, and no killing takes place.

I did not make these points to Betty across the dinner table, partly because it seemed like bad manners to argue with our hostess, and partly because I knew it was just so much wasted breath—those who support foxhunting are never going to be persuaded out of their convictions, and those who oppose it are not going to be moved by arguments about its historical importance, or its value to horse breeding or the human character. As for the hunt itself, like most hunts its internal politics were so complicated, and the rifts between different factions so deep, that they were inexplicable to any newcomer, beyond the basic division between old money and new, and between the members who were, or considered themselves to be "gentry" (i.e. those who owned a considerable amount of land), and those who weren't. I talked horses, instead, a far less controversial subject (hardly anybody is opposed to horses), and thereby no doubt left behind me the impression that Margaret and I were going to be "active" in the hunt.

Sheila Melville's farm, down the road from us, perhaps a mile and a bit away, represented another and rather less respectable faction of the hunt. The Melvilles had been around for at least three generations— long enough to have the road past their property named after them—as substantial landowners, although Sheila's life was more in the pattern of a Surtees character than that of Betty Davis. The hard-drinking, hard-thrusting, noisier members of the hunt seemed to gather around Sheila, and her house had a certain eighteenth-century quality to it—a graceful, curved staircase with a chandelier hanging above it as you entered the hall, lots of handsome hunting prints on the walls, but with the run-down atmosphere that comes from many dogs, lots of smoking and drinking, and too many people trooping in from the barn without bothering to take off their boots and spurs. Lord Scamperdale, the hunting peer in *Mr. Sponge's Sporting Tour*, would have been perfectly at home in it, and indeed in some ways it resembled a smaller version of Woodmansterne, the earl of Scamperdale's seat, with its comfortable furniture, much used and worn by dogs, and the general ambience of a sporting tavern.

Somewhere in their lives, the Melvilles had descended slightly, perhaps even precipitously, from the *grandeur* of their parents and grandparents, but they still owned not one but three houses on the property, none of them in particularly good repair, in addition to a rather noisome roadside facility in which one of Sheila's brothers raised and slaughtered veal calves, and which even Hustle didn't like to walk past, as well as a barn and an indoor ring.

Sheila, whether from financial need or simply the love of company, took in boarders, so she never had less than twenty or thirty horses on the place. Sheila's parents were born in an age when people "knew their places" and were expected to stay in them. Indeed, many of the photographs and prints on the walls of her house showed quite a different world. Horses, dogs, and ponies proliferated, of course, but the clothes and posture of the senior Melvilles and their friends at hunt meets and hunter paces and in the show ring made it clear that theirs was still a world in which the social barriers between gentry and "help" were clear-cut and observed, particularly the barrier between hunt servants and the members of the hunt—and especially between hunt servants and the daughters of the members. The Crash and World War II had no doubt wiped out most of this, but like a lot of people in similar circumstances, Sheila combined the imperiousness of a landowner and member of an old Dutchess County family with a more modern and democratic determination to have a good time with whomever she damned well pleased. It was impossible not to like her, and as neighbors go, she was undemanding, allowing us to ride on her land whenever we liked.

Perhaps because of this, we had given her the impression of being rather more interested in foxhunting than we actually were, and had grinned and waved cheerfully at her as the Rombout Hunt went out "cubbing" on our land off-season or crashed across our fields in pursuit of a fox (or, at least, their own hounds) during the season. We did not, however, join in.

Riding Hustle down to the opening meet was therefore something of a major step for me, and I was at pains to look my best, carefully trying my white silk stock—the real kind, from England, made of thick silk, which in the seventeenth century was originally intended to be used in emergency as a bandage for the leg of an injured horse or a sling for a rider's broken arm, hence the large gold stock pin, resembling an out-size safety pin, which fixes and adorns it—and wearing my best boots, brought to a high gloss. Roxie had been up long before dawn weaving intricate patterns in the horses' manes and tails and grooming them until they glowed.

A photograph of the three of us, taken by Richard as we rode through the front gate, showed us from behind, with Margaret and Roxie both wearing long braided pigtails that matched the horses' tails, and all three of us dressed in black, Roxie riding Sundance.

Horses that don't normally hunt tend to get more worked up about it

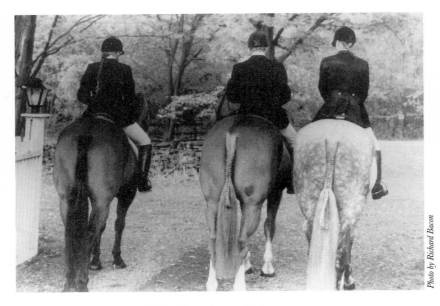

Photo by Richard Bacon

Roxie, the author, and Margaret.

than almost anything else. In the first place, all the preparations alert them to the fact that something unusual is about to happen, and in the second place, a field full of strange horses, hounds, and crowds of people milling about makes them understandably nervous—and that's before the really exciting stuff starts, when the master moves the hunt off, the hounds begin to "give tongue," and the huntsman and his helpers begin to blow their horns and shout directions at the hounds, while everybody jostles and jogs after them, trying to get into a good position for the first jump. All of this produces in most horses (except experienced hunters) a high level of anxiety, and tends to make them hard or impossible to handle. Once we got down to the lake, however, Hustle was remarkably calm. We kept to one side a bit—no point in tempting fate—taking up a position on a rising slope where our presence would be visible, in my case with the kind of fixed smile that people have who are about to do something obviously stupid and dangerous.

Just to our left, the trail led alongside the lake, across another biggish field, and on into some woods, winding past the stone wall where we had seen the tiny fox cubs on the day when we rode Missouri and Hustle back to the farm. No doubt the little foxes were full-grown by now, if indeed they were still alive, but the more I thought about them, the less I felt like hunting them, and the more I thought about the stone wall, the less I felt like jumping it, squeezed into a mob of other riders and horses, despite Hustle's competence.

I pulled Hustle out, waved to Margaret and Roxie, turned him around, and walked him home. To give Hustle his due, he didn't seem disappointed. If his blood was up, it was hard to stop him—aim him at a fence, and once he had made up his mind to jump it, there was no point in changing your mind, because he was going over it—but he had a pretty good sense of the rider's commitment, and no doubt he could tell that I wasn't in the hunting mood. That was okay with me. We got home, I gave him a carrot, and we never went out hunting again. Eventually I gave away my hunting jacket, let my velvet cap gather dust, and passed my white stock on to Margaret, who found it heavy and cumbersome to tie. I never missed it, either. I liked the little foxes we saw out riding in the woods a lot better than hunting, and moved, step by step, to the point where we eventually closed our land to the hunt, to Betty Davis's pained regret, though Sheila Melville took it in her stride.

The author and Margaret, opening meet, on Hustle and Missouri.

As for Hustle, he went on being the perfect horse, a little underutilized in the sense that I wasn't making full use of his talent and ability, as Roxie never tired of hinting. She and Margaret took him to competitions, but I was content to hack him in the mornings with Margaret, and never doubted that whatever I did, Hustle would get me safely home.

Since he was a young and healthy horse, it was disconcerting when Mike Murphy, then our vet, came into the tack room looking concerned after Hustle's regular examination. He hemmed and hawed a bit—Mike was never in a hurry to come up with really bad news—but the bottom line was that Hustle was showing signs of skin cancer. I raised an eyebrow. I hadn't even realized that horses developed skin cancer, though it was perfectly logical that they should, now that I thought about it. Horses with large white patches were particularly liable to it, Mike explained—it had something to do with exposure to the sun. He didn't need to tell me that Hustle's distinguishing mark was a large white patch, or blaze, down the middle of his face. It was an endearing mark, but it was to prove, unfortunately for Hustle, a deadly one. He did indeed test positive for cancer, and eventually it metastasized to his eye. He looked the same, he was as good to ride as ever, but he was in deep trouble, and since there was nothing else we could do, Richard and Roxie took him up to the School of Veterinary Medicine at Cornell, where the eye was removed and the lids sewn shut over the empty socket.

Margaret and I were away when this happened, which was probably just as well, but when we came back, Hustle had a sad but faintly piratical look, an expression—though one tries not to anthropomorphize about these things—of resigned suffering, a look of the holy fool, in the Dostoyevskian sense. Oddly enough, he could still jump like clockwork, and seemed to enjoy it as much as ever. You had to line him up carefully so he could focus his good eye on the jump; then he would move his head back and forth until he was sure of himself, but he never put a foot wrong, and didn't seem to miss having two eyes (and binocular vision) a bit. People who saw him said, "Poor Hustle!" but Hustle didn't seem sorry for himself, and we all toyed with the hope that he would go on for years, one-eyed but otherwise in good shape. Then, very shortly afterward, the cancer returned, and Hustle had to be put down, buried behind the paddock in which he had so often eaten grass, under a huge old apple tree.

Of all the horses I've owned (or ridden) I remember him best, and wish I'd spent more time on him or reached out a little further to compete, and taken advantage of at least some part of his talent. I often look at the photograph of the three of us riding through the front gates to the opening meet of the Rombout Hunt, with Hustle and me in the middle, as the best and most promising moment of my relationships with horses, the moment when it all seemed to come together, the autumn leaves beginning to turn, the horses' coats gleaming in the sun, the three of us, Roxie, Margaret, and myself, all dressed to kill in our best hunt clothes.

I have that picture facing me at home, by my desk, at work, on my desk, and every time I look at it, I feel a certain nostalgia, the sense of having captured, even for a few moments, the kind of pleasure that Surtees wrote about in *Mr. Sponge's Sporting Tour*, the feeling, not always easy to produce, that it all makes sense—the country, the barn, the amount of money it costs, and the constant angst of finding and keeping barn help, the overwhelming reality that we're doing something anachronistic, cranky, old-fashioned, and overwhelmingly difficult, but *worth* it.

I still miss Hustle. I've had other horses, before and after him, but none of them has ever been as good as Hustle, or as gentle, or as reliable, and very few of them have had as much "character." Even in his last days, when the cancer was spreading fast, he had a certain nobility of character, an expression—made all the more striking by having only one eye—that suggested a sense of humor, as well as an eagerness to please. He was a very nice horse.

Hustle

CHAPTER EIGHT

The Sporting Life

"The Rider's husband" —

1   *and 2*

'VE ALWAYS TRIED to avoid a single-minded obsession about horses—or about anything, come to that—but it fascinates me to know people for whom such an obsession is ordinary. Years ago, about the time we bought our country house (before we started thinking of it, let alone referring to it, as "The Farm"), in my capacity as editor in chief of Simon & Schuster (a role I still play), my then boss and good friend Richard E. Snyder, the famously hard-nosed and abrasive CEO of S&S, called me into his office one evening to express to me his determination that we were going to have "the best god damned sports editor in book publishing" working for us. "Somebody," he added, "with class."

I waited to hear who this person was, but was dismayed to discover from Dick that he apparently thought it was *my* job to find and hire him (the idea that it might turn out to be a woman was not likely to occur to either of us in those days).

Now, if there's one area of book publishing I know nothing about, it's sports books, nor did I have a clue who the "hot" sports editors were, though it was clear enough that nobody on our editorial staff at that time qualified, at least in Dick's eyes. Our sports books, such as they were, were mostly edited by Peter Schwed, an older man who had been Dick's principal rival for the presidency of the company, and whom Dick particularly disliked. Peter liked golf books, which was good, because they sold a lot of copies, and tennis books, which was okay, too, but his specialty was the "nuts and bolts" books about how to improve your swing or your backhand, rather than the big "celebrity" sports books—ghostwritten autobiographies by football and basketball stars from other publishers—that were cluttering up the top half of the non-fiction bestseller list week after week, to Dick's dismay.

Obediently I canvassed a few names and set out to meet with them. It was a dismaying experience, like being stuck on a desert island—or, to be more exact, stuck in a patent leather booth in a dark West Forties cocktail bar—with the late Howard Cosell at his most contrary and talkative. The sports editors were mostly bulky older men, eager to drink on somebody else's expense account and heavy smokers to a man, and all of them talked, loudly, hoarsely, endlessly, in language I only vaguely understood, about sports with which I was more or less unfamiliar—baseball, football, ice hockey, basketball. I hadn't a clue which one of them would seem to Dick "classy," if any, and had not read any of the books they had edited. I have never been a sports spectator or fan to begin with, and the only sports I knew anything about were things I had done myself, like riding, skiing, and soccer—the latter then virtually unknown in the United States and dismissed by the sports editors as a pansy version of football, played by Brits and Europeans.

Eventually a friend came to my rescue by telling me that the classiest sports editor he knew in New York might in fact be looking for a job with a larger book company than the one he was at, and that is how I came to meet William Steinkraus, a member of the United States Equestrian Team for over twenty years, its riding captain for sixteen, who rode in five Olympics and won four medals, including the individual gold at Mexico City in 1968—the first individual equestrian gold medal ever won by an American rider. Here was "class," as Dick had demanded. In fact Steinkraus exuded so much class across the luncheon table—was so clearly a gentleman in every sense of that word—that it crossed my mind that S&S, notoriously an authoritarian roughhouse of a place, might not be the ideal place for him to work and that I should probably try to discourage him from coming there. On the other hand, I told myself, I liked him, and if Dick Snyder wanted class, well, here it was, on the hoof.

We had a common interest in the shooting sports—Steinkraus was a first-rate shot and hand-loaded hundreds of cartridges a week in a small armory on his Connecticut estate because he shot so much to keep in practice—but what sold me on the idea of hiring him was that he was, by any measure, one of the finest competitive horsemen America had ever produced. I had seen him, in fact, on his last ride in the Garden. The perfect timing with which he took the jumps, as well as the way he galloped flat-out like a teenager on a dirt bike between them to make the time, was a sight to behold, one, in fact, that brought the entire audience to its feet. He looked the part, too, even off the horse—a smallish man, wiry, muscular, with the hands of a concert violinist (he was in fact a gifted musician), a narrow waist, broad shoulders, and a sharp-nosed, cleanly chiseled face on which there was not a hint of superfluous fat. He wore a dark tweed suit of impeccable tailoring that would not have looked out of place in a London club, and his bespoke shoes gleamed.

Steinkraus, I quickly discovered, was an omnivorous reader and a man of considerable cultivation—he knew a lot about books, but he also knew a lot about the market for sports books, which was more than I did, though his interest in sports was rather more rarefied and upper-class than what Dick had in mind—fly-fishing, the shooting sports, riding, and dog training were some of the things that interested him, and I have to confess that I may have underplayed this WASP elitist side of Steinkraus when I described him later to Dick over a glass of vodka in

Dick's Rockefeller Center four-window corner office at the end of the day. Upland bird shooting wasn't Dick's idea of sport, I reflected, nor grouse shooting on the Yorkshire moors, still less three-day eventing or dressage. Basketball and hockey were more in Dick's line, and especially since our parent company Gulf + Western had bought Madison Square Garden, he had become an ardent Knicks and Rangers fan. Sports that weren't played professionally by tall black men or French Canadians on skates hardly even registered on Dick's radar screen. Still, he was impressed with what I told him. "*Four* Olympic medals?" he mused from behind his feet, which he perched on his desk, his chair tilted all the way back.

"One of them an individual gold," I emphasized.

"An individual gold? I'll bet there isn't another house in town with a sports editor that has an Olympic gold medal. Not even Knopf or Farrar, Straus."

"That could be. You *said* you wanted class."

Snyder nodded. He always wanted to hire class, though once he had it, he didn't always know what to do with it. A trace of concern crossed his face. "Are you sure he'll *come* here?" he asked, in a rare moment of self-doubt.

"He says so."

"Hire him."

So we hired Steinkraus, and he moved right in, a neat, spare figure, always impeccably dressed and polite, with a firm handshake and the bright, clear-eyed gaze of a bird of prey. Rather to his credit, I thought, his small office did not put any of his successes as an athlete on display— there were no photographs of him standing on the podium receiving his gold medals at the Olympics or winning at the Garden, or being presented with a trophy by the queen of England—no hint, in short, of the fact that he was himself something of an athletic legend and a star. He arrived early every morning in his English raincoat and a jaunty green Tyrolean hat, of the kind worn to shoot chamois in the Austrian Alps, and got right to work; he took a short lunch break, and left for his home in Connecticut carrying his briefcase promptly at five o'clock. If Dick had supposed that Steinkraus would be hanging around his office through the early hours of the evening exchanging sports stories over a glass of vodka, he had the wrong man.

In fact, he *did* have the wrong man, as it turned out, particularly as the company changed, having been bought out by a major conglomerate. First of all, Steinkraus was just as stubbornly determined to do things his own way as Dick Snyder was—Steinkraus had the firm jaw and unyielding eye contact of a man who was more accustomed to giving orders than receiving them, and while unfailingly courteous and soft-spoken, he wasn't a bit afraid of Snyder. Secondly, the sales department soon started sending up alarm signals to Snyder about the fact that our sports list was becoming too esoteric. "What the fuck is upland bird shooting?" Dick yelled at me over the telephone one day—no doubt in response to the same question from the sales reps—and after I had explained what it was, he thought for a moment and said, more calmly, "Maybe class wasn't what we needed after all."

Steinkraus took his departure with his usual grace—he was not surprised by it—and left as quietly as he had arrived. We promised to keep in touch, and from time to time I called him when I had a horse problem, which became more frequently the case as Margaret began to compete more and more actively.

Years later, when I went to visit Steinkraus on his Connecticut estate, which jutted out into Long Island Sound, I realized how great his patience must have been at these queries. It was not just that the estate might have served as a portrait of what life was like for those who had *old* money, in the days before the great bull market of the 1920s when "old money" still really meant something; it was also that here, at home, was the evidence of Steinkraus's riding career, the cups and plates and trophies, the ribbons, the framed photographs of innumerable victories, the gifts, the worn and faded red Olympic hunt coat, the crops and bats and ivory-handled hunting whips, the famous photograph of Steinkraus and the queen (hung, no doubt from a wry sense of humor, in the downstairs lavatory, of all places), the rows of beautifully kept hand-made riding boots, creased and worn but still polished to a steady luster and kept in shape by wooden boot trees, made back in the days when the trees themselves, not just the boots, were carved to the exact shape of the rider's leg.

It isn't just that horses are an integral part of Steinkraus's life; it's that the competition side of it is never altogether absent from his thoughts—it comes to him as naturally as breathing. He quotes the great American expert on rifles, Townsend Whelan, who said, "Only accurate rifles are interesting," and points out that the same applies to horses—it's only the horse with potential to compete and to win, in whatever area of equestrian competition, that truly interests him. He walks me through the stable, which is huge, cavernous, elegant, a neo-Gothic relic with towers, turrets, carved stone, and a slate roof, from the days when there were probably forty horses or ponies on the estate, plus carriages of all kinds, and points to a photograph of a racehorse in the winner's circle, probably from the 1930s, to judge by the men's clothes and the women's fashions. "One of the Nasrullah line," he says, waving at it. "Winners, but they'll take your arm off if you offer them a cube of sugar." He shrugs, as if to say that it's a racehorse's job to win, not to prove that he's a nice guy, or a suitable substitute for a child's pony.

The aisles of the Steinkraus stable are wide, with great open cavernous tiled spaces where horses must once have been harnessed to carriages, or where lots of horses were prepared and kept waiting for a full complement of foxhunters to take out on a crisp autumn morning, and a beautifully detailed indoor ring. Everywhere there is a sense of space and classical design—the stable was in fact designed by the same architect who did the one at the U.S. Equestrian Team facility in Gladstone, New Jersey, which, with its rotunda, decorative brickwork, enormous stalls, and elaborate tiling is one of the most beautiful stables in the country, built in an age when the rich spent almost as much on their horses as they did on their yachts and their homes. Everything here is about competition; the faded, browning photographs on the walls of the office and tack room are of hunters and polo ponies, racehorses, steeplechasers, all ridden by people with the lean, wiry look of Steinkraus himself and surrounded by elegantly dressed people of wealth and substance. Outside there is a dressage ring, a space that was once a polo field, what appear to be miles of crushed-stone trails. It all seems like something out of another age, as indeed it is—the age when Long Island was still horse country and when the gentry foxhunted over land that is now covered in tract housing or whole new suburban towns. Steinkraus is aware of this, of course; he knows that the estate is an anachronism, but it's a glorious one, and when we drive through the guarded gateway that links the family's land with the mainland, it's like entering a separate country, with two-car garages instead of stables built in the style of a cathedral or a castle and fast food franchises and car washes instead of carefully preserved woods and croquet courts. It's perhaps in this context that Steinkraus remarks that three-day eventing, which used to be military, has been taken over by foxhunters who don't have any place to hunt. As usual he's dead right. Three-day eventing is the ideal sport for people who don't have the land, or the foxes, to fox-hunt anymore, giving the rider all the thrills and dangers of foxhunting without having to shock the neighbors when the hounds tear the fox to pieces, as Surtees would instantly have recognized had the sport existed in his day.

Steinkraus is not only a witty man; he has a rare ability to put things in perspective in one pithy phrase. He describes the ideal riding position for the horse in terms that go to the heart of the matter—"Get his hind end underneath him, and his head down—the back should be rounded, not hollow; then you've got him ready for anything." This is the wisdom of whole books and theories of riding in one graphic phrase, and I actually can *see* what he means, even feel it every time I ride a horse whose hind end *isn't* underneath him, whose back is stiff and hollow, and whose whole body is strung out. This isn't the way Steinkraus would want the horse to look, I tell myself, trying to put myself into the correct riding position from which it will all magically happen, as if the horse were saying to itself, "Hey, this guy knows what he's doing!" But knowing how to get the horse into the kind of position that Steinkraus talks about is hard, often beyond me, although most of his advice is practical, easy to understand, and to the point. He'd have made a great teacher—like Lao Tzu, every sentence stops you in your tracks and makes you think, which explains why in an emergency I didn't hesitate to call him with a problem, even years after he had left Simon & Schuster.

Most of my problems were commonplace ones, far removed from Steinkraus's level of expertise, as Margaret and Roxie began to push Hustle and Missouri a little higher in the local competitive world. I remember calling Steinkraus once to ask him about trailers when it became apparent that we were going to need one, and a vehicle of our own to tow it, and having him point out dryly that it made more sense to spend money on the best horse you could afford than on the fanciest trailer, and of course he was dead right about that too.

The competitive side of owning horses was increasingly beginning to take over our barn. It was not just that Margaret had an enormous drive to resume where she had left off in the days before her marriages, when she was still living in England, but Roxie too, who had spent a good part of her life preparing horses for other people to compete on, was eager to do some competing herself. So long as I was not obliged to compete myself, I saw no reason why this shouldn't be a good idea—after all, we had horses that could win, so why not let them? Time-consuming it might be, but it was not, in those days and at that level, a particularly expensive proposition, and a sizable number of people were doing it. Within a couple of miles of our front door there were at least two barns that put on regular horse shows, not to speak of the annual Pleasant Valley Horse Show, with its own grounds, down a dirt road off Rossway Road, just past the Four Brothers Pizzeria, a local Chinese take-out restaurant, and the car wash. There was Rhine Valley Farm, set back in the woods, not more than a twenty-minute drive away in the other direction, and of course beyond that Deb Dows's Southlands, perhaps half an hour away near Rhinebeck—there was no shortage of places to compete within easy distance, and still more if one crossed the Taconic Parkway and went out toward Millbrook, or farther on toward Connecticut. On a summer Saturday or Sunday morning the local roads were full of horse trailers on the move, from modest, rusty one-horse ones hitched behind the family station wagon to vast great gleaming rigs that carried four, six, or even twelve horses, and were towed by full-size trucks in the farm's colors.

It would be gilding the lily to claim that equine sports are, or ever have been, "democratic," but it was not just the gentry, or rich folks from the city up for the weekend, who were on the move at first light. It was just as likely to be the plumber's daughter, small girls with ponies, teenage daughters from families for whom keeping a horse represented a considerable financial sacrifice—they all competed too, usually accompanied by the whole family as a cheering section. Almost everybody in our town, and the surrounding countryside, had, or had had, a daughter who had been "crazy about horses" and had competed at local shows, most people acknowledged with a sigh, though there was a tendency for all this to end in high school, when some combination of boys, the ambition to go to college, and thoughts of a career put a stop to it. Still, you would never have guessed this looking out toward our road in midsummer, as rig after rig, trailer after trailer, went by, all of them on the way to compete somewhere. With all these horses on the move, it was of course unthinkable that our own should be simply standing at home chewing grass and swishing their tails after an early-morning trail ride, with the rest of the day to kill.

In hardly any time at all, it seemed to me, the horses were groomed to within an inch of their life and Margaret and Roxie were off, first in the borrowed trailer, then in a brand-new two-horse trailer, towed behind a Chevy Blazer, then in a western stock trailer, which Missouri seemed to like, and eventually—a meaningful moment—in a big, glossy Trail-et gooseneck trailer, with its own dressing room, the whole rig painted to match Margaret's new big Ford truck in the "farm colors" of blue and silver (originally green and red, then blue and red, but at some point Margaret had a change of heart, which resulted in the vehicles being painted in different colors from those of her helmet cover, back protector, and so forth, and making it difficult to decide what colors to paint things).

Quite apart from Bill Steinkraus, there was hardly anybody nearby, I was soon to discover, who did not have an opinion on the subject of horse shows and horse trailers, and they were all eager to share it. Hardly anybody who lived in or near our small town had not, at some point in their lives, had a daughter who was bitten by the horse bug. At Cady's, the local bar, at the post office, at both of the two feed stores (plus the Agway, a few miles away), at the hardware store, I could always be sure of running into guys who were an unfailing source of advice, solicited and unsolicited. Everybody had their own formula for how often (and how tightly) the wheel nuts should be torqued down, how much slack there should be in the safety chains, whether the ball should be greased or left ungreased, the ideal tire pressures, and how the trailer brakes should be adjusted "just so," so that they came on just before or just after those of the truck. Forget the safety chains: there was no slack at all in people's opinion; you did it their way, or lost your trailer on the highway. One of these days you would look back in your rearview mirror and see your trailer bouncing off the road and into a ditch with the horses in it, and that was that, "Good-bye was all she wrote," and then where were you? Up shit creek without a paddle, that's where, all the more so since it would be Margaret and Roxie sitting in the Blazer watching Missouri and Hustle vanish off the road. So buying a trailer was the easy part of the deal—keeping it in good shape, and above all keeping it safely attached, was a whole different story.

At the time it was the general opinion that this kind of thing was the business of menfolk—i.e., Richard and me—and I therefore considered it my duty to go along to Jim's Trailer Barn and look solemn and wise when Margaret bought her first trailer, and afterward I bruised many a finger and thumb as Richard showed me how to hitch and unhitch the trailer once we got it home. The hitch had to be hauled out of its storage place in the garage and laid out on the ground in pieces, then put together in the right order, the stabilizer bars and safety chains offering the maximum opportunity for sudden, painful injuries, not to speak of lower back problems, since some of the parts were unexpectedly heavy. I made a prudent purchase—a pair of thick leather work gloves from the local department store—but was happy to discover that since it was Margaret's trailer, she was determined to learn how to hitch and unhitch it herself with the minimum of help from anybody else. In any case, Richard was around to torque the wheel nuts, grease the wheel bearings, and adjust the brakes, and since Roxie would invariably be accompanying Margaret, he had a powerful incentive to make sure they didn't run into any kind of mechanical trouble.

Margaret's sturdy independence when it came to hitching up was matched by her determination to learn how to back her "rig" up without "jackknifing." Here I drew upon my experience in the Royal Air Force, and what it taught me was not to try. At one point as a recruit I had been selected to take a driving course, success in which depended on being able to back around a corner a giant "Scammell" lorry—in which one sat like the driver of an old London bus, about five feet above pavement level, with a huge, horizontal steering wheel, and a gearshift and clutch both of which required the strength of an Olympic weight lifter to move—while towing a large trailer. The main attraction to passing the course successfully was that you were then issued a dashing sleeveless leather jerkin to wear over your battle-dress blouse, and a license that enabled you to drive just about anything in the British armed forces short of a tank. After four attempts, however, during the course of which I got the rig hopelessly jackknifed, knocked over all the orange cones, and very nearly ran over the flight-sergeant instructor, he heaved himself up the metal steps of the cab until he could look me straight in the eye from under the polished visor of his cap and said,

"That's it, laddie, hand over the bloody keys—I've seen monkeys who could back up a lorry better than that."

Since nothing had happened in the ensuing twenty-five years to improve my skill in this area, I decided to leave it to Margaret. After all, if she was going to go to horse shows, she would have to learn how to back up into a tight space and get out of it. Very fortunately, she turned out to be an ace at it, and continues to be some twenty-four years later, but then as now, I limited myself to standing behind and to the side, making encouraging or frantic hand gestures like somebody on a carrier flight deck, which for the most part she ignores.

Still, I made my contribution. If there is one thing I *do* enjoy doing, it is buying motor vehicles of any kind, and the Blazer was no exception. I remember that when I explained to the salesman the purpose to which we intended to put the vehicle—towing a horse trailer—he fixed me with a glittering eye and said, "Let me just give you one phrase you'll always thank me for: *four-wheel drive!*" So indeed it proved. Parking areas at horse shows are usually chosen because they're unsuitable for outdoor rings, which is to say that they are seldom flat, and when it rains they are likely to become muddy bogs, in which vehicles sink to their hubcaps or beyond. The Blazer had what is now the old-fashioned kind of four-wheel drive, in which you had to squelch through the mud to lock the front hubs to engage it, but never mind—in bad weather you could count on it to get you out of the parking area and back to the road, as opposed to all those other competitors waiting for a neighboring farmer to appear with his tractor and a chain and haul them out at the end of a long day. To this day, my preparations for watching Margaret compete anywhere, even on the clearest and sunniest of days, include throwing a pair of knee-high rubber boots, a Barbour raincoat, and a hat in the trunk of my car. Experience has taught me that, if nothing else.

Indeed, my first memory of Margaret competing on Missouri was at a "hunter trial" on a windy, rainswept hill, not far from home, before I had figured out the importance of waterproof boots, with Roxie standing beside me in a state of high nervous anxiety, while Richard, in the parking area, coopted on his day off, went round the trailer checking tire pressures and worrying about the hitch. Every time Margaret approached a coop, a fence, or a wall—they were mostly low and "friendly" jumps—Roxie, who never swore, would mutter at Missouri, though he was a hundred yards or more away, "Come *on*, you little bugger!" though in fact he did just fine, ears forward, and perfectly happy, as was Margaret.

The weather was that curious mixture of sunny periods and light rain that is particularly English (and Irish), against a background of the leaves just beginning to turn, and it occurred to me that this was pretty good. Margaret was in her element—she already knew a lot of the riders and the horse people—and I almost immediately settled into the soon-to-become-familiar role of "the rider's husband," dressed, I thought, nattily for the occasion (*too* nattily, given the periods of rain) in beige corduroy trousers, a suede leather jacket, shooting glasses, and a Nikon with a telephoto lens. There is a lot to be said for the camera, starting with the fact that it gives one something to do, and the appearance of some serious purpose, as well as providing a good reason not to stand around holding the horse, or be asked to help groom it. Other husbands, I noticed, were carrying well-worn towels looped over their belts, or pails and brushes with hoof picks in the back pocket of their trousers, and it took only a minimum of intelligence to see that a camera was a better deal.

In later years, as Margaret became a more serious competitor, friends would often ask if they could come and watch her ride, but unless they were seasoned horse people we tried, not always successfully, to discourage them. Most of them, we soon discovered, had in mind some version of an elegant, well-catered tailgate picnic, the kind of scene you might see on the cover of one of the pricier outdoor-life mail-order catalogs, showing elegant people in their best tweeds and cashmeres, Labradors and shooting sticks at their feet, silk scarves and binoculars around their necks, gathered around a wickerwork English picnic basket from Asprey's of London, fitted with gold-monogrammed china, silverware, and linen, disgorging a lavish spread of pâtés, cold chicken, and salads to eat while sipping a nice dry white wine and watching a grand outdoor spectacle worthy of a Degas painting. Unfortunately, the reality was usually less glamorous. The competitor (in this case, Margaret) is usually far too keyed up and busy to be social, everybody around her is busy cleaning tack, or grooming the horse, or hauling buckets of water, and there are very few places where the pace of the competition isn't slow and tedious for the spectator, quite apart from often having to stand around ankle-deep in mud, or shiver under a piece of sodden canvas along with a couple of wet horses and their grooms, or swelter on a hot summer afternoon in a cloud of mosquitoes, while munching a candy bar or a greasy bacon cheeseburger from the food concession, served on a disintegrating paper plate and quaffed down with lukewarm tea from the breakfast thermos or Gatorade drunk straight from the bottle.

Of the many amateur forms of competition, it is hard to say which one is the most trying for the spectator. Typically, eventing consists of short periods of intense activity, much of it beyond the sight of the spectators, followed by hours of waiting around for the next ride, exposed to the elements. Show jumping, though easier to watch since it takes place in a ring, features an apparently endless succession of horse and riders taking exactly the same series of jumps at more or less the same speed, the only excitement coming when a horse "refuses" a jump or a rider falls off, and at the more modest level involves a lot of standing around in swirling clouds of thick, manure-scented dust. Watching somebody you love do this is one thing—there are endless reasons to support a spouse or a child with your presence—but for people who aren't interested in horses (or in love with one of the riders), the fascination wears off pretty quickly.

The thing about any kind of competition is that you've really got to be interested in *horses,* to start with. (Thoroughbred racing is a different matter, of course, since it involves betting, and, at a few of the more famous tracks, a certain degree of social excitement—the opportunity at least to rub shoulders with the rich and the locally famous—while rodeo involves a whole lot of things that aren't necessarily centered on horses at all, from bull riding and greased pig contests to live country and western music.) Still, in most forms of equine competition, the horse is the central object of attention, and people who care about horses can watch for hours just to catch a glimpse of that moment when the horse and the rider get it right—that moment when the will, the musculature, and the forward motion of horse and rider seem to combine in one glorious, fluid motion.

You have to have an eye for this sort of thing, as you do for most sports, and I can't say that I ever developed it to any meaningful degree. Of course it's easy enough to tell the riders who can't produce that kind of image, however fleeting, who get "left behind" (that is to say, the horse jumps before they're ready for it, so they're still sitting back in the saddle, with their weight in the wrong place), or who, unable to judge the distance or the right takeoff point, come forward too soon and look as if they're about to break their nose against the horse's neck, or those who just aren't ready for it when the horse puts in a bigger jump than they expected and look as if they're about to be launched in mid-air like a rocket, but it's less easy to recognize that elusive moment of perfection when everything comes together just right. Then too, appearances count—a handsome, energetic, graceful rider looks better on a horse than one who is overweight and physically graceless, even though, in the final analysis, all that matters objectively is whether the horse cleared all the fences within the prescribed time limit.

When it comes to dressage shows, of course, all this is true in spades. Those who are interested (and care about horses) can watch breathlessly as horse and rider trot around the ring, but to the uninitiated it's like watching grass grow. Again, it may be possible to tell when a horse and rider are hopelessly out of sync, but the moments that make more knowledgeable spectators ooh and aah are likely to be invisible; at any rate, they were, and for the most part remain, invisible to me.

The one thing I did learn about dressage competition is not to say, "Great ride!" until the rider, or somebody knowledgeable like Roxie Bacon, has said it first, since very often a remark like that merely prompts the reply that I must be blind, or wasn't paying attention. Only if the rider (Margaret in my case) is smiling when her time in the ring is over, or if the judge seems to be in good spirits and keeps her in front of the judge's booth for a good long time to talk about the ride, do I feel emboldened to offer a few words of congratulations; otherwise I have learned to wait for my cue. It is equally gauche (and unnecessary) to say anything like, "That looked really good, except for the moment when he stumbled just before breaking into a canter," since presumably the rider either already knows this (and knows what it will cost in additional points), or is still blissfully unaware of it and will find out soon enough when the judge hands her the score sheet. In riding, as in other sports, nobody is looking to hear bad news from husband, lover, or best friend.

In any event, Margaret and Roxie frequently went off to compete together, which occasionally put a certain strain on their relationship, since neither of them much liked to be beaten by the other. In the meantime Missouri (and to a lesser degree Hustle) began to develop a certain reputation for winning, enough to cause people to look admiringly at the horse as well as the rider. Missouri actually seemed to flourish as he picked up ribbons and trophies, and his walk took on a certain swagger. As with any other athlete, competition brought out the best in him, not just mentally, in the form of a real will to win, but physically, as he put on layer upon layer of hard, solid muscle. He did not take well to being ridden by a man (in fact, he didn't like men much at all, even when they were on foot), but he got on well with Margaret, though he retained a certain amount of high spirits and an independence of mind that made him a real "character" both in and out of the show ring. On a hot day, for example, he enjoyed a can of soda, preferably Pepsi or Dr Pepper, and he drank it straight from the can if you held it at the right angle for him—an unusual taste for a horse. (I even took a photograph of this and sent it to the company with the suggestion that it would make a very funny advertisement, but the idea was rejected, showing, perhaps that nobody in the canned beverage business had ever read *Black Beauty*, or gauged the feelings of young girls for horses.)

Photo by Michael Korda

It was not necessarily easy to get Roxie to take on the job of "coaching" Margaret, since she was also a competitor, and the rivalry between herself and Margaret, while kept under control, was nevertheless always there, but Roxie was in fact pretty good at coaching, with a keen eye and an exact sense of the right moment to shout out, "Now show him who's boss!" or "Don't let him get away with that!" the two key phrases of riding instruction.

Of course all good instruction leads somewhere. You don't work hard with a horse just to stay at the same level, doing the same thing. Without my consciously recognizing the fact, Margaret was developing her competitive instincts. The few ribbons became many, then many more, until Richard finally built an elegant Plexiglas-covered display case in the barn, which when it was first screwed into the wall, looked big enough to contain a full lifetime's worth of ribbons, but which in fact was soon filled to overflowing, so they began spreading into the house.

I remember going over to Southlands one afternoon to watch Margaret compete, early on in Missouri's rise to stardom. In those days, twenty years ago, Southlands was a hive of activity, a noisy, lively place, the center of horse activity around us, very much formed by the imprint of Deborah Dows's character, quirky personality, and family money, for it was not only her creation, a kind of equine Oz, but her life. It was in consequence on the one hand a very special place, but on the other, not unlike thousands of other horse establishments, eastern and western, all over the United States, where on a Saturday afternoon pretty much the same genial chaos reigned, whether involving, to take two extreme opposites, barrel racing or hunter-jumpers. At heart, after all, it doesn't matter whether the defining object is the Stetson or the velvet-covered hunting helmet, cowboy boots and jeans or English boots and riding breeches. The place is instantly identifiable—many paddocks, run-down barns and outbuildings, usually a big indoor riding ring, several dusty (or muddy) outdoor rings, horses, dogs, trucks, trailers, and children everywhere, the noise of an old-fashioned outdoor loudspeaker system booming out messages, announcements, and the current status of competitors (*"A clean round for Betsy Brinkley on Muffin. . . . Will the person who parked a silver Dodge truck in front of the entrance to the main barn move it before we have it towed? Is anybody missing a large dog with a red handkerchief around his neck instead of a collar?"*), the smell of frying hamburgers from the food concession mingling with that of horse dung, and everywhere the overwhelming presence of horses and ponies, patiently waiting in a trailer or tethered to one, being walked, rubbed down, washed, or groomed, shifting restlessly at all the commotion in their stalls, or grazing on any available patch of grass, often held by a child, right between the picnic tables and the secretary's tent.

Southlands, because of Deb Dows's all-embracing feeling for animals and generally laissez-faire way of running things, added to all this
geese, ducks, a seemingly unlimited number of cats, and goats, but this
too is not uncommon, on either side of the Mississippi—this kind of
horse place generally adds to the horses the equivalent of an animal
pound and a small petting zoo, as well as children, horse-struck young
girls, and leather-lunged instructors. It's all part of the ambience, along
with the star instructor and his coterie of admirers, the snooty young
rich kids on the expensive horses their parents have bought for them,
the hell-for-leather tomboy, riders on horses as rough and perfunctorily
groomed as themselves, and the older, more serious riders, easily distin-
guishable by their well-cut jackets and by their expression, which,
despite eyes shielded by the peak of their hunt caps and designer sunglasses, clearly signifies, "I mean business—keep out of my way!"

Southlands was all this, and more. Wealthy and odd, with a certain
resemblance to the late English character actress Margaret Rutherford,
Deb Dows ruled her extensive property overlooking the Hudson
River—a developer's dream—with an iron whim. Indeed, keeping
would-be developers at bay seemed to be one of her reasons for living.
Touring the place in a golf cart, accompanied by swarms of dogs, she
missed nothing—the small children on ponies, who had a certain
generic sameness to the casual eye, were instantly recognizable to her as
the daughters or granddaughters of women who had learned to ride on
her farm, while horses and dogs she knew on sight, although the names
and faces of adults on foot were apt to challenge her memory, unless
they were Southlands "regulars," for there were plenty of grown-ups
whose life revolved around Southlands almost as much as Deb's did,
who were there every day, and who depended on Southlands for a daily
"fix" of horsiness, as well as for much of their social life. The chief
instructor, manager, and social director of the place was a small, energetic man named John Craven, whose task was to keep the pot boiling,
to interpret Deb's wishes (for there was a certain aristocratic remoteness
to her), and insofar as possible keep her from being involved in the

messy details of running a place that catered to so many people's different fantasies.

This was a world very different from anything I had ever known before. In some ways, of course, it resembled a much larger version of Claremont Riding Academy, equally ramshackle but spread out over several hundred acres, though lacking the visible iron hand and undisguised profit motive of Mr. Novograd, and with a much larger cast of characters, many of whom spent their whole day here, rather than just an hour or two. Then too, here I was only a visitor, "Margaret's husband," and she herself did not keep a horse here but only came over to compete. Still, while it was recognizable as a riding establishment, in some aspects it also made one think of Disneyland, with a tendency toward fantasy that included costume parties on horseback for children and a general tendency for people to dress up and act out the role of the gentry. In fact, Deb Dows herself, with her vast hats, secured with a flowing, flimsy scarf, and her annual "pig roast" (a much coveted social occasion), was one of the last remaining examples of this class.

Although neither Margaret nor myself had any real need to take Deb seriously, she bore a certain resemblance to the Queen of Hearts in *Alice in Wonderland,* so that on the rare occasions when you glimpsed her at close range on her own turf, you were forever expecting her to shout "Off with his head!" or "Off with her head!" In fact she was mostly mild enough, with the slightly puzzled expression of somebody who was not only short-sighted but had been running the equivalent of a three-ring circus for over four decades. On closer acquaintance, I was to discover that she was amiable and shrewd. Certainly she was good, even in her old age, at frustrating the combined efforts of bankers, developers, real estate men, and state bureaucrats who plotted to build something, *anything,* on her land, or to build roads across it.

Whether Southlands (which she managed to convert into a "foundation" before her death, so as to continue frustrating developers and politicians even from beyond the grave) was profitable or not, a subject of intense speculation among the people who rode there, was irrelevant; it is unlikely that Deb Dows even bothered to think in those terms. What family money remained to her, she used to preserve and protect not only her land but the whole idea of a place that revolved around horses, and that catered to almost every level of rider.

The one thing you could say for Southlands is that it wasn't snooty, like some high-level jumper barn, in which everybody has a six-figure horse and their own professional trainer and coach. Small children on ponies and nervous beginners learning to walk, trot, and canter in the ring were as much a part of the Southlands scene as more serious competitive riders. A certain rough, homespun equality was maintained, perhaps because to a person of Deb's advanced age almost everybody seemed like a child, even middle-aged mothers of teenagers. In any case, wealth, social celebrity, and glamour counted for very little at Southlands (not that the last was in great supply). What did matter was enthusiasm and a certain clubbiness, which is to say the willingness to think of Southlands as the center of the world and to accept its many unwritten rules, most of them reflections of Deb Dows's old-fashioned view of herself as the lady of the manor and the last word on horsemanship.

Well, that's easy enough to forgive in somebody old enough to remember riding over to FDR's home in Hyde Park to tie up her pony and chat with the president, and who liked to recall that her father could remember FDR electioneering by driving a horse and trap over the dirt roads of Dutchess County to talk to the local farmers when "Franklin" was still an ambitious young man running for state office. He stood on the back of the trap in shirtsleeves, she said, to talk to the voters of nearby Staatsburg, while one of them held the horse and the rest listened politely, though when he had finished they explained, a little sheepishly, since he was a neighbor and like themselves, of Dutch descent, that they always voted Republican on principle.

Sometimes it occurred to me that Deb might be making these stories up, the way she made up the rules at Southlands, but one night, at her annual pig roast, she took me through her decaying and dilapidated mansion, with layers of dust everywhere and unpleasant animal drop-pings underfoot. From under piles of old papers, magazines, and dis-carded clothing she unearthed an old photo album, and lo and behold, there she was as a child, with the pony, standing up in the stirrups to chat with FDR on his porch. Delving more deeply into drawers, files, and suitcases, she emerged with an even older photograph, stained and brown, of the young FDR, tall, upright, and shirt-sleeved, wearing a straw boater, standing up in the back of a trap to address the stout burghers of Staatsburg, most of them bearded and wearing bib-overalls, with expressions that must have made it clear to him that even though he had been born not ten miles from here, he shouldn't count on his neighbors' votes to get him to the State Assembly in Albany.

It was here at Southlands that Margaret began to join the competi-tive world—at a low level, to be sure. Still, it was at Southlands, though she didn't board her horses there, that it became obvious she was in it to win, not just for the pleasure of spending the day sitting around with a lot of other horse people in boots and breeches. There was a firm set to her jaw, from the very beginning, that meant business, and in Missouri she had the kind of horse who could be relied on to give his all.

Of course a lot of people at the lower levels of competition are hardly in it to win at all—they ride because it gets them out of the house for the day or the weekend, or because they enjoy the social life that revolves around it, or because they like the way they look in the clothes. Of course competitive riding does offer all this: it's a perfect way of fill-ing up time, joining a group, even of becoming a "groupie" of sorts, since most riders tend to gravitate toward a single professional, who very often finds the right horse for them, trains it, and gives the rider instruction on it. In many cases the horse stays in the professional's barn, the owner goes over there every day for a lesson, and all the pro-fessional's "students" go to the same event or show together, *en famille*, as it were, with the horses packed into the professional's big rig, a kind of equine flying circus in which everything revolves around the profes-sional's experience, reputation, teaching skills, and charisma. Most of these instructors—but by no means all—are stars of varying degrees of brightness, top-flight riders who can get on the horse themselves and show how it ought to be done, while others prefer to coach "on the ground," and not a few of them are demanding, impatient, and push their pupils hard, some of them as hard as Prussian drillmasters. Still, there's a tremendous loyalty in these little groups of followers, and the competition scene would hardly survive without them. This is also one of the few ways in which it's possible to make any money at all in competitive riding, apart from the track, of course, and the upper reaches of big-time professional rodeo, where the top riders make the kind of money basketball professionals and stock car racers do, with their own private jets, and endorsements of every kind. A good professional sells his pupils horses, trades them back and forth when they don't work out, keeps them at his barn, charges their owners for board, lessons, and training, supports a blacksmith and a vet, and in general, rather like a certain kind of southern preacher, makes his living from his flock. At events and horse shows, the professional is also supposed to argue on behalf of his pupils, lodging a protest when they're scored unfairly, and in general looking after their interests. Needless to say, the job calls for the maximum of patience. Pupils who don't win, especially if they've been dumped headfirst into the water jump in front of a crowd of spectators, or eliminated in the show ring, aren't likely to be happy campers.

It was Margaret's good fortune that she had her own barn and, in the person of Roxie, somebody who could help her, so she wasn't obliged to become a member of a small group centered on a single figure. With her own barn, her own trailer (and the ability not only to drive it, but to back it up), and her own help, she was therefore, from the beginning, independent. Of course the disadvantage is that you're not part of a group, but some people need that, and some people—certainly the truly competitive ones—don't, and she didn't. Nevertheless, in that small world, you could hardly help getting to know people, even if you weren't part of their riding group. It is perhaps appropriate that at Southlands, the local center of horse activities, she became friendly with Ina Schoenberg, a tall, poised, beautiful blond who, like Margaret, was a city person in the process of putting down roots in the country and reverting to a childhood love of horses. Ina was married to a dashing, bearded, Saville Row–suited Wall Street *macher* and bon vivant named Freddy, and like Margaret seemed to have had enough of the party scene and the international good life.

Having settled down in a rather ramshackle farmhouse in nearby Milan, New York, Ina adopted John Craven of Southlands as her riding guru and friend but eventually moved her horses elsewhere, finally to the care of a Czech professional named Pavel, whose praises she repeated endlessly to Margaret, who was fairly skeptical, not from any lack of respect necessarily for Pavel himself, but because Ina was one of those people who tended to compete in a mild state of white-knuckle terror.

None of that is to say that Ina didn't look great on a horse, or couldn't ride at all, or was a danger to herself or others, but nothing anyone had so far done in the way of coaching seemed to increase her confidence much. This is not an uncommon phenomenon—Ina loved horses, loved the social life that came with owning a horse, could happily fill a day with horse care, and horse talk, and horse companionship, not to speak of visits to the barn and the tack shop and phone calls to the vet and the blacksmith, but the actual riding was in some ways the least of it, not nearly as important or fulfilling as feeling oneself to be a part of the horsey world, of *belonging.* A certain kind of person can spend the entire day, from early morning to late at night, in riding breeches, without once getting on a horse. Ina's house was decorated with the horse motif in every possible form—ceramic, glass, and bronze, as well as stuffed pillows and upholstery and horse prints— while her bathroom was almost impossible to use, what with the quantity of tack hung there to dry. The amount of time she spent during an average day actually riding a horse, however, was something of a mystery, even to her husband Freddy, who sometimes (he had that kind of sense of humor) claimed the whole thing was an elaborate illusion, behind which she led a secret life.

Though Margaret had talked about them, I first saw Ina, in, of all things, a "pairs" class, which she and Margaret had been preparing for over some time. They were both slender and blond, they both owned dapple-gray horses, and after a good deal of discussion over the telephone, much like teenagers trying to decide what to wear for school the next day, they decided to ride in matching beige riding breeches, black boots and hunt caps, white turtlenecks, and turquoise sweaters.

A pairs class is, by and large, about as dull as it gets for spectators of horse competition (though conformation classes may be slightly duller), since essentially all that happens is two people ride around the ring, stirrup to stirrup, at the walk, the trot, and the canter. Of course, as in dancing, a certain modest degree of synchronization is called for—at a walk, the horses should be moving at the same pace, not fighting to get ahead of each other; at the trot, the riders should try to synchronize their posting (the moment at which they rise out of the saddle); and at the canter, they should both be on the correct lead. The pinpoint accuracy of the Spanish Riding School is not called for (and is in any case very seldom delivered by amateurs), but the general impression should be harmonious and appealing, and if possible the two horses should be of similar size and color, and not look like the equine equivalent of Mutt and Jeff.

Southlands was full of this kind of thing, Pony Club stuff, much of it intended for children but also done by adults, some of it outright kids' stuff, like dressing up in homemade knights' costumes on horseback with wooden swords, with somebody on a pony to play the dragon. (Lest anybody think that this kind of thing is limited to the effete East Coast or to England, let me point out that on a holiday in Montana I was once persuaded to compete in "strip barrel racing," in which the entrants had to gallop across a field, take off all their clothes except their underwear and throw them in a pile, gallop back to the starting point and around a barrel, then back to the pile of clothes, dismount, grab a shirt, jeans, boots, and hat, dress, and gallop back again around the barrel, the winner being the first one to cross the finish line fully dressed, no matter how tight or loose the clothes he or she had grabbed. Obviously, there was no time to be fussy or to look through the pile for your own if you meant to win).

In any case, the fact that Margaret and Ina had dressed alike, and were both blond and striking—really almost like sisters from a distance—was the icing on the cake, and it would have been hard for the judge *not* to award them a ribbon. As they walked their horses around the ring, their faces were set in an identical firm, polite smile, as if to suggest that while they were taking this as seriously as could be, they were also having the time of their life—the precise expression preferred by judges in everything but those extreme horse sports, like the stadium and cross-country phases of three-day eventing, or serious jumping. In those classes, only a winning time and perfect performance—no refusals, no rails knocked down—gets you a ribbon, and a tortured expression, a look of terror, or a great splash of mud across your face doesn't count against you at all.

Photo by Michael Korda

Ina and Margaret.

Freddy Schoenberg, tall, bearded, and affable, arrived late, and realizing somehow that I was the other husband—first of all, there was not exactly a crowd of spectators, and then, who else would have been standing there with a motorized Nikon, taking pictures as if this were the Olympics?—introduced himself and said, "When does the action start?"

"This *is* the action," I explained.

He raised an eyebrow. "They just ride around the ring dressed the same?"

I nodded. "You've got it."

"*Goyishe nachas,*" he said, sotto voce.

Although this was to become the beginning of a great friendship between the four of us (we even went riding together on safari in Kenya, though Fred was anything but a horse person), it was also the moment at which Margaret decided that she and Missouri needed something more challenging. Hunter trials and hunter paces were a little tougher—you had to ride a cross-country course over fairly modest "natural" jumps, stone walls, coops, fences, and so forth, and Margaret won a lot of ribbons doing this, with Roxie beside her to form a pair team—but this kind of thing didn't really get the adrenaline going. She entered the local horse shows, in which there was plenty of jumping and a fairly serious standard of competition, but it still wasn't what she was looking for, partly because there was too much waiting around, partly because there wasn't any real sense of danger and excitement to jumping in the ring at this level; it was either something you and the horse could do, or it wasn't.

Eventing was something else again. Sometimes referred to as "three-day eventing" because at the highest levels the three different phases of the event are carried out over three days (at the lower levels, they are squeezed into one or two days), but properly referred to as "combined training" (the governing body of the sport in this country is the U.S. Eventing Association), eventing is unique in combining precision with excitement and a certain element of danger. First you do a formal dressage test, in which it is imperative to do well (it is almost impossible to recover from a bad dressage score in the next two phases), then a cross-country trial over natural and artificial obstacles (often including, at higher levels, a water jump complex, steep up and down banks, ditches, and so on), and finally stadium jumping, a complicated course in the proper sequence over numbered and usually challenging jumps in an outdoor ring, against the clock. Not too many people can contrive to get themselves hurt riding in the dressage phase, but the cross-country phase can be dangerous, and injuries are not infrequent (it was a fall in the cross-country phase of an event that led to Christopher Reeve's injury). Since the cross-country phase presents horse and rider with big, challenging jumps and obstacles and has to be ridden at a fixed, fairly rapid pace, it is a real test of horse and rider—of the horse's strength, boldness, speed, condition, and athletic ability, and of the rider's skill, judgment, courage, and absolute control over the horse. Margaret made no secret of the fact that eventing was what really interested her, not show jumping.

Although the time had not yet come when eventers would be obliged to wear back protectors (some with shoulder pads that made them look like football players), they already wore a more serious helmet, with a full chin strap that had to be fastened before they even mounted the horse, and on which they usually sported a decorative cover in their "racing colors." At the time, Margaret was in her red-and-green period, and I have an early photograph of her galloping Missouri toward a fence at an event in Millbrook, New York, dressed in white breeches and a green polo shirt, with a red and green helmet cover, her expression determined (no smiling for the judge here!), with Missouri the perfect picture of controlled power, caught by the Nikon in midstride. Both horse and rider are looking straight ahead, getting ready for the next obstacle, determined to get over it cleanly.

The Millbrook Hunt Horse Trials was a fairly big one, firmly fixed in my memory because there I first met Karen Forgione, a friend of Ina's, who had become a friend of Margaret's. I had been told that Karen was petite, beautiful, fiercely determined, and had wonderful horses on which she was thought by some to be "overmounted." A fashion designer, she lived with Michael, a somewhat mysterious real estate developer who was Fred Schoenberg's best friend. The horse world has a way of bringing very different people together, particularly the husbands of riders, who, because they have to show up and look interested at events, soon form a close bond, like people who have shared the same lifeboat together. Karen was an enthusiastic eventer who favored big, powerful, expensive horses. At Millbrook that day, I didn't see her until she appeared out of the woods, moving much faster than seemed to me wise. I heard somebody mention that it was Karen Forgione, so I raised my camera, thinking that she might like to have a photo of herself as a present from Margaret, and just as she came into sharp focus, rising over a huge, thick log, beyond which was a steep drop down toward the field in which I was standing, I saw her part company with the horse, land headfirst on the steep slope, and come to rest on her back more or less at my feet.

I let go of the camera and leaned over. She was lying absolutely still and rigid, looking straight up at me, eyes wide open, her head propped at an uncomfortable angle by the back of her helmet. At times like these, my RAF emergency medical training tends to come back in a rush, which would have surprised my instructors, most of whom complained that I wasn't paying attention and would regret it when the man next to me was wounded, or if I was wounded myself and had to apply a field dressing.

"Don't move her," I shouted dramatically—half a dozen spectators were running toward her. "She may have broken her back."

Karen's eyes looked up at me unflinchingly from under the visor of her helmet. It crossed my mind that she might be unconscious. Still, she might just be dazed, so I leaned over and in my best bedside manner said, "I'm going to take off your helmet very carefully, and try to slip something more comfortable under your neck—my sweater, rolled up, maybe."

"Don't touch me," she said firmly, through clenched teeth.

"You'd be a lot more comfortable without the helmet. . . . I'll be very careful not to move your neck, I promise. It *is* your neck you're worried about?"

She blinked. "It's my *hair* I'm worried about," she said. "Leave the helmet on."

It's impossible not to like somebody who is worried about her hair when she may have a broken back or neck, and it was the beginning of a friendship that endures to this day, some twenty years or more later.

The next time I was to see her on the event course was equally unforgettable. Unlike most eventers, Karen insisted on her comfort. It is, by and large, depending on the weather, either a muddy or a dusty sport, in which it's hard to stay clean, rather like warfare. Between the mess the horses make (not to speak of innumerable dogs), the way the trucks and trailers chew up the parking areas and the rough dirt roads, and the fact that you have to wade through marshes, mud puddles, and creeks to walk the course or get a view of the action, it is hardly surprising that it's not a dressy sport, nor that for most people a pair of rubber Wellington boots or galoshes is standard kit. What's more, events are usually held out in the open, a good long distance away from barns, houses, indoor riding rings, and of course indoor toilets. When it rains, you get wet. When there are insects, you get bitten. When you want to go to the bathroom, you slog through the mud to the nearest Porta-Potti, which will have been used by a hundred wet, muddy people before you, not always with a finicky care for the next person. All that is part of the charm of the sport, its rural roots showing through, and explains why Barbour rainwear and its Australian equivalent sell so well in tack shops around the country. Heavy canvas soaked in wax, rubber boots, and a waterproof hat are the way to go—even on the sunniest of days they should be kept within easy reach—and those in the know fill their pockets with Kleenex, tear-open packets of disposable wipes, Deep Woods Off!, and toilet paper.

Among many other things, the idea of Karen being muddy was unthinkable—somehow she always seemed well groomed and gleaming from head to foot. Like Margaret, she had her own truck, trailer, and groom, in her case a solidly built and muscular young woman named Pam, who not only did everything for Karen but looked as if, had a tire needed changing, she could have picked up the truck with one hand and loosened the wheel nuts with the other, without bothering with a jack. Pam was about as strong as they get, in a part of the country where young women who work around horses are likely to be built for strength in any case, and it seemed to be her mission in life to look after Karen, who was, to put it kindly, thought to be of a demanding nature. One rainy, soggy day I was squelching my way gingerly from the parking field, where I had left my car to sink in the mud, to where Margaret was about to compete in the dressage phase, when I saw Karen ahead of me, heading in the same direction with Pam. As usual, Karen was perfectly turned out—black hunt hat, spotless breeches, an immaculate rain slicker, without a trace of mud on it. In front of them, where the ground was low and sloping, the rain had cut a gully, like a small stream, and there was no way over it. For a moment I thought Karen might turn back—though that was not her nature—but she said something to Pam, who was walking beside, covering her with a big umbrella. Without breaking stride Pam furled the umbrella, picked Karen up, and carried her across, so she didn't get her boots wet and muddy. On the far side she put Karen down, opened the umbrella, and they continued on toward the dressage, as if nothing unusual had happened.

Pam took care of everything, allowing Karen to sit in her truck, warm, clean, and dry, and emerge only when it was time to get on her horse, unlike almost everybody else in the horse world. Other competitors—those who were of a disposition to notice—suffered from frizzy hair, sunburn, sweat, insect bites, stains from mud, manure, and horse liniment on their clothes and boots, broken fingernails and chapped hands from cleaning tack. Karen, even on the worst of days, managed to look like a photograph from Miller's catalog of riding clothes, improbably neat and clean. At the last minute, once Karen was mounted and ready to enter the ring or the start box, Pam would pull a cloth from the back pocket of her jeans to give Karen's boots a final rub, just in case a few specks of dust had settled on them. She was probably the only rider in the USCTA who was better groomed than her horses.

Though they seldom rode together—Ina was into hunter-jumpers, rather than eventing, while Karen did not always share Margaret's very English indifference toward the weather—the three became friends, and I tended to think of them (and refer to them) as the "Three Graces." Riding was what held them together, even during the long winter months when, in our part of the world, competition came to a halt while snowdrifts blocked the barn doors and buckets of water turned to ice as if all nature was a giant freezer. In those early years (was our blood thicker?) Margaret and I would bundle up in heavy down-filled clothing head to foot, Roxie would smear Crisco into the horse's hooves with a rubber kitchen spatula to prevent them "balling up" (forming balls of ice in their feet that would make them slip or slide), and we would go cantering down the side of our rural road the morning after a heavy snowstorm, the horses snorting as their hooves threw up long plumes of snow, floundering through heavy drifts, while the howling wind brought the wind-chill factor down to the sub-teens.

Well, we *were* younger then, and in those days there were fewer snowmobiles, less traffic in general, and the highway department's big orange snowplows didn't get around to plowing and sanding our road in any hurry. When you got off your horse after a ride, you were unable to move for a few moments, between the sheer bulk of your clothing and the frostbite in your hands and feet, while the horses had icicles forming at the nose and mouth, their coats covered in snow as fine as powdered sugar, steaming as they waited to be dried and groomed.

Then, in the evenings, on the weekends, fingers still stiff from holding the reins, we would meet at Ina and Freddy's house for dinner, and while Freddy, Michael, and I talked about the stock market, or exercise, Margaret and Karen, dressed to kill, would sit on the sofa with Ina and talk about the events and shows to come, once the snow melted and the ground began to soften, talk doubtless going on from Virginia to the Canadian border, wherever serious riders gathered.

The most serious riders—those who were rich enough, anyway— moved south with their horses to warmer climates during the winter months, to Southern Pines in North Carolina or to Ocala or Wellington in Florida, outside West Palm Beach, and continued to ride and event in places where the ground didn't turn as hard as concrete, and ice or snow drifts weren't a problem. In northern New York State and New England, however, you dressed yourself in layers of stuff from the Eddie Bauer or the L. L. Bean catalog and went on riding, looking like a Himalayan mountain climber, with nothing showing except your eyes and the tip of your nose, the latter glowing bright red like the taillight of a car. A favorite Christmas present was a box of chemical foot warmers or hand warmers, little foil packets that you shook hard, like a cocktail shaker, and placed in your boots and gloves, and which produced a momentary scalding warmth, which, as it ebbed, made your toes and fingers feel colder than ever.

This was the period in which the USCTA *Omnibus*—which lists in meticulous detail the events for the next season—was consulted, along with the atlas of road maps of the fifty states, over cocktails, dinners, and after-dinner drinks, while the wind shook the storm windows and the big snowplows roared in the distance. Was Maryland too far to go, and could one get there, compete, and get back in time to recover and make it up to Woodstock, Vermont, for the Green Mountain Horse Association summer event? What was the most direct route down to Gladstone, New Jersey, or up to King Oak, Massachusetts? Was Canada simply too far, or was that just an illusion? How long would it take to drive through the Delaware Gap to an event in rural Pennsylvania? These questions posed no difficulty for Michael, Freddy, or me— we were all three enthusiastic drivers and motorcyclists, and would have gone just about anywhere for the sheer pleasure of getting there. And after all, *we* wouldn't be the ones traveling with a truck, a trailer, one or two horses, a trainer, and a groom, or having to compete. In any event, in mid-February, with the snow deep on the ground outside, all these plans sounded good to us, and events and shows at great distance and in the most inaccessible of places—towns where you need to get out a magnifying glass to search for them on the map in a spider's web of secondary roads, and where the nearest motel appears to be miles away from the competition site or the stabling—sounded just fine too.

In the end, it was Margaret who would travel the farthest when spring, finally, came. Having spent most of her adult life staying at places like the Connaught Hotel in London, or the Plaza Athénée in Paris, or the Beverly-Wilshire Hotel in Los Angeles, she descended without any apparent regrets or difficulty to Howard Johnson motels, where the deciding factor was how long it took to drive to where the horse was stabled for the nightly barn check, and how far away the nearest diner was. Having our own barn and keeping our horses at home had opened out a whole world of local trails and backwoods to us that we would never have seen, or even suspected the existence of, from the road. Traveling to compete would very shortly make us familiar with the back roads and byways of countless states, as Margaret cast her net wider and wider for places where she and Missouri could compete.

I had bought the Blazer and the horse trailer with no real expectation that they would ever be used except to go to local horse shows and hunter paces, but to my surprise they were in constant use, while Margaret and Roxie developed a whole technique of packing; everything that the horse might possibly need had to go with him, and be quickly reachable. This part of horse competition I recognized easily too, from my military service experience. Things had to be packed so they could be unpacked in the right order—Roxie (and Leslie, who came after her) had a whole system for packing, which exactly resembled that of the

Leslie at work at an event—G.M.H.A., Woodstock, Vermont.

supply sergeant in every unit of a first-class army, and her own mental checklist that was apparently infallible. It occurred to me often, as I watched the proceedings, how very different this sport was from most. All a golfer or a tennis player has to remember is her clubs or racket, whereas transporting a horse means carrying along enough equipment to fill the back of a large vehicle, the absence of any item of which might prove critical. Bandages, towels, sweat sheets, medications, leg wrappings, tail wrappings, hay bags, bags of shavings, liniments, water in big plastic jerry cans, boxes full of grooming stuff, horse treats—the horse traveled with as much luggage as a movie star. The rider needed almost as much: boots, spurs, black hunt coat, helmet, the right kind of gloves, stock and stock pin, rain gear, overalls (so as not to get dirty while working on the horse), regulation back protector, and, in Margaret's case, good luck charms (a gold sovereign, a silver dollar, four-leaf clovers worn in the socks). The dressage phase required the most formal clothes, of course, while the cross-country phase required the equine equivalent of combat gear, and the stadium jumping something in between. (The cross-country phase was very shortly to be revolutionized, in appearance at any rate, by the introduction of form-fitting one-piece stretch suits, rather like those worn by Olympic skiers and skaters, in bright colors and complicated designs, a change that naturally favored the better-looking female riders. Color coordination—truck, trailer, tack trunk, saddle pads, and leg bandages, the rider's cross-country outfit, helmet cover and back protector, the horse's headband, and almost anything else you could think of or find in the major riding catalogs all in one's own colors—became de rigueur for those who wanted to look their best, even, in a few year's time, down to the polish women riders used on their fingernails.)

These heady days were in front of us, way back when Margaret and Missouri started out on the event trail, and for some time the differences between eventing and other equestrian sports remained unclear to me, except that even I could tell eventing was more consuming and dangerous than anything else except steeplechasing, and amounted to more than the sum of its parts. The fact that you and your horse could turn in a good (i.e. low) dressage score was all very well, but then you had to change clothes and ride at high speed over a cross-country course that required physical strength, quick reflexes, and raw courage, and then change again and put in a faultless round of stadium jumping. Plenty of riders (and plenty of horses) are good at *one* of these things, but eventing requires you to be good at all three of them, very often on the same day, and despite whatever the climate might throw in your way. A fractional mistake in dressage might start your day off with a poor score; a slight hesitation or going a fraction of a second too slow or too fast might drop you even further, to the point where even the most perfect stadium round can't pull you up into the top couple of places at the end of the day. To win reliably, you really have to ride a dressage test that brings smiles from the judge (and dressage judges don't smile easily), then throw your heart over every jump in the cross-country and have a fast, flawless, successful ride. Most of the better riders can put in a faultless round of stadium jumping, so you really have to be in first place by the time you get into the jumping ring if you want to win, or if you are in second place, hope that the rider ahead of you "pulls a rail." That, for Margaret, meant that the part of it that interested her least—dressage—was something she had to become good at if she wanted to win blue ribbons and silver trophies. There was no point in being good at the high-adrenaline part of eventing, riding hell-for-leather cross-country over all sorts of natural and unnatural obstacles against the clock, if you had already put in a lousy dressage test.

Fortunately, dressage was something of a specialty for Roxie, who had, after all, worked for Janet Black and for Katy Boyer, for both of whom dressage was a religion, the only real reason to be on a horse at all. Missouri, as it turned out, had something of a gift for dressage himself—you couldn't exactly say he *enjoyed* it, like cross-country, but insofar as horses have expressions, you could almost see him screwing up his face in concentration, while he worked to get his end of things right, with Roxie standing in the center of the ring shouting things like "Feel your seat bones!" or "Make him get his hind end under him!"—instructions that make no sense to people who don't do dressage but, to a rider who knows what she is doing, make instant sense, however hard they may be to put into practice on the move. The object, to quote the endlessly quotable Fillis, is "the complete equilibrium of the animal in all his movements. . . . The loins, hind quarters and hocks are flexible, the hocks stoutly press the mass forward, the shoulders are free and movable, the neck is high and the jaw readily obeys the feeling of the rider's hands on the reins, and all the parts of the horse being in action and equally enterprising, combine to form an energetic, harmonious and light whole." Fillis being Fillis, he goes on to demand from the rider "the delicate and constant play of the fingers," which, he points out helpfully, should be "compared to the fingering of a piano as regard delicacy and speed."

In other words, the rider must be firmly, gracefully seated, with a straight back and neck, as she pushes the horse forward with invisible pressure from the legs and the seat bones with quiet hands, and by a deft combination of weight and pressure move the horse through a complex repertoire of classical movements at the correct pace. The horse has not only to get every step of the dressage test right but to show a willing, eager spirit, instant obedience, athletic flexibility (no evidence of stiffness to one side or the other), and, for the few minutes that the dressage test takes, present itself in exactly the "frame" the judge expects, collected, showing no evidence of constraint, each muscle working harmoniously. This is a tall order. Some horses never get it right, and many riders—indeed most riders—don't have either the patience or the gift for it. It is slow, hard work, the coming together of a great many small details, and very hard, if not impossible, to get it right without an instructor. Then, too, it seems the very opposite of just what a lot of people take up riding for in the first place. It isn't freedom, or the kind of riding you see in *National Velvet;* it's a painstaking physical art form, overseen by gimlet-eyed judges looking for a kind of perfection in motion that is alien to most people in the twenty-first century, and whose standards are every bit as idiosyncratic and cranky as those of figure-skating judges.

Of course respect for perfectionism on horseback is not limited to the East Coast. Many years ago I made a trip to visit Larry McMurtry at his home in Archer City, Texas, to attend the Archer City Rodeo. As McMurtry's readers know, the Pulitzer Prize–winning author of *Lonesome Dove* is, among other things, more or less the poet laureate of rodeo, if such a role existed. *Moving On* is perhaps the only major American rodeo novel, at least in the sense that a substantial part of its almost 800 pages takes place in and around the rodeo world, and many of the characters are rodeo people, or drawn to the rodeo, or, in the case of its heroine, Patsy, become repelled by the rodeo world. Rodeo, in short, plays the same central role in *Moving On* as whaling does in *Moby-Dick.*

Since McMurtry and I were originally drawn together by a mutual interest in rodeo (everybody else in the New York book publishing world read the manuscript and complained that there was too much about rodeo in it, while I felt there could have been more), I was eager to take advantage of his invitation, particularly since small-town rodeo is a very different thing from big-time professional rodeo. Hardly any town in West Texas is too small to have its own high-school football team and its own annual rodeo, and many of the football players do double-duty steer wrestling in the rodeo, an event for which football playing is pretty good training.

McMurtry is knowledgeable about rodeo, but not exactly an enthusiast. Coming from a family of ranchers, he was naturally brought up as one—traces of that experience can be found in *Leaving Cheyenne; Horseman, Pass By,* and much of his work—but early on he decided that reading interested him more than riding, and books more than cows or horses, and once he had made his escape from ranch to college, he did not look back on his years in the saddle with any nostalgia, however well he eventually came to write about cowboys past and present. Although after living in Houston, Washington, D.C., Los Angeles, and Tucson he would eventually gravitate back to Archer City and his parents' ranch house, he did not give the impression of being a man who cared whether he ever saw a cow or a horse in the flesh again, and occasionally he expressed a mild distaste for both. He had seen enough of horses as a boy to last him a lifetime, he would say, but he nevertheless retained an affection for small-town rodeo and tried never to miss the one in Archer City, at the beginning of June.

We prepared for our night at the rodeo with a family picnic in the dusty park outside the rodeo ring—McMurtry has a large family, many of whom resemble characters in his novels. All around us people were cooking on grills and open fires. Our own picnic featured ribs, hamburgers, several different kinds of deer sausage cooked over an open fire, and bowls of coleslaw and potato salad—the kind of food that sticks to the ribs. Behind us, under the lights of what looked like a basketball court, a few sub-teenagers were dancing in the purple twilight to country music, while all around us small children ran, tripped, dropped their ice-cream cones, and wailed. Ahead of us, beyond a few stunted cedars and mesquite bushes, the big lights of the rodeo ring were coming on, bringing with them clouds of insects. Among the things that McMurtry had suggested bringing to the rodeo was my own supply of Off!, and he was not wrong.

The air was richly scented with popcorn, barbeque, and horse and cow manure, and it was astonishing how many horses were present, tied to the stunted trees or to trailers. The horse has long since retreated from urban life in the East, but in the West it still remains a visible part of small town and city life. I had, in fact, just come from Amarillo, where I had given a speech to the managers of Hasting's, a large southwestern book and record chain, and I was surprised to discover that at breakfast time half the vehicles parked outside fast-food places and diners seemed to consist of pickup trucks towing an open trailer with a horse standing in it, already saddled and bridled, ready to ride.

There's something odd, to an easterner, about the sight of a whole bunch of horses chewing away at their hay in the parking lot of a Burger King, but in Amarillo it didn't raise an eyebrow, and on rodeo night in Archer City (compared to which Amarillo might as well be Paris) the horse was omnipresent, dozing, chewing on hay, flicking at insects with its tail, and of course producing manure and piss while peacefully waiting for the action to begin. We weaved our way between them in the dark to take our seats on the bleachers.

Almost everybody who mattered apparently aimed to make an appearance on horseback during the course of the evening—the town fathers, the local Kiwanis and Rotarians, groups of all sorts gathered to ride around the ring, mostly solid, middle-aged, overweight men (mounted on equally solid, overweight horses) wearing a Stetson, jeans, and a white western shirt with pearl snaps, and looking ever so slightly uncomfortable and out of place in the saddle, which they had long since given up for the adjustable leather contour seats of a Cadillac. The girls who were to do the barrel racing rode around the ring, a good deal more confident in the saddle than their fathers, and a parade finally formed behind a tall man on a palomino carrying the Stars and Stripes and a pretty girl in sequins with the state flag of Texas, while the loudspeakers blared out both anthems.

For those who don't know rodeo, a lot of it seems closer in spirit to a state fair than to anything they would recognize as an equestrian event, which is partly because most rodeo events—except perhaps for barrel racing—derive from what working cowboys used to do for a living, and partly because rodeo has deep rural roots. We sat through a number of events involving steers and cowboys, a clown act, any amount of rural humor and commentary, a free-for-all in which kids ran and tumbled all over the ring trying to catch a greased piglet. All this was interesting, though not riveting, and the spectators reflected that—they were noisy, cheerful, shouting to friends and to people they knew in the ring, urging the kids on to catch the piglet, busy eating and drinking sodas.

Then, all of a sudden, during a pause between events, a boy of about twelve rode out into the ring on a nice-looking palomino pony. There was nothing special about him—he wore jeans, a Stetson, and a checked western shirt, and his face was set in a serious expression. First he walked around the ring, while the noise and the hubbub went on and hardly anybody paid him any notice; then he picked up a trot, and I started to look at him more closely. His back was straight, his legs motionless, the seat of his jeans appeared to be glued to his saddle, and his horse was perfectly "collected," neck high, head tucked in, mouthing the bit nicely, his legs well under him. He was "in the frame," as dressage teachers describe it, and James Fillis, had he been alive and present in Archer City, would have been, I thought, mighty pleased. Here was "complete equilibrium," just as he had defined it, the "energetic, harmonious and light whole" he had sought for all his life, not to speak of fingers holding the reins as dexterous as those of the finest concert pianist.

The boy kept trotting around the ring, so perfectly seated on his horse that he might have passed for an adolescent centaur, while gradually, but very noticeably, the noise level among the spectators decreased, then fell away to silence as the boy picked up a canter. The canter was slow, collected, perfect, as good as anything you might see in the Spanish Riding School in Vienna, and by now the spectators were completely absorbed. Then a largish man rode out into the arena on a dapple-gray quarter horse—the spitting image of Missouri, it occurred to me—and joined the boy, riding stirrup to stirrup with him. It was obvious without being told that he was the boy's father—their features were identical, and he rode with the same easy perfection, making it look completely effortless.

By now you could have heard a pin drop—there wasn't a sound except for the thud of the horse's hooves and their steady breathing. Neither father nor son *did* anything fancy or unusual, a couple of figure eights with a perfectly timed change of lead, but they didn't *need* to do anything fancy; they were simply demonstrating perfection. This was an audience that still had, for the most part, ranching roots. The men might be working in the oil industry now, or driving a semi, or a bulldozer, or keeping a store; most of them probably hadn't been on a horse in years, perhaps not since they were kids themselves, but they were close enough to the past to recognize and respect great horsemanship when they saw it, and to appreciate it the way you might appreciate any other skill displayed perfectly. Many of them probably had fathers, or grandfathers, or uncles, maybe some still living, who had spent their working lives with horses, and for whom a man's seat in the saddle mattered almost more than anything else in defining his place in society, much as it had when Cervantes lived in Spain.

They watched, smoking, or chewing tobacco or gum, transfixed, as if the spectacle before them was somehow ennobling, giving them, in their turn, merely by looking at it and recognizing it for what it was, more dignity than they would ever get on the seat of a bulldozer. Something was happening out there in the ring that was no longer part of their lives and never would be, but which had been, until recently, part of everyone's life around here, and under the bright, buzzing lights, hissing and popping as insects brushed against them and burst into flame, one brief and unmistakable moment was almost religious, a feeling like that of the crowds solemnly watching a procession of *penintentes* in New Mexico, not so far from here, when they carried their huge crucifixes and relics of saints up the steep hills toward Taos. These people, here in Archer City, would not necessarily be impressed by the Spanish Riding School, with its crystal chandeliers and nineteenth-century Habsburg uniforms, still less by the National Horse Show in Madison Square Garden, with most of the audience in dinner jackets or evening gowns and the riders in their red coats and black velvet hats, but unlike most of the audiences at both those events, they knew the real thing when they saw it, and by their silence they paid homage to it.

When father and son slowed their horses to a walk with nothing more than an almost imperceptible shift of their weight in the saddle, and moved out of the ring into the darkness, there was no applause—just a long collective sigh. Then the announcer cleared his throat, the music came back on, and the rodeo resumed at its normal frenetic, noisy pace, except for a few misty-eyed old men, who were, no doubt, looking at their own past, when you rode into Archer City sitting tall in the saddle, instead of driving into town in a car.

I found out later that father and son were from a family famous around these parts for their horsemanship. The father rode "pickup" at rodeos, riding in close to the bull to pick up a bull rider who had been thrown and was in trouble, a much admired kind of horsemanship requiring skill, courage, and a perfectly trained horse—a single moment of hesitation from horse or rider could get two people killed, not just one. Horses and horsemanship were in their blood, and from generation to generation they apparently produced a succession of flawless riders. Their riding together wasn't an "event," or a planned part of the rodeo, it had been spontaneous, just something the boy felt like doing in the interval between two events, and his father had ridden out to join him, one of those natural "father-son" moments that you can't fake, or plan for.

Doing something so perfectly that it looks simple is no easy task, particularly when it has to be done in concert with a horse, who doesn't get anything out of it—no ego boost, at any rate. Ring work isn't dangerous or thrilling; there is none of the adrenaline reward that usually accompanies athletic contests, even for horses—you just have to do something exacting and difficult right, and make it look as easy as eating pie. Out of Margaret's ambition to succeed at the sport, and Missouri's natural intelligence and physical potential, without either one of them becoming a "dressage freak," they persevered well enough to go on to a long and successful eventing record over many years, and photographs record the way in which Missouri put on the muscle and the weight to become a spectacularly successful all-round competitor, a horse to which attention must be—and was—paid.

Apart from a taste for Pepsi-Cola and a dislike of men, he developed a strong and recognizable character as he went on from win to win on the northeastern eventing circuit. Although good-tempered, he was feisty and insisted on being treated as the number-one horse in the barn. He knew his place as the firstcomer, and insisted that other horses recognize it. Out on a ride he insisted on being in the lead—he had a precise sense of everybody's place in the herd, and of his prerogatives—and disliked being crowded. He wasn't a kicker, but he was capable of a quick, neatly administered bite when there was any dispute about seniority, and very good at maneuvering himself so as to block off other horses if they tried to pass him. In certain places on our own land, he felt—very strongly—that he had attained the right to stop and graze grass, and nothing in the whole world would move him past those places when he was out on a ride. There didn't seem, to the human eye, to be anything different about the grass in Missouri's favorite spots, but to him there clearly *was* a difference, and he wasn't about to be cheated of a few mouthfuls of it. As with most western-born and -bred horses, snow and ice didn't stop him. He was terrific at scraping the snow and ice away with his front hooves to reach a favorite spot, while the other horses stared goggle-eyed in amazement, without apparently feeling inclined to try it themselves. There was something clownish about him, a sense that he was having fun, or perhaps joining in the fun, rather more like a dog than a horse. At the sight of Margaret approaching at any time of the day or night, he would amble across to meet her for the expected treat, not in a slavish way but rather like one old friend greeting another and getting his deserved due. On and on he went, winning blue ribbons at more and more difficult events, without showing any strain, as if he was determined to make it look easy. He left horses that had cost many, many times what Margaret had paid for him in his dust, and time after time he brought her in safely from a challenging cross-country course and kicked up his heels at the end of the event as he did his victory gallop around the ring, a blue ribbon fluttering from his bridle, while Margaret held aloft a silver plate or a tray or whatever. He was that rarest of horses, at once safe and bold—Margaret could ride him bareback with a halter and a lead rope out to the fields to graze, or down to the stream to water (like most horses, he was fussy about his water), but when you got him tacked up to compete, he was all there for you, absolutely determined to win. I seldom rode him, first of all because he was Margaret's horse, and secondly because, docile as he was for her, he was jealously possessive of her, and only too happy to throw me if he could. He saw me, I think, as a rival for her affections, and this naturally affected our relations. Anyway, I had a horse of my own, Zapata, which I bought to replace poor Hustle, so there was seldom an occasion or a need for me to ride Missouri, which suited both of us just fine. Then too, since he was Margaret's competition horse, I didn't want to run the risk of bringing him home lame, or even with a shoe missing.

Missouri went on to acquire modest fame as he and Margaret began to be regular winners—his picture appeared in the *Poughkeepsie Journal* and even *People* magazine, trotting on the lawn in front of the house for our photographer friend Stanley Tretick. He gave the distinct impression that he knew he was a star, and that he was more comfortable around people than with other horses. Some horses are like that—they take so naturally to people that it almost seems as if they think they're a person, which tends to make them impatient with other horses. Missouri had that quality—as if only a rude accident of fate kept him out in the fields at the end of the day, or in the barn, instead of sitting in the house by the fire with Margaret—and it did not necessarily endear him to the other horses, nor them to him.

Eventually, as the years went by and Missouri racked up win after win, he began to show signs of aging, until the day when we were forced to retire him from his competitive career and let him resume the more leisurely one of pleasure riding, out on the trails. Today, at twenty-nine—old age for a horse—he still looks remarkably fit. Like most dapple-gray horses, he has turned pure white with time, and he has stiffened up a lot—in fact, like a lot of old men, he is lame, stiff, cranky, and impatient with youngsters—but he can still be ridden, and when we go out riding, he likes to tag along with us, like a large dog.

At first, for a long time, Margaret "ponyed" him, holding onto a lead rope attached to his halter as she rode, but gradually it became apparent that this wasn't necessary—Missouri is happy to come along, doesn't stray far, and very often pushes his way past to get in the lead. (Margaret carries a coiled rope attached to her saddle, just as a precaution, but it has never proved to be necessary.) What is more, when we go on longer rides and Missouri is in the lead, he remembers trails we have forgotten. On trails we stopped using years ago and that are now overgrown and half-blocked with fallen trees or newly built homes, Missouri can navigate around the obstacles and find his way down deer trails and pathways that he hasn't seen in ten or fifteen years, ever since he gave up trail riding for eventing, and that we haven't seen either, as we began to ride shorter distances.

How does he remember, and why does it matter to him? Well, as we all know, horses have a terrific memory, and a firm sense of geography—they can always find their way home, and if they've been down a trail once, it's imprinted on their memory forever. *We* may not be able to remember how we used to get from the far side of our neighbor Cal Smith's property through Mr. Litt's woods, and eventually back to our barn. What with one thing and another, it's been a while since we've done it, and a lot has changed (among other things, the hunt doesn't look after these trails anymore). But Missouri, ranging ahead of us on his own, turns left into the woods and plunges into the untrimmed vegetation and second growth without a moment's hesitation, knowing the old hunt trail exactly, even though it's invisible to the naked eye, stopping every once in a while to look back at us with surprise and impatience, as if he were saying, "What's the matter with you guys? Can't you see this is the way?"

Sometimes he gallops ahead a little too exuberantly, and ends up having to take a rest of a day or two on "bute" (the anti-inflammatory phenylbutazone, the horse aspirin) for whatever combination of arthritis, rheumatism, and the simple aches and pains of old age that afflict him when he overdoes things, but he's not usually happy at being left behind. He's like those old men who keep going only by sticking to what they've always done, and for whom a brisk daily walk is part of what keeps them alive—put them in a Florida "retirement community" to rest and play shuffleboard, and they'd be dead within a few weeks. The same is true for Missouri. Given a routine, a sense of purpose, and a good helping of physical exercise, he seems likely to go on forever. The list of supplements in his feed is awesome, like reading a veterinary medicine catalog, but what keeps him going isn't medical, it's getting on with his job of accompanying Margaret on her rides.

Admittedly, she's usually on another horse's back these days, but that's all right. Missouri doesn't necessarily want to be *ridden;* he just wants to be there, in charge, and share in whatever the excitement of the day is, whether it's Star's foolish (and typically thoroughbred) tendency to spook at things Missouri would walk right by without hesitation—deer, a section of new fencing, a piece of tarpaulin flapping in the wind—or Margaret's taking Dundee, her young Irish horse, over the jumps, which Missouri watches from a certain distance with calm,

unruffled professional judgment (been there, done that!), between crop-
ping mouthfuls of grass. Age, he seems to feel, has its privileges, and one
of them is watching the youngsters put in the hard work, and stopping
for a bite to eat whenever he feels like it. True, there's a certain brightness in his eyes that seems to suggest he's thinking, "Put a saddle on me,
and *I'll* show you how it's done!" After all, who can count the number of
blue ribbons he's won, and victory gallops he's led? But in a deeper
sense, he's content.

On the way home he stops at certain spots to drink—only these will
do; he has an exact routine, here, at this stream, here, at this water
feeder, and it all has to be done in the right sequence. Does the water
taste different, is it a matter of connoisseurship, or is it the places that
matter to him, the fact that right here, where the overflow from Cal
Smith's pond—a quiet, placid place, in the lee of several big hills and
home to a small and noisy family of wild ducks and occasionally a few
Canada geese seeking peace and quiet from the big flock—runs across a
bed of stones and gravel, has always been one of his favorite spots for a
drink? Even in the days of his youth, when Cal Smith first said it was
fine by him if we rode on his land, you couldn't get Missouri past this
place without giving him a chance to drop his head and take a few sips
of water, and even then he always managed to secure his place on the
left, upstream, so he wasn't drinking water that had been muddied by
the other horses' hooves but got it fresh and clean—a prerogative that
he defends today with just as much determination, pushing his way in to
where he wants to be, where he *belongs*, in his view, by right. He can't
kick—he was never much of a kicker, actually—because his hocks are
too stiff, but he humps his back and gives a kind of make-belief kick
when he has to, just to put the other horses in their places, and show
them who is boss. The herd only has one leader, and Missouri, old as he
is, has no doubts about who that should be.

These days his coat is thick and curly, not just because of the cold but
one of the symptoms of Cushing's disease, a hormonal imbalance that
can lead a horse to founder, a painful ailment of the hooves for which

there is usually no happy outcome, but he is kept clipped so he doesn't get overheated when he's out on one of his extended walkabouts.

When we approach the roads, people stare at us—two people out riding, with a white horse beside or ahead of them, going without a saddle, a rider, or a lead rope—wondering what's going on, and perhaps afraid that Missouri will take it into his head to gallop across the road and cause a ghastly accident, or be killed messily by a speeding truck. No doubt some of them think us irresponsible, but the fact is that Missouri is as cautious as they come—he stays away from the road, he lets the other horses go first when there is any possibility of danger, he keeps his eyes on the ground so as not to stumble on a half-hidden rock or put a hoof into an animal's hole, and he slows to a walk at the sight of farm machinery, not afraid, but not about to take any unnecessary risks. "I've made it this far," he seems to be saying, "and I plan to make it a lot farther."

At any time of the day or night, he is eager to eat a Starmint peppermint candy, if it is unwrapped for him, but above all he lives for his daily outing, waiting by the gate to join Margaret as she rides out on one of her younger horses. If the weather is really terrible, with cold rain pouring down, he sometimes stays in his run-in shed, keeping dry, and elects not to follow, looking out with an expression that seems to say, "Not *me*, baby."

Above all, he exercises, watches the world with curiosity but without fear, eats slowly, taking his time to chew, and stays as close as he can to Margaret, the love of his life, if horses can be said to have a love. When she comes back from an event, he's always waiting, ears forward, as if he wants to know how she did, what the ground was like, how good her dressage score was—he knows what it means when she arrives back in the big blue-and-silver rig, tired, smiling, and happy; he's *interested*, his ears tell you that. As for the blue ribbons and the silver trophies, he's won as many of them as any horse is ever going to in a lifetime, including the long ones that they hang around the neck of the horse, and the embroidered horse blankets, and all the rest of it. He is willing to leave the laurels to younger horses now, and rest on his own. He's earned the good life, and a decent degree of respect from man and beast, and doesn't appear to have any guilt about enjoying it as much as he can and as long as he can.

Plenty of older human beings could learn from him.

In the twenty-three years since we've owned the farm, things have changed—housing developments have grown closer, cats have come and gone, *we've* changed—but Margaret owned Missouri before we bought the farm, and he's still here on it, the one constant, the horse she always dreamed of owning, what old-time horsemen used to call "an honest horse."

You don't get many of those in a lifetime.

CHAPTER NINE

"Horse for Sale"

Zapata eventing

O H, THE JOYS of looking for a new horse! Of course there's a level at which it's easier: you go to a professional's place—having first called to tell him what you're looking for (and what your price range is), and find out what he's got on hand—then look at the horse in his ring. Invariably, the horse is well turned out, groomed to within an inch of its life, and ridden by somebody who knows what she is doing, if not by the professional himself. Then you get on and try it out yourself.

There are lots of people around who trade in horses—enough so that it sometimes seems as if the automobile hadn't been invented at all—and if there's one thing the more prestigious ones know how to do, it's make a horse look good. If you go up to Vermont, to Denny Emerson's farm, say, or to David Hopper's, or to the equivalent places in Virginia, Maryland, Florida, or North Carolina, you're sure to see the horse performing at its best for you. (A lot of these people move south in the winter, so the areas around Ocala, Florida, and Southern Pines, North Carolina, are both hot places for high-end horse trading and horse sales, in the months when there's snow and ice on the ground in the Northeast.)

In general, the sales pitch at the higher level of selling horses is very different from that at the lower levels, and in no way resembles the kind of sales pitch that luxury car dealers favor. Hyperthyroidic enthusiasm and the genial man-to-man assumption that a person of your refined taste, judgment, social position, and income wouldn't be comfortable with anything less than this car, or be willing to live without full leather upholstery, heated programmable orthopedic seats, all-wool floor mats, and genuine burled walnut trim, aren't how horses are sold—in fact, the pitch is so laid-back that it's hardly a pitch at all. Generally, the question is more whether you are good enough for the horse than the other way around.

At the very highest level of show jumping, where it's not uncommon for people to spend in the high six figures for a horse that can take a daughter or a wife to the Garden or the equivalent with a chance of winning a major trophy, this kind of salesmanship reaches its peak, of course. A show jumper with a good record of wins is as a rule so obviously better bred and more attractive than the person buying it (or for whom it is being bought) that the matter is hardly worth discussing. Devotees of Hollywood movies about horses will be disappointed that, generally speaking, there are very few surprises in show jumping—the rider with the most expensive horse and the best trainer/personal coach is very likely to win, and the odds on a rider with "a backyard horse" doing well are very long indeed. This is not by any means as true of combined training, and not necessarily true at all on the track, where people are betting on genetics as much as anything else, and the occasional genetic surprise crosses the finish line first.

In the meantime, horses are being bought and sold all over the country, advertised like used cars in magazines, the classified section of the local newspaper, in whatever the local giveaway paper is (the *Pennysaver,* in our neck of the woods), and on plaintive cards pinned to the bulletin boards of gyms, delis, and the A&P: "Horse for sale." Very often there's a snapshot of the horse, but unlike cats and dogs, mostly not. Horses don't usually have "take me home, please" expressions, or a wistful look in their eyes.

One reason why there are always a lot of horses for sale is that people's lives change—girls outgrow their pony, or go away to college, or get married, or have a child, and all of a sudden the pony or horse has to go. Of course it's harder to sell a pony or a horse than it is to sell a dog or a cat—dogs, cats, and kittens don't necessarily demand major life changes or big sacrifices, but a horse is a big, and expensive, responsibility, requiring more from the owner than most animals. You can't drop it off at the vet for a few days or weeks if you're going on vacation; its food comes in bales and sacks that are hard to store and heavy to pick up; and it is weather-sensitive and requires a blacksmith at regular intervals. The failure to plan ahead for all this, or the inability to keep on providing it, explains the vast number of "Horse for Sale" ads to be found almost everywhere in the country, and in not a few cities.

Every once in a while, one gets drawn into the lower levels of this world, hope springing eternal even in the most jaded and experienced human breast. Not so long ago, when I was looking for a horse for myself—something robust, comfortable, and easy-going for trail riding, not a candidate for show-jumping fame or winning eventing ribbons— Margaret drew my attention to an ad in the *Chronicle of the Horse* for just such a horse, a young quarter horse–draft horse cross with a sweet disposition, which I liked the sound of, offered at what seemed like a reasonable enough price. The place was a horse farm, perhaps three hours or so from where we live, and it didn't seem like a bad idea to drive up and have a look at the horse—or horses, for a conversation with the owner revealed that she had several for sale, any one of which would be perfect for my needs. If we wanted a few days of trial time to have one of them at our place, that would be okay too, provided we paid a deposit.

Accordingly, one cold, rainy morning just as winter was giving way to spring (reluctantly, slowly, and by fits and starts in our neck of the woods), we put a couple of saddles and our riding boots and helmets in the back of the car and drove off to have a look. Our mood was one of cautious optimism—cautious in the sense that we were taking the car, not the truck and trailer, as the lady had suggested we should do, promising that when I saw these horses I would want to take one of them home. We debated that possibility for about two minutes, and decided against it. If we liked what we saw, we could always make arrangements to have it picked up later, after all.

Driving through the back roads of the Catskills did not lighten our spirits much—we passed through one small, run-down, half-deserted town or village after another. Since the collapse of the Jewish summer resort business a couple of decades ago, accompanied by the simultaneous decline and fall of the small farm and the dairy business, there's nothing much to see back here but abandoned farms, collapsing dairy barns, and motels and trailer parks that have been left to decay by the roadside. A very few of the resorts have been turned into Buddhist temples, and some of the trailer parks have become fortified outposts of outlaw biker gangs, which fled the big city years ago as blacks began to threaten their turf. A farm that bred Shetland ponies was the one bright spot, and Margaret was prevented only with difficulty from buying one and bringing it home in the back of the car, but otherwise there was nothing much to write home about, including the local diner, decorated inside from floor to ceiling with pigs in plastic, paper, and cloth, and in which most of the customers as well as the cook and the slatterns behind the counter had a distinctly porcine appearance—so much so that I suffered from guilt pangs as I ordered a BLT.

The horse farm, when we found it, was anything but scenic. A dozen or so horses, shabby and out of shape, looking as if they had been clipped with electric pruning shears, stood listlessly, ankle-deep in thick, gluey mud that resembled the kind they used to have onstage for the naked-women-mud-wrestling act in *Nachtlokalen* on Hamburg's famed Reeperbahn. The fencing relied heavily on strips of black rubber from old tires and barbed wire, and even from a distance the horses showed puncture wounds from the latter, and what looked like tread marks from the former.

Here, pleasant as everybody was as we slogged through the malodorous mud to meet them, there was no pretense at having the horses look their best for the customer. The first one was brought in covered with mud, given a quick once-over-lightly with a brush, and tacked up so that the owner's daughter could ride it for us in the ring, the mud surface of which had just been smoothed out with what looked like a modified lawnmower for our benefit. Bean, as the horse was named, was about three-quarters quarter horse and one-quarter draft, and gave the impression that he might eventually clean up to look like something fairly respectable, I thought, and as billed, he was of an amiable disposition.

When I got on him, however, it became instantly clear that he was pretty much completely untrained—he had no idea how to respond to the signal for a turn, and at a trot and a canter showed an alarming tendency to drift into the center of the ring and come to a halt, or to bump into objects rather than go around them. Also, his gaits were so short and choppy that I was bounced out of the saddle at every stride—the ten minutes I spent on him felt like an hour. I got off him, relieved that we had decided not to come up with the truck and trailer, and prepared to let the owner down gently, but she beat me to the punch. Bean was a sweetheart, of course, she said, but he was a youngster (I pegged him for five, at least) and perhaps needed a little more schooling than I was probably prepared to put into him. What I wanted was a "shake-and-bake" horse, one who would go for me just as he was. Goldie had "a few more miles on him" than Bean, and would suit me a lot better, she thought, so the daughter was sent off to bring Goldie in.

Goldie, when he arrived, was as shaggy and covered with puncture wounds and scratches as an old sofa in a house full of cats, and it was difficult to tell what his ancestry was. He was described as "part thoroughbred," but what part was hard to say. The size of his head and ears and the shortness of his neck argued against any significant thoroughbred blood, and his back was as long as the spine of a good-sized New England fishing skiff. This is not a desirable characteristic in a horse—a short back is more comfortable for the rider and less likely to produce orthopedic problems for the horse, besides which, one wants a compact animal that fits within a frame, rather than a gangly beast whose back legs don't seem to be connected to the front ones. Stubbs, like the other great horse painters of the eighteenth and early nineteenth centuries, specialized in making the ideal horse seem longer and slimmer than most horses are in real life (rather the way Vargas and other pinup artists portray women), in order to give the illusion of speed to his paintings, in much the same spirit that the horses' owners were always portrayed as thinner and taller than they actually were, and for a while long-backed horses, built rather like greyhounds, were the fashion as a result, but with the age of photography horses quickly reacquired their normal appearance. There are exceptions, of course, and Goldie was one of them—you could have landed an airplane on his back. He chewed on his bit reflectively as I mounted him.

Before I had even picked up the reins or thought to touch him with my legs, he was off at a brisk, jolting, walk, then lurched into a fast trot. Getting him to canter was no problem—he simply sped up until it was easier for him to canter than to trot, and no amount of pressure on the reins appeared to slow him down. In fact, he didn't even notice pressure on the reins, so I gave up any pretense at finesse and yanked on them unmercifully. Goldie put his head down and plowed on, throwing up a wake of mud behind him, while the three onlookers shouted helpful advice from the sidelines like "Watch your diagonals!" or "You're on the wrong lead!" or "Sit tight!" as I tried desperately to keep him from bumping into oil drums and jumps and the rusty old kitchen steps that served as a mounting block. When we were both reduced to breathlessness, I finally managed to steer him head-on into the fencing around the ring. Even then, it seemed to me possible he might just break through and keep going. I dismounted and stood in the ankle-deep mud with the owner. "He likes to go, don't he?" she said proudly.

There was no denying this. "Yes," I agreed, "but I didn't even touch him with my legs. I just got on him, and off he went."

She nodded. "He's a self-starter, all right. Forward-moving, no doubt about it. Just what you want—you won't have to push *him*. He'd make a great trail horse."

I tried to contemplate riding Goldie on the trails. If he could take off without any signal in the ring, what would he do if, say, a horse broke into a canter in front of him on the trails? And if you couldn't slow him down, even in the ring, not even by sawing and pulling unmercifully on the poor animal's mouth, what would he do out in the open countryside? But I knew exactly what he would do—he would run away with his rider.

I explained, as tactfully as I could, that Goldie was perhaps a bit *too* forward-moving for me, and his owner nodded sagely. "Well," she said, exchanging a glance with her daughter, "there's always Jack. One thing about Jack, he won't give you any trouble."

Jack, when he was brought out of his field, was a dark horse of no particular breed. Given that he was caked with mud, it wasn't easy to guess at his color, except that it was of the brownish persuasion, and while he too was a youngster, he had a mournful expression, like that of a little old man, which I found it hard to understand. "A lot of people don't want him because of his head," the owner said. "That's the only reason why he's still here."

I hadn't noticed anything wrong with his head, but when I took a closer look, I realized that there was a huge declivity in Jack's forehead, a crater about the size of half a grapefruit. It was hard to tell whether it was an old injury or a birth defect. It certainly wasn't recent, the owner explained—the horse had come to her like that, and there was no visible scar tissue. I didn't think it was a birth defect—it looked to me as if the horse had been kicked in the forehead hard enough to indent the bone and leave a permanent mark, probably when he was quite young.

On the score of looks, it didn't help him a bit, but I consoled myself with the thought that of course I wouldn't be looking at the horse's forehead when I was riding him, so we transferred my saddle to Jack and led him down to the ring.

I asked how old he was. "About five," I was told, which might have been true, I thought. I wasn't too sure about him—quite apart from his head, he wasn't the kind of horse you'd necessarily look forward to riding every day; he definitely lacked presence, and would certainly not cause other riders to shout out enviously, "Great looking horse!" but on the other hand he had four legs, and here we were, after all, three hours from home, having come here to try out horses, so I mounted and pressed him gently with my legs. Nothing happened. He seemed to be asleep. I clucked with my tongue. He slept on. I applied my legs more vigorously. "Give him a tap," the owner called out, so I gave him a tap with my crop. At that, he woke up just enough to lurch in a slow but determined manner over to the gate leading out of the ring and stand there, looking longingly toward the field he had been taken from. Eventually he was led by the bridle into the middle of the ring, but no amount of effort on my part could get him to move more than a few steps.

"*He* won't run away with you," his owner called out, looking at the bright side, as usual. "Jack's as reliable as the day is long."

Yes, I thought to myself, and dead safe too, if all you want to do is sit on a horse without moving for an hour or two. I dismounted and said thank you as sincerely as I could manage—never knock somebody else's merchandise, is my motto—though in fact all three horses struck me as the kind that old Mr. Novograd would have turned down as being unsuitable for hiring out to ride in Central Park.

The owner held onto Jack's bridle, unnecessarily I thought, since he wasn't any more likely to go anywhere on his own than he was with a rider. "What are you asking for him?" I said, out of curiosity. The other two horses had been reasonably priced, by local standards—either one of them could have been bought for $5,000, probably for much less.

She thought for a moment. "Three thousand?" I raised an eyebrow.

She looked at my expression and shrugged. "Well, just for today only, I might take two," she said. I shook my head. "You stick around," she said. "Stay here long enough, there's no telling *how* low I may drop his price."

I said there was no need—I would think about Jack, and Bean, and Goldie, and give her a call—then I pulled off my boots and got back in the car. Margaret shook her head. "One who won't steer, one who won't stop, and one who won't go," she said with a sigh.

And that about summed it up, which is why it's nearly always a good idea to buy a horse from somebody you know, and who knows you, if possible, well enough to have a reasonably good idea of what you're looking for.

These thoughts went through our heads when it came time to find me a replacement for poor Hustle, and as Margaret began to compete on a more ambitious basis, which would require more than just one horse. Missouri could do the job, up to a certain level, and went on doing it for many, many years, but he couldn't be expected to do it every weekend. She needed a backup.

My own needs were fairly simple—I wanted a sound, reliable, presentable horse that would do for trail riding, the very occasional hunter pace, and perhaps a little really low-level competition, if I ever felt so inclined. It didn't seem like a tall order, and it wasn't. Within a few days Katherine Boyer called to say that she had found a young dapple-gray gelding who seemed to be what I was looking for, so Margaret, Roxie, and I drove over to her farm to look at him.

Handsome Devil, as he was called, was a little on the small side, but then I've never been one for owning big horses, and what he lacked in height he more than made up for in presence, personality, and muscle. He had, for his size, a short, thick neck. Purists don't like this, and even Katherine, who was selling the horse, wished his neck was a little longer, but I've never minded this much—given a choice, I prefer compact horses, and if there was one thing you could say about Handsome

Devil, he was compact. When we got my saddle on him and I mounted him in Katherine's ring, he felt a little like a pony, in fact, and I wondered if my feet would be dragging along the ground. I reminded myself that the shorter the horse, the less far it is to fall, which is undeniably true—not that I had any intention of falling off the horse in front of Katherine, of all people. Because of his short neck and robust, compact build, riding him was a bit like driving a van, from which you look out onto the road without any hood in front of you—Handsome Devil's ears seemed very close to my hands, and I felt that if need be, I would have no problem leaning forward and talking directly into his ear.

Riding around the ring under Katherine Boyer's eagle eyes was in any case hardly conducive to relaxation. Even at her most genial, Katherine didn't miss a thing—one felt, even as a customer, that one was being judged, and that the smallest mistake would be noticed and remembered, if only with a raised eyebrow. From time to time she made a small, snorting sound of dismay or disapproval, as if to say, "Well, if you can't even tell that you're on the wrong diagonal, I'm not going to point it out to you, but then don't blame the horse because he doesn't know what you want him to do, please."

But none of that mattered because the truth was that it was love at first sight—Handsome Devil was as comfortable and as smooth as a horse can be, easy to ride, undemanding, and cheap. He was not, as Katherine was the first to admit, her cup of tea—she liked bigger horses, with more breeding, whereas Handsome Devil was more like a cow pony, and would in fact have looked perfectly good in a western saddle, had I cared to put one on him. He had something of the allure of a small sports car, in that he was flashy, attention-getting, nimble, and quick to respond, and in that sense he reminded me a lot of my first car, a Triumph TR-2, back in the days when you got into an English sports car as if you were pulling on a shoe, and could reach over the top of the cutaway door and touch the pavement, if you cared to. I'd hardly gone around the ring twice before the sale was as good as made, despite a certain doubtful look on the faces of Margaret and Roxie.

"He's got a lot of personality," Katherine said when I'd finished my ride and dismounted, without making it clear whether she thought that was an asset or a problem. "He's been some kid's backyard horse, used to getting all the attention—a little spoiled, frankly. He likes people a lot more than he likes other horses. He was probably cut late too."

The question of when a male horse is castrated is one of some importance. If it's left until too late, the horse has a natural tendency to retain certain characteristics of a stallion. Certainly Handsome Devil, small as he was, had the thick neck of a stallion, and a stallion's quick intelligence as well. Horses cut too late tend to be what horse people call "studdy," which is to say, quick to bite other horses, touchy, competitive, proud, and something of a pain in the ass, as horses go, the kind of behavior described by the phrase, "Too full of himself for his own good," whether applied to a horse or a man.

The general feeling was that Handsome Devil would probably not present any problems that Roxie couldn't take care of—after all, Katherine had trained Roxie—and that he was a bargain, sound, comfortable, and ideal for me, so I bought him on the spot. (I've never found that with horses it pays to hesitate and worry over the decision—once you've seen the horse and ridden it, you know what there is to know, subject always to the vet's examination for soundness and good health, and it's unlikely that staying awake at night worrying about it will tell you more.)

Anyway, that took care of my problem, though not Margaret's. At the time—partly because of my friendship with Larry McMurtry and partly because of the success of *Lonesome Dove*—we were in a western mode when it came to naming horses. There was Missouri, and a nice little horse we'd owned for a while whom we renamed Sundance, so Handsome Devil didn't seem the right kind of name for my new horse at all, and I came up with the idea of calling him Zapata. Some people think that changing a horse's name is bad luck, like changing the name of a boat, but I have never subscribed to this—besides, a lot of horses are given such silly or inappropriate names by their owners that changing them seems like doing them a favor.

Anyway, Zapata he became (and remains to this day), and like most horses he eventually settled in, though not without great difficulties. The routine of one barn is pretty much like the routine of another—as long as a horse gets fed two square meals a day (appropriate to its size and the amount and type of work it's doing), is kept warm and dry when the weather is cold, and has plenty of space to graze and stroll when it's outside and a supply of good, fresh water, it is unlikely to grieve over the change in residence. Horses don't sit around looking sad, or starve themselves to death yearning for their former owner, as dogs are reputed to do. Horses are used to humans, put up with the demands of humans, may even form a kind of personal attachment to a human, as Margaret's do to her, but in general, if they're moved on to a new home and owner, they take it philosophically—certainly they don't pine away. It's one of the advantages of being a herd animal. The horse's first concern is for its place in the new "herd" in which it finds itself, be it ever so small, and this place, once it's established, has to be fought out over and over again, every day, and of course reestablished every time there's a change in the horse population. However peaceful horses may look grazing in their fields or dozing solemnly on their feet in their stall, they are always busy, in the sense that their mind is constantly aware of their status, and brooding over anything that might seem likely to change or challenge it. In short, it ain't easy being a horse—and particularly being the new horse in the barn, since your very presence upsets the social order (I hesitate to use the phrase "pecking order" about horses).

Domesticated horses do not fight near or to the death for control of the herd, the way wild mustang stallions sometimes do, but they can and do make a lot of trouble for each other, resulting in severe injuries. Hence, however pretty it may look to have a whole lot of horses grazing together in a field, most serious horse people prefer to keep their horses separated, in individual paddocks, from which they can see each other (which is vital to the peace of mind of herd animals), but where they are prevented by fences (if necessary, electrified) from harming each other. Even their play is apt to turn dangerous, with a lot of biting and kicking involved.

Of course who knows what goes on in a horse's mind? Sometimes that kind of fighting between horses looks like play, a little bit on the rough side, like that of schoolboys in the playground, but it can quickly turn nasty, and lead to real wounds, with the vet having to be called to put in a few stitches. This is a major factor in the design of any barn—ideally the horses should be able to see each other by sticking their heads out over the top of the stall door but not be able to reach each other, since this is likely to result in bites, whether out of boredom or because the horse is still trying to settle its place in the hierarchy of the herd from behind the locked door and protective grills or bars of its stall. Anybody who has ever been bitten by a horse is likely to remember it—and unlikely to behave as if all horses are "My Friend Flicka." A serious bite from a horse is not something you're likely to forget in a hurry, and even a playful nip is enough to give the most ardent and sentimental horse lover a certain respect for those front teeth.

In any event, Zapata, after a brief period of biting every horse in sight and what appeared to have been a series of psychosomatic illnesses caused by moving to a new barn, eventually settled down, apparently willing to concede to Missouri first place in our little herd—though Zapata remained, by nature, something of a "nudge" (to use the Yiddish word for somebody who is a constant pain in the ass), as horses go, always pushing his way to the front, and the center of any kind of equine mischief—Peck's Bad Boy, in short.

He suited me fine—riding Zapata, with his thick, short neck and his compact body, was as much like riding a motorcycle as a horse can get, and he had the same kind of instant response and quick pickup as a motorcycle too. He was a good jumper—a good deal better than I deserved—though not always a reliable one. Competition brought out the worst in him, and better riders than me—Roxie, Margaret's goddaughter Tamzin, Tamzin's mother Nancy—went home without a ribbon after Zapata had put the brakes on unexpectedly in front of a jump that should have given him no trouble at all. Any chance that he might be a useful event horse was nullified by his refusal to jump ditches, for no reason any of us could work out. We even had special, "friendly" little ditches, "ditch-lettes" as we called them, dug on our land, sited so Zapata could have a good, long look at them on the approach, and so shallow and narrow that a Chihuahua could have jumped them with ease, but it made no difference. From a hundred yards away, Zapata registered "ditch," his ears went back, he plunged on at full speed, giving the rider the illusion that for once, this time, he would go over it, then, at the last possible moment, just as you were coming forward in the saddle, he put on the brakes and came to a full stop, looking down into the ditch with interest while the rider tried to disentangle himself from his mane, having been thrown forward with his arms around Zapata's neck by the sudden stop. Either that, or you just kept going and ended up on the ground.

No amount of training ever reconciled Zapata to ditches, though sometimes he would capriciously jump one just to keep everybody's hopes up, or perhaps to demonstrate that he *could* jump ditches if he wanted to. Elaborate attempts, involving many people, were made to cure Zapata of his phobia against ditches, major productions in which Roxie cracked a long lunge whip and two people pulled on a piece of rope drawn around Zapata's rear end with all their might, but Zapata simply dug his feet in and refused to budge. Threats of force, force, outright bribery, such as having somebody stand on the other side of the ditch with a handful of "treats," carrots, an apple, "Starmint" peppermints—none of these made the slightest impression on him. He didn't do ditches, and that was that.

His worst habit was his ability to suddenly drop a shoulder and make a sudden, uncalled-for sharp turn at high speed. Because his neck was so short, this had the result of making you feel that there was suddenly nothing in front of you, and it was difficult to prevent yourself from being hurled off headfirst. You could curse him until you were blue in the face—indeed, the first time that Nancy Blinkhorn competed on him while visiting us from England, I heard an amazing and impressive string of curses coming from her lips as she pushed Zapata over a stone wall at high speed, after he had refused the two previous jumps—but the one thing you could say for him was that he was small enough so that it was never a problem to get back on him after he got you off.

The other thing you could say for him was that he had character, in spades—what he lacked in size, he more than made up for in personality. Of course, if it had been my ambition to compete and win, Zapata would have been a complete bust, but since I never had the slightest desire to enter competitions, I was happy with him. Ironically, as I write this, I can see, pinned above my mantelpiece, the orange-and-gold first-place ribbon Margaret and I won at the Newtown Bridle Lanes Association "Frost on the Pumpkin" pace, and I still have a photograph of Margaret and me jumping side by side over a fence there, on our way to victory—though you wouldn't have known that looking at our faces in

Author on Zapata (foreground); Margaret on Cheyenne, on right.

the picture. Judging from the glum expression on my face under the visor of my helmet, I seem to be asking myself, What am I doing here? (a good question), but Zapata looks mighty pleased with himself, while Margaret, bent forward gracefully, seems to be saying to herself, We might win this if only he doesn't screw it up at the last minute! a thought that would come easily enough to anybody who had Zapata and me as their teammates.

Zapata also seems to have won a ribbon (a lowly red) at the Golden's Bridge Hounds Hunter Trials in the same year, with Nancy riding him, which must have represented the peak of his success. This may have been partly because these paces and trials didn't present Zapata with any ditches, and partly because he was out riding side by side with a stablemate—Missouri, or whatever horse Margaret was on at the time—rather than on his own, or with a strange horse. Zapata was a great believer in companionship, however "nudgy" he might be toward it, and if a horse he knew was prepared to go over a fence, then Zapata was usually willing to take a chance and go over it with him, unless of course a ditch was involved, in which case all bets were off.

Still, I can never look at these ribbons, however lowly, without surprise that at some point in my life I actually won any of them, and on Zapata of all horses, who was notably lacking in the spirit of coop-eration that is said to be at the heart of the horse-and-rider relation-ship. Zapata had his own priorities, but reliability was not among them. He might go over a fence perfectly eleven times, but on the twelfth, for no particular reason, his ears would go back at the first sight of it, and just at the moment when you were leaning forward to go over it, he would put on the brakes sharply, and like as not send you flying over it headfirst. When you *did* come off him, he was capable of being a real pain in the ass too. He did not, like some horses, appear to feel ashamed of himself, nor was he certain to stand there and take a few mouthfuls of grass, waiting for you to get back on. On the con-trary, the moment you exchanged a seat in the saddle for a trip through thin air, Zapata was off and running, kicking, breaking his reins, galloping flat out, letting off thunderous, triumphant farts in a wild ecstasy of motion.

Once, when he dropped his shoulder and turned sharply away, like a missile unexpectedly changing course—leaving me to keep going in a straight line until I landed on my right shoulder with a painful thump that brought tears to my eyes—he dashed back and forth so fast that I thought he was going to trample me, something in the nature of a game, I hoped. Immobilized momentarily by pain (not to speak of humiliation), I held my good arm over my head as Zapata's hooves thundered and clattered past me, missing, it seemed to me, by inches, while I screamed at him to get away. Eventually he lost interest, and put his head down to eat. Once I had managed to push myself up into a sitting position—I had done something so drastic and medically interesting to my right rotator cuff that to this day it fascinates doctors and physical therapists—Zapata calmed down enough to let me mount him again, with Margaret's help. The sight of him galloping straight for me, though, from a worm's-eye view on the ground, reins and stirrup leathers flapping on either side of him, was not something that I was ever likely to forget, and remained a powerful incentive to stay on him for the rest of our relationship together. What mattered most to me was that he was comfortable.

Comfort is a big issue when it comes to horses. I myself think of comfort first, unlike competitive riders, who are willing to put up with a good deal of discomfort if the horse can put in a winning performance. For me, however, comfort counts. I don't want to be bounced up and down, or feel in the saddle as if I were being run out of town on a rail; I don't like narrow horses, or horses with a choppy way of going. I like a horse that's got some breadth to it, and nice, soft gaits, a horse that comes as close as it can to make sitting in the saddle feel like sitting on a sofa. And Zapata was in fact like riding a sofa, when it came to comfort—you could have ridden him for hours, even days, always provided, of course, that you could stay on him.

Every once in a while I will read about somebody who is planning to ride a horse all the way across the country, or be tempted when Larry McMurtry tells me about people who reenact the cattle drive in *Lonesome Dove* (from the Rio Grande in Texas to Montana) every year. I'll think to myself, I could have done that on Zapata, and it's probably true that he could have been ridden the whole way without giving his rider a sore butt, although whether his legs would have stood up to the journey is another matter, not to speak of the fact that he would probably have thrown me at the very first sight of a cow close up—Zapata never reacted with anything less than shock and hysteria at the sight of our neighbors' dairy cattle, even from a distance, so cow ponying would likely not have been a natural thing for him. Nor was he the kind of horse about which you could say, "Well, he'll get used to it." What he didn't like, he didn't like permanently, and he wasn't about to change his mind, and cows were high on the list of things he didn't like.

Not everybody's ideas about comfort are the same, of course, and I have often been given a horse to ride that somebody else finds comfortable, only to find it intensely uncomfortable myself. The saddle has something to do with this, of course—it is always best to use your own saddle, since other people's, however expensive and highly praised, nearly always turn out to be too hard, or too slick, or to have seams or welts in odd places that rub you raw in no time at all. As a result, people who own a comfortable saddle will go to any lengths to preserve it, from a total rebuild to repairing it with duct tape, and a lot of the good ones don't start to get comfortable for decades if you buy them new. Some of the most expensive and prized saddles in the world seem hard and uncomfortable to me, although since they're not only used, but in some cases designed by top Olympic riders, I may be the one at fault.

In any case, important as the saddle is, the most comfortable saddle in the world won't help a bit if the horse doesn't go comfortably in the first place, with a nice, smooth action. Alas—like beauty in a woman— a horse is either born to be comfortable, or it isn't. The elasticity of its joints, the proportions of its legs and back, its build and "conformation," come together naturally to produce a happy result, or they don't. Zapata's did, so I was willing to forgive him a good deal.

From time to time I talked, half-jokingly, about putting a western saddle on Zapata, but neither Margaret nor Roxie was amused, being English riders by definition. The truth is that while I've ridden in a western saddle often enough, it's never felt altogether natural to me. Still, if I'd taken Zapata on the *Lonesome Dove* trail ride, I'd have put a western saddle on his back, and I don't suppose he would have cared or noticed. As it was, there was something about Zapata that seemed to call for western trimmings. I often rode him wearing chaps, and once, on a visit to Los Angeles, when I discovered an expensive tack shop on Rodeo Drive in Beverly Hills (no longer there), I bought a silver-trimmed western bridle, with braided, silver-trimmed reins, an outfit suitable for Buffalo Bill (or Danny Dakota) and which, needless to say, neither Roxie nor Margaret would put on the horse, so it was relegated to the wall of my office as decoration, along with western roweled spurs and a braided quirt.

At some point, when an injury to Zapata's mouth or a problem with his teeth—I forget which—made it uncomfortable for him to deal with a bit, Roxie suggested riding him in a hackamore (a device that works by applying pressure to the horse's nose, rather than on his tongue) until his mouth was healed, which meant taking the western bridle down from the wall and actually using it. I was delighted, and saw myself riding Zapata like a cutting horse. Certainly he looked terrific in the Beverly Hills outfit, with the silver conchos and fittings gleaming in the sun. The only problem with it, as I very soon discovered, was that Zapata, who was never exactly easy to slow down or stop at the best of times, ignored the hackamore altogether. The more you squeezed his nose, the lower he dropped his head and the faster he went, so that it was like driving a car without brakes. Despite many adjustments to the hackamore and a lot of coaching from Roxie, Zapata never adjusted to a western bridle at all—he either didn't get it, or just didn't like it—and it went back up on my wall, where it hangs to this day.

·   ·   ·

We were to have a long and mutually respectful relationship together for many years, and when Zapata's legs finally started to go—his tendons had never been his strongest point—and I began to find, after prostate cancer surgery, that even riding a horse as comfortable as "Mr. Z," as we all called him, was more than I could do for the moment, I let him go at last to Rita Dee, who keeps old horses at her farm. From time to time I heard rumors that in his retirement he was being used to give lessons to small children, and thought to myself, Well, at least he will teach them to fall on their feet! and also hoped that they were always obliged to wear a good, strong helmet with a proper chin harness when riding him. As it turned out, when I finally went to visit him, giving lessons to small children was something he enjoyed, perhaps because none of them wanted to jump ditches, or enter him in horse shows, or ride him anywhere near cattle, while of course from the child's point of view, there was something comforting about Zapata's size. He was bigger than a pony, certainly, but not so big as to be physically intimidating, and like most ponies had a distinct personality, in his case that of a four-footed prankster.

It's often an emotional mistake to go and visit in its retirement a horse one has owned—witness Margaret's experience retiring Tabasco to a farm that had been highly recommended to her for the purpose, only to be so shocked by the sight of him when she went to pay a visit that she took him back—but Zapata, though age had turned him white and stiffened him up a good deal, had hardly changed at all. Since Rita Dee's horses aren't fenced in paddocks or stalls in the barn but come and go on their own, like free spirits, in keeping with her own views about life, I did not at first recognize Zapata in the small mob of horses wandering in and out of the barn, into the fields, across the driveway, and around the house. But then one of them put his head down and made a mock charge at me, heading straight for me at top speed, then veering off with a buck, a snort, and a kick at the last moment, missing me by inches, long white mane and tail flying in the wind, big black eyes focused directly at me. He came to a stop, and we stared at each other, and if a horse could do such a thing, I would swear I saw him grin.

You don't often get a horse with a sense of humor, or at least one that's recognizable to human beings, but Zapata came as close as a horse can. If he hadn't been too old, too stiff, and as stubborn as ever, I'd almost have been tempted to ask for him back, but then again, I reflected, he was happy where he was. I didn't need any further damage to my rotator cuff, and anyway Rita Dee loved him, and had memorialized him in a superb painting—a faintly dappled white horse with a flowing mane (rather like the one on the horse in David's portrait of Napoleon crossing the Alps), turning his head to look at the viewer, every muscle tensed, eyes glistening, ready for everything (except perhaps ditches), the kind of picture that makes you understand why mankind's relationship with horses is like that with no other animal, even today.

The years with Zapata were good years, from my point of view (and probably from his). True, he didn't do well at horse shows, but early on in our relationship I had abandoned the idea of competing in horse shows after he took the bit between his teeth and charged the judge, who very fortunately had the presence of mind to drop her clipboard and leap from the ring. Shortly after that I also gave up the idea of eventing him, when he refused a fence and took off into a crowd of spectators, aiming straight for the food stand, and had to be led off in disgrace. Basically, this was all right with me. I had no competitive ambition (I get enough competition in my regular life as a book editor to satisfy any needs I have in that area) and was very happy to leave that side of riding to Margaret, who was becoming a more and more serious (and successful) event rider. I was happy enough to hack out for a brisk hour's ride in the open countryside around us, and so was Zapata, provided there was an apple in it for him at the end of the ride. He was usually good for a few modest jumps, although he tended to approach them at the speed of a missile being launched, and reserved the right to change his mind at the last moment if there was something about the jump he didn't like. If another horse went in front of him, however, to "give him a lead," as riders say, he was usually happy enough to follow, puffing and snorting like a locomotive. In short, our limitations dovetailed, which is a pretty good recipe for happiness. I didn't have high ambitions, and neither did Zapata, so we got on fine together. Zapata did not pine when the trailer pulled away from home, taking Margaret to an event somewhere—he was pleased enough to be left behind, and to leave the glory, such as it was, to others. Another day at home, another chance to graze on the best patches of grass instead of having to stand around in a trailer and then be asked to jump ditches, might as well have been his motto. If he'd been a person, he'd have called out between mouthfuls, "Lots of luck!" to Missouri, as Missouri went bumping down the driveway in the trailer on his way to compete somewhere.

Margaret, however, needed at the very least a backup to Missouri. Eventing is physically taxing for a horse—you can't expect to compete one every weekend without eventually breaking it down—and Zapata had clearly declared himself not a candidate for the role. The search for a suitable horse to compete alongside Missouri was to take many years, and involve a lot of different horses (and horse sellers), proving, if nothing else, how lucky Margaret had been when Katy Boyer produced Missouri for her.

The concept of "need" here is relative. Given the proliferation of vehicles in the United States today, nobody literally "needs" a horse, let alone more than one, but for active competition it can be argued—and certainly was by Margaret—that one is not enough. Horses go lame, get ill, have off periods (just like people), so a backup horse is a good idea in principle. Cowboys, when they joined a cattle outfit, usually picked three horses out of the remuda (or herd), broke them, and became responsible for them so long as they stayed with the outfit, a system remarkably similar to the way Indians got their horses, while the old army idea of one trooper/one horse was among the many reasons why it was always difficult to keep enough cavalry in the field to meet the

Indians on equal terms, despite the former's decisive advantage in weaponry. A trooper whose horse went lame was at once useless and helpless until he was remounted—a man in heavy boots and spurs, standing around holding a McClennan saddle, a saddle pad, a bridle, a revolver, and a saber, waiting for the remount sergeant to find him another horse and fill out the necessary paperwork, is of no use to anybody, and still less of a threat—while the Indians not only traveled light but generally had two or three horses apiece, so if one was hurt, they could mount another and get back into the fight without delay or looking around for an officer to sign forms in triplicate.

Much the same applies to competition, and Margaret was also hoping to find a horse that would eventually take her to a higher level. Beyond all this, there's the space factor. When we bought our house in the country, it had a barn with six stalls. It is a natural tendency among horse lovers to want to fill every stall, if possible, which explains why our neighbors down the road have twenty-three horses on their property (at last count) and why it's a mistake to build your wife a barn with twelve stalls unless you want to own twelve horses. If there's one thing a horse person can't stand the sight of, it's an empty stall, and the same is true of fields, paddocks, and corrals. Just as cat lovers can always find a good reason for adopting one more stray cat, no matter how many are already in the house, horse lovers are almost incapable of resisting that next, truly desirable horse.

Of course there's a difference between cats and horses—cats require very little upkeep, do much of their personal cleaning themselves, and produce shit in relatively manageable amounts, while horses, as we've seen, require intensive looking after and grooming, none of which they contribute to, and produce huge amounts of horseshit and dirty bedding to be disposed of every day. One more cat, in a house that has several, is not necessarily impossible to squeeze in or deal with, but every horse represents a major commitment, particularly in these days, when vet bills can run into thousands of dollars, and when the blacksmith's monthly bill makes it seem that the horses are being shod in sterling silver rather than iron. Adding another horse to the barn doesn't just mean adding a few more cans of Fancy Feast to the shopping cart at the supermarket and throwing in an extra bag of kitty litter—it's a complex, expensive undertaking. Each of those horses out there in the fields, no doubt improving the scenery by its presence and gracefully embellishing the view, needs somebody to feed it, water it, clean out its feet, groom it, put its warm clothing on in the winter and fly spray in the summer, check it for colic or other ailments, exercise it on a regular basis, and of course clean out its stall or shed daily. Every horse you add is an addition in terms of time, money, and labor—a commitment, in other words.

What's more, unless they're sturdy old retirees, every horse requires exercising, training, a regular schedule of work and riding, which means, unless you have your own trainer, the more horses you have, the more your own time is going to be filled up with riding them, and the more you ride them, the more tack there will be to clean, and so forth, which is why people who own barns and quite a few horses can often be found still wearing their riding breeches and smelling of horses way past the cocktail hour, having risen at or before dawn.

Except for the very rich, the days when you could saunter down to the stable after breakfast, ride, come back, and hand your horse to a groom and your boots to your valet, confident that everything—horse, tack, boots, and clothes—will be taken care of and ready for you at the same time next morning have long since gone. Instead, the day is more likely to open out as an endless series of chores, especially since everything to do with horses requires cleaning immediately after use. It is, of course, tempting to shuck off your boots and leave them until tomorrow, but as every horse person knows, that is the first step on the slippery slope toward decay and ruin. For horse people, as for sailors, neatness, cleanliness, and stowing things away where they belong is the golden rule—tack that isn't cleaned and stored properly after use will not only deteriorate but most likely break at just the wrong moment; horses whose hooves aren't regularly cleaned and checked will develop thrush (a potentially crippling hoof ailment), or go lame, or lose a shoe. Thus not only appearance is at stake in keeping things spick and span, but the rider's safety and the health of the animal.

The U.S. War Department's *Basic Field Manual of Animal Transportation* (FM 25-5, edition of 1939), for many years the cavalry bible, whose authors never waste words, puts the matter, as usual, very simply: "Grooming is essential to the general health, condition, and appearance of animals. The value of grooming depends on the thoroughness and speed with which it is done. Men should be encouraged to work hard and rapidly and to do a thorough job in a minimum time."

Amen to that, every horse owner will say, as well as to the long list of hard and fast rules that follow, all of them full of common sense and reduced to the form in which even the dimmest recruit can understand and remember them. FM 25-5 makes it clear that cleanliness, routine, and attention to detail are essential in even the humblest of tasks, and that the good condition of horse and tack must be the rider's first concern. Nothing has happened since 1939 to invalidate any of the *Field Manual*'s rules, which in any case merely represent the accumulated wisdom of several thousand years, and have been as familiar to the armies of Xerxes or Alexander the Great as they are to anybody looking after horses today. The hoof pick carried by Genghis Khan's mounted troops was identical to the one in use today; and the need to use it regularly to remove stones and debris from the horse's hooves, just as generally understood (though failure to do so was no doubt more strictly punished in the days of Genghis Khan). Keeping the horse fit and sound doesn't require anything in the way of arcane knowledge—indeed, even in the days of my father's youth, at the turn of the nineteenth century, most people outside the big cities knew the basics of looking after horses, and had some idea of how to handle and care for them. Still, the one thing that was always true is that caring for horses is hard, tiring work, and the more of them you have, the more work there will be.

It's hard to say—and differs from person to person—at what point you go from a part-time hobby to a full-time occupation, but in our case it probably happened when we went beyond three horses, one for me, one for Margaret, plus the aging but still lively Tabasco. Like so many transitions in life, it occurs without drama or a conscious decision, and once it has, you never look back. In part the desire to expand is natural—one more dove in the dovecote, as it were, though these are thousand-pound doves—in part something depends on having willing help like Roxie, for whom one more horse is an interesting challenge rather than a burden to complain about.

In this case the opportunity came about through Southlands and, in a roundabout way, because of our friendship with Ina and Freddy Schoenberg. John Craven, who managed Southlands for Deb Dows, was a witty, acerbic man, as much an entrepreneur as a riding instructor, or at least as much of an entrepreneur as you could be in the horse business while managing a large barn. John, for some years, had been going to England and buying horses, which he sent back to New York, and either kept as school horses at Southlands or sold to private customers. This, let me say, is an established part of the horse business, and has been for centuries. Lots of people today still go out west and buy a "string" of horses to bring back east (as Arno Mares does every year when it's time to get horses for his summer camp in the Catskills), and enterprising horse people have always gone looking for horses in places where they are cheap and plentiful, for obvious reasons. It's still possible to pick up a string of horses from a dealer out west at five hundred dollars a head, or less, and bring them back east, where the average price of a riding horse is in the thousands. Needless to say, a certain percentage of these horses are hopeless, and end up pulling carriages in Central Park, or, worse yet, as dog food; nevertheless, somebody with a good eye for a bargain can usually keep the wastage to a minimum and pick up a nice bunch of horses fairly cheap.

For people who are interested in hunters and horses for three-day eventing, England (or Ireland) are what the West used to be—places that still have plentiful rural backwaters, and where plenty of people still breed horses and, equally important, *know* horses. Foxhunting in both countries, like cowboying in the West, tends to weed out the ones who don't have solid bone, a good constitution, the willingness to go forward, and a placid disposition. You can pick up lots of solid, useful horses for a fraction of what they would cost back on the East Coast of the United States. Craven had hit on this fact some years back, and made a regular trip to England to go horse shopping. At some point he persuaded Fred Schoenberg to make "an investment" in the business, which in practice meant that Fred put up the money for Craven to go to England and buy horses, and would, of course, share in the profits, if any, once they rolled in.

Like a lot of Wall Street guys who pride themselves on their financial smartness, Fred was in fact a sucker for any kind of get-rich-quick scheme that *didn't* involve selling stocks or trading foreign currency, and over the years of our friendship acquired part ownership of a whole variety of unlikely and doubtful businesses (and even more doubtful partners) in the country around us, including a health food store, an apartment building for college girls around Bard, a deli, and an athletic shoe shop. Part of the attraction was that these investments gave him something to do and places to go on the weekend, part was that at least some of them involved pretty girls, but a major part was also a sincere, if ill-founded, belief that each of these enterprises would pay off handsomely. In most cases it was the old story of the city slicker undone by the slow-talking country shrewdies. If you had tried to sell Fred stock, he would have brought to the matter his native shrewdness and caution, but once the deal involved something other than engraved and printed paper and took place in the country rather than on Wall Street, enthusiasm often overcame his basic common sense.

Of course, there was nothing inherently implausible in the scheme of buying horses overseas and selling them in America, but the fact is that it's always easier to buy a horse than it is to sell it, and all the time it's waiting to be sold, it has to be fed, groomed, vetted, and shod—not to speak of the cost of flying the horse over from the UK in the first place and taking it through the U.S. Department of Agriculture's quarantine stable before it can enter the country. Even then, you can't just park a horse on the lawn with a FOR SALE sign the way you can a car, which means that your money comes in slowly and erratically, while your stock continues to consume bales of good hay and bags of oats and sweet feed.

To make a long story short, Fred's investment in importing English horses never paid off for him financially—he quickly reached the stage where he was talking about it as if he'd gone into it in search of a really good tax loss, always a sign of putting the best possible face on disaster—but it did produce a certain number of good, solid horses, one of which, Berry Fox, rapidly became a favorite in Southland's school. Berry Fox was a sixteen-hand thoroughbred-pony cross, a dark bay horse with the lines and the stamina of a thoroughbred and the good, thick bone of a pony, typical of the kind of horse that foxhunters prefer in England and Ireland. "Berry," as almost everybody called him, had looks and character. If you pointed him at a fence, he went over it, and that was that. He had his quirks, of course—pony blood tends to make a horse a little stubborn and mischievous—but he was basically good-natured to a fault, and eager to please. Indeed, his placid nature and his slow walk could sometimes lull the unwary into believing he was just a lovable old plug, but once he got

Berry, in his prime.

going, Berry liked a good gallop and didn't pay much attention to efforts to slow him down, which he shook off with a toss of his head. When in the right mood, he could put in the occasional buck too, though not the standing-still, stiff-legged kind that is lethal.

In any case, whenever Margaret brought up the subject of buying another horse, Berry's name came up. Everybody, it seemed, wanted her to buy Berry. Everybody loved him. John Craven, of course, was anxious to sell him because it was going to be hard to raise the money from Fred Schoenberg for another buying trip to England when most of the horses from the last trip to England were still standing around the barn at Southlands unsold, eating their heads off and wearing out their shoes; Ina Schoenberg, like everybody else who knew Berry, simply wanted him to go to somebody who would love him and look after him; and Fred Schoenberg just hoped to see one of the horses he had invested in "move." In short, the unanimous opinion was that Berry Fox should belong to Margaret, and eventually Margaret came to the same opinion herself. Margaret not only liked Berry (as did Roxie), but argued forcefully that he needed "a good home," to which I might have replied that he wasn't exactly *homeless*, had I not known it would be a waste of breath.

"He's earned it," she would say, "he's paid his dues," applying to Berry the same logic that she uses in rescuing stray cats from the fields around us, who get food left out for them, then get brought into the barn for the winter as "barn cats," in the hope that they will put in a little light mousing in return for their keep, then promoted to the warmth of the tack room (where they are entitled to snacks from people's doughnuts at coffee time) and the laundry room, and finally, when they've put in their time, brought into the house itself, which most of them never leave, except for an occasional stroll around the garden in good weather to contemplate their good fortune. Once the argument in favor of Berry had become a humanitarian one, I knew it wouldn't be long until he was in our barn, and that it was time to have a brass plate engraved with his name for the door of his stall.

Berry wasn't cheap, but in the small horse world of Rhinebeck, New York, he was something of a local celebrity; the only question was whether he would pass the vet, and on this score, he just squeaked home. God alone knew what his story had been in England, and how much mileage had been put on him there, but basically the vet reported that he was sound enough. With his tough pony genes and blood, Berry could be expected to be "as tough as an old boot" and stick around for a long time, though nobody back then, including the seller, could have guessed that he would still be going strong as I write this, about twenty years later, having just come back from an hour's ride over the countryside with Margaret on him, in which he got in a couple of good, long gallops, trotted at a smart pace, and took a couple of small fences as if just to show that the last two decades have been kinder to him than to me.

So much has happened to us over the past twenty years—my cancer and heart attack, Margaret's broken back (a riding accident, of course), huge changes in the countryside around us and in the lives of ourselves and our friends—that it's hard to remember that Berry Fox has survived all that basically unchanged. Oh, to be sure, he's a little stiff, he stumbles easily, so you need to keep his reins short in case you have to pull his head up sharply, and he can be a little grouchy first thing in the day, no doubt from the minor aches and pains of age and a general lack of tolerance for younger horses that don't know their place, but seen from a distance, and even close up, he's still the same solid, sensible horse he always was, with a broad back and kindly eyes, and once he gets moving, as unstoppable as ever. Like most of us, he doesn't seem to want to retire. On his days off, when he gets a rest, he watches us go out on other horses with a certain resentment, or perhaps just hurt feelings—"Why not me?"—but age hasn't changed him much, and he'll take you pretty much anywhere you want to go, provided you're careful with him over rocky ground and let him pick his own way. In the winter—the pony blood again—he grows a coat like a grizzly bear's, and his thick black mane seems to sprout in every direction, which only increases his charm. On the whole, he's one of those gentle, even-tempered horses about whom everybody says, "Good old Berry!" giving him a pat on the rump or the neck as they go by, which he accepts with the dignity of somebody who's been around a long time and has seen vets, blacksmiths, and barn managers come and go over the years.

Of course his competition days are long since over, but in his day he won a lot of eventing ribbons and performed, just as Margaret had intended, as a backup to Missouri. You wouldn't necessarily have guessed it, if you looked at Berry standing in a field, head down in the grass, but in the right hands he could put in a winning performance, though what you needed even more was a strong pair of legs, to push him up to the bit and keep him moving. Roxie had as strong a pair of legs as any rider I've ever seen, and she could make Berry strut around the ring, neck bowed, head down, legs flying, as if he were being auditioned for the Spanish Riding School in Vienna. Even in his old age Libby Dowden, who managed the barn for us for years, could still make him look like a champion, but on the few occasions when I was talked into having a lesson on him, I was never able to do it—I don't have the knack for dressage, and Berry figured that out on day one. On the other hand, a jumping lesson on Berry, back in the days when he was still doing a lot of jumping (and I was still doing a little), was always a pleasure, since no matter what you did, or how badly you rode him, he always went over the jump cleanly and brought you down safely on the other side, though with a slightly reproachful sideways look, as if to suggest in a gentlemanly way that perhaps you could have done *your* part of the job a little better. Not too many horses can succeed in looking reproachfully pained, but Berry had that down pat, though his chief characteristic was a blend of high spirits and good humor rare enough in a person, let alone a horse.

He was also what is known as "a good keeper," which is to say that he liked his chow, and in his own quiet way got down to the task of eating it, whether it was his feed, hay, or grass, and thrived on it. Most old horses get skinny, and their ribs start to show, but Berry, even at an advanced age today, is still solid, rounded, and filled out, obviously chosen by nature to be Falstaff as opposed to Cassius. Some horses are fussy about their feed (not every horse "eats like a horse"), though picky eating is sometimes just the result of a tooth problem that the owner has ignored, but Berry eats his grub neatly and swiftly, then stands around in his stall with his eyes closed, in a trance of well-being, before starting in on his hay. Like a lot of horses—most, in fact—he doesn't much like to be left behind if he's out with a group, so left to himself he'll dawdle along at a walk, taking in the scenery, but when the horses in front of him break into a canter, his ears go forward and he runs to catch up with them, huffing and puffing like an old-fashioned steam engine and building up to an impressive rate of knots as he narrows the gap between himself and whoever is in front of him.

Still, the same basic good nature that made Berry Fox such a pleasant horse to have around didn't prevent him from being the ideal horse to take Margaret to the higher levels of eventing. Berry was willing to try; you could rely on him to take you over the jumps, he put in a great show at dressage, and in his day he even had the killer instinct that makes for eventing winners.

At this point, let me say, I was still only dimly aware that there was this whole world out there of "combined training," which went right up to the Olympics, with local and national boards of directors, and with a thick rule book that any serious eventer had better know by heart and keep up to date with. Rather like Berry, I could see that the dressage phase was a stern test of skill, that the stadium jumping required not only good jumping skills but the ability to memorize a complicated course from one jump to the next, and that the cross-country phase was hell-for-leather fun (if you enjoyed dangerous fun), involving not only fences and walls but banks, ditches, water jumps, and all sorts of ingenious obstacles. Not every horse wants to jump without hesitation into water of unknown depth, gallop through it, then jump out of it over a stiff fence and keep going on dry land again, and not every rider has the sense of balance and the sheer balls for that kind of thing either. At every serious event I'd seen horses refuse at the very edge of the water, or riders lose heart and fall off into the water as their horse galloped off toward the trailer parking area, reins and stirrups flapping. "Horse loose on course!" from the announcer over the loudspeaker was an automatic heads-up, even for unknowledgeable spectators, at every event, only one step below the more alarming "Ambulance to fence number six, please!"

The first big-time event I went to, up in Massachusetts on a searing hot summer's day, a horse cleared a fence, then went crashing to the ground, dead of a heart attack in mid-jump, and a rider was carried off in the ambulance with a shattered leg. Things like this don't happen very often at dressage shows, or even at jumping shows, but eventing has its danger-

*Margaret on
Zenith.*

Photo by Cindy Arendt

277

ous side, which for many is half the attraction. It took actor Christopher Reeves's accident, which left him paralyzed, to bring home to the outside world, and even to many eventers, just how risky a sport it is, and that even the required regulation back protector and helmet with a harness and a chin strap may not protect you if you hit the ground at the wrong angle.

The sight of Margaret plunging down steep drops or taking off to jump fences that looked solid enough to stop a tank gave me some indication of what was to come at the higher, more "serious" levels of eventing, and a couple of disastrous tries at it myself at the very lowest, local level on Zapata were enough to convince me that I had no more business doing it than I had going out on the racecourse at Lime Rock driving a formula racing car—a brief adventure that ended after I bought myself a Nomex fireproof suit, fireproof shoes and gloves, and a Kevlar helmet, and found myself one blazing hot afternoon in a real honest-to-God race, harnessed tightly into an open V-formula racing car and beginning to realize, hot and sweaty-palmed, as other cars (mostly driven by crew-cut aggressive entrepreneurial businessmen in their forties and nineteen-year-old kids with no sense of danger) skidded past me around the S-turns, engines thundering and tires screaming, just why you needed to be wearing all that fireproof stuff in the first place. Above all the noise of the engines, I could hear a small voice whispering over and over again in my head: "Are you crazy? This is *dangerous!*"

While it is admittedly difficult to catch fire riding a horse, any kind of equestrian competition is also a dangerous business, and not for the faint-hearted. The regulation back protector and helmet help, of course, but the greatest safety element is the horse itself, and the rider's skill.

In any event, as Margaret sought to fill her barn, she cast her net wider and wider for the right horse, none of which, however fond we became of them, seemed to turn out to be what she had in mind. There was Cheyenne, an Appaloosa, a sweet horse with real ability who suffered from narcolepsy and had a disconcerting habit of falling asleep and landing in a heap with a puzzled expression that seemed to be saying, "How did *that* happen?" Cheyenne fell asleep instantly—one moment you could be riding him, the next moment you were on the ground—which made him a poor candidate for competitive success, though when he was awake, he was terrific. He was followed by Lonesome Dove (named with the blessing of Larry McMurtry), who was good but had leg problems, then Zenith, who was terrific, a great competitive horse and a big step up for Margaret, but who began to go lame on her and eventually had to be retired to Rita Dee's old-age home for horses, then Topper and Nimbus (no western names for them), who were good horses too, then, at last, Nebraska, an Appaloosa mare, with whom, from the very first moment, it was obvious that Margaret bonded.

It was love at first sight.

CHAPTER TEN

A Great Lady

'M NOT NORMALLY FOND of "Apps"—nothing personal, mind you—particularly the ones that are pink around the eyes, with wispy tails. I've seen "leopard Apps" (the ones that have jet-black markings like ink spots against a white background) that were stunning, but I've always suspected it's possible that the best looking Apps tend to stay in the West, where they're bred and greatly admired (some of the best ones are still bred by the Nez Perce Indian Nation), rather than being brought east. Many of the ones I've seen aren't that gracefully built, either, color apart—they tend to look chunky, with a kind of Indian pony look that comes off better in Remington paintings than it does in real life.

So when Margaret called me in the city to say that she thought she'd found the horse she was looking for, after so many that hadn't worked out in the end, and that it was a registered Appaloosa mare, my heart sank slightly. The only Appaloosa we'd ever owned was poor Cheyenne, and I'd never thought he was a handsome horse, even setting aside his tendency to fall asleep at the crucial moments in his life. Margaret loved him, but of course she loves all her horses, and since they're like her children, none of them ever seems ugly to her. But I found the pinkish cast to Cheyenne's face mildly off-putting, though in other respects he was a nice enough horse when he was awake.

I was prepared to be disappointed by Margaret's new horse, but one look at Nebraska, as her new horse was named, was enough to sweep away any prejudice I had against Apps—she was a stunner, maybe the best-looking horse we'd ever had in the barn.

Margaret had found her (her original name was Sally Gee) in an ad in the *Chronicle of the Horse,* which is a little like finding the man or woman of your dreams in the personal column of the *New York Observer.* The horse was being sold by Karen Norton, a horsewoman in Connecticut who had too many horses on her hands and, reluctantly, had to give one up. This is a song one hears all the time when horse shopping, but in this case it turned out to be true. Nebraska was everybody's favorite, and putting her up for sale was a traumatic experience for Karen, mitigated only by the fact that in Margaret she has found an obviously kindred spirit.

Karen and her husband Bob were typical of people of relatively limited means—i.e., very far from "big rich" like the Tobers, whose whole life seemed to be concentrated on their horses. Karen was an eventer herself, who, as I was to discover later, was one of the very few people who competed successfully on a stallion. When she went to events, her truck and trailer were always surrounded by empty space, no matter how crowded the rest of the parking lot might be. That was because whenever somebody started to pull in beside them, Karen or Bob would say, "Hope you don't mind, but we have a stallion," and people would swing their rigs away without even stopping, in search of a safer place to park.

Except for a habit of kicking out the tires of the trailer when he got bored, her Trakhener stallion Seydlitz was in fact a nicely enough man-

nered horse, but stallions scare many horse people, particularly if
they've got a mare. "His father was snorty and off the wall," Karen says
of him. "But he's a real sweetheart." On the other hand, he likes to get
his way. Once when she was leaving his stall, he grabbed her by his teeth
"on the meat of her butt" and dragged her back in. "I guess that kind of
thing is why I'm such a tough person," she says more reflectively.
Indeed, she is—as Margaret puts it—"a toughie," high praise from one
horse person about another, one of those people who, like Margaret
herself, will compete even with a back so badly hurt that she can hardly
walk upright. If there's one thing horse people believe in, it's going on
with whatever they're doing despite injuries and pain that would put
most other athletes on the sidelines. For that matter, one of the things
that Karen liked about Nebraska, right from the get-go, when she
picked her out from an Appaloosa breeder in—where else?—Nebraska,
was that the mare herself looked like "a toughie," so much so that
shortly after arriving *chez nous* she acquired the admiring nickname
"Miss Army Boots" (an unlikely nickname for a horse) because she
seemed virtually indestructible. Injuries, bad weather, sloppy footing
that would make most horses think twice about going on never stopped
Nebraska—she had, as they say, "heart."

Apps are a "color breed," of course, like paints or palominos, so they
don't necessarily run to type, and inventive cross-breeding over the
years has produced some interesting, even startling, variations, particularly in size and build. Color apart, Nebraska had a lot of quarter horse
in her at first sight, with the massive chest, thick neck, and big, muscular
rump that are quarter horse characteristics, but somewhere in her background there was a lot of thoroughbred too, for she had the small ears,
the graceful lines, the long, cleanly sculptured legs of the typical thoroughbred, along with a thick black tail—nothing skimpy about *her*
tail—and a black mane that grew straight up, like a crew cut, or the
manes on Greek and Roman sculptures of horses, and which resembled
the "Mohawk strip" that was, at about that time, becoming fashionable
for the more extreme and daring teenagers.

There wasn't a trace of pink showing on her. Her markings were a deep russet brown against white, her head was a solid reddish brown, and her eyes were dark, soulful, and intelligent. Graceful as she was, she was solidly built ("Built like a brick outhouse," as we came to say of her), with perhaps the most beautiful coat I've ever seen on a horse of any kind—thick, sweet-scented, soft, and lustrous—running your fingers through it was a sensuous experience, as was leaning your face against Nebraska's neck.

A certain amount of courage was required to attempt this kind of intimacy with her, however, because she snapped her teeth and bit at the slightest opportunity. If you were *really* close to her, of course, beside her neck, she couldn't reach around and bite you, but with her ears flat back against her head, her teeth snapping like castanets and her eyes giving off warning signals, she wasn't an easy horse to cuddle up to.

It took a while to realize that Nebraska didn't much care for most other horses—though she would eventually bond with Missouri, in old age—and much preferred women to men, so far as people were concerned. When she was in her stall, she had a way of reaching out at you as you walked down the aisle past her, neck extended, ears back, and teeth snapping, that led us to refer to her affectionately as "the snapping turtle," although there was nothing turtle-like about her in other respects. Both Margaret and Roxie soon learned that in Nebraska's case, the old adage that "her bark was worse than her bite" did not apply—her bite was serious and memorable.

Her ears were flat back against her head—a major warning signal—so much of the time that it was hard to photograph her with them in the more desirable alert, upright position, but it was very soon noticed that when Nebraska was in full motion, cantering toward a stiff jump, for example, or galloping cross-country to make up for lost time, or just being ridden at a brisk pace out on the trails, her ears were forward, and she looked completely happy. What she *didn't* like was standing around, it appeared, or being fussed over when she was in her stall, which she seemed to regard as an invasion of her space. A natural athlete, she was happiest when in motion. Even her walk was a revelation—fast, springy, covering a lot of ground with each step. Nebraska could walk faster than most other horses can trot, and without being pushed.

Better still, with her broad back and solid build, she was comfortable, maybe the most comfortable horse I've ever ridden—not that I was allowed to ride her much once her career as an eventing star began to rise. You could trot her all day without jarring your back, or sit back in the saddle totally relaxed while she cantered, as if you were lounging in a La-Z-Boy easy chair; she was simply the gold standard when it came to comfort, which very rarely goes hand in hand with being a first-rate competitive horse and having a real will to win.

None of that necessarily explains why Nebraska and Margaret bonded, but bond they did, from day one, as if their character and personality dovetailed. On Nebraska, Margaret looked not only totally confident and at ease—she does on most horses—but somehow as if she and Nebraska were one, completely attuned to each other's mood and happy in each other's company. Others could ride Nebraska—me occasionally, as a treat, Roxie to exercise her when Margaret had other horses to ride, or to fine-tune her in the dressage ring—but it wasn't the same. Nebraska would make any rider look good, but with Margaret aboard she seemed to skim over the ground effortlessly, so responsive that it was as if she were reading Margaret's thoughts rather than responding to a signal.

And perhaps she was, at that. I'm not a skeptic when it comes to that kind of communication between animal and person, and in fact there is a level of riding that's only possible if horse and rider are communicating mentally. Anybody who has ever watched a good roping team, horse and rider, working has to realize that there are two minds in communication there, and the same is true at the higher levels of eventing, dressage, and show jumping, as well as racing, where at the critical moments the horse's mind and the jockey's have to be in sync.

Horses are good at absorbing a rider's thoughts—it's why a lack of self-confidence in the rider is so fatal: the horse can sense it instantly, without any physical signals, and very naturally jumps to the conclusion that if the rider, who is sitting up there in the saddle and supposed to be in charge, feels uneasy about what lies ahead, then there's probably something to be afraid of, and the best thing to do is either to stop or take off, a horse's only choice when confronting a dangerous situation. By the same token, self-confidence, determination, and a sympathetic understanding of the horse's problems communicate themselves instantly from rider to horse, and the horse allows itself to become, though animate and a separate personality, an instrument for the rider to play, alert and responsive to the rider's wishes. It's a trust, a bond, one that is immensely difficult to achieve and fragile, all too easy to break in one careless or thoughtless moment. That in part explains why Margaret was always a little reluctant to let anybody else ride Nebraska, right from the beginning, though the truth was that Nebraska was a tough horse, with a mind of her own, very much what you'd expect a western-bred horse to be, and was remarkably patient with strange riders, if not always exactly enthusiastic. A rider who really knew what she was doing, like Margaret's goddaughter Tamzin, Nebraska would accept without hesitation, and never put a foot wrong, and to a lesser degree that was true of Roxie too—after all, Nebraska saw Roxie every day, so she was used to her.

When I rode her, I could always tell by her ears (and the gnashing and clicking of her teeth) that she was doubtful ("*Now* what?" she seemed to be saying), but she also knew that I wouldn't put her through her paces, or take her over big jumps, if only because the last thing I wanted was to bring Nebraska home lame, so with me she always knew that not much was going to be asked of her, and so long as I didn't lean on her mouth, she was quite willing to be ridden by me. She never made trouble, or showed off. She was all business, absolutely reliable—she didn't buck seriously, she didn't shy, she didn't stop or hesitate, she was always the perfect lady, except for the ears and the teeth, signaling, no doubt, nothing more than her impatience with and general intolerance of any rider who wasn't Margaret.

The search for a worthy backup to Missouri had been a long one, and not without its intense disappointments. Cheyenne had seemed like a winner until we discovered that he was narcoleptic (who even knew that horses suffered from narcolepsy?); Lonesome Dove, Zenith, Topper, and Nimbus all had their good points, particularly Zenith, a striking black Dutch warmblood mare, but each of them turned out to have some kind of problem. The cross-country phase of eventing, unlike most forms of equine competition, takes place over rough ground, often rocky or badly broken up, or bone-dry and hard in the summer months. It is not a forgiving environment, and even a horse that is sound enough to perform well in the dressage and the stadium jumping phases may still go lame in the cross-country. Hard pounding over rough ground or through thick mud brings to the fore all those little "problem areas" that vets are supposed to pick up when the horse is X-rayed and turns them very quickly into a case of full-fledged lameness, which may have been what happened to poor Zenith, who was a terrific performer for a while and did very well for Margaret but wasn't, in the end, up to the task.

Zenith was a winner, earning blue ribbons for Margaret again and again with an appealing personality and dramatic good looks, but none of that makes any difference if the horse can't take the pounding and the shock of eventing. After all, when a horse takes a big jump, as it lands it puts tons of pressure on small bones in its front feet that are hardly larger than those in a human being's finger, so the smallest trace of a problem there is bound to cause trouble. It's one of the peculiarities of the horse that so much weight and power rests on such a delicate bone structure—it's as if a human being walked on his extended index fingers—and although a horse's hoof looks like a solid structure, it is in fact complex, intricate, and easily damaged or bruised, and contains within it an even more complex structure of delicate and tiny bones, all of which have to mesh together smoothly and without friction if the horse is to go sound. "No hoof, no horse," goes the old horseman's adage, and it's true enough. No matter how good the horse may look, if all those tiny bones—and the ligaments, muscles, and tendons that support them—aren't in proper alignment, or are impeded by injury or strain or by arthritic changes, the horse isn't going anywhere, not for long, anyway, and certainly isn't going to be competing successfully. Given the Rube Goldberg architecture on which it moves, the fact that the horse can run and jump at all is something of a miracle, let alone that it does so carrying another creature's weight on its back.

Nebraska had the kind of solidity that inspired confidence from the very start. She was a horse with "a leg at each corner," as horsemen say, standing four-square, front legs straight and separated by a broad chest, hind legs also well separated, the four legs forming, if you were to draw the horse from below or from the side, as close to a square as possible— in short, the ideal horse, one with the same layout as the modern sports car, in which the wheels have been pushed as far apart (giving greater width of track) as they can go, and as far out to the corners of the car as possible (thus eliminating as much overhang as possible at both ends).

That great artist and anatomist Leonardo da Vinci drew horses exactly the way horses ought to look, unlike those of painters of later periods who had a tendency to make them look a little like enlarged greyhounds. In any event, Nebraska would have pleased Leonardo, even standing in a field doing nothing—her muscles seemed to ripple, and she fit exactly "within the square," or "in the frame," as dressage people, with their roots in classical antiquity, like to describe the way a horse should look when working in the ring, and as Leonardo painted and modeled them in his work.

.   .   .

This isn't some kind of effete eastern (or European) concept—the sculptures of Chinese T'ang period horses are "in the frame," thickly muscled neck held high in front of a gracefully curved back, head vertical, ears alert, legs placed geometrically under the body, just like the horses in classical Greek sculpture or in the Spanish Riding School in Vienna. The ideal western horse looks pretty much the same, as do the Paso Finos in Latin America. Most horses, to be sure, can eventually be taught to do this, though horses with a long back or a long neck are at a disadvantage, but it may require more time, skill, hard work, and talent than the average rider has to invest. On the other hand, some horses seem naturally endowed to hold themselves in the correct way, and even without a rider on their back tend to fall into a posture of classical perfection automatically. In some ways it's like ballet—most little girls can be taught the rudiments of the classic positions if you start them early enough, and some of them will take to it more naturally than others, however even among the latter group not all of them will grow up to become Maya Plisetskaya.

It's important for a nonrider to understand that none of this is esoteric—on the contrary, it is all founded in practical horsemanship. A horse with its neck and head in the correct position and its legs well underneath it is more easily and more precisely controlled than a horse that is sprawled out sloppily. Of course, for some things this is not an issue. Thoroughbreds on the racetrack stretch out because the only objective is speed—the last thing the jockeys want to do is to slow them down or stop them, and in any case the jockeys, who are perched above the horse on their knees, are not in a position to exert all that much control over their mount; their job is to stay on and make the horse go fast. If speed is the only issue, precise control is secondary—when the Scots Greys made their famous charge at the Battle of Waterloo, the troopers were ordered to take the bit out of the horse's mouth beforehand, so that even had they wanted to restrain the horse or slow it down, they couldn't—think of it as driving a car with no brakes or steering, and the accelerator pressed down flat against the floorboard. Without a bit, the horses, no doubt in a state of frenzy or panic at the noise, the smell of blood, and the confusion, could only charge at a full gallop straight at the enemy, crashing into the French lines at full speed, each trooper riding stirrup to stirrup with the man next to him, holding on to the horse's mane with his left hand and wielding his saber with the right. It is one of the more famous moments of British military history, captured in a huge, memorable, and famous painting by Lady Elizabeth Butler, in which the Scots Greys are depicted charging from the enemy's point of view, a long line of horses galloping out of control straight toward the viewer, eyes wide open with fear—more like an armed stampede than an orderly military maneuver. Certainly it put the fear of God into Napoleon's Garde Impériale and the gunners behind them, which was no easy thing to do.

But that, of course, is the exact opposite of what most riders want—for the most part, what riders require is a firm degree of control over the horse, the very reverse of what happens on a racetrack, or when a horse bolts in a panic. A horse that bolts won't be—*can't* be— stopped, not even at the risk of its own life, let alone that of its rider. Nineteenth-century foxhunters' memoirs are full of grisly stories about what happens when a horse bolts, galloping out of control under low branches that knock the rider off, often with a broken neck, or in one case into a low tunnel in which the rider is decapitated, the moral being that the horse must always be controlled, and never allowed to surrender to its own fear. (The introduction of the railway train gave horses a dramatic reason to bolt in the Victorian era, as the introduction of the motorcar would in the Edwardian era—horses dislike new and noisy inventions that spout steam or smoke.) Once the horse gives in to fear and bolts, no amount of pulling on the reins will help; in fact it will only make matters worse by giving the horse something to pull *against*, while increasing its fear by the application of pain. (A strong rider may be able to pull the horse's neck around sharply so that it starts turning in a circle, but while this is recommended, it isn't easy to do, and may require more strength—and presence of mind—than the rider is likely to have.) Anyone who has ever been on a horse that bolts is unlikely to forget the experience in a hurry. The only thing you can do is to hang on for dear life and hope you can stay on until it reaches the stable, which is almost always where it's heading to. For all these reasons, control of the horse matters a lot, and much of the way the horse is taught to hold itself is designed with this in mind—a question of aesthetics and practicality coming together. The object is to get the horse to respond to small and delicate signals rather than getting into a test of strength that the rider is only too likely to lose and which can only increase the horse's panic and discomfort, which are making it run straight for home in the first place, ignoring whatever obstacles may be in the way.

The gracefully curved neck carriage, the head carried vertically, the way the horse "mouths" the bit (that is to say, chews on it gently, as opposed to fighting it), all add up to a horse that is responsive and paying attention, and that takes the signals it receives from the rider seriously rather than fighting them. A good western rider only has to touch the horse's neck with the rein to get it to turn in the opposite direction, and can stop the horse by simply raising his or her little finger to increase the pressure of the bit by an infinitesimal amount. English riders can move the horse sideways by the most gentle of pressure with a short, blunt spur, nothing more than a well-placed, modest nudge, and can stop a horse by simply tightening their fingers on the reins—indeed, many well-trained horses will even respond to a limited range of voice commands ("Walk!" Trot!" "Canter!" "Halt!") when they are given in a low, firm, but above all nonthreatening and consistent tone of voice. The aim of riders everywhere is to maintain control of the horse with the bare minimum of effort and force, and to do so gracefully, harmoniously, and within the limits of the possible, with the horse's full cooperation. Thus the importance of balance, both in the way the rider sits on the horse and the way the horse holds itself when ridden. Balance not only looks right; it puts the horse in a position from which it can

respond to the rider's aids without confusion or doubt, with the minimum of friction for either party.

The brisk forward movement of the well-trained horse—a "forward-
moving" horse, as horse people call it—is again not only good looking
but a major factor in control. Just as a becalmed or slow-moving sailboat
is almost impossible to steer, whereas one that's well under way will
respond quickly to the helm, the horse that is moving forward at a brisk
pace brings a certain momentum to turns and movements, while one
that's just plodding along will be much harder to turn, and slower to
react, even to quite large and powerful promptings from the rider.
Getting a horse to turn when it's standing still may require heroic pushing and shoving, or even leaning against its shoulder to get it to move if
you're on the ground, whereas the same horse if it's moving forward
briskly can be turned by nothing more than a change of weight in the
seat or a slight tightening of one rein. Forward motion—willing, natural
forward motion—is the key to controlling a horse; without that forward
impulsion the horse is a thousand-pound lump, and a constant test of
the rider's strength and patience; with it, anything is possible.

In any event, beyond all other things, forward impulsion is what a
horse person looks for in a horse, and Nebraska had it in spades. Her
walk was bold, "animated" (another favorite word of horse people), and
free-moving, her trot was springy, her canter bold and smooth, and at
any gait she covered a lot of ground with each stride. Her walk carried
her ahead of most other horses, which she didn't mind, since she wasn't
afraid of being in front, but unlike a lot of other horses she didn't make
trouble if you wanted her to go behind—her ears would flatten back to
register her objection, but she didn't buck or try to break into a gallop to
catch up. Still, her preference was for rapid movement, and she had a
certain lack of tolerance for slowpokes, either on her back or in the
form of fellow horses. Wherever you were going, she wanted to get
there at a good, smart pace. If I were going to cross the United States on

a horse—there is almost always somebody doing this in the summer months—Nebraska would have been my first choice for the job. She would have eaten up the miles, day after day, and been pretty good company too, as horses go. As our farrier Tom Pavelek once said, her feet would certainly be up to it.

Perhaps fortunately, this was never a realistic possibility, partly because I would never have had the time, and partly because Nebraska wasn't my horse, after all; she was Margaret's, and what Margaret wanted to do was win events with her, not cross the country from sea to shining sea on horseback, though now that I think about it, she could probably have been talked into the journey, provided we camped out for the night in places where she could plug in her hair dryer. All the same, Nebraska's willingness to go the extra mile was never in doubt from the very beginning. When other horses were getting hot, sweaty, and tired and looking for a chance to stop, she just kept going, with her long, swinging stride. Weather didn't seem to bother her—heat didn't bring her out in a sweat, fierce cold didn't matter to her a bit. In the winter she grew a noticeably thicker coat—you could sink your fingers deep into it—but even in the summer she still retained a pretty thick coat, unlike a thoroughbred, for example, which probably served her as insulation against temperature extremes, a useful thing for a horse from a state like Nebraska. She always looked good, the way some horses do, maybe because her remarkable color had the additional advantage of not showing the dirt, maybe because she was just one of those horses that seem slightly fastidious, "a real lady," in fact, as everybody who met her sooner or later came to say of her. Toward the end of her life she acquired the new nickname "Mrs. Braveheart" (in homage to the Mel Gibson movie about Scotland), and brave she certainly was. Like all good competition horses, Nebraska seemed to want to win, and one of my favorite photographs of her was taken during a victory lap at Groton House Horse Trials, in Massachusetts, as she galloped around the stadium field with Margaret holding a blue ribbon up in the air. Insofar as a horse can have an expression, Nebraska looked modestly pleased

Margaret and Nebraska—a victory lap.

with herself, and also as if she could have gone on galloping for another hour or so without even breaking into a sweat.

From the very first, Nebraska was a terrific competitor—dressage, which many horses are reluctant to accept, as if they just don't see the point of it all, she took to naturally, and despite a certain subliminal prejudice among dressage judges in the East against Appaloosas (and in favor of thoroughbreds and European-bred horses), she scored well from the very beginning. The cross-country phase she simply enjoyed, the way any good athlete enjoys what she is good at.

Nebraska won seven novice level events in one year and was the novice champion of our area (the Northeast) in three years, then overall champion, and was soon regularly winning a place at the national USCTA level, as well as competing on numerous winning teams. Ribbon after ribbon, trophy after trophy, filled the house, not to speak of embroidered presentation blankets and saddle pads, and photographs of Nebraska with a blue ribbon pinned to her bridle. Year after year, during the eventing season that stretches from May through November in our part of the country, Margaret would come home from the weekend having won, and Nebraska would descend backward down the ramp from the trailer daintily, looking as pleased with herself as her owner. Applause, praise, admiration, she took in her stride—her "personal best" was almost always enough to win, often against far more expensive horses, for Nebraska had been that miracle everybody in the horse world seeks, the perfect horse going for a reasonable price. She became, admittedly in the rather limited world of lower-level eventing in the Northeast, something of a celebrity as horses go, yet you could still have put a child on her in perfect safety—she had no vices, no tricks; she would go in front or behind without making a fuss, and didn't spook at anything.

To see Nebraska compete at an event was to see real class. She not only looked good, she looked as if she were having a good time, and gradually began to acquire a small circle of admirers and enthusiasts, almost a fan

Photo by Reflections of Killington, Inc.

"Class!"

club. It was a pleasure to drive up to Woodstock, Vermont, to the Green Mountain Horse Association event, or to Groton, Massachusetts, or down to Maryland, where the *Chronicle of the Horse* team championships took place, and find, when I arrived there, that Nebraska was always in the lead. She managed to make winning look easy, but beneath the easy self-confidence she, like Margaret, always made the maximum effort, instinctively took the right line, never slackened off at the end of a long day, when a moment's inattention will bring down a rail in the stadium jumping and cost you your hard-won first place. She was a natural competitor, maybe the best $7,500 event horse that anybody could buy, and worth many, many times that if you measured her in money, which nobody did.

Nebraska in some respects changed Margaret's life. She began to see herself as a serious competitive rider, somebody whose life revolved around the sport, rather than somebody whose hobby it was. On the

Nebraska and Star

principle that you should never put all your eggs in one basket, we acquired from time to time some more seriously expensive horseflesh, including Star, a thoroughbred whose half-brother would win a silver medal in individual three-day competition at the Sydney Olympics, and Jiminy Cricket (known, more easily, as "Jimmy"), another thoroughbred with an impressive record of wins, but who turned out to be difficult to keep, unhappy during the winter, with hooves that kept Tom Pavelek busy making all sorts of therapeutic horseshoes and pads. Star was explosively spooky, though never in competition, but Jimmy was a "high-maintenance" horse whose back required special pads, acupuncture, massage, and expensive injections, and not an easy horse to ride. Successful as both these horses were, Nebraska just kept going, giving no trouble, winning whatever she was entered in, as well as being the perfect horse to hack out on the trails.

When it came to Nebraska, you didn't need magnetic saddle pads, or acupuncture, or expensive back specialists; you just put a saddle on her and got on with it. Jimmy might hate cold weather—you could actually *see* how miserable he was—but Nebraska loved a brisk ride on a cold winter's day, with icicles forming from her nostrils as she cantered through the snow, her glossy, sweet-smelling thick coat covered with gleaming ice crystals. She was, in fact, the least temperamental of stars.

Still, much as Nebraska seemed likely to go on forever, Margaret decided she needed a young backup. Besides, she would have the fun of training a young horse who could take over one day from Nebraska, who could then give up competition and go on into a long and honorable retirement. Margaret's friend Mark Weissbecker eventually found her just the right horse, a four-year-old Irish sport horse, who had a good, solid build and was a rather flashy rose-gray, a color I didn't believe until I saw it—rather like a photographic negative of an Appaloosa, he was a dark rose-gray with silver spots and a silver mane and tail.

Margaret named him Dundee—explaining to those who asked that it was spelled "as in the marmalade," for Dundee is a city famous for its marmalade. Dundee was earnest, young, easily bored, like a teenager, which is exactly what he was in terms of horse age. Like all Irish horses he was a good jumper (the national passion for foxhunting assures that), but dressage bored him, and he tended to lean on the bit and mouth it as if he were chewing gum—not likely to please a dressage judge. As time went by and Margaret took him out competing, she would find that Dundee, unlike Nebraska, had a natural gift for screwing up at just the moment when it looked as if he might be winning. He was also, like many another teenager, given to spurts of growth. He had not been a small horse when she bought him, but he seemed to put on weight, height, and muscle overnight until—there was no denying it—he became quite a large horse with every sign of getting a good bit larger before he hit his stride.

It did not seem that he would ever grow up to be another Nebraska, but fortunately the real Nebraska was there and likely to go on competing for a good many years more, so training Dundee was rather more of a hobby than a necessity. Or so it seemed.

Year after year, Nebraska had kept going, never showing her age, as handsome and solidly built as she was the day Margaret first brought her home. Then, at the age of twenty, in the dead of winter, she suddenly went lame—unusual for "Miss Army Boots," but one of those things that happen. Horses slip, or hurt themselves lying down or getting back up on their feet again (more often the latter), or step on a rock and bruise themselves, or a million and one other things that have made horses go lame from the day man first tried riding one. Even the most carefully looked-after field may contain a sharp hidden rock that a horse may step on too hard; even the tamest and most phlegmatic horse may be startled by something and take off in a hurry, pulling a tendon, ripping off a shoe, or in some other way damaging itself. Most of these things can be cured—or cure themselves—with time and care, and are, as horse people like to say, "a long way from the heart," meaning that they're not life-threatening.

Nebraska's problems went deeper, alas. X rays, poultices, injections of "bute," bandaging—nothing seemed to help. Gradually, as winter set in for good, it became apparent that we had a very sick horse on our hands, not just a lame one. Almost every day brought a visit from Paul or his partner Jeff, to try out something new or change her medication. Nebraska, who was never ill, and seemed to be indestructible, was clearly succumbing to something. It was a process we had lived through with poor Hustle, as his cancer spread—a long, slow downhill slide, in which you look at the horse and try to convince yourself that it's getting ever so slightly better, or that whatever the vet is doing may be beginning to work. Of course there are moments when things do seem to be getting better, too, but they don't last long, and pretty soon the vet is coming daily instead of weekly, or even twice a day, and his visit produces long moments of silence, in which everybody stands in the barn in a mournful group, swaddled in down jackets and wool hats against the cold, looking glumly at the patient. Tom and his partner Tim, who had shod Nebraska and all our horses for many years, looked equally glum, sadly recognizing a bad situation which wasn't going to get better, however artfully they worked.

The fact was (though nobody wanted to say the word) Nebraska had "foundered," a disease which I'd always associated with ponies who break into the feed room and eat too much grain, or horses left out too long in rich grass. In Nebraska's case, however, she was dying of complications of Cushing's disease, a hormonal imbalance that was causing physical changes, including the swelling of the sensitive laminae that make up a horse's hoof (and your nails, which are formed much the same way). It's what finally happened to Secretariat, perhaps the best looked-after horse in America, so it can happen to any horse.

A horse that's foundered can sometimes be brought back to usefulness, but not often, and one of the first signs of what's gone wrong is that the horse "points" its front feet forward, trying to keep its weight off them and on its hind quarters. Even the slightest amount of weight on the front hooves becomes increasingly painful for the horse. In some ways, of course, winter is the worst time to deal with the disease—the horse can't stand outside because the ground is frozen solid, hard as rock, which means keeping it inside twenty-four hours a day, in a stall piled high with sawdust to give it a soft surface to stand on. The shoes have to come off, of course, and eventually the front feet have to be protected with layers of plastic foam, held on with duct tape and changed at frequent intervals. The horse, in acute misery, can only move in a painful shuffle. Medications can help, up to a point, but there is no miracle cure or magic bullet, and progress, if any, is slow, with frequent episodes in which things get worse suddenly, just when you thought they were improving. Juan, who works in our barn, was wonderful with the mare, patiently rebandaging the foam pads that gave her the look of a girl trying out high heels for the first time, and gently walking her back and forth from one stall to another, across the aisle, on a well-worn path of sawdust. Calm and optimistic, he seemed to have the power to give the mare confidence, despite the pain she was in and the unfamiliar sensation of walking on thick pads. Between him, Leroy, Libby, the vets and the blacksmith, and Margaret, Nebraska was painstakingly cared for, night and day, but no miracle took place, despite the almost daily attendance of the vet, and Tom and Tim, the farriers.

One night in the deep winter, when we were in the city, we came to the conclusion that things were hopeless, and decided to have Nebraska put down. She had become increasingly listless and unresponsive and was clearly in pain, and there seemed no sensible alternative. The horse was declining rapidly and seemed to be resigned to death. The kindest thing would be to put her down, as we both knew, but putting down a horse is never easy, and in the winter in one part of the country it's harder still, since the ground is frozen solid, making it almost impossible to dig a grave for a horse.

Since we were in the middle of a brief thaw, however, it seemed like the right opportunity, and Margaret got on the phone to the vet, then to our friend Detlef Juerss, who would dig the grave, and made the necessary arrangements between them for the next morning. That night we drove up to the country, arriving late, and Margaret decided to pay a visit to the barn to commune with Nebraska, who to our surprise was standing in her stall looking 100 percent better and more lively, cheerfully eating an apple when it was offered to her. Her eyes, which had been dull and lusterless, were bright and shiny again, and she had even regained enough energy to snap her teeth at me when I appeared.

I looked at Margaret and shrugged my shoulders. In view of this unexpected revival, it was impossible to imagine putting Nebraska down in the morning. Instead, we were up early to cancel all the arrangements that had been made, with a deep sense of relief. Everybody else was relieved, too, including the vet; indeed the only cautious note came from Tamzin, Margaret's goddaughter, who was in England, and said that when a horse in Nebraska's condition rallied, that was the time to put it down, rather than using it as an excuse to put the decision off. It is almost needless to say that Tamzin turned out to be right, as usual.

The recovery was deceptive and short-lived, but having lifted the death sentence once, it became just that much harder to reinstate it. Inevitably Margaret found reasons to put it off from day to day: a new drug, a story from somewhere about a miraculous recovery on the part of a horse that was at least as sick as Nebraska, or worse off, a new procedure for gluing plastic shoes to the hoof without the use of nails. . . . Prayers were offered from well-wishers in the form of get-well cards, and it seemed for a time that they might be answered.

But it was not to be. To even the most lovingly self-deluded eye, Nebraska was declining. Paul Mountan, our vet, looked more and more mournful every time he came, which was once or twice a day again. He had X rays taken that were more depressing still, showing the rapidly deteriorating situation in her front hooves, as the aptly named coffin bone rotated closer and closer to the point where nothing more could be done for her. I took him out of the barn for a chat one evening, out of Margaret's hearing, while Nebraska was receiving her treatment. What, I asked him, was the next step? Paul looked out across the cheerless fields, looking their worst at this time of year, frozen mud covered with ice, slush, and lumps of frozen horseshit. She could lose the sole of her hoof, he said, or the hoof itself might deteriorate to the point where it couldn't be saved. That was not a possibility I thought we wanted to face, and I asked if he would let us know before that time came. Paul agreed solemnly, despite the fact that like most horse vets he is a born optimist, but as it turned out, that would not be necessary. As I should have known, when it came time to bite the bullet, Margaret would bite it herself before anybody else.

I knew too how close the relationship was between this horse and this rider—Nebraska had been a part, perhaps the most important part, of Margaret's progress from somebody who competed from time to time to somebody for whom competition was the central focus of her life, the horse that had taken her from championship to championship and filled the house with ribbons and trophies. Losing an animal you love is never easy, but losing this one was going to be very hard indeed for Margaret. It might mean losing a whole part of her own life too, for Jimmy, the "high-maintenance" winner, had been injured during the previous season and eventually had to be retired, while Star had suddenly reached the age when he had "gone sour" on competing—he would win, as he always did, in the dressage phase, then throw it all away by refusing a jump in the cross-country or stadium phase. Maybe something hurt—as with an aging athlete, that was possible, even though nothing significant showed up on X rays beyond the normal wear and tear—or maybe he had just had enough of it, taken one jump too many and decided not to do it anymore. And Dundee was still a problem—a young horse who *could* win, but didn't seem to want to. In any case, all of a sudden Margaret had gone from being a rider with four potential winners to a rider with none, and all of it happening as her favorite horse, the one with whom she bonded most closely, was dying by slow degrees, day after day. She was, perhaps, saying good-bye to more than Nebraska, and so the decision was doubly difficult for her.

"Putting a horse down" isn't that easy to begin with, emotions aside. The cavalry manual, always pragmatic, ends its section on caring for horses with a graphic illustration of how to put one down when care has failed, showing a trooper standing in front of the horse, with the lead rope in one hand and a cocked .45 caliber Colt automatic pistol in the other, aimed about two inches above the horse's eyes, right smack in the middle of its forehead, with the muzzle almost touching the horse (Bill Mauldin, the great World War II cartoonist, caricatured this perfectly with a cartoon of an old U.S. Cavalry sergeant major covering his tear-filled eyes with one hand as he holds his .45 pistol against the hood of his broken-down Jeep).

These days private owners, at any rate, prefer to leave this kind of thing to the vet, and the horse is usually tranquilized first, then given a lethal injection. Then, of course, it has to be disposed of, not an easy matter in itself. Partly, it's a question of size—a horse is a large animal to dispose of, and a dead horse is not an easy object to move. You cannot take it down to the vet and come back the next day to pick up a discreet little box of ashes.

In the past, in sporting circles, this problem was solved (and still is in serious hunt country) by "sending the horse to the kennels," that is, by taking a horse that's old or lame over to the hunt's kennels in a van to be slaughtered and butchered to feed the hounds. In hunting circles this is not only still done, but stoutly defended as the cheapest way of feeding them, without which the cost of keeping a pack of hounds would rise dramatically, making it a sport only for the rich (which most people have always assumed it was anyway). Racehorses that don't win and aren't worth breeding are slaughtered to provide meat for *boucheries chevalines* in France and Belgium, where horse meat is regarded as a delicacy, and for pet food in the United States, where it is generally not regarded as food for gourmets.

Most private owners with feelings for the horse (and enough land in which to indulge them) prefer to have it buried on their own property (cremation is not a practical alternative for an animal weighing a thousand pounds or more), but that too raises problems. In the winter it's hard to dig a deep enough grave, and if the ground is solidly frozen, it may be impossible; then, too, does one take the horse to the grave before injecting it—with the risk that the sight of the open grave may panic it—or have the horse put down, then transported to the grave (which requires a bulldozer or a forklift, and is not a pretty sight to see)?

Of course people used to be accustomed to this sort of thing—even in the late nineteenth century dead horses were a frequent sight on big city streets, mostly having died from exhaustion pulling the trams and the heavy wagons, or from slipping and breaking a leg during icy winter weather, and the European battlefields of World War I (and even World War II) produced hundreds of thousands of dead horses (both the German and the Soviet armies in World War II remained largely horse-drawn)—but these days a dead horse is a rarity, and all the more shocking for that.

Besides, the larger an animal is, the harder it is, for some reason, to accept its death. When told that killing an elephant is a crime (or ought to be), the character modeled after John Huston in Peter Viertel's *White Hunter, Black Heart* replies, "No kid, it's not a crime; it's a *sin*." There is indeed a sinful quality about killing something so large and so full of life, particularly when, like the horse, it isn't dangerous and doesn't fight back. It is hardly surprising that many buffalo hunters of the mid- to late-nineteenth century seem to have found their work deeply depressing—the buffalo were large, pacific (even benevolent), and weren't being killed for their meat, except by the Indians, and it was in fact the object of the buffalo hunters to starve the Indians into submission by slaughtering the vast buffalo herds on which they lived. The larger an animal is, the more it seems a crime against God to kill it, all the more so when it has more or less voluntarily allowed itself to be domesticated. Even the most tame and overweight of house cats never completely trusts human beings—there's always a secret feline reservation in those watchful eyes, a warning that it may turn wild again in an instant—whereas most horses put themselves in the hands of human beings without any reservations, completely trusting and in the end all too often, alas, deceived.

As the winter wore on and Nebraska's condition continued to worsen, to the point where her discomfort was obvious and no medication gave her any relief, Margaret sadly gave in to the inevitable. I had anticipated that there would be no real point in trying to talk her into it, and that it wouldn't be necessary, in the end, for Paul to warn her that the time had come—Margaret would *know*, and once she knew, she would act as quickly as possible. And so it proved. The horse was trapped, really, hardly even able to shuffle from her stall across the aisle, despite a thick, cushioning layer of sawdust and pieces of foam duct-taped to her feet. The date that had been postponed was reinstated.

This time there was to be no last-minute recovery, and no last-minute reprieve. Detlef was called in to dig a grave in one of the fields nearest the house (because we had once kept Margaret's pigs there, it is known as "the pig field"), and we selected a flat place on the lawn that was about as close as we could get her to the grave without her actually seeing it, or having to walk over rough ground. In the morning, after the vet had put her down, Detlef would move her body to the grave with his backhoe (no details about how this would be accomplished were asked or were necessary—Detlef simply suggested that Margaret should not be present for it, which was enough to guess how gruesome the procedure was likely to be).

The next day, the weather contributed to the mournful quality of the occasion—a damp, gray, dreary morning, with a leaden sky and a cold wind blowing. Paul and his assistant arrived in his big SUV, and for a few minutes we all stood around, avoiding the inevitable. Then Margaret hugged Nebraska's neck one last time and led her, walking gingerly, out of the barn and onto the lawn, close to the field in which she was to be buried.

This was not my first time. I had stood close to Tabasco when he was put down, and it's an experience I would always prefer to avoid. Somehow, the horse always seems to guess what's about to happen at the last moment, perhaps simply from the mood of the people it knows, perhaps along some more complicated internal path of knowledge. Be that as it may, horses tend toward resignation and fatalism. They don't fight back, even though they sense that something bad—fatal—is about to happen. They have no way of pleading, of course, and unlike people—and wild animals—they have long since come to accept human beings as authority figures; indeed it's almost their first lesson, and all subsequent training, one way or the other, is designed to reinforce it. The horse's fate is in our hands, and somehow the horse knows it, even at the very end. Perhaps we make them more comfortable by surrounding them with familiar faces—it would be nice to think so. More likely it merely makes it that much easier for the horse to pick up from our expressions and our tone of voice the solemnity of the moment.

Paul quickly gave Nebraska the injections, and within seconds the mare buckled and collapsed. It could hardly have gone more quickly, and, I suppose, more "humanely," but it's still awful to watch something so big and full of life as a horse transformed suddenly into an untidy heap on the ground—it seems such a lot of life to take, and all in one quick moment.

Then we looked around and realized that something was missing. Neither Detlef nor his backhoe were present.

The mare lay on her off side, legs stretched out on the grass under a gentle, intermittent rain, sprawled in a position that no living horse would have assumed—somehow, few dead things seem as dead as a dead horse—while Paul packed his things away, eager to be off.

Margaret kneeled down on the sodden grass beside Nebraska and covered her with one of the blankets she had won, embroidered with her name and the event, while the rest of us, at a decent distance, used our cellular telephones to try and reach Detlef on his. What had promised to be a pretty agonizing morning to begin with was being drawn out unbearably. Somehow, the wrong time had been communicated to Detlef, and he was still miles away, on his way to a building site to pick up his backhoe. He would be with us "as soon as he could," not at all news likely to comfort Margaret. I managed to get Margaret back into the barn—my thought was that a cup of coffee in the tack room might be a good idea while she waited for the next act—but once she was there, she looked out the window and gave a cry of alarm. "Crows!" she said.

I looked out. Indeed, crows were beginning to appear, gathering in the trees, circling in the air, some of the more courageous landing near Nebraska's body. Of course in our part of the country we don't have buzzards, as they do out west, or vultures, as they do in Africa, but crows are carnivores and scavengers too, and though smaller, they are just as determined and relentless, once they've made sure that whatever is lying there is dead. From the trees all around us they croaked and screeched at each other, bringing flocks more of them to gather in the trees.

Margaret sat beside the mare in the rain, shooing the crows off. I brought her over a rain slicker and something to sit on, but I didn't suggest that she come indoors. I knew there was no way she would abandon Nebraska to the crows, however long it took for Detlef to arrive. I also knew that she was not only saying good-bye to a beloved horse, but perhaps to a whole way of life built around eventing and competing. Knowing better than to intrude on her solitary grief, I backed away.

For what seemed like hours, Margaret sat there alone, at once grieving and protective, waving her arms at the hordes of black birds that circled around her. It was a blessed relief when the noise of Detlef's backhoe finally made itself heard above the cawing of the crows. Detlef dismounted, full of apologies, and between the two of us we persuaded Margaret to leave Nebraska's side.

I stayed—out of some sort of obligation, I'm not sure what—and watched him transport the body to the grave, drop it in, and cover it up. The next day Juan, who had cared for Nebraska with such patience, planted on the site an azalea bush that Libby had bought—a spontaneous gesture of respect and affection for a great lady.

CHAPTER ELEVEN

"I Can Never Get Enough of Looking at Horses"

 OOKING AFTER HORSES tends to bring out the best in people, partly because it's hard work, partly because the horse, unlike a cat or a dog, can't be carted off to the vet in a box for a quick visit when it's sick or injured. Because horses have always been intrinsically valuable animals, on which the owner's life very often depended in the past, veterinary care for horses was for many centuries far more advanced (and more effective) than medical care for people. In the early nineteenth century, when repeated bleeding, the application of leeches, and huge doses of emetics and laxatives were still the basic medical arsenal for human beings, horse vets already had a pretty rational sense of how to treat the more common equine problems, based on practical experience and observation as opposed to folklore, and produced impressive results. Indeed, except for the quantum leap of antibiotics, advanced pharmaceuticals, and X rays, most horse treatments have been around for centuries, in one form or other, and still work.

Generally speaking, the horse got saner, safer, and more successful medical treatment than its master (or mistress) until well into the twentieth century. Vets were washing their hands for many years before physicians were finally (and reluctantly) persuaded to do so by the discoveries of Dr. Ignaz Semmelweis, who was booed by the Vienna Medical Society for suggesting that the death rates of infants and mothers might be reduced if obstetricians would only wash their hands in hot water before delivering babies. While madame (and her baby) were dying upstairs in the house of puerperal fever, the vet was out in the barn delivering endless numbers of healthy foals, most of whose mothers survived, without anybody bothering to ask why that was so, or to suggest—God forbid!— that doctors might have something to learn from vets.

Now, of course, veterinary medicine is struggling to catch up with the huge advances in human medicine, the limiting factor being how much money people are prepared to spend on their horses' medical care, as opposed to that of themselves or their family. Except for the most valuable of horses (Triple Crown winners, and so on), there is obviously a limit to how much it is worth spending on a horse, some point at which sentiment is outweighed by common sense. Still, horse care, while retaining its links to the past in the form of such old-fashioned remedies as liniments, "firing," and "tubing" for colic, has become increasingly sophisticated, complex, and of course, expensive, in recent years.

The main difficulty remains the patient, whose size poses all sorts of problems. In the horse operating rooms, where they exist, the horse is fastened to the table while it is upright, then anesthetized, then the table is revolved into the horizontal position, along with the horse—not the kind of thing that comes cheap, and which explains why some equine surgery is still done on the spot, like early-nineteenth-century battle surgery. When my horse Zapata had to be "nerved"—an operation that involves severing the nerves in the lower legs to relieve persistent lameness—our friend Paul Mountan performed the procedure on the front lawn, outside the barn, with Zapata lying on the grass after having been fully anesthetized, and staggering to his feet groggily after the procedure had been successfully completed and the anesthetic had worn off. There is good reason to do surgery this way—the horse isn't traumatized by unfamiliar surroundings, you don't need a multimillion-dollar facility, there's plenty of light and room to work—and it favors the kind of surgeon who works quickly and decisively. Of course it has echoes of the heroic past of veterinary surgery, when vets commonly performed complex surgery on horses that nobody had thought of attempting on a human being.

Still, caring for the horse remains hard work—the patient, after all, weighs half a ton or more, can't explain what hurts, isn't necessarily cooperative, usually won't lie down, and produces its own unsterile conditions—not the ideal subject for nursing. In the old days, grooms and stable hands were pretty good at this kind of thing, but people with that kind of experience are hard to find nowadays, and a lot of owners end up doing it themselves, learning firsthand how hard it is to keep a wound clean in a large barn animal or how tiring it is to hose a leg down with cold water every hour on the hour for days on end.

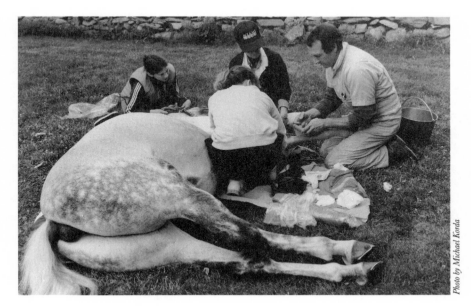

Dr. Mountan operates on Zapata on the lawn.

And yet something about horses brings out that kind of dedication in people—even people who aren't necessarily from the country, and haven't been brought up around horses.

Prisoners, for instance.

Given my interest in horses, I get a lot of mail asking me to join this or that organization to protect them (not as much as Margaret does, to be fair, but I'm better at ignoring it). One that caught my eye, however, was for the Thoroughbred Retirement Foundation, partly because it had some pretty horrifying accounts of what happens to thoroughbreds who don't do well at the track (and of course most don't), and also because the abused or injured horses, in many cases saved from the slaughterer in the nick of time, are cared for and, when possible, rehabilitated by prisoners. Where possible, the horses, once they're sound, go to good homes; the ones that can't be made sound again are often adopted as "lawn ornaments" by people who simply want to see a handsome thoroughbred grazing in a pasture, and don't care that it can't be ridden. The foundation is in the business of providing happy endings.

This, I thought, I have to see, which explains what I was doing driving to "The Farm," at Wallkill Correctional Facility, on the Hudson River more or less opposite West Point, one bright day in the early fall, when the Hudson Valley is at its most beautiful. This, in fact, is the beginning of the "leaf season," when the roads, inns, bed-and-breakfasts, and restaurants are full of tourists who have come to see the leaves turning orange and red, but none of them, I guessed, had put the Wallkill Correctional Facility on their itinerary, and the surrounding area, mostly flat farming country, was deserted, except for the occasional pickup truck or tractor. Wallkill CF doesn't exactly advertise its presence, and if I hadn't had precise directions from the indefatigable Diana Pikulski, director of the Thoroughbred Retirement Program, whom I had met at a book signing, I might have driven in circles for hours looking for the prison. As it was, when I stopped for an early lunch at an old-fashioned diner, I knew I was on the right road—the photographs on the wall were all of New York State correctional officers in various recreational pursuits, hunting and bowling being the two favorites, with fishing a close third, and most of the customers were big, solid men with crew cuts, carrying pistols and hand-cuffs under their windbreakers. Their eyes tended to have that penetrating, challenging stare that goes with the job, and which is hard to lose even when you're off duty and eating farm-fresh sausage, bacon, and eggs.

The flat countryside means that traffic for miles around is visible from the prison towers, though the prison itself, set in something of a rolling hollow in the land, doesn't appear until you're almost on top of it, looking from the driveway rather like the Smithsonian Institution at first glance, all red brick and Victorian architecture, at least so far as the administration building is concerned, with a glimpse of huge, grim cell blocks, high walls, and rolls of razor wire stretching to the horizon beyond it. A cheerful woman CO checks me in, inquires if I have a weapon to deposit in the armory, and asks me to wait. The atmosphere is institutional but not in any way threatening, and decidedly low-tech—big doors, big keys, the kind of furniture that looks as solid and heavy as the walls. The serious security is farther back, behind the big, locked doors.

Diana soon turns up, an attractive and chatty young woman from Vermont with a mission—two, in fact. Mission number one has to do with the horses. The thoroughbred industry, about which she talks cautiously since much of the foundation's money comes from there (one of the biggest endowments comes from the late Paul Mellon's estate), is tough on horses, first of all by breeding far more thoroughbreds than it needs, and secondly because the only thing that matters for thoroughbreds is winning races. That means pushing the horses hard when they're still young and growing, with soft bones, keeping them racing even when they're injured, and getting rid of the ones that don't win races or are too badly injured or lamed to keep on trying. Of course, at the top, it's an industry that contains a lot of very wealthy people, some of whom have a sentimental streak about horses (and can afford to), but below that level it's largely an industry of small-timers, operating on the proverbial shoestring, dependent on paying low wages for immigrant labor, and taking marginal horses to tracks you've never heard of.

Admittedly, the word *thoroughbred* conjures up a glamorous image, but in fact the racing world is a tough, cutthroat business, and the average thoroughbred isn't Secretariat but more likely the product of over-breeding, inbreeding, or just poor judgment or plain bad luck in breeding. Horses like this get pushed hard too soon, often on the kind of cheap, small-time track where the footing is poor and the turns aren't properly banked, so they develop potentially crippling leg problems early on, and when that happens, they aren't going to be put out in rolling green pastures to recuperate, like the horses in television ads around the time of the Kentucky Derby; they're going to be sold to the killers for between four hundred and five hundred dollars, and will either be sent to Europe—lean thoroughbred meat is regarded as a delicacy superior to beef in Belgium and France—or to pet food factories here in the United States. (In case anybody thinks this is a small business, in the year 2000 nearly 50,000 horses were slaughtered in the United States, and another 26,573 exported to Canada for slaughter there, of which some 4,000 to 5,000 were racetrack thoroughbreds.) For the small owner, there isn't much choice—a horse that can't win, or worse yet can't run, costs just as much to feed and care for as one that can, and sending a horse to the killers is at least money in your pocket. "You have to sell the losers to the killers on a Friday to feed the others over the weekend," as one of the trainers explains the economics of small-time horse racing.

This is the downside of lower-level racing, which nobody wants to monitor, or even think about, the unglamorous side of a glamorous sport, and it's Diana's determination that you look it right in the eye—her primary mission is saving horses from the killers and then, when possible, rehabilitating them so they can go to decent homes where they're wanted. Her second mission is saving souls, for the foundation sends the horses it has rescued from slaughter to the prisons, where the rehabilitation process is carried out by prisoners, who find in the horses something rare in prison life—creatures whose needs are greater than those of the inmates, and who desperately crave care, attention, and love. The inmates work to rehabilitate the horses; in turn, the horses have the potential of rehabilitating the inmates.

Two large men come over and introduce themselves, George McGrath, deputy superintendent of Wallkill CF, dark-suited, genial, but with the unmistakable look of a man whose job is running a prison, and Jim Tremper, more casually dressed, who manages the Thoroughbred Foundation's farm here and is somehow able to combine a look of firmness with the infinite patience you need to look after horses. Both men have bone-crushing handshakes, a certain country-bred reticence and formal politeness, and a real devotion to the cause. There are not a lot of humanizing aspects to the New York State prison system. You just need to look behind the ornate administration building at the vast, grim blocks of cells, the guard towers, and the glitter of tightly coiled razor wiring to guess what life is like back there—we've seen it often enough on television and at the movies—but the horses are one of the more visible attempts to give the prisoners a glimpse of something more hopeful, and since the majority of the inmates are city boys, different.

We pile into a car and drive about a mile away from the prison to a neat, white-buildinged farm with numerous well-fenced pastures. The view looking downward to the west is spectacular—we can see the Hudson River, with the woods beginning to turn red and yellow on both sides of it. Looking back to the east shows us the prison blocks on the horizon, surrounded by a high fence. "Everywhere you drive here, you're in sight of the guard towers," Deputy Superintendent McGrath says unnecessarily, since it was my first thought—the roads are laid out here so somebody with a pair of binoculars can keep track of every vehicle. It seems likely that McGrath means this to be comforting—Big Brother is not only watching you, but can summon up help whenever it's needed.

The prisoners are back at Wallkill having their lunch, McGrath explains, but Jim Tremper takes the opportunity to show me around. The horses are outside, in their pastures, but he walks me around the beautifully kept barns, which have about forty stalls, the schoolhouse, where, he tells me, the inmates receive a lecture every day on horse care, often given by a farrier or a veterinarian, the special stalls for horses that are sick or injured, "problem cases." In the schoolroom there is a huge wall board showing every possible kind of horseshoe, including some I've never seen before, made by one of the prisoners (there's no shortage of time for big projects like this, in a place where five, ten, or twenty years is all part of the deal), elaborate four-color charts of the anatomy of a horse, pictures of every possible type of bit. The prisoners not only get taught about horses, from forty-five minutes to an hour and a half a day; they are tested at regular intervals, and their progress is noted in their Education Record and Employability Profile, both of them key documents at parole hearings.

The prisoners put in about five hours of work a day, Tremper explains, much of it heavy physical labor, and all of them have chosen to work with horses, which requires something of a sacrifice on their part, since inmates only get paid ninety-five cents a day on the farm, whereas those who do "industrial-type" work inside make between a dollar fifty and five dollars a day—a big difference in terms of snacks, cigarettes, and the other small items that prisoners can buy. The prisoners (most of them serving between five and fifteen years) who work with the horses *want* to do it—it's a privilege, which explains why although there's no prison fencing around the farm, nobody has ever tried to walk off.

We lean on the fence and look at some of the horses. They're all thoroughbreds, some of them great looking but most of them showing, even to my relatively untutored eye, the physical consequences of accidents, breakdowns, and injuries—bowed tendons, enormously swollen joints, badly sutured scars, swollen hocks. Tremper knows the history of every one of them, and in most cases it's being raced too soon and pushed too hard. A few of the horses show the horrifying scars of "pin firing," one of the more inhumane and old-fashioned quick treatments for tendon problems. Plus, he adds, most small-time trainers and owners don't want to call in a vet, which costs serious money, and prefer to deal with problems themselves, often using rough and ready methods that cause more trouble than the injury itself—pin firing being a perfect example. He shakes his head and sighs.

A van appears, its windows covered with meshed wire, and a tall, muscular, immaculately uniformed corrections officer carrying a clipboard gets out and unloads the prisoners, eight men in denim pants and sweatshirts. The men aren't wearing uniforms—there is nothing to identify them as inmates, beyond a certain caution as they pass the guard—and the corrections officer, who gives me another bone-crusher of a handshake and introduces himself as Officer Petrie, isn't carrying a gun; indeed, his only weapon seems to be a two-way radio and a clipboard. On the other hand, Petrie has the look of a man who wouldn't need a weapon to deal with trouble. He is not only conspicuously fit but positively radiates an air of absolute authority, apparently without effort or conscious thought. Despite his prison guard's baseball cap, he reminds me instantly of the Centurion in the Bible: "I am a man under authority . . . and I say to this man, Go, and he goeth; and to another, Come, and he cometh; and to my servant, Do this, and he doeth it." Without raising his voice, or even looking in their direction, Office Petrie manages to send his charges moving at a rapid pace toward their tasks. Like a British sergeant major, he appears to have eyes in the back of his head—without looking around, he tells one of them to get a move on, and another to double-latch a gate who is about to single-latch it.

He is also—which explains his being here—a horse person through and through. All this, he says—indicating the horses, rather than the men working around them—is the result of irresponsible breeding and irresponsible racing. You breed a lot more thoroughbreds than anybody needs in the hope that one of them will turn out to be a winner and make money, and in the meantime you have a lot of horses that you run to death on backwoodsy tracks before they're ready to race, and when it doesn't work, you sell them to the killer for four hundred bucks or so for dog food. Officer Petrie is less diplomatic about the racing industry than Diana—he scowls under the brim of his cap. "It stinks," he says.

Petrie has actually adopted a couple of the horses himself and keeps them at home. He and his kids ride them—they go trail riding and camping on horseback in the nearby parks; the horses are part of the family. He's the kind of man who not only knows horses but can do his own horseshoeing, and doesn't have a lot of patience for horse owners who can't, and like a lot of New York's upstate correction officers, he's an avid outdoorsman and hunter. He has brought his kids up to understand that responsibility is part of horsemanship, he says. They learned early on that you didn't get to ride unless you kept the horse clean and well looked after, and put it away the same. Responsibility matters, and that's exactly what the prisoners are supposed to learn by working with horses.

Petrie knows each of the thirty or so horses here, and what their history and problems are, and knows his inmates just as well. Nodding toward an older man who is gently hugging a lame horse whose leg he has been treating, Petrie says, "Second-degree murder, he's done fourteen years—sixty-four years old; he should be getting out soon." He shakes his head glumly at the thought. It's a problem, he says. The guy's probably better off in here, working on the farm, than he'll be back outside. The horse farm prepares the prisoners for jobs they probably can't get, partly because in New York State they're paroled back to the county where they committed the crime, which for most of these men means the mean, tough streets of Brooklyn, Harlem, or the Bronx, where they got into trouble in the first place, and where an expert knowledge of horse care isn't likely to come in handy; then too, getting work at the tracks, where they could put what they know to good use, is very tough, because the tracks won't hire anybody who has a record of narcotics use or sale, or extortion, or illegal gambling, and most of these men have all those crimes and worse on their records, or they wouldn't be here in the first place. "Caught between a rock and a hard place, is what they are," Petrie says, gruffly greeting a prisoner, a heavily muscled young man wearing a T-shirt despite the cold weather, who has his arm around a horse's neck, with obvious affection, as he grooms it. "He's is going to come out of here knowing everything we can teach him about horses, and he's great with them, got the touch, but where's he going to get a job, you tell me that?" Petrie shakes his head at the irrationality of the system, which still seems to amaze him after twenty-three years on the job.

Petrie, though he's a guard, isn't above pitching in. He grabs a shovel and demonstrates to one young prisoner how to "put his back" into shoveling manure—Petrie works at a furious pace, piling his shovel high, then grabs a hoof pick from another young prisoner to show him the best technique for cleaning out hooves. "The young guys," he says, as we move on, "they don't always have the same kind of enthusiasm as the old ones. Some of them think it's going to be easy outdoor work, you know, and it's part of my job to teach them they're wrong. But given time—and time is the one thing everybody here has lots of—they come around eventually."

And if they don't?

"They get kicked off the unit. This is a privilege, working here. No hassles, no fences, minimum security, a chance to learn something different . . ." He shrugs. "It's not for everybody, though. You've got to be motivated."

I ask Petrie how many of the horses work out. "Quite a few," he says. "I mean, a lot of these are good horses—we had one here won over $400,000 until he bowed a tendon and got sent off for dog food." This isn't unusual, as it happens. Even a successful and well-known racehorse like Exceller, who won nearly $2 million in his career, ended up in the slaughterhouse when he stopped winning races. The racing industry isn't a sentimental business, Petrie points out, his expression blank. "But it takes time to make something of these horses, you know," he says. "They've got to be gentled, and taught to stop, which they don't have to do on the track. Some of them go on to be dressage horses, quite a few go to places where they do equine-assisted mental health therapy, riding programs for handicapped children, and so forth. . . . We don't have a riding program here, but some prisons do, so the inmates learn to ride as well as how to look after horses." He shakes his head in wonder. "Amazing, isn't it?"

What about the horses that can't be rehabilitated, I ask?

Petrie points to a big old thoroughbred mare with a huge lump on her leg, perhaps an old injury that never healed, or surgery that went wrong. She limps over to the fence slowly and puts her head out to him. He reaches into his pocket, finds a Starmint, unwraps it, and holds it out to her in his hand. She takes it, crunches it between her teeth slowly—not hurrying the pleasure—and gives him a look of frank adoration. "They stay," he says. "Lifers. None of them is going from here to the dog food slaughterhouse," he says, patting her, "that's the main thing."

Of course the most amazing thing is to watch the connection between the men and the horses. It still seems to amaze Petrie, for that matter, or at any rate to fascinate him. Most of the horses require substantial amounts of special care—bandaging, massaging the legs, hosing injuries and bowed tendons, dealing with scars and injuries. It all takes time and huge quantities of patience, and it's all being done by men who in their outside lives acted impulsively, impatiently, violently—yet here they are, hand-feeding a fussy eater, gently rubbing liniment on sore legs, preparing poultices and bran mashes, painstakingly preparing the horses for the night. The horses have led a tough life too, and many have been rescued at the last moment from the slaughterhouse, so a lot of them start out with an attitude problem toward humans, which has to be transformed into trust.

Petrie looks on critically as his men work, but with a certain satisfied gleam of approval in his eyes. You would not necessarily want to run into one of these men on a dark street late at night, he admits, but when it comes to these horses, they care deeply about them, and it shows. One of them, the big, muscular guy, with a speech impediment of some kind is whispering to one of "his" horses as he gets it ready for the night, and there's a look in his eyes of something hard to place, a certain fear, perhaps, or a reluctance to leave this quiet barn and the friendly, trusting horses for whatever is waiting for him back at the prison. Just there, over the hill, is the noisy, brutal world of steel bars and crowded cells that the movies and television have made familiar to us, while here it is hushed, everything is made of old wood, polished to a fine gloss by time and wear, and the only noise is coming from the horses, as they chew their evening meal and give an occasional soft snort of satisfaction. "Let's go," Petrie says, hurrying him on, but in a kinder, gentler tone than his usual clipped voice.

The van has returned, and the driver is waiting, leaning against his door, chatting with Jim Tremper as they admire the sunset. From here you can see the river, and beyond it the low hills, beginning to turn dark now. Petrie pauses and admires the view too—it's impossible not to. "It would be quite a place to build a house, wouldn't it?" he says, counting off his prisoners as they get into the van. He pauses and shakes his head. "But then you wouldn't want to live in a prison, even with a view like that."

Of course it doesn't feel as if we are in a prison, despite Petrie's uniform and spit-shined shoes, or the clipped corrections-officer chatter from the two-way radio in the van. The prison itself is visible only as a blur of lights beyond the last field, silhouetting three thoroughbreds as they stroll across it after their meal. There are no high walls or guard towers here, not even any razor fencing; the only thing that keeps the prisoners here from walking away is that they'd be taken off the horse program and put back into the general labor pool, but that's apparently enough, buttressed by Petrie's absolute moral authority.

"I don't know what it is," he says, "but I can never get enough of looking at horses." The prisoners apparently feel the same way. You can see them turning their heads in the van for a last look at the horses on the horizon as they get driven back to the bright lights, loud buzzers, and clanging doors of another evening in the prison. As one of the prisoners says to me, "The horses keep me sane. I think about them when I'm back in there, and plan out what I'm going to do with them the next day. . . . It's something to look *forward* to, you know? And when they get better, it's a great feeling, it's like you did something *useful?*"

A good deed in a wicked world, I am about to say, but don't. Everybody has warned me about the dangers of getting into this kind of conversation with the prisoners, and with the importance of keeping to the subject of horses, and with good reason. Most of them have a story to tell—basically the same story that they've been telling since their arrest—whereas on the subject of horses and horse care they're pretty straightforward, and even knowledgeable. They defer to Officer Petrie when he's in sight, but by now most of the more intelligent ones have developed their own routines, and have a pretty good instinct for what to do, and more important, when to ask for help. This is a place where I'd be happy to send a lame horse, were that possible, and all the lectures and examinations in the little schoolroom have paid off—the older guys, who have been doing this for some time, know what they're doing. It's probably a function of long incarceration, but they have in spades that most difficult of qualities, patience. They don't expect—perhaps even don't want—sudden miracles (when you're doing time, the natural tendency is to slow things down, and wring the most time out of any job). They're perfectly willing to settle for gradual improvement, and to accept that at the end the horse may still be flawed, a situation rather like their own, for they too are being "rehabilitated," if you believe the New York State Department of Corrections, in a long, slow process, but are not expected to be without flaws when they finally get released (otherwise we wouldn't need parole officers). In short, they and the horses are in pretty much the same boat at Wallkill CF, though horses are the more authentic victims. It explains the deep bond between the animals and the men who look after them, which is the first thing you notice here.

Except for small children and their ponies, you don't often see a person hugging a horse, but you see it here often enough to amaze you at first. At first, it amazes the horses too—most of them don't come here with a great deal of faith in human beings—but they soon get used to it.

Of course the "touchy-feely" side of the relationship between people and horses is very much in fashion these days, not only in prisons, but also in innumerable riding programs—for the mentally handicapped, for retarded children, for the physically challenged. The horse has, in fact, become the beneficiary of a whole new role as an adjunct to therapy, with apparently limitless possibilities. In Los Angeles, for instance, "Horses in the Hood" was founded to "introduce the Watts community to the joy of caring for and riding horses," and sponsors camps in which "at risk" children from the African-American and Hispanic communities in Watts (site of the infamous riots) are brought to day riding camps and taught to care for and ride horses. Ultimately, the goal is to bring to Watts a dedicated riding facility, but in the meantime the horses and ponies are transforming the lives of children, most of whom are educationally deprived and live in single-parent families, often beyond the reach of city social services. In a recent attempt to expand this already ambitious effort, Horses in the Hood sponsored a five-day horse camp to bring together children of the African-American and the Korean-American communities, recognizing that "in some areas, time has still not delivered a comfortable understanding between the two cultures" (something of an understatement).

Thus the horse has been assigned a new and unusual role. It is being used not only to give people of all ages with physical or mental handicaps a greater sense of personal control, balance, and achievement—the ability to reach beyond their handicaps—but to bring together the children (and perhaps, through them, the adults) of mutually hostile ethnic groups by making them cooperate in learning to care for the horse and to ride it. It may seem optimistic to imagine that ethnic difficulties and hostilities can be eased by horses, but in this case, at any rate, it seems to have been successful. As one participant puts it simply: "It works!"

The benefit for the horse is that it doesn't necessarily need to be young, 100 percent sound, or have perfect conformation to be led around a riding ring at a walk with a child on its back. Retirement to Horses in the Hood or a physical therapy program is a good deal better than being sent to the slaughterhouse to be made into canned dog food, and certainly better than an old age spent in, say, New York City, pulling carriages full of tourists around the city in the blazing heat, breathing in diesel fumes from passing buses and stabled at night in a straight stall so narrow that it's impossible to lie down. Looked at from this point of view, the use of horses for therapeutic purposes can only be a win-win situation.

In the long history of the horse and humankind there have been high points and low points, perhaps the lowest point having been reached toward the end of the nineteenth century, when horses were worked to death ruthlessly by the hundreds of thousands, then turned into leather and glue and mattress stuffing, the lowest point of all being reached, for horse as for man, in World War I, when casualties among horses on the western front provided an additional and very visible element of pain and suffering that affected even the most hard-bitten of trench veterans, and that Picasso later used to such dramatic effect in that most overwhelming of antiwar paintings, *Guernica*.

The fact that horses are now becoming part of the healing process, and given, in these circumstances, a second chance in life when they can no longer be usefully ridden, is a small down payment on the immense debt we humans owe to horses, accumulated over centuries of exploitation, cruelty, and suffering, when the word *horsepower* was taken literally, since the horse provided (along with oxen, the mule, and the donkey) the only source of power beyond the strength of a man's own arms. Thrilling as it is to watch the Budweiser horses at state fairs, pulling their gleaming beer wagon in front of cheering crowds, we need only look at photographs of pre–World War I street scenes—Edward Weston and Edward Steichen come to mind—to realize how different the reality of it was when teams of four or six or eight great horses pulled huge loads in wintertime over slick, cobbled streets coated with ice, horses often slipping and breaking a leg, so that a policeman would have to put them down where they lay, with a pistol bullet to the head.

The Teamsters' logo today still features a wagon wheel and a draft horse's head, as a reminder of the days before trucks, when "teamsters" still handled a team of horses, and had to be strong enough not only to load and unload their wagons but to control big horses that weighed a ton apiece, calm them when they were scared or spooked by city traffic, and drive them forward even when they were exhausted and overburdened, or skittering around on icy paving and rain-slick tramlines. Properly harnessed, horses can pull amazing weights at speeds much higher than oxen, and continued to do so until well into the industrial age. Only when Henry Ford finally produced a cheap means of transport that didn't need to be fed, shod, and groomed was the horse swiftly put out of business, even on farms, where it had been thought of as indispensable, and eventually in the world's armies, where the horse had been seen as not only indispensable but a potent status symbol and an even more potent weapon. The Polish army stuck with cavalry to the bitter end, hence the futile charges of massed Polish cavalry units against German tanks in 1939, while the British army gave up horses reluctantly and only under great pressure to "modernize" in the 1930s ("The cavalry has been 'modernized' only in the sense that its horses have been taken away from it," commented one acerbic British military critic on the outbreak of war, and the historic lancer, hussar, and dragoon regiments that were converted unwillingly and with much foot-dragging to petrol and armored vehicles nevertheless continued to insist that their officers and noncommissioned officers should be able to ride properly, even though they would eventually do their fighting in tanks or armored cars). Even in the most "modern" army of them all, the German, the social gulf between cavalry officers and infantry officers remained unbridgeable; infantry officers were still expected to ride at the head of their company as late as 1940 (see the photographs of the German army entering Paris), and most of the transport and artillery that followed the infantry was still horse-drawn and proud of it.

Nobody can say that those who depended on horses gave them up easily or without a struggle, least of all cowboys, who are still fighting a lonely rear-guard action against pickup trucks, four-wheelers, and helicopters to this day, and seem likely to win it, since the horse not only has tradition going for it but in fact remains a useful and environmentally friendly means of rounding up cattle, as well as a good reason to go to work wearing boots, spurs, and chaps, as opposed to overalls, for those who do the rounding up. The cowboy has managed to remain mounted, not only in the national imagination but in reality, whereas the cavalry-man has been reduced to ceremonial functions even in the British army, where the sentimental attachment to the horse on the part of senior officers and the queen herself is as strong as among cowboys in America. Even if Japanese four-wheelers could be used to round up cows better than horses, it seems as unlikely that cowboys will ever be willing to make the change as that the Household Cavalry in the United Kingdom will take to guarding the queen of England in armored cars and battle dress instead of on horseback, in uniforms that go back to the seventeenth century. The horse symbolizes something—not just an attachment to the past, though that is certainly a part of it, but also the relationship between human beings and animals, which is very different from that between humans and machines.

Nor is that attachment limited to girls and their ponies, or to women who love horses—it includes New York City mounted cops, Canadian Mounties, cowboys, many of them tough guys (and these days, gals), who, like the inmates at Wallkill CF, nevertheless aren't ashamed of hugging a horse, and don't hold back their tears when it's sick or injured. The horse, in short, brings out the sentimentalist in even the most unlikely of people, even if that hasn't done much to protect horses over the past few thousand years, or even today.

Ronald Reagan was also an unabashed sentimentalist when it came to horses, as well as being the first president since Theodore Roosevelt who enjoyed riding, rode well, and rode regularly. (Lyndon Johnson liked to be photographed on a horse at his ranch, but that was par for the course in his day for Texas politicians, and you only need to look at the photographs to see how much LBJ is looking forward to getting out of the saddle and back in his Cadillac.) Reagan had ridden since he was a child, and his riding skills were honed by experts when he became a movie star, since he was expected to look good on horseback in westerns. Somewhere along the way it took, and the closest way to his heart was to talk to him about horses.

I can testify to this because I edited his memoirs, *An American Life,* as well as his collected speeches, and one of the reasons why the president and I got along so easily and so well from the very beginning was that Reagan saw in me a fellow horseman—and in Margaret a fellow enthusiast. I would often come into a room at home to find Margaret with the telephone pressed against one ear, absorbed in conversation about her horses, only to find that it was President Reagan on the phone, from the White House. At such times, I knew better than to interrupt. At other times, I would pick up the phone to hear a familiar voice say, "Uh, is Margaret there? This is Ron Reagan." Other presidents had the White House operators place their calls, but Reagan liked to place his own, for some reason, and was always happy to talk to whomever picked it up. He and Margaret developed a kind of "phone pal" relationship on the subject of horses, and he sent her many photographs of himself on horseback, to which she responded by sending him photographs of her competing on *her* horses, for which he thanked her in handwritten notes signed "Ron." Whenever he spoke to me, he never failed to ask how Margaret and her horses were, and could only with difficulty be steered onto the subject of his book.

None of this would have come as any surprise to Mrs. Reagan. Even in the days when she was still wooing him, in the aftermath of his divorce from Jane Wyman, one of Nancy Reagan's cleverer moves was to go riding with Reagan. Photographs of them together on horseback seem to me to reveal a combination of nervousness and determination on Nancy Reagan's face, while Reagan simply looks as if he is having the time of his life, as he almost always did. He is among the few presidents (along with Washington, Grant, and Theodore Roosevelt) who would have agreed with Winston Churchill's comment, "No hour of life is lost that is spent in the saddle."

Before I actually met the president, I was under the impression that he usually rode western, perhaps because of the number of cowboy movies he had made, and also because that used to be the norm for southern California and for movie stars, back in the days when you could keep a horse in Beverly Hills and when the median between the two lanes of Santa Monica Boulevard was a bridle path. That, however, like many things about Reagan, was an illusion—he had always preferred to ride English, and favored well-cut English riding breeches and boots and an English saddle. Being Ronald Reagan, he sometimes topped this outfit off with a battered Stetson hat, but his off-camera presence on a horse was that of an easterner, not that of John Wayne. It was customary, once he became president, when he traveled abroad on state visits, for him to ride when his host was a fellow enthusiast, not just because it was a good camera op but because he really enjoyed it, and he always wore English breeches and boots, even when, as with the president of Mexico, riding western might have seemed more natural. The British press was bitterly disappointed when he went riding with the queen, since they had expected Reagan to be dressed up as a cowboy, instead of which he looked like any upper-class English horseman, in a tweed hacking jacket and beige whipcord breeches. Except for his hair, he might have been mistaken for the duke of Westminster.

On my very first visit to Reagan's Los Angeles office, I discovered that his enthusiasm for horses was genuine. The ambience was distinctly horsey, rather like "21" in the old days—Remington sculptures, paintings of horses, a collection of tooled fancy cowboy boots. He graciously took me to a kind of trophy room, where he showed me a dazzling collection of gold- and silver-trimmed western presentation saddles, all given to him by admirers over the years. He had, even before Alzheimer's set in, a reputation for a less than reliable memory, but when it came to horses he could remember the name of every one he had ever owned, and what they were like to ride. He remembered horses he had owned twenty years ago or had only ridden a few times in a movie as clearly as a horse he might have bought today, despite a certain fogginess that overcame him when he was asked about events in the

White House. Horses were different—he knew a lot about them, and more important, cared a lot about them, a lot more than he cared about, say, his secretary of state.

The president's interest in horses was such that it took only the prospect of spending a few hours in the saddle to cheer him up, and I could tell when he came to work on the book in the morning in jeans and cowboy boots that he was planning to play hooky from his memoirs in the afternoon. Writing the memoirs didn't interest him nearly as much as horses did—not, of course, that he was actually writing them himself. Reagan *could* write perfectly well—he composed his own speeches and radio talks in longhand on yellow legal pads—but that was because he was going to deliver them himself, and had a perfect ear for the kind of line he could deliver with authority, or humor. Nobody could prepare Ronald Reagan material better than Ronald Reagan, after all, but when it came to words that would be read in book form, he took the businesslike view that it was a writer's job to produce them, not his, much as he had back in his days as an actor, when it was the writer's job to produce script, and his to act it. Though unswervingly polite, he clearly felt it was a waste of his time to hang around while we discussed the manuscript, and from time to time he looked out the window with the faraway expression of a man who would rather be on a horse.

I found that I could usually bring him back to the task at hand by calling for a coffee break and asking him to show me the photographs of his and Nancy's horses on the wall outside. He could remember when he had bought each horse, and how much he had paid for it, and how it had worked out—his memory, on this subject at any rate, was not only sharp, but phenomenal. He was also one of those old-fashioned hands-on horsemen who enjoy nothing better than getting their own horses ready. He had the big, strong hands of a manual laborer. The way he loved clearing brush and chopping wood at his ranch had been much commented on by the press, at first with disbelief, then with a kind of qualified approval, but the fact that he liked working with his horses drew less attention. He liked the feel of brushing down a horse, picking out its hooves, tacking it up; he even enjoyed cleaning the tack after his ride, and the kind of silent communication between man and beast that can only come from working on the horse with your own hands. Of course he had barn help, but he was probably the first president since John Adams who liked the feel of a pitchfork in his hands and who enjoyed lifting bales of hay. Certainly he was right that the only way to know your own horse is to look after him yourself, though not too many people want to do that these days, or ever have, probably.

It certainly took the queen by surprise, when she paid a reciprocal visit to the president's ranch and went for a ride with him, to find him in the barn getting the horses ready himself. The royal stables at Windsor Palace and in the mews behind Buckingham Palace are run along almost feudal lines, with small armies of grooms to look after the horses and tack in a state of gleaming perfection, so it must have been startling to find the president, brush in hand, about to saddle up the horses.

Not that Her Majesty would have disapproved, on the other hand. I have to admit, however, that in this department I am a reluctant participant. My ideal is for somebody to hand me the horse, tacked up and ready to go, and to hand it back when I return from the ride, and in general that has usually been the case. I wouldn't mind handing my boots over to be cleaned and polished as well, but we have never run to that kind of establishment, alas—I long to be the Duke of Omnium, and live surrounded by valets, but it seems unlikely to happen. I *can* brush a horse, clean tack, and pick hooves, if only because I was taught to ride by people who considered all this and more to be an integral part of the learning process, but I'd just as soon have somebody else do it. As for mucking stalls, I am neither good at it, nor willing, unlike President Reagan.

All the same, getting to know the horse, to really bond with it in any deep way, is very clearly dependent on caring for it, so that its welfare, good health, and spirits become as familiar to you as your own. The notion that the horse has a special lesson to teach people (beyond the value of hard work), however, is a relatively recent one. Making a kid look after his own horse was a lesson in responsibility deeply valued in every rural society, whether farm families like my father's in central Hungary or American Plains Indians, but the *spiritual* qualities of the horse were not widely appreciated. Today, of course, as a glance at the bookshelves and magazine racks will demonstrate, the horse has been vested with a whole new set of values. It is not just Horses in the Hood, in which the horse promotes peace between ethnic groups in conflict (neither of which, in the case of Korean shopkeepers and African-American ghetto residents, is historically a horse culture); endless numbers of people and organizations are devoted to the horse as an instrument of healing and mental peace. Here, in the normally staid pages of the *Chronicle of the Horse,* is a tribute to Kathy Havens, who is shown riding her horse, The Rocket Man, while wearing on her back oxygen tanks because of the cancer that would eventually kill her, and being helped by her horse "to communicate with souls along the way"; meanwhile, the actress Bo Derek, in her new book *Riding Lessons: Everything That Matters in Life I Learned from Horses,* "uses her intuitive understanding of horses to explain the secrets of the male mind." These spiritualists follow in the best-selling path of Monty Roberts, the original "horse whisperer," who uses what he has learned about horses from his unconventional training methods to show parents and employers how to deal with children and employees—the wisdom of the horse (and of equine nonverbal communication) applied to seminars for big business and modern family life, a fast-growing trend.

In *Horses Don't Lie,* Chris Irwin, a "coach for horses and riders" (not, one gathers, the same thing as a riding instructor), explores "the spiritual connection" between "human and equine nature," emphasizing that horses have a lot to teach us about empathy and patience (all too true, alas), and that "a horse knows what you know" (maybe, but maybe not always). In *She Flies Without Wings—How Horses Touch a Woman's Soul,* on the other hand, Mary D. Midkiff writes about the horse beckoning us from across a pasture, summoning us into a magical world in which the horse releases the strength within a woman's soul, "teaching us compassion and acceptance" and revealing a world in which "women and horses emerge . . . as a huge tribe of spiritual sisters."

Ms. Midkiff is far from being alone in seeing the horse as a spiritual sister. Rebekah Ferren Witter, in *Living with Horsepower: Personally Empowering Life Lessons Learned from the Horse,* covers substantially the same ground, showing how humans can learn from the horse, among other things, integrity, humility, patience, honesty, and experience in coping with loss.

This is heavy psychological baggage for a horse to carry as well as a saddle, and much as I like horses, I can't say that the ones I've been close to have ever seemed to me to have the qualifications of a therapist, but then perhaps I'm not the right kind of "animal person" for that. I am, for example, doubtful that *Astrology and Your Horse,* by Vicky and Beth Maloney, will help me "understand [my horse's] deepest needs and behavior," or even "what colors [he] feels happiest wearing," so it is possible that I am simply out of sync with those who seek "spiritual knowledge and enlightenment" from horses, though certainly I wish them well. I have always been under the impression myself that the horse is basically color-blind, so the color of his saddle pad or leg wrappings seems unlikely to disturb him.

Lord Melbourne's favorite piece of advice that "the best thing for the inside of a man is the outside of a horse," remains more in the spirit of my own view—the horse offers us healthy exercise, communication of a kind with a different species, and a vigorous pursuit of the outdoor life. That's not to say that I don't think people have something to learn from animals in general, horses included, though it seems to me that it may have been best summed up by Walt Whitman:

> *I think I could turn and live with animals, they are so placid and self-contain'd,*
> *I stand and look at them long and long.*
> *They do not sweat and whine about their condition,*
> *They do not lie awake in the dark and weep for their sins,*

They do not make me sick discussing their duty to God,
Not one is dissatisfied, not one is demented with the mania of owning things,
Not one kneels to another, nor to his kind that lived thousands of years ago,
Not one is respectable or unhappy over the whole earth.

You have to hand it to old Walt, he managed to sum it up perfectly, for all time. No doubt he too would have been puzzled at the notion of the horse as a kind of four-legged therapist, or that to the other burdens a horse has to carry should be added the responsibility for teaching parents how to deal with their children, or big corporations how to negotiate with their employees, or women how to liberate themselves from the constraints of their lives. He would have been the first to recognize that to begin with, a horse in the wild is a very different creature from a domesticated horse, and that much of the admiration for the horse's "humility" and "patience" comes from the fact that in the domestic horse's world man (or woman) is the master, while in the wild horses fight each other for leadership of the herd and control over the herd's mares, not exactly the kind of lesson that Ms. Midkiff, Ms. Witter, and Ms. Derek have in mind, one supposes.

We have a kind of sentimental displacement here, almost exactly the reverse of what Whitman had in mind, in which people bring to the horse their own problems, unhappiness, and human confusion, in search of answers that will come from the horse's superior (but silent) morality. None of this has anything much to do with the horse, nor, we may suppose, is it on the horse's mind. Horses, as Whitman points out, unlike people, "do not sweat and whine about their condition," they are "placid and self-contain'd," and, although Whitman does not mention it, they have a long-nurtured respect for the potential for cruelty of their two-legged masters and mistresses that makes most of them cautious around us. What horses are supposed to make of people who "sweat and whine about their condition" to them, in expectation of some kind of explanation, is hard to say.

In much the same spirit, there is a tremendous vogue these days to make the horse a symbol of liberty and freedom, a theme often expressed in contemporary heroic sculpture—the horse portrayed as the symbol of the fall of communism being a typical and popular example in front of banks and hotels in the American West, galloping free through the ruins of the Berlin Wall. In truth, once domesticated, horses are no freer than dogs, and in fact rather less so. They are kept locked up in fenced paddocks, corrals, or barns; they have traded, involuntarily and without their consent, their liberty for absolute dependence on humans. The fact that this dependence is, in many places in the Western world, a more or less loving one does not alter the fact that the horse is as dependent on us as the house cat is, and less able to survive on its own. Far from a symbol of liberty, the horse, except for the few surviving wild mustangs, is as much a prisoner as was poor Dr. Alexandre Manette, patiently working away at his cobbler's bench in his cell in the Bastille, and like the good doctor in *A Tale of Two Cities* the horse is largely dependent on good behavior and a highly developed sense of routine for survival.

That the horse has more dignity than most of the people around it is obvious, as a look at the people standing around the horses at any racetrack will reveal, but then too, whales have more dignity than tourists leaning out of a boat trying to photograph them, and elephants seem many times nobler than the wealthy European and American businessmen in safari outfits who have paid a fortune for the privilege of shooting them. In general, as Whitman points out, almost any animal has more dignity than man, and horses are no exception. That does not necessarily give them any superior wisdom, however, let alone a message to impart to humans.

In *Living with Horsepower,* Rebekah Ferran Witter quotes one woman as saying, "When I am with or on a horse, it's as if I feel the Breath of Mother Earth coming through the horse into my body." On the face of things, that sounds like a nice feeling to have, but it ignores the fact that the only reason she can be on the horse in the first place is that the horse has been carefully bred, trained, and conditioned to accept the unnatural imposition of a saddle and a rider. It isn't "Mother Earth" who has fashioned the horse to be ridden; it's man who has turned a wild animal into a tame and useful one over thousands of years. It is possible, as another of her riders says, that "when you get closer to your horse, you are closer to your maker," but this seems to imply that our maker intended the horse for us to ride, which seems as unlikely as the notion that he created the great whales so that human beings would have an ample supply of whale oil for their lanterns, or to lubricate their watches.

It is typical of human beings to assume that their exploitation of animals is all part of God's great design, and even those who, like Ms. Witter, believe that the horse incarnates "spiritual potency" for our benefit in fact subscribe at bottom to a utilitarian view of the horse's role. In the end, it's the horse's fate to be maintained "through human management and domestication," for the purpose of being ridden, which is a significantly one-sided relationship, more practical than spiritual. Admittedly, there's everything to be said for Monty Roberts schooling horses with a more gentle approach than that of the traditional "horse breaker," but the fact remains that the animal is still being trained to do what *we* want it to do, to accept *our* authority, however quietly expressed, as absolute, and to subordinate its own desires to ours.

To look to it for spiritual enlightenment as well seems a little excessive.

CHAPTER TWELVE

The Grass Isn't Always Greener on the Other Side of the Fence

The New water feeder

OU DON'T SEE the passion for horses clearly until you get a glimpse of it in other people. Particularly when it grows cumulatively—one horse, then another, and so on—it all seems to make perfect sense, and rather like collecting (or drinking), there's no one single point at which you're likely to say to yourself, "Hey, this is getting out of control!"

Of course this is true of a lot things. Most forms of collecting, for example, fall into this category. People who set out to collect, say, nineteenth-century American pocketknives, or salt-and-pepper shakers in the shape of a Mexican taking a siesta in the shade of a giant cactus, with a sombrero pulled down over his face (no, no, I kid you not, I have seen two such collections with my own eyes*), don't start with the *intention* of having their collection come to dominate their life; it just hap-

---

*One belongs to my editor, Larry Ashmead; the other to the former co-owner of New York's Four Seasons restaurant, Tom Margittai.

pens. At some point, something that has filled perhaps a couple of desk drawers or shelves begins to fill a whole room, then the whole house, and before you know where you are, there's no way out except by creating one of those weird, out-of-the-way, little back-road museums, of which America is so full. Of course horses are different—you can't put them in showcases, like the Museum of American Dolls—they're living, breathing animals, and worse still, unless they all belong to you, they come with human owners.

To give credit where it's due, Margaret has never gone beyond the six horses for which we have stalls in our barn, however strongly tempted she has sometimes been to enlarge the barn, or perhaps even—a barely thinkable idea—keep some of her horses elsewhere for a time. But the latter is not an attractive notion to her; she likes to walk out the front door and see her horses, and they, it must be said, like to see her.

On the other hand, it also has to be said that she has always firmly resisted the very idea of boarding other people's horses, no matter how insistent and persuasive our good friend and business adviser Jay Watnick and our accountant, Stuart Yonteff, have been on this subject over the years.

Not that they're *wrong*, mind you. Yes, of course, once you've got income, then many of the inevitable expenses of keeping horses at home become tax-deductible—the salaries of barn help, installing water feeders in each paddock, barn repairs, new horse clothing, tractors, horse treats, fencing, the growing tidal wave of bills from farriers, vets, builders, the feed store, the hay and straw man—in short, all the inevitable financial consequences of the decision to keep horses in a barn of one's own that monthly threaten to swamp the family economy can be turned, at one stroke, into a humongous tax deduction, multiplied by the endless state and federal tax advantages of running a farm, on the condition only that there is, somewhere in the picture, at some point, an honest-to-God income—the blessed sound of money coming in instead of the steady, dismal noise of money going out. Simple as this seems, this goal has remained out of our grasp for over two decades.

After all, even the most overblown, glamorous, and preposterous of establishments—a barn with crystal chandeliers in the aisle, rare wood paneling, and a heated swimming pool for horses, to take one glaring example from nearby Millbrook—can be presented (and written off) as a perfectly sensible and prudent farming business, provided some part of it is able to show an income.

Racehorses used to provide one of the better known and more glamorous ways of combining pleasure and the potential of social celebrity with a hefty tax deduction, which of course explains the large number of thoroughbred farms started in New York State twenty years ago, most of which now lie abandoned to the weeds since the state tax laws abruptly changed again, leaving the breeders high and dry, despite intense and anguished lobbying by the New York thoroughbred industry. The New York State tax code transformed thousands of acres of rapidly declining family-owned dairy farms (declining despite intense tax protection and federal price support for milk) into glamorous thoroughbred farms almost overnight, complete with countless miles of expensive "Secretariat fencing," showpiece barns, and even full-size racetracks, by the magic of just a few lines in the state tax code, then ended it all as quickly as you might turn off a light. Many horsemen in our part of the country are still wondering what hit them.

Still, if you want to write off the expense of keeping horses, there remain ways to do it, in every state. Horse breeding can satisfy the IRS, as can buying and selling horses, and of course boarding horses, any of which need only produce an income, and even—though this is a more doubtful proposition—a profit, once every seven years.

Horse breeding has never been our cup of tea (though Margaret has often expressed her regret that we didn't breed poor Nebraska in time to enjoy a new generation of Nebraskettes), and it is by no means the easy business it sounds. Selling horses is out of the question for us—once they come here, they are family, assuming they bond, as they do with very rare exceptions—and the obvious problem with boarding other people's horses is that you have to deal with their human owners and riders. Problem horses are one thing, problem *owners* quite another.

This explains why, although we have a prominent sign on the road that reads "Stonegate Farm" (with a picture of a horse on it), as well as "Stonegate Farm" sweatshirts, polo shirts, and even one-size-fits-all baseball caps for friends, there's nobody home here but our own horses, and of course no profit. Every once in a while somebody will pull into the driveway and ask if we board horses, or rent out horses, or give riding lessons, but most people can see at a glance that ours is not a "commercial" establishment without getting out of the car, even before we've explained to them that this is a private barn. It doesn't have the look of a commercial barn, somehow; it's too tidy, too neat, there isn't enough parking, there's no "office," and at first glance there's nobody in charge. Besides, we look like the kind of people who would normally be more concerned about pleasing ourselves than pleasing the customers, which, God knows, is true enough.

When I heard that our neighbor Sheila Melville was selling Locust Hill, her family home and horse farm, to an attractive young couple who intended to keep it going as a business, that was in fact my first reaction—who on earth would want to buy themselves that kind of *tsouris?*—particularly since the husband, in this case, was reputed to be a high-powered computer executive, constantly on the move worldwide, and his wife was an airline flight attendant, so they could hardly be expected to oversee the operation twelve hours a day, seven days a week, like old Mr. Novograd back at Claremont Stables in New York City, hunched over his ledger.

Not of course that Sheila necessarily had a hands-on attitude toward the business herself. Sheila's clientele consisted largely of foxhunters, not surprisingly, since she herself was a keen foxhunter and a power in our local hunt. Weekend fox hunters are notoriously unfussy about their horses—so long as the horse is tacked up and ready to go on hunting days, they don't notice or care about much else. Foxhunters also contribute to a barn a certain raffish ambience—they tend now, as in the nineteenth century, to be a loud, hard-riding, heavy-drinking, clannish group, "the unspeakable in full pursuit of the uneatable," as Oscar Wilde memorably described them, a judgment with which even more people would agree today, at any rate in the United Kingdom, where foxhunting looks like being legislated out of existence. (You and I might have thought that British prime minister Tony Blair must surely have more important things on his mind than sticking a thumb in the eye of the rural middle and upper classes, but that is to underrate both the complexity and the deep emotional currents of the English class system, as well as its capacity for turning molehills into mountains.)

In any case, long before foxhunting came under attack over there, Sheila had already adopted here at home the defense posture of embattled British foxhunters today, which is to claim that it is in fact a democratic sport that embraces all social classes, not just the landed gentry, and that a great many country people make their living off foxhunting as well—farriers, vets, boarding stables, and so on—so that it benefits the rural economy. Sheila's boarders did indeed include a few local diamonds-in-the-rough—among others, an electrician, the owner of a home heating oil service, and a landscape and gardening contractor—but if not "gentry," they were hardly proletarians out of *Les Misérables*. The majority of the members were from the city: stockbrokers, currency traders, doctors, and their women. To hear her talk about it, however, foxhunting was the great leveler, bringing all classes together in a healthy outdoor sport with strong rural traditions, while protecting the stock of poultry farmers.

Since the last poultry farmer around us went out of business many years before we moved to the country, and the vast majority of locals buy their eggs in the supermarket, this was not necessarily a strong pro-foxhunting argument, and I had my doubts about how much Sheila herself believed it. In truth, I think she simply enjoyed living like a character out of Surtees (a female Lord Scamperdale, as it were), surrounded by people tramping through the living room of her great, ramshackle house in muddy riding boots and spurs looking for a drink, or a convenient sofa on which to nap. It was the social life of foxhunting, as well as the sense of being queen bee of the hive, that kept Sheila in the boarding business and wearing hunting pink—that and the self-imposed obligation to keep the Melville estate intact, and more or less the way it had been in her father's day, when the Melvilles had been local *echt* gentry, with the road past their estate named after them. Her father gazed down from above the fireplace, painted on his hunter, in his Rombout Hunt pink coat, holding a coiled whip and looking every bit the pre-Crash landowner-sportsman.

In the event, Sheila's fierce devotion to the past turned skin-deep eventually. She put the whole place up for sale, barns, horses, and all, and moved to Long Island, about as far away from foxhunting and horses as she could get while still remaining on the North American landmass, and never cast a look back. The likelihood, I thought, then and now, was that Sheila had simply had enough of the demands of country living—the house itself, the impossibility of getting or keeping decent help, horses breaking out of their fields and onto the roads on foggy nights, the demands of her boarders, pumps burning out, electric wires coming down, leaks at crucial places in the roof, horses going lame. At some point she simply and abruptly severed the connections between herself and her property, which must always have seemed to her, as they did to everyone else, the strongest and most important part of her life; then lo and behold, one day she was gone, with all the speed and lack of ceremony of somebody driving out of a trailer park to a new life with all her worldly goods in the trunk of her car. It occurred to me that here was a rural gentry version of *Thelma and Louise,* except in this case the woman in question was driving away from the complexities of country living—especially running a large boarding barn—toward the simplicities of a small, modern house in which the roof didn't leak, and a life that wasn't governed by lame horses, ailing pets, and whether the blacksmith would arrive to tighten a loose shoe on so-and-so's horse in time for him to make the meet.

There are those who run toward sanity, often without knowing it, and those who run equally blindly away from it, as everybody knows who has read *The Odyssey.* The gods simply even things out in the end. When we heard that Sheila was, presumably, running toward sanity, we were happy for her, though our greatest fear, of course, was the dread word *developer,* since the worst thing your neighbor can do to you in the country is to sell out to a developer who plans to bulldoze the woods, "landscape" the fields, and put up a couple of dozen houses or more on what for many generations had been a perfectly nice farm.

Despite Sheila's firm commitment to her land over the years, a certain premonition had persuaded me some years ago to buy the forty-four acres of woodland opposite our house, which acted as buffer between our property and hers. Margaret had objected, with some reason, to the purchase—the land was steep, and where it was not it was as boggy as a World War I battlefield, heavily wooded with second growth, and of no earthly use to us or anyone else. It *could,* of course, be turned into useful pastures for the horses, but since this would be a project only slightly less expensive than the building of the Great Pyramid of Cheops, involving the cutting down and removal of thousands of trees, a drainage system, and a king's ransom of fencing, roads, and plumbing for water feeders, I refused to even consider it. The only useful purpose the land served, as I explained to Margaret, was that in the event Sheila Melville were ever to sell up—a proposition that seemed admittedly far-fetched at the time—we would have a kind of DMZ between ourselves and any development. *Not* buying the land might mean waking up some morning to see a bulldozer chugging away just across the road, in full sight of our bedroom window, and a sign going up offering two-acre building sites; buying it meant that whatever happened over there beyond the trees, at least we weren't going to see it. In the circumstances, we sighed, signed the check, and later breathed a sigh of relief at our good judgment when we heard about Sheila's sudden decision to cut her ties to the Melville past.

Soon we heard even more heartening news down at Mackey's Tin Whistle Pub at lunchtime—that the rumor was true that one of Sheila's boarders, together with her husband, was buying the property, and that they would keep the place going much as it had been under Sheila's ownership. There was talk of "improvements," of course—good news to the electricians, plumbers, and landfill contractors who sat at the bar of Mackey's at lunchtime—but there would be no development, no rows of vinyl-sided houses replacing horse pastures, no new blacktop roads and drives or excavations for foundations and septic tanks, no big floodlit sign on the road announcing the entrance to "Locust Hill Houses" or some such.

Up where we live, *improvements* is a good word, *development* is a bad one. *Improvements* means work for carpenters, plumbers, tree surgeons, fence builders, blacktoppers, painters, and so forth, but with a decent chance that the property will remain the same, only better, whereas *development* means rows of houses, unruly kids with dirt bikes and .22 rifles trespassing on your land, and fields and trees giving way to asphalt, aboveground swimming pools, crazy paving, and plastic gnomes in the garden. The suburbs were moving north toward us, surrounding us like a rising tide, as fast as they could be built. Here, for another few years, though, they would be held at bay by Sheila's decision to sell to people who wanted to keep the business, such as it was, going, and the dominant theme would remain horses instead of barbecue pits.

The Lynns—Jeff and Sue—when we first met them had the slightly dazed look of people who were already overwhelmed by the reality of their dreams having come true. Sue, it turned out, had always wanted to have a horse farm of her own, and like Shelia Melville apparently saw herself as the central figure of a horsey little community, surrounded by people who loved horses and loved to ride. She had boarded her own horses for some time at Sheila's, and was therefore familiar with the place and the cast of characters. Buying Locust Hill Farm when it came up for sale was the culmination of a lifetime's ambition, the kind of life she had always no doubt dreamed about on layovers or when her flight was delayed, as far away from passing out headphones or preparing dinner trays in the galley of an airliner as you could possibly get. There were advantages, of course—no matter how difficult and demanding the boarders and the foxhunters might be, they could hardly be worse than a full load of airline passengers. And having boarded her own horses at Sheila's farm, Sue had a pretty good idea of the problems of finding and keeping decent barn help—always the most crucial factor in operating any kind of a horse facility.

We had had ample opportunity ourselves to discover just how difficult it was to find and keep barn help when the Bacons suddenly left to make a new life for themselves in Colorado. For nearly eighteen years we had never had to think about barn help—Roxie was always there, like the Rock of Gibraltar. The greatest help problem we had in all those years was finding her an assistant who was competent, but whom Roxie (and Richard) wouldn't suspect of upstaging or replacing her.

Hiring replacements over the years, on the other hand, was a more formidable task. People didn't turn up for interviews, or turned up only to reveal that they knew nothing about horses or barn work, or, if they did happen to have some experience, usually turned out to have impossibly complex problems involving ex-husbands, vehicles, or child care. Candidates who answered Margaret's ads included an exotic dancer, an arboriculturist, and any number of people who simply liked the idea of working with horses, without necessarily ever having tried it. Even my command of Russian, such as it is, was put to the test when a couple of swashbuckling, heavily bearded Georgians of gangsterish appearance showed up with a purported cousin (no visa, of course) who had zero horse knowledge but would, we were promised, work his heart out for us. When it turned out that he had no place to stay—and of course no vehicle—his "cousins" explained that we were not to worry about any of this; he would sleep in the tack room or even one of the stalls, he was used to worse at home. If he failed to satisfy us in any way, we should just call them, and they would drive over to discipline him for us.

Those who turned up for "trial periods" often had combative tempers, their own strongly held ideas about how horses should be cared for, or unsuitable-looking boyfriends who came over and stationed themselves in the driveway to keep an eye on them during the day. Dramatics, hysterics, angry scenes, and endless complications became, for a long time, a normal part of life in the barn, with changes of personnel so frequent that the ladies in the classified advertising department of the *Poughkeepsie Journal* and the *Pennysaver* actually began to recognize my voice when I called, and had the wording of our "Barn Help Wanted" ad up on their screen and ready to go. When finally we hit upon reliable, professional help who actually turned up in the morning, we gave a sigh of relief so loud that the Bacons could probably hear it all the way out there in Colorado.

This, mind you, was for a barn that contained five or six horses, and only two riders to please, so the notion that the Lynns were going to take over a barn with nearly *thirty* horses, and more than twenty boarders, left us momentarily speechless—particularly since they not only planned to do it part-time, without giving up their jobs, but also looked on the whole thing as something like a hobby, a pleasurable interruption to their high-flying and fast-paced working lives. It took only a few weeks before Sue Lynn had the trademark harried, distinctive look of somebody running a busy horse establishment, which consists of wearing riding breeches without the boots all day, and, when possible, right through the evening, as if it was a uniform, along with enough layers of Polartec fleece for an Arctic expedition and a pronounced tendency to fall asleep over dinner, however early.

The Lynns had two cars, two careers, and something like thirteen cats, each of which they seemed to have rescued from the animal shelter with some kind of severe medical problem that required constant care and attention, and none of which were able to go outdoors. To say that we were bowled over by the sheer scope of what they were taking on is putting it mildly.

Even today, after twenty-three years of living in the country and keeping our own horses, when you might suppose nothing would be likely to surprise me, I occasionally look at our own barn, our paddocks, our indoor riding ring with its fragile Rube Goldberg watering system (not to speak of our house), and say to myself, "How on earth did we get into all this?" On days when Margaret's horse has lost a shoe the day before going to an important event, when a major tree has fallen on the lawn during a storm in the night just after the tree service man has told us he's going on vacation, or when a blocked gutter has backed up, causing water to leak in sheets down the wall of the dining room, I sometimes say to myself, "How do we ever get out of this?" but there is no good answer to that question, either. We have put down roots, it seems, like the tree, and it's a question of facing up to the problems and dealing with them, or going down with a crash.

Even at these moments of doubt, however, with the electricity out, with one of the horses sick and the vet on call somewhere on the other side of the river, and somebody in a rain slicker carrying a flashlight turning up in the driveway just as we're about to crawl into bed, exhausted, to warn us that one of our neighbor's cows (or possibly steers, he isn't sure, in fact they might even be bulls) is loose on our property, we have learned to say to ourselves—and each other—that things are probably at least as difficult at the Lynns', and the odds are that it's true. It's a comfort.

Even by the standards of our house, which was built in 1785 and whose numerous problems were, literally, enough to fill a book (*Country Matters*), the Lynns' seemed to have a remarkable number of unimaginable problems, ranging from wet rot and dry rot to the need to dig up all old underground fuel tanks, which were leaking, remove the contaminated dirt, and replace them with EPA-approved aboveground tanks. Chimney and fireplaces needed to be rebuilt, new wiring installed, leaks caulked and repaired. The house seemed from a distance to have acquired a permanent addition of scaffolding, as one group of specialists after another—the entire lunchtime contingent from Mackey's Tin Whistle Pub—struggled to replace what was rotten and fix what was broken, and deal with all the things that Sheila had managed to put up with, or simply ignored, for most of her adult life, from missing lightning rods and shingles to collapsing gutters.

Of course, no house that contains more than a dozen cats in various stages of ill health is ever likely to resemble something that Martha Stewart might admire, and any visit to the Lynns was likely to test severely the degree of one's fondness for cats. Everywhere you looked there were litter trays, an array of humidifiers that made the atmosphere resemble that of a greenhouse for tropical plants, and cats walking across every piece of furniture, including the dinner table. The Lynns not only had every problem we had with our house, they had problems we hadn't yet experienced or imagined. When you opened the door of their freezer, for example, the interior resembled a frozen Niagara Falls—great cataracts of ice cascading down, dripping away at the bottom to melt under the kitchen floor, no doubt causing more damage somewhere beneath it. Like us, they had toilets that failed, fireplaces that smoked, doors that stuck, windows that wouldn't open, and leaks that seemed to spring up from nowhere, so that you had no sooner fixed one than another one appeared. Housekeeping had never been one of Sheila's obsessions, and all the little things that had been ignored over the years, or that Sheila had simply learned to live with, were now making themselves known, one after the other. Every time I saw Jeff, he had the grim and slightly haggard look of a man who has spent the morning on the telephone, leaving messages with repairmen and contractors who never call back.

And all that, as he never failed to point out, was without even beginning to assess the problems of the barns, and the indoor ring, and even the outdoor ring, which had to be dug up, have drainage laid down, and be resurfaced with many layers of exotic materials, or the fencing, miles of which simply needed to be rebuilt from scratch, or the water supply to the far-flung pastures. . . .

At some point a certain friendly rivalry, not unnatural between friends and neighbors who keep horses, crept in. For example, water feeders. Margaret had invested a lot of money in installing automatic water feeders in the paddocks around our barn, and after admiring them, the Lynns finally bit the bullet and did the same, though the distances and the size of their fields vastly exceeded ours.

Distance, as it happens, is the key factor in what it costs to provide a freezeproof watering system in each field. You start by having to dig a well and put in a pump (which means running electricity to it underground, of course); then you have to dig a trench to each place where you've decided to put a water feeder, for obvious reasons digging deep enough so that the water pipes are below the frost line—about four to five feet down, in our neck of the woods. An electric line has to run alongside the water line, since the bowl of the water feeder has to be kept warm enough so that it doesn't freeze over. Obviously, the farther away your fields from the house or the barn (and the bigger the fields), the more it is going to cost. It doesn't take long before you discover why oil and gas producers are so determined to kill environmental legislation that would force them to put their pipelines underground—several thousand feet of six-foot-deep trench can add up to a substantial amount of money, especially in a place like Dutchess County, where due to the Ice Age bedrock sometimes lies just a few inches below even the greenest of pastures.

On the other hand, what do you do about water without water feeders? Sure, a generation ago (in fact not even that long ago, while Roxie was still working for us), you put a tub in each field, and in the winter somebody (mostly Roxie, in our case) walked out through the snow to each tub with an old claw hammer and broke the ice from time to time so the horses could drink, except for the fields near the barn, where you could put an electric heating coil in the tub and run a thick orange extension cord to the nearest electric outlet. Quite apart from the labor involved, it was an inefficient way of doing things, and below a certain temperature, particularly if there was a strong wind-chill factor, the tubs froze up more quickly than you could get to them with the hammer.

Water feeders eliminate all those problems, and what's more, they have built-in filters that remove rust and minerals and dirt from the water, which is important because horses are more finicky about water than almost anything else, but need a lot of it. It's not for nothing that the adage "You can lead a horse to water, but you can't make it drink," has passed into the language and remains in current usage by people who have hardly ever seen a horse—it's the one thing, in fact, that everybody, however urbanized, knows about horses, and one of the few such statements to be undeniably true.

Our water feeders were a widely admired blessing, once they were installed and working, and added a neat, space-age look to our pad-docks, like small rocket ships, although cleaning the filters at regular intervals was a delicate and fussy job that Margaret would delegate to nobody, involving boiling water, corrosive chemicals, and tiny brushes, because of the high mineral content of our water.

Naturally, the Lynns' water was much the same as ours, and we heard all about the trials of installing and maintaining their water feeders, since of course the same people who put ours in, put theirs in—the usual way of small-town life. What with all the cats, and the horses, and the boarders, there was always plenty of news from Locust Hill Farm, from horses breaking out of their paddocks to the fact that Sue Lynn came home late at night once, weary from flying and looking after the farm, and got out of her car to pick up the mail. When she turned around in the dark to get back into the car, it was gone—as if it had simply disap-peared. Once the shock wore off, she instantly realized what hap-pened—exhausted, she had put the shift lever in neutral instead of park, with her back turned to the car, and it had run downhill and plunged into the pond, where it quietly sank. That was certainly worse than any-thing that had happened to us, but not nearly as odd as the rumor that none of the horses would drink at the Lynns' new water feeders.

Horses are slow to accept change, and fairly timid about most innovations; still, automatic water feeders are something they have usually been exposed to at some point in their lives, and sheer curiosity, added to thirst, is usually enough to get them to try one. Once they have, they adapt quickly—all they have to do is put their muzzle in the bowl, and it fills at once with clean, filtered water. Even the dimmest of horses only has to try it once to realize that it's an improvement. Of course the feeders have to be adjusted so that the bowl doesn't fill up so fast that it alarms the horse, but mostly it's a pretty foolproof mechanism.

The men who had installed the feeders spent a good deal of time adjusting them, changing the filters, and having the water itself tested, but there didn't seem to be any good reason why the horses wouldn't drink from them until one of the workmen leaned over, put a finger in the bowl himself, and jumped back in surprise. The water had given him a mild but distinct electric shock—it was electrically charged.

That set everybody to thinking, or at any rate to standing around the water feeder with their hands in the pockets of their overalls, in deep conversation. There were, it turned out, two possibilities. Either there was a break in one of the wires that had been laid alongside the water pipes, all of them now buried under six feet of soil, or somewhere on the property there was an old electric line, from way back in Sheila's early days, that had gone bad, and was leaking a low-voltage charge through the ground to the water.

Any way you looked at it, it was good news only for the guy with a backhoe, since locating the source of the current was going to be looking for a needle in a haystack, if you can imagine a haystack buried six feet underground. . . .

In the end, that's the great comfort about having friends and neighbors who keep horses. On any given day, through thick and thin, there is always somebody out there whose problems are at least as bad as your own, and on days when your own horse has lost a shoe, or developed a curious rash from allergy to insect bites (or something else), or cut itself inches deep requiring an emergency visit from the vet late on a Sunday evening, we always ask what's going on across the way at Locust Hill, secure in the knowledge that it will very likely make our own troubles seem more bearable, and no doubt vice versa.

We felt that all the more strongly when, out of the blue, the same problem struck *our* water feeders, in midwinter, of course, when you would need dynamite to get down to where the pipes and electric cables were buried. The Lynns' problems had at least prepared us for ours.

If that isn't neighborly, I don't know what is.

CHAPTER THIRTEEN

Star

The new champion

HEN SPRING COMES at last, and Margaret begins to take Dundee out on the road again, hesitantly at first, it suddenly seems as if all Libby's hard work, and her own, in the dressage ring since Nebraska's death may have paid off—either that, or it's at last occurred to Dundee that if he doesn't shape up, he might get shipped out.

He starts bringing home ribbons—firsts, seconds, never anything less than thirds—and his whole demeanor has changed, as if he's become serious about competing at last. Of course he's still growing—to Margaret's dismay, he seems to be turning into a giant (with a giant's appetite), but in his own good-natured, unruffled way, he gets out there and tries to win. At the 2002 Stuart Horse Trials, a huge and lavish event up in Iona, New York, complete with bagpipers and an outdoor competitors' banquet, with over four hundred fifty horses entered—this is big-time eventing—Dundee takes a second in novice, and comes home in his trailer looking relaxed, proud of himself, and ready for more.

He's beginning to look like a pro, in fact, and Margaret has put to one side her thoughts about giving up eventing, even though she sometimes wonders how long she will be able to go on doing it. She's looking for an understudy to Dundee now, as well as a younger "barn horse," a good, solid young horse to take out on the trails, now that Missouri and Berry Fox have definitely reached the status of old-age pensioners and enjoy a stately walk, rather than a real ride.

At Fitch's Corner, a week after Stuart, with a big Saturday-night "Blue Jeans Ball" and a lot of first-rate competition, as Dundee appeared out of the woods in the haze of a hot, humid day and sailed smoothly over a big fence toward the finish, somebody near me said, sotto voce, "He looks like Margaret's next Nebraska."

And who knows? Maybe he is.

Margaret on Dundee.

PATRON
The Stuart Horse Trials 2002

In the meantime, I have inherited Star, a surprise to both of us.

It's a warm, beautiful day in early June, with a soft breeze blowing from time to time, briefly relieving the humidity of the Hudson Valley. Margaret is away at an event, where Dundee will unfortunately fail to continue his winning streak for the moment.

Star likes his exercise; on the other hand, he has to be ridden with some care, since like most thoroughbreds he's always eager to go, and though he's not Missouri's or Berry's age, he's no spring chicken, however good he looks. He needs to be held back a bit, not pushed on.

I am afraid that much as I recognize the importance of doing things for myself, I am only too happy to let other people do them for me, so Star has been cleaned and tacked up for me by Toby, who works in the barn, and knows more about horses (and trucks and cars) than I am ever likely to learn. I *can* tack up my own horse—I used to do it for years, when Margaret and I kept our horses at Claremont, on Frank's day off, and later at the Sleepy Hollow Country Club stable, where we usually rode very early in the morning, before the help arrived—but I don't feel I have to, or even that it's character-building anymore. I am reminded of the story about the legendary actor John Barrymore in his old age, in

Hollywood, where he insisted on having a couple of men just out of the camera field to hold up a big board with his lines of dialogue written on them, to the intense annoyance of the crew. One day, the young director of the movie in which Barrymore was appearing was infuriated to see that the board contained one line only—"Good morning!"—and confronted Barrymore in a rage on the set. "Mr. Barrymore," he said, "you are a member of America's greatest acting family, and yet am I to believe that you can't even remember the line, 'Good morning!'?" Barrymore stared haughtily at the director for a moment, then said, "Young man, I *can* remember my lines, but thank God, I don't *have* to anymore."

I feel the same way. I *can* tack up a horse, but thank God I don't have to. I do walk around the horse once, an old habit from the Royal Air Force, where you always walked around an aircraft, just to make sure everything was as it should be before taking off; then, once I'm mounted, I check the girth for tightness, which is basic prudence. When horses are saddled, they learn to puff their stomach out just as the girth is being tightened; when the rider mounts, the horse lets its breath out, and the girth, which had seemed so tight a moment before, is suddenly loose and, from the horse's point of view, comfortable. If it is left this way, however, the rider is likely to find the saddle slipping inexorably to one side, or even slipping so that it's under the horse, with predictable results. It should be second nature to check the girth (or the cinch, in the West) for tightness from time to time, and also to make sure that the stirrups are the right length, if there's a chance that anybody else may have used the saddle since the last time you did. With Toby tacking up a horse, none of these things is likely to happen, but it's the responsibility of the person riding the horse to make sure everything is in order.

Star clip-clops briskly down the short stretch of blacktop behind the barn (an innovation resisted for many years successfully by Roxie, who was convinced the horses would slip on it), then past the fenced-in paddocks and across a long stretch of grass in front of the indoor ring, down past another couple of larger paddocks to a gate. In one of the paddocks a deer is standing with her two fawns, the size of smallish dogs. Star flicks an ear in that direction, but he isn't interested or alarmed. He's seen this little family group before—they hang around picking at the horse's leftovers—and anyway, four-footed animals that graze don't ring any warning bells for horses. Herbivores don't spell danger. I've owned horses that didn't like cattle a bit, but I've never seen a horse alarmed by a deer, or vice versa. I lift the gate off its stop and lean over to undo the chain, then Star and I go on down the long side of a paddock and out onto the land.

The barn and the paddocks are behind us now, hidden by the dense green foliage, which has to be cut back every year to make riding trails. We're still walking, but Star has picked up the pace a bit. He likes the great outdoors, and unlike a lot of horses, he's relaxed on his own.

He flicks an ear to the left, and snorts. I look that way and see a couple of deer standing in the undergrowth stock-still as if frozen, staring at us, which I would surely have missed. Star, on the other hand, doesn't miss anything—his vision appears to be as acute as ever, and his sense of hearing, perhaps even more important for a horse, is as precise and accurate as radar. He doesn't move his head about much, but his ears are in constant motion, picking up sounds and analyzing them. Every once in a while a rabbit zigzags across the trail, but rabbits don't interest Star much.

We pass a series of ditches, over which Roxie used to school me when I owned Zapata, in the vain hope of getting him used to jumping ditches. In his jumping days, Star would jump anything, but these days he doesn't feel obliged to.

We wheel to the right and go down a steepish, muddy trail, with a lot of rocks underfoot—in bad weather it turns into a streambed—and Star slows down a bit and focuses on the ground in front of him. Going downhill may hurt him, and he does it with caution. Bad ground—in this case a rough, muddy trail, cut by rain gullies and strewn with small, sharp-edged rocks—makes it even more difficult for him, and he appreciates being kept clear of that kind of thing.

I am conscious, as always, that I am wearing a baseball cap instead of a proper helmet. Years of riding motorcycles have taught me the wisdom of helmet laws, but there's something about riding a horse that doesn't seem to go with helmets. If I were planning to jump, I tell myself, I'd wear one, and of course if I were competing it would be mandatory, but somehow a gentle morning hack on my own land seems different. I reflect that this is fatuous reasoning for a grown-up, in an age when people on roller skates or a bicycle wear head protection, but there it is.

At the bottom of the path Star and I come to what we call "the power-line field," a good ten acres or more of grassy land that undulates down to where the Central Hudson power lines run overhead, at the very bottom. East of it is a wooded property with a large man-made lake; to the west, rising steeply, our own woods. We bought the field many years ago, as part of a varied parcel of some thirty-five acres all told, of which the power-line field is the gem, really.

Back in the days before she had acquired Star, Margaret used to take all the horses down here in the spring and summer, after we finished riding, often riding Missouri bareback with a halter and a rope, dressed in her bikini, to lead them, and bringing them back the same way at the end of the day, when it was time for their supper. The field was wired, there was enough good, sweet grass to keep the horses eating all afternoon, and a small stream gave them water. Since the field was tucked away out of sight, they were not likely to come to any harm, and it was a kind of Shangri-la, hidden away and unapproachable unless you knew the way, hard to get to on foot and almost impossible to get to with a vehicle—in any case, hardly anybody knew it was there. The previous owners of our house had lived here for over thirty years without knowing there was a field back here. Once, many years ago, thirty-five or forty at a guess, it had been a cow pasture, and as a result the grass was exceptionally good. Margaret had tried to get it hayed, but that never worked out, and she finally settled for mowing it until it looked like an English park, except for the presence of deer and wild turkey. The woodchuck holes had either been filled in or marked, a few interesting fences had been put up for jumping, and most of the dead wood and wild shrubbery had been removed. A few years ago—ten at least, maybe more—Margaret stopped bringing the horses down here together for the afternoon, partly because by then we had built plenty of paddocks closer to the barn, where the horses were in sight, partly because as she began to compete more seriously she no longer had the time, and partly because one of our horses, Sundance, was shot by a bow hunter out here during deer season, which, even though the horse survived, had to make you think twice about their being that far from the house.

Star is a little moody on the way down the rough path, just a hint of reproach, as if he were saying, "Hey, this ground is no fun at all for an old guy like me!" but once he's in the field he cheers up instantly and breaks into a trot to the top of a grassy rise from which we can see the whole field spread out before us, like parkland. His ears are forward now, and he gives a couple of snorts, presumably of approval. This is a place he associates with good feelings—long grassy trails, perfect for a thoroughbred. There's a long trail down the middle of the field, perhaps half a mile in length, and Star trots down it without being pushed, taking big, vigorous strides as his muscles begin to stretch and warm up, and no doubt his minor aches and pains recede. An elderly runner might feel the same kind of exhilaration as he begins his run in a favorite spot and feels his muscles loosening up.

At the bottom, I can either swing to the left and come up one side of the field, next to the woods, or swing to the right and come up the other side, with a view of the lake. Star doesn't appear to have a preference, really; it's my choice. I opt for the lake view, which is okay with him, but either way, he knows there's a good long uphill canter ahead, and he's eager for it. I give him the signal, and it's as if Star has lost ten years. Nobody looking at him would imagine this was an old horse—his canter is smooth, regular, balanced, he's moving at a good, steady speed—you can actually *feel* his pleasure. It's as if I have dropped ten years or more too—I can remember cantering up this pathway, with the lake visible through the woods on my left, when we first moved the horses to the farm, when Margaret would be riding Missouri ahead of me, her long blond hair flying behind her, while I came up behind her on Hustle. . . .

I come forward, out of the saddle, to get my weight off Star's back as he crests a hill; then he skirts a big old jump, designed to look like a park bench, and knowing there's an even steeper hill ahead, with a sharp turn to the right, he snorts and gives it all he's got. The wind is in my face, I can hear the regular thud of his hooves against the grass, I get my full weight down into my stirrups, braced so that hopefully I won't fly off forward if Star spooks, but spooking isn't on his agenda today. The reins are short, but loose, with just enough contact on the bit to remind him that I'm there, but he takes the final hill at a full gallop, turns to the right as if we were barrel racing, and comes to a halt back at the top of the field, both of us looking down the length of it as if to say, "Well, *that* was a good one." Star is huffing and puffing now, not out of breath at all (his flanks aren't heaving) but with the sheer pleasure of movement and speed, a noise something like an old-fashioned steam locomotive, deep, regular, loud, as he blows air out of his nose. He gives a few deep snorts—always a sign that he's pleased with life and himself—and I move him forward, since it's not good for horses to stand still after any exertion. "*This* is the life!" I think he'd say, if he could talk.

I walk him down the whole length of the field to let him catch his breath, though he isn't even breathing hard, and put my hand against his neck to see if he's sweating, but no, not a bit of it. A flock of wild turkeys crosses the field in front of us, and for a moment I think Star may be about to spook—horses usually hate the noise wild turkeys make, all that chattering and clucking gets on their nerves, and wild turkeys have a habit of taking off suddenly with a wild beating of wings, then coasting for twenty or thirty yards to get out of the way, which is usually enough to alarm most horses—but he merely gives a couple of extra-loud snorts, just to show the turkeys whose field this is, and bears down on them without slowing his pace, as if he means to go right through them. They give a squawk of alarm, like pedestrians who have just noticed an eighteen-wheel semi coming down the street toward them, and rush headlong into the long grass, out of Star's way. He gives a contented snort, as if to say, "I showed *them!*" and as we get to the bottom and turn left this time, breaks into a slow, controlled canter uphill, which takes him back into the turkeys again in a few hundred feet, only this time the turkeys have had enough of him, and the whole flock takes off, headed for the woods. I put just enough pressure on the reins to keep him cantering slowly, since I don't want him to run away with me—after all, he *is* a thoroughbred, and once he really gets moving, he flies—and when we get near the top of the field, I slow him down to a walk, so he doesn't go galloping up the steep part of the hill. It isn't a problem to keep him to the speed you want—all you have to do is sit back, deep in the saddle, and keep a firm grip on the reins with your fingers, and slowing him to a walk doesn't require much more than thinking about it, so well tuned are Star's responses. He's really too fine an instrument for me to play.

I'm not sure that Star is much on abstract thought—he's a gelding, so he would hardly be likely to see himself as part of the sisterhood of horses and women, or even the brotherhood of horses and men, and I don't suppose that he's aware of "the breath of Mother Earth," either—but that doesn't mean that he can't communicate, or that he isn't totally conscious and aware. My good mood—it's one of those rare summer days (rare around here, anyway) with zero humidity, a crystal blue sky, and just enough of a breeze to keep the insects away, and what's more, it's a Saturday morning, so my telephone answering machine isn't picking up messages from the office, e-mails aren't piling up in my laptop, and I don't have any errand more pressing than driving to Adams, our local farm market, to pick myself up something for dinner and maybe take my car through the car wash on the way home—communicates itself unmistakably to Star, and *his* good mood and pleasure at having what older horsemen used to call "a pipe opener," a chance to stretch out, gallop a bit, and clear the lungs, is palpable.

A horse's face isn't designed to enable him to smile, but if Star could, he would. I see that expression on the faces of older runners as they pass our house on the road, a combination of pleasure at still being able to run and the sheer physical well-being of feeling the muscles and the lungs work. Star can't put any of this into words, but it's the same feeling. Physical sensations matter a lot to horses. They don't have the capacity or the need (perhaps fortunately for them) to worry about death, disease, money, or taxes. They live in the present—they don't torment themselves over the past, or concern themselves about the future—and what they experience now, *right* now, is all that matters to them. They are creatures of habit; they thrive on regularity and are never bored by routine, but at the same time they get the most out of every good moment, and put up with the bad moments with monumental patience. You can, in fact, learn a good deal from horses without necessarily believing that the Earth Mother is speaking to us through them, or that they have useful advice to offer us about the human condition.

Star could do with a good, brisk, long walk, I decide. He's cool enough, but there's no point in pushing an aging horse, particularly one as game as Star, who would probably carry you at a gallop until he dropped. In any case, Star's reached the age when he rather enjoys what is called in German a *Spaziergang*, the kind of leisurely walk that old German and Austrian gentlemen used to take after meals—you could see them, even after the war, in spas, walking in pairs, each wearing a loden cloak and a hat with a chamois brush and carrying a cane, looking just like Kaiser Wilhelm II and King Edward VII at Bad Homburg. After a brisk canter, a *Spaziergang* is just Star's cup of tea, and indeed I myself, when I have time, enjoy a slow ride around the perimeter of our property, which, between what we own and what we lease, comes to about two hundred acres, allowing for a good, long ride of about three-quarters of an hour to an hour.

All this is familiar ground to Star, and like most horses he reacts to even the slightest changes along the way. Whether Star thinks of himself as a "spiritual sister" to Ms. Midkiff is not for me to say—though I personally doubt it—but what I *can* say is that Star has a capacity for memory that would put mine, or Ms. Midkiff's, to shame. He remembers things I have hardly even noticed, and the slightest change attracts his attention. Anything that has been moved, repainted, or fallen down attracts his attention just the way it would that of a sergeant major in the British army—that is to say that Star has a perfect eye for detail, and an infallible memory for anything or anyplace he's seen before.

In the old days, farmers returning from someplace late at night in their buggy would drop the reins, doze off, and let the horse find its way home. "The horse knows the way" was the old refrain, and by and large it's true—the horse *does* know the way, and can be relied on to get back to the barn where it lives. It's not that Star is in any special communication with Mother Earth, but he remembers distinctly what we hardly see at all, a pattern of leaves, a fallen rock, a patch of wild grass; he can orient himself as accurately as a human being with a GPS system— maybe more accurately, in fact. He knows where he is, how far it is to the barn; his mind is always hard at work on the landscape, like that of every other horse.

The thing about horses is that they possess remarkable qualities, even if they're not necessarily spiritual. We go down the edge of a couple of big fields, cross into a smaller one that has been carefully set up with jumps—two of them have been moved, which Star examines closely and registers, even though he's no longer in the jumping game—down a steep decline, Star grumbling a bit, and out into the woods at the far end of our property. Star knows his way here too, though he leaves it up to me to steer him clear of rocks and roots—after all, I'm up there in the saddle, so that's my job, not his. We squelch through a couple of muddy patches, and I lean down to check that he hasn't lost a shoe—thick mud has a way of sucking the shoe right off the horse's foot—then down past the stone wall and wire fencing that separates us from the old Plankenhorn farm.

The Plankenhorns themselves are dead or retired, but the place is still meticulously farmed as a hobby by Dr. Simon, who has just hayed the big field on my right and left dozens of big rolls of hay to dry. Star gives each of these rolls a worried look as we pass by, and tries to move over to the left as far as he can, just in case they turn out to be a threat of some kind. He's seen plenty of them before, but not *here*, and it's easy enough to tell what's going through his mind: "Those don't look like a problem, but you never know . . ."

Well, you can see his point. Who knows what a lot of big rolls of hay look like to a horse? Anyway, from Star's point of view the important thing is that they weren't here yesterday. A Martian spacecraft sitting in the Plankenhorn field would get much the same look of suspicion from Star. It isn't moving, but it wasn't here yesterday, he'd think. Since the rolls of hay haven't made *me* sweat, or raised my heartbeat or my blood pressure, he's willing to accept them as harmless until proved otherwise, however. That's not to say that he necessarily ascribes any degree of special wisdom to me, but when it comes to human artifacts, he's willing to accept my estimate of their danger or harmlessness—natural hazards, from steep, rough ground to angry stray dogs, he can make up his own mind about without my help.

Really, this is what people miss who are looking to the horse for some kind of horse-to-human spiritual wisdom. The horse has its own agenda, and within the limits of its nature, its own view of the world, but it's a here-and-now world, in which thinking about what went wrong yesterday, or what might happen tomorrow, or whether God does in fact know what He's doing, plays no part. Human beings have become part of the horse's world, but that isn't to say that horses spend their time thinking about us—we are background noise. Fate has given us the power to set down and enforce the rules under which horses live, and horses have adapted to that, even benefited from it, but it's not their job to make us feel good about it.

We're past the rolls of hay now—a sigh of relief from Star—and turn sharp left alongside the road, separated from it by only a screen of shrub. When we first moved up here, this was a quiet rural road, and we used to trot the horses down the side of it, but these days it's got far too much traffic to make that a good idea, and most of the drivers are no longer rural people who understand about horses. Nowadays they don't bother to slow down, they're impatient, they honk or rev their motors, they drive too close to the horse. Star isn't worried about vehicles, and even big, noisy trucks roaring down the road at twenty or thirty miles an hour over the speed limit don't alarm him much—they're part of my world, so he expects me to deal with them—but lots of horses do worry, so we no longer use the road at all. We follow a trail through some heavy brush, then come to a wide open, grassy space, and I give Star another (short) canter, then cut through Margaret's stadium field, past the jumps, across another open field, past the house of our neighbors, whose kids, when they were little, used to wave at Star from the back porch, past the old cow barn we rent out to Detlef Juerss as a workshop, and all of a sudden the farm is in sight. Star gives a good old snort of pleasure at the sight. He knows the tack will be off in a few minutes, he'll get an apple as a treat—it's part of the routine—be washed down, then spend the rest of the day in his stall, eating hay and watching the other horses out of the corner of his eye. Another good day, in Star's book, and who would argue with him?

I dismount, unfasten his girth—big sigh of relief from Star, like a fat woman getting out of a foundation garment—take the saddle off and put it on the saddle rack for cleaning in the tack room, select an apple, and come back to feed it to him. He cuts it neatly in two pieces with his front teeth and chews it slowly, savoring the juice. Some horses prefer carrots, and Star will certainly take a carrot if it's offered, but he prefers an apple, the juicier the better. He closes his eyes for a moment, thinking "This is the life!" Something like that, anyway. I'm happy for him.

Well, and for myself. I've had a good ride, and as Winston Churchill said, that's never a waste of an hour. Did I learn anything from Star? Did he communicate anything to me? Not consciously, no, and certainly no messages directly from Mother Earth, but some things, yes, absolutely: To live in the moment, to enjoy what the day offers, to notice the all-important pattern of little things, to feel yourself a part of all creatures, great and small, to live *on* the earth, not imagining yourself to be lord and master of it (at one with the U.S. Army Corps of Engineers and the land developers, as it were), but just a small part of its endless changes, to slow down enough to appreciate nature, and speed up enough to feel the well-being that comes from using one's own body. In his own way Star feels all these things, though he can't express them in words, and if that isn't a lesson for humankind, then I don't know what is.

I don't believe in whispering to horses, but I think we might all benefit from listening a lot harder to what horses have to whisper to *us*.

Riding into The Sunset

Star   Trader

ACKNOWLEDGMENTS

I OWE MY THANKS to too many people to list, but most of them are mentioned in the text. My particular thanks are owed to my beloved wife Margaret, whose story this in part became, to my agent Lynn Nesbit, who suggested I write it, and to my dear friend and editor Larry Ashmead, and to his assistant Krista Stroever, whose support, judgment, and unfailing enthusiasm have been invaluable and deeply appreciated. I am very grateful to Miranda Ottewell, who brought to the job of copy-editing the manuscript a real knowledge and love of horses, and to Amy Hill for her patience and superb taste in design. Thanks are also due to Tom Pavelek and his associate Tim, to Libby, to Juan, Leroy and Toby, and to many, many others.

Finally, my special thanks are owed to our horses over the years: in Margaret's case, Tabasco, Missouri, Berry Fox, Nebraska, Harold, Star, Jimmy, Dundee, and Trader as well as Cheyenne, Lonesome Dove, Zenith, Topper, and Nimbus; in mine, Malplaquet, True Grit, Sundance, Hustle, Zapata, and—may she rest in peace—the big mare.

> Think, when we talk of horses, that you see them,
> Printing their proud hooves i'th' receiving earth. . .
>
> —William Shakespeare, *Henry V*

"The Big Mare"